CWSP Guide to
Wireless Security

By Mark Ciampa

THOMSON
COURSE TECHNOLOGY

Australia • Canada • Mexico • Singapore • Spain • United Kingdom • United States

CWSP Guide to Wireless Security

is published by Thomson Course Technology.

Vice President, Technology and Trades
Dave Garza

Acquisitions Editor
Nick Lombardi

Quality Assurance Coordinator
Christian Kunciw

Marketing Director
Deborah Yarnell

Cover Design
Abby Scholz

Editorial Director
Sandy Clark

Product Managers
Amy Lyon, Donna Gridley

Technical Editor
Nicole Ashton,
Green Pen Quality Assurance

Senior Channel Marketing Manager
Dennis Williams

Text Design and Composition
GEX Publishing Services

Executive Editor
Stephen Helba

Production Editor
GEX Publishing Services

Manufacturing Coordinator
Susan Carroll

Senior Editorial Assistant
Dawn Daugherty

Developmental Editor
Deb Kaufmann

Contents

BRIEF

TABLE OF

Contents

CHAPTER SIX
Enterprise Wireless Hardware Security   181

CHAPTER SEVEN
Designing a Secure Wireless Network   219

Introduction

There are two critically important topics in information technology (IT) today. The first is wireless access. Airports, hotels, coffee shops, colleges, and homes are all installing wireless local area networks (WLANs) at a record pace, making wireless the network of choice among consumers. Organizations have also discovered that WLANs in the work-place can increase productivity, save valuable employee time, and reduce costs. The use of wireless networks by large businesses is estimated to grow at a rate of 47% through 2008.

The second critical topic in IT is security. Despite increased efforts and a heightened awareness of the dangers posed by lax security, attackers continue to wreak havoc and steal billions of dollars annually. Over 100 new phishing attacks are launched each day, and one out of every five computers in the U.S. is infected with some type of virus, worm, spyware, or Trojan Horse.

It comes then as no surprise that these two topics—wireless and security—converge to create one of the most highly demanded skill sets in the workforce today, namely wireless security implementation and management. It is important that today's network managers and system administrators understand the complexities of securing wireless LANs. *CWSP Guide to Wireless Security* provides the information you need to protect a wireless network. This book takes a comprehensive view of attacks and defenses of wireless networks. It examines the technology that helps make wireless networks secure and offers practical tools, tips, and techniques to protect a WLAN. *CWSP Guide to Wireless Security* helps you understand and use the latest wireless security technology.

CWSP Guide to Wireless Security also prepares you to take the Certified Wireless Security Professional (CWSP) examination. This certification, administered by Planet3 Wireless, Inc., is the leading vendor-neutral WLAN security certification and is considered one of the fastest-growing certifications today. Based on the Version 2006 objectives published in January 2006, *CWSP Guide to Wireless Security* will equip you with the knowledge and skills necessary for taking this exam.

Approach

Vulnerabilities in the original IEEE 802.11 WLAN standard have allowed attackers to exploit these weaknesses and steal information or inject malware onto wireless networks. Since 2003 improved security protocols based on IEEE 802.11i have been approved. These standards, known as Wi-Fi Protected Access (WPA) and Wi-Fi Protected Access 2 (WPA2), vary in their specifications and technologies. *CWSP Guide to Wireless Security* covers the latest information about wireless attackers, their attacks, and how these standards, as well as enhanced hardware and software, can protect a WLAN. This coverage of the major IEEE standards and enhanced technology gives you the flexibility to use the wireless network equipment that is available to you.

With the growth of online delivery of computer courses, it is essential that a textbook be flexible enough for use either in the classroom or as part of an online Web course. This book is intended to meet the needs of students in a traditional classroom setting as well as in an online delivery of the course materials. Hands-on activities can be performed using either enterprise-level Cisco equipment, which is typically installed on college campuses, or home and small office-level Linksys equipment, which can be obtained easily by students at a low cost. This flexibility allows students to perform similar wireless activities in either a classroom computer lab with other classmates or at home in an online course. And for those institutions that teach in the classroom but do not have Cisco equipment installed, Linksys equipment can be substituted, providing students with a rich environment for mastering wireless technologies.

A strictly wireless classroom computer lab is not necessary in order to perform the hands-on activities in *CWSP Guide to Wireless Security*. A standard wired computer lab can be easily converted to a wireless lab simply by inserting inexpensive wireless Universal Serial Bus (USB) network interface adapters into each computer and installing one or more access points. This allows the computer to fully function as a wireless device (although it is not mobile) to send and receive RF signals.

Although wireless networks provide a number of advantages, many organizations are still reluctant to invest in wireless technology because of the security risks. *CWSP Guide to Wireless Security* devotes attention to the design of a secure wireless LANs along with advanced technologies that can be used to identify imminent attacks and prevent them from damaging a wireless network.

Intended Audience

This book is intended to meet the needs of students and professionals who want to master wireless local area network security. A basic knowledge of computers and networks is all that is required to use this book. Those seeking to take the Planet3 Wireless, Inc., Certified Wireless Security Professional (CWSP) exam will find the text's approach and content especially helpful, because all CWSP Version 2006 objectives are covered in this book. For more information on CWSP certification, visit Planet3 Wireless, Inc., Web site at *www. cwnp.com*. Yet *CWSP Guide to Wireless Security* is not strictly an examination preparation book: it covers all aspects of wireless networks while satisfying the CWSP objectives. The book's pedagogical features are designed to provide a truly interactive learning experience to help prepare you for the challenges of wireless networking, with particular emphasis on wireless network security. In addition to the information presented in the text, each chapter includes Hands-On Projects that guide you through implementing practical security hardware, software, and network configurations step by step. Each chapter also contains a running case study that places you in the role of problem solver, requiring you to apply concepts presented in the chapter to achieve a successful solution.

Chapter Descriptions

Here is a summary of the topics covered in each chapter of this book:

Chapter 1, "Foundations of Wireless Security," begins by explaining how wireless is used today and also outlines the advantages and disadvantages of wireless networks, why wireless security is important, and the wireless standards organizations and regulatory agencies. In addition, the IEEE wireless LAN standards are discussed along with wireless certifications.

Chapter 2, "Wireless LAN Vulnerabilities," lists and explains the types of security protections that were part of the original IEEE 802.11 standard and the vulnerabilities of these and other WLAN security protocols.

Chapter 3, "Passive Wireless Discovery," begins by describing how attacks can obtain data from wireless networks without actively attacking the network itself. These attacks include general information gathering, wardriving, and using wireless packet sniffers.

Chapter 4, "Active Wireless Attacks," explores different types of wireless vulnerabilities and how they can be exploited by attackers. This chapter details the different types of active wireless attacks.

Chapter 5, "WLAN Security Models," examines the common security models used in WLANs, including IEEE 802.11i, Wi-Fi Protected Access (WPA), and Wi-Fi Protected Access 2 (WPA2).

Chapter 6, "Enterprise Wireless Hardware Security," looks at the different types of wireless hardware that can be used to ward off attacks. In addition, this chapter discusses hardware security features that can be implemented.

Chapter 7, "Designing a Secure Wireless LAN," explains the principles involved with the layout and design of a secure WLAN and how network segmentation, hardware placement, and wireless device security can provide additional layers of protection.

Chapter 8, "Secure Wireless Authentication," introduces authentication used in wireless network security.

Chapter 9, "Secure Wireless Transmissions," explains how encryption can be used to prevent unauthorized users from viewing material transmitted over a WLAN.

Chapter 10, "Managing the Wireless Network," describes how to monitor and maintain a WLAN. In addition, the importance of wireless intrusion prevention and wireless intrusion detection systems are discussed.

Chapter 11, "Wireless Security Policy," explores what a security policy is and how it is developed. It also lists and explains the different types of wireless security policies that should be used.

Chapter 12, "Operational Support and Wireless Convergence," explores the features of a secure and scalable WLAN and also what is involved in operational support. Finally, the chapter discusses the convergence of different types of wireless networks.

The three appendices at the end of this book serve as references for the wireless networking professional:

Appendix A, "Certified Wireless Security Professional (CWSP) Examination Objectives" provides a complete listing of the Planet3 Wireless, Inc., CWSP certification exam objectives and shows which chapters and sections in the book cover material associated with each objective.

Appendix B, "Wireless Web Sites" gives a sample of useful Web sites for the wireless network professional.

Appendix C, "Sample Acceptable Use Policy" provides a template of an acceptable use policy for a wireless environment.

Features

To aid you in fully understanding computer and network security, this book includes many features designed to enhance your learning experience.

- **Chapter Opener.** At the start of each chapter a real-world example of how wireless security is used and why it is important is found in "The World of Wireless Security."

- **Chapter Objectives.** Each chapter begins with a detailed list of the concepts to be mastered within that chapter. This list provides you with both a quick reference to the chapter's contents and a useful study aid.

- **Illustrations and Tables.** Numerous illustrations of wireless LAN security concepts and technologies help you visualize theories and concepts. In addition, the many tables provide details and comparisons of practical and theoretical information.

- **Hands-On Projects.** Although it is important to understand the theory behind wireless security, nothing can improve upon real-world experience. To this end, each chapter provides several Hands-On Projects aimed at providing you with practical wireless network experience. These projects cover both Cisco and Linksys equipment using Windows operating systems as well as software downloaded from the Internet.

- **Chapter Summaries.** Each chapter's text is followed by a summary of the concepts introduced in that chapter. These summaries provide a helpful way to review the ideas covered in each chapter.

- **Review Questions.** The end-of-chapter assessment begins with a set of review questions that reinforce the ideas introduced in each chapter. These questions help you evaluate and apply the material you have learned. Answering these questions will ensure that you have mastered the important concepts and provide valuable practice for taking the CWSP exam.

- **Case Projects.** Located at the end of each chapter are several Case Projects. In these extensive exercises, you implement the skills and knowledge gained in the chapter through real design and implementation scenarios.

Text and Graphic Conventions

Wherever appropriate, additional information and exercises have been added to this book to help you better understand the topic at hand. Icons throughout the text alert you to additional materials. The icons used in this textbook are described below.

The Note icon draws your attention to additional helpful material related to the subject being described.

The Caution icons warn you about potential mistakes or problems and explain how to avoid them.

Each hands-on activity in this book is preceded by the Hands-On icon and a description of the exercise that follows.

Case Project icons mark Case Projects, which are scenario-based assignments. In these extensive case examples, you are asked to implement independently what you have learned.

INSTRUCTOR'S MATERIALS

The following additional materials are available when this book is used in a classroom setting. All of the supplements available with this book are provided to the instructor on a single CD-ROM. You can also retrieve these supplemental materials from the Thomson Course Technology Web site, *www.course.com*, by going to the page for this book, under "Download Instructor Files & Teaching Tools."

Electronic Instructor's Manual. The Instructor's Manual that accompanies this textbook includes additional instructional material to assist in class preparation, including suggestions for lecture topics, recommended lab activities, tips on setting up a lab for the Hands-On Projects, and solutions to all end-of-chapter materials.

ExamView Test Bank. This cutting-edge Windows-based testing software helps instructors design and administer tests and pretests. In addition to generating tests that can be printed and administered, this full-featured program has an online testing component that allows students to take tests at the computer and have their exams graded automatically.

PowerPoint Presentations. This book comes with a set of Microsoft PowerPoint slides for each chapter. These slides are meant to be used as a teaching aid for classroom presentations, to be made available to students on the network for chapter review, or to be printed for classroom distribution. Instructors are also at liberty to add their own slides for other topics introduced.

To the User

This book is designed to be read in sequence, from beginning to end. Each chapter builds on preceding chapters to provide a solid understanding of wireless networking administration. You can also use this book to prepare for Planet3 Wireless Inc.'s CWSP certification exam. The summary grid on the inside covers of the book and Appendix A pinpoint the chapters that cover each exam objective.

Hardware and Software Requirements

Following are the hardware and software requirements needed to perform the end-of-chapter Hands-On Projects:

- Cisco Aironet 1100 or 1200 series access point with an IEEE 802.11b, a, or g radio installed

- Linksys WRT54G or equivalent wireless router

- Wi-Fi certified IEEE 802.11b, a, or g wireless network adapter

- Windows XP Professional or Home Edition

- An Internet connection and Web browser (i.e., Internet Explorer)

Specialized Requirements

Whenever possible, the need for specialized equipment was kept to a minimum. The following chapter features specialized hardware:

- Chapter 3: Cisco Aironet IEEE 802.11b, a, or g Wireless CardBus Adapter

Free downloadable software is required in the following chapters. Instructions for downloading the software are given in the chapters:

- Chapter 1: ShareEnum, PasswordSafe,
- Chapter 2: SMAC
- Chapter 3: Cisco Aironet Client Utility, NetStumbler, Airopeek NX
- Chapter 4: Pong, CommView, Eicar, AOPAR
- Chapter 7: Windows Defender, Blacklight
- Chapter 8: Adobe Acrobat
- Chapter 9: Putty, Pretty Good Privacy, Hamachi
- Chapter 10: SuperScan, Attacker, WiFi Manager

ACKNOWLEDGMENTS

Despite the fact that only the author's name appears on the cover of a book, in reality it is the work of an entire team that creates what is inside. The team that produced this book was excellent. Executive Editor Stephen Helba demonstrated his excellent vision by directing the scope of the book to meet the needs of the readers. Product Managers Amy Lyon and Donna Gridley were very supportive and helpful in keeping this project moving forward. Production Editor Gina Dishman was great in finding my mistakes and making excellent suggestions. Technical Editor Nicole Ashton and Peter Stefanis and Danielle Shaw of Quality Assurance carefully reviewed the book and identified many numerous corrections. The team of peer reviewers evaluated each chapter and provided very helpful suggestions and contributions. I thank Bruce Hartpence of the Rochester Institute of Technology; Laraine Koffman of the City College of San Francisco, and David Pope of the Ozarks Technical Community College.

And special recognition goes to Developmental Editor Deb Kaufmann. Deb was again marvelous at answering questions, reminding me of deadlines, identifying problems, making suggestions, and turning my rough work into polished prose. Despite my numerous delays, she always did her work with joy and enthusiasm. Without question, Deb is simply the very best there is.

The entire Thomson Course Technology staff was always very helpful and worked very hard to create this finished product. I'm honored to be part of such an outstanding group of professionals, and to these people and everyone on the team I extend my sincere thanks.

Finally, I want to thank my wonderful wife, Susan. Her continual support, patience, and love helped see me through yet another book. I could not have typed the first letter on the keyboard without her.

DEDICATION

To my wife, Susan, my sons, Greg and Brian, and daughter-in-law, Amanda.

PHOTO CREDITS

Figure	Caption	Credit
Figure 3-4	Convertible tablet	Courtesy of Fujitsu-Siemens
Figure 3-5	Slate tablet	Courtesy of Fujitsu-Siemens
Figure 3-6	Handheld PC	Courtesy of Psion Teklogix
Figure 3-7	PDA	Courtesy of Fujitsu-Siemens
Figure 3-8	USB wireless NICs: (a) standalone USB device, (b) USB key fob	(a) Courtesy of NETGEAR (b) Courtesy of SanDisk Corporation
Figure 3-9	Wireless NIC PC Card adapters: (a) CardBus card; (b) Mini PCI card	(a) Courtesy of 3Com Corporation (b) Courtesy of Intel Corporation
Figure 3-10	Wireless CompactFlash card	Courtesy of Linksys
Figure 3-12	Global positioning system (GPS)	Courtesy of Garmin Ltd.

FOUNDATIONS OF WIRELESS SECURITY

After completing this chapter you should be able to do the following:

➤ List the advantages and disadvantages of a wireless local area network

➤ Describe the functions of the wireless LAN standards and regulatory agencies

➤ List wireless networking and security certifications

➤ Define information security and tell why it is important in wireless networks

➤ List the five types of IEEE WLANs

The World of Wireless Security

Google has actively branched out beyond its original Internet search engine business. Google e-mail, desktop search, hardware search appliances, mobile Web search, and satellite imagery are just a few of the areas in which the company is engaged. Now there is one more item to add to Google's list: providing city-wide wireless local area networks.

In November of 2005 Google received approval from city officials in Mountain View, California, to begin building a WLAN that covers the entire city. Located 56 kilometers (35 miles) south of San Francisco, Mountain View is home to over 70,000 residents and Google's main campus. All of the installation and annual maintenance costs will be paid by Google, and any utility costs paid by the city will be reimbursed by Google, which may run up to $4,000 per year. Also, Google will make annual payments to the city of about $12,600 to place wireless access points on city-owned light poles.

Google intends to use the Mountain View wireless network as a proving ground to show officials in large metropolitan areas that Google can be a provider of wireless access throughout a metropolitan area. Google has also approached city officials in San Francisco to promote the benefits of free, city-wide wireless service, in hopes of becoming the provider of that service. Google already provides WLAN service in Union Square, a popular outdoor public area in downtown San Francisco.

The Google plan to wirelessly connect Mountain View is not a done deal just yet. Parts of the city have streetlight poles that are owned by another utility and not the city itself. Google has said it will work with this utility to gain access to these poles or to develop alternate equipment to provide WLAN coverage to these parts of the city. Also, some of the city's residents are concerned about their privacy and health problems that could occur because of the radiation emitted from the wireless transmissions. At this writing, Google has not specifically addressed these concerns.

The explosive popularity of wireless local area networks (WLANs) has dramatically changed how we read our e-mails, surf the Internet, and access data. Can you recall the last time you visited a local coffee shop that did not have a wireless network that you could use while you drank your cappuccino? How long has it been that you were on a college campus and could not find wireless access in the library, classrooms, or student common areas? When was the last time you saw a billboard for a hotel that did not advertise "High-speed Wireless Internet"? This remarkable transformation has occurred since WLANs first became available in 2000. No longer a novelty, WLANs are now a must-have for businesses and individuals, a standard that is increasingly relied upon and expected.

In spite of the popularity of wireless networks, one factor that has prevented them from being even more widespread can be summed up in a single word: *security*. Because of the nature of wireless transmissions and the vulnerabilities of early wireless networking standards, WLANs have been extremely vulnerable targets for attackers. Because the network signals are not restricted to a cable in a wall or buried underground, attackers can easily intercept an unencrypted wireless transmission and read its private contents, steal its passwords, or even change the message itself. An attacker sitting in a car across the street with a radio frequency jammer can perform a denial-of-service attack and bring the network to a crashing halt. Older wireless security mechanisms were not sufficient to defend against such attacks, and WLANs were seen as an open invitation for attackers to enter an organization's network and steal, plunder, and destroy valuable information.

However, there have been many changes and upgrades in WLAN security in the last few years. The technology and standards are now available to provide the same level of strong security for WLANs that wired users enjoy. Implementing a robust wireless security infrastructure can also create a more secure platform for related wired network segments.

This book aims to give you all the knowledge and skills you need to design and implement secure wireless networks. This chapter provides an overview of wireless networks and security, beginning with how wireless networks are used today and their advantages and disadvantages. The chapter then introduces wireless security, and organizations and agencies that regulate wireless networks. Finally, you will review the different types of WLANs.

WIRELESS IN OUR WORLD

The degree to which wireless technology can be found across a broad spectrum of industries is truly astonishing. Wireless LAN applications can be found in every industry whose employees need or want to conduct business without being confined to a specific location. This section describes how some leading industries use wireless technology.

Business

A characteristic of the business world of today is "flatter" organizations: instead of employees working at their desks with a supervisor overseeing their work, much of an employee's work is done in teams that cross functional and organizational boundaries. This means that employees are involved extensively in team meetings that occur away from their desks. Yet the need for immediate access to network resources exists even while these meetings are taking place.

In the pre-wireless era, these meetings were typically held in conference rooms where employees were away from the data that they need to help make decisions. And those conference rooms that did have wired network connections were not always convenient for meetings: data ports were located around the perimeter walls while the meeting took place with members sitting at a table in the center of the room. Employees had to remember to bring a patch cable for their laptop computer and had to compete with other employees for a free port to connect to the network.

Wireless technology has dramatically changed how and where business meetings take place and has made the meetings more focused and productive. Team members now bring their wireless laptop computers to the conference room and remain connected to the network and their data. The ability to access their data to make decisions helps make more timely decisions while everyone is present instead of waiting until the next meeting occurs.

WLANs have made it possible for businesses to improve services, reach new markets, and improve overall productivity, while reducing IT and administrative costs. A study conducted by NOP World Technology found that wireless LANs delivered the following benefits to businesses:

- *Increased productivity*—The mobility afforded by WLANs increased workers' access to the network by up to 3.5 hours more per day, which resulted in a productivity increase of 27 percent.

- *Time savings*—The ability to access data from almost anywhere on the business campus at any time saves employees 90 minutes each day.

- *Financial savings*—Based on an average IT salary of $64,000, the employees' time saved had an annual dollar value of $14,000 per employee.

One emerging WLAN technology that many organizations are particularly excited about is **voice over wireless LAN (VoWLAN)**. VoWLAN uses the existing data WLAN to make and receive telephone calls. Just as a WLAN gives users mobility for accessing data, VoWLAN provides that same freedom for voice communication. Users no longer have to wait in their office for a phone call but can take with them just one mobile device that works everywhere: in the office, elevator, hallway, cafeteria, and even in the car or train. In addition, VoWLAN devices can forward business calls to their mobile phones during regular business hours. Table 1-1 illustrates the importance of VoWLANs based on a survey by Forrester Research on how businesses plan to use WLANs.

NOTE

VoWLAN is also known as wireless voice over IP (wVoIP), voice over IP (VoIP), and VoWi-Fi.

Table 1-1 Business plans for WLANs

Application	Percentage planning to implement
Employee mobility	66%
Conference-room access	56%
Voice over WLAN	24%
Asset tracking	22%
Wired port replacement	21%
Other	12%
Unsure	5%

Travel

Traveling is all about mobility, and the travel industry has been a leader in adopting wireless technologies. Most airport terminals provide wireless access hotspots, and it is estimated that in 2006 over 1,000 airports worldwide will have wireless access. Airports generally charge a fee to use their wireless networks, allowing passengers with wireless laptops to surf the Internet or read e-mail. Several major airports also use wireless technology to keep track of passenger luggage. One airport reported that the number of lost bags in the airport terminal was reduced by 96 percent using this technology.

NOTE The Pittsburgh (Pennsylvania) International Airport decided to offer free wireless Internet access. Travelers who pass through the airport can surf the Internet from any food court or from their seats at the gate at no cost. Pittsburgh International installed free wireless in the hope that it would bring more connecting travelers. So far it is working: several large companies are routing employees through Pittsburgh International when they travel because of its free wireless service. Airport executives estimate that the wireless LAN, which consists of 60 access points and cost approximately $25,000 to install, will pay for itself in one year.

Travelers are not the only ones to benefit from wireless access at the airport. Wireless PDAs now replace the walkie-talkies that firefighters and other emergency response workers used in the past. These wireless devices allow workers to file reports and updates directly instead of recording information on paper and then entering it on the computer when they return to their office. In addition to providing airport authorities with the latest information online, workers have found that using wireless devices allows them to give a much more accurate record of events as they are happening instead of relying upon their notes or memories several hours later.

The communication between air traffic controllers and aircraft typically uses voice radio systems that haven't changed much in 50 years. Important communications about the weather or route changes between pilots and company dispatchers or air traffic controllers occurred on overcrowded voice radio circuits that resemble an old-fashioned party line telephone system. Many of these connections are of poor quality. Some airlines are turning to a new wireless data service. WLAN technology is used to communicate with the aircraft once it has parked or is taxiing on the ground. This allows the airline to automatically upload and install software updates for onboard computers or the avionics system before the next flight. Other airlines are using wireless LAN technology for flight maintenance information. Aircraft maintenance personnel with wireless LAN laptops can have immediate access to an online database that stores important information about each type of aircraft and maintenance procedures. This information is much more current than that found in printed manuals.

NOTE Wireless connections are also being offered to airline passengers during flights. United Airlines will offer in-flight WLAN service on domestic U.S. flights beginning in 2007. Other airlines, such as Lufthansa and Japan Airlines, currently offer the service on international flights.

Wireless LAN technologies are not restricted to airplanes. Many trains, such as the French TGV and trains running between San Francisco-Oakland and Montreal-Toronto have WLAN access for riders. Also, ferries that cross Puget Sound in Washington offer WLAN access to the Internet. The Texas Department of Transportation has installed free WLANs at all of its 84 safety rest areas and 12 Travel Information Centers, to encourage drivers to make regular stops and help reduce driver fatigue.

Education

Wireless LANs are an ideal technology for colleges and schools. In fact, educational institutions were some of the first adopters of WLANs because of their dramatic advantages in teaching and learning. Teachers can create classroom presentations on the laptop computer in their office and then carry that computer with them right into the classroom. They do not have to spend time plugging and unplugging cables to attach to the campus data network. Instead, their laptop device automatically makes the wireless connection as they walk into the classroom. In settings where students bring their own wireless devices to class, teachers can immediately send handouts directly to students sitting in the classroom.

NOTE According to the 2005 Campus Computing Project report, 77 percent of campuses participating in the survey had wireless classrooms, up from 67 percent in 2003.

Wireless LAN connections also offer students an important degree of freedom. Students no longer must go to a specific computer lab or the library to access the school's computer network. Instead they can access the school network wirelessly from almost any location on campus. And as they move to different classrooms in different buildings they can remain connected to the network. Most schools publish maps, like that shown in Figure 1-1, showing the location of wireless access points and the coverage areas in buildings across campus. Schools that require students to own a laptop computer are now requiring that those same computers have wireless network interface cards. This wireless education model makes computing resources available from anywhere and at any time to students.

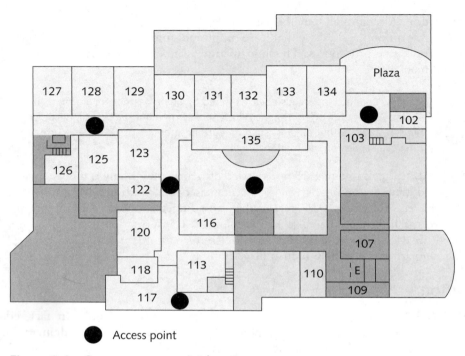

Figure 1-1   Campus access point locations

Wireless LAN technology translates into a cost savings for colleges as well. Traditional classrooms become fully accessible computer labs without the expense of additional wiring and infrastructure. And colleges no longer have to consider the expense of adding multiple open computer labs for students because everyone can access the resources from anywhere on campus.

NOTE   Wireless networks are also used to promote safety and security. Some schools are installing wireless security cameras, and public safety personnel can view the live feed from any of the cameras using hand-held personal digital assistants (PDAs).

Health Care

The health care industry, including hospitals, physician's offices, and clinics, has embraced wireless technology to improve patient care. For example, in a hospital, properly administering the right medication to the right patient at the right time in the right dosage is critically important. Typically, medication printouts are posted at the medication area. As medications are given, they are crossed off the list and initialed. However, because the paper record cannot always be updated immediately, there is a possibility that a patient could get an extra dose of medication before an order for a new or changed medication was processed.

Wireless LAN point-of-care computer systems allow medical staff to access and update patient records immediately. Many hospitals use laptop computers on mobile carts with barcode scanners and a wireless network interface card connection. Health care professionals can document a patient's medication administration immediately in the computer as they move from room to room without connecting and disconnecting cables. Nurses first identify themselves to the computer system by scanning their own personal bar-coded ID badge or wireless tag. The patient's bar-coded armband is then scanned and all medications that are currently due for that particular patient are brought up on the screen. The medications to be administered are sealed in a pouch with a wireless tag or bar-coded bottles. Nurses scan this barcode or tag before opening the package. An alert immediately appears on the screen if the wrong medication or incorrect amount is identified.

The system immediately verifies that medication is being administered to the correct patient in the correct dosage, which eliminates potential errors and documentation inefficiencies. The documentation process now takes place at the bedside where care is delivered, which improves accuracy. In addition, all hospital personnel now have real-time access to the latest medication and patient status information.

WIRELESS ADVANTAGES AND DISADVANTAGES

With any technology, there are advantages and disadvantages to be considered. Wireless LANs are no exception. The following is a summary of the advantages and disadvantages of the technology.

Advantages

There are many advantages to using wireless networks. These include mobility, easier and less expensive network installations, increased network reliability, and disaster recovery.

Mobility

The primary advantage of wireless technology is the freedom to move about without being tethered by wires. This mobility enables individuals to use a laptop computer that is always in contact with the network no matter where the user may roam within range of that network. Many occupations that require workers to be mobile, such as field repair technicians or inventory clerks, find that wireless technology is vital to their work.

With the change in today's business environment even more workers can take advantage of the mobility afforded by a wireless technology. An increasingly mobile workforce is one characteristic of today's business world. Workers today are being equipped with laptop computers and other portable communication devices to enable them to be mobile.

However, these employees still need immediate access to data on the company network. WLANs fit well in this work environment, giving mobile workers the freedom they need but allowing them to access the network resources that they need. With a wireless network, workers can access information from almost anywhere.

WLAN technology is also being incorporated into other devices to provide an even greater degree of mobility. For example, digital cameras are now available with embedded WLAN technology. Users can take photos that are immediately transmitted to a computer, printer, or even the Internet.

Easier and Less Expensive Installation

Installing network cabling can be expensive, particularly in older buildings. These buildings were constructed long before personal computers and networks were ever even thought of. It is difficult to run cable through thick masonry walls and plaster ceilings. Many older buildings used asbestos when constructed. Following today's regulations, the asbestos may have to be completely removed before any major cabling infrastructure can be installed. And sometimes there are local or national restrictions that prevent modifying older facilities that have historic value.

In these instances a wireless LAN is the ideal solution because the need to run cables is eliminated. That means that historical buildings can be preserved, dangerous asbestos is not disturbed, and difficult drilling can be avoided by using a WLAN system.

Reducing the need for installing cabling will result in a significant cost savings. With cable connections costing from $1 to $3 per connection, a wireless network can easily pay for itself by eliminating the need for a network connection in each office.

The time required to install network cabling is usually significant. Installers must pull wires through the ceiling and then drop cables down walls to network outlets. This can usually take days or even weeks to complete. During that time employees must somehow continue their work in the midst of the construction zone. Installing a wireless LAN reduces these disruptions.

Wireless networks also make it easier for any office—in an old or new building—to be modified with new cubicles or furniture. No longer does the design for a remodeled office first have to consider the location of the computer jack in the wall when relocating furniture and setting up a computer. Instead, the focus can be on creating the most effective work environment for the employees. The computer can be connected to the network no matter where it is placed in the cubicle.

Wireless technologies also allow businesses to create an office in a space where the traditional infrastructure doesn't exist. Typically, an office space must be wired with computer cables for network connections for it to be useful. With WLAN, this expensive cabling infrastructure no longer is necessary. This means that usable office space can be created almost immediately with little expense. For example, a hotel conference room that may not have the infrastructure to support a wired network can quickly be turned into a wireless networked office environment.

Increased Reliability

One of the main sources of wired network problems is network cable failure. Moisture from a leak during a thunderstorm or a coffee spill can erode metallic conductors. A user who shifts the computer on his or her desk may break one or more of the wires in a patch cable. A cable splice that is done incorrectly can cause problems that result in intermittent errors that are very difficult to identify. Using wireless LAN technology eliminates these types of cable failures and increases the overall reliability of the network.

Disaster Recovery

In today's environment with fires, tornados, hurricanes, floods, and even terrorist attacks, disaster recovery must be a prime concern of every business and organization. A documented disaster recovery plan is vital if an organization is to quickly get back on its feet after a calamity. Any business that is not prepared to recover from these or other disasters will find itself crippled or out of business.

Most organizations have plans in place to move to another site from which to run their operations in the event that the primary site is no longer available. Known as a **hot site**, this is generally run by a commercial disaster recovery service that allows a business to continue computer and network operations to maintain business continuity. A hot site has all the equipment needed for an organization to continue running, including office space and furniture, telephone jacks, computer equipment, and a live telecommunications link. If the organization's data processing center becomes inoperable, it can move all data processing operations to a hot site, often within an hour.

NOTE Typically, a business has an annual contract with a company that offers hot site services for a monthly service charge. Some services also offer data backup so that all company data is available regardless of whether a hot site or cold site is used.

However, the contract for maintaining a hot site is very expensive and not all businesses can easily afford this expense. An alternative is a **cold site**. A cold site provides office space but the customer must provide and install all the equipment needed to continue operations. A cold site is less expensive, but takes longer to get an enterprise in full operation after the disaster. Many businesses use cold sites and WLANs as a major piece of their disaster recovery plan. Laptop computers with wireless NIC adapters and access points are kept in reserve along with backup network servers. In the event of a disaster, operations are quickly relocated to the cold site. No consideration has to be given to network cabling. Instead, laptop computers are distributed to the resettled employees and access points are quickly installed. The network can be immediately up and running so that business may proceed in as normal a fashion as possible.

Disadvantages

Along with the many advantages of WLAN technology there are disadvantages and concerns. These include radio frequency interference, health risks, and security.

Radio Frequency Interference

Wireless devices operate using radio signals, creating the potential for two types of signal interference. Signals from other devices can disrupt wireless transmissions, or the wireless device may itself be the source of interference for other devices.

There are several different types of devices that transmit a radio signal that may interfere with a WLAN. These devices include microwave ovens, elevator motors, photocopying machines, certain types of outdoor lighting systems, theft protection devices, and cordless telephones. These may cause errors or completely prevent transmission between a wireless device and an access point. And because WLAN devices operate within the same radio frequency, they may "return the favor" and likewise interfere with other wireless devices.

NOTE Interference is nothing new for a computer data network. Even when using cables to connect network devices, interference from fluorescent light fixtures and electric motors can disrupt data transmission. The solution for wireless devices is the same as that for standard cabled network devices: locate the source of the interference and eliminate the interference. This can be done by moving an access point away from a photocopying machine or microwave oven.

Health Risks

Wireless LAN devices contain radio transmitters and receivers that emit radio frequency (RF) energy. This is similar to cellular telephones and other mobile wireless devices that emit low levels of RF while being used. It is well documented that high levels of RF can produce biological damage through heating effects (this is how a microwave oven is able to cook food). However, it is not known if or to what extent lower levels of RF might cause adverse health effects. Although some research has been done to address these questions, no clear picture of the biological effects of this type of radiation has emerged to date.

However, in the United States, the Food and Drug Administration (FDA) and the Federal Communications Commission (FCC) set policies and procedures for some wireless devices. A recent FDA update stated that "the available science does not allow us to conclude that (wireless devices) are absolutely safe, or that they are unsafe." The report went on to say that "the available scientific evidence does not demonstrate any adverse health effects associated with the use of (wireless devices)." Currently, no scientific studies have revealed health problems associated with the absorption of low levels of RF energy by the human body.

Security

The greatest disadvantage to wireless LANs is security. Many organizations have resisted implementing wireless on a broad scale because of the lack of security for wireless communications. A survey by *Network Computing* in 2005 indicated that just under 50 percent of business respondents said that "lack of adequate security technology" was a barrier to WLAN adoption in their organization. A number of different attacks on wireless networks, such as denial-of-service attacks, stealing passwords, altering messages, and other attacks make many organizations reluctant to use wireless technology.

Because of these concerns, wireless security remains the major issue in WLANs. Although newer types of WLANs have improved security features, wireless security must be properly addressed to ensure that data is protected.

INFORMATION SECURITY AND WIRELESS LANs

Knowing how to defend a wireless network against a wide array of attacks begins with an understanding of what information security is. It is also important to know why it is so difficult to defend against attacks and why wireless security is particularly important. Each of these topics will now be discussed in detail.

What Is Information Security?

The term **information security** is frequently used to describe the tasks of guarding information that is in a digital format. This digital information is typically manipulated by a microprocessor (like on a personal computer), stored on a magnetic or optical storage device (like a hard drive or a DVD), and is transmitted over a network (such as a local area network or the Internet). You can understand information security by examining its goals and how it is accomplished.

First, information security ensures that protective measures are properly implemented. Just as with national security, information security cannot completely prevent attacks or guarantee that a system is totally secure. Rather, information security creates a defense that attempts to ward off attacks and prevents the collapse of the system when an attack occurs. Thus, information security is *protection*.

Second, information security is intended to protect information, which has high value to people and organizations, and that value comes from the characteristics of the information. Three of the characteristics of information that must be protected by information security are:

- *Confidentiality*—Confidentiality ensures that only authorized parties can view the information.

- *Integrity*—Integrity ensures that the information is correct and no unauthorized person or malicious software has altered that data.

- *Availability*—Although a secure computer must restrict access attempts by unauthorized users, it must still make the data immediately available to authorized users.

Information security attempts to safeguard these three characteristics of information (sometimes known as CIA). Therefore information security *protects the confidentiality, integrity, and availability of information.*

However, information security involves more than protecting the information itself. The third objective of information security is displayed in Figure 1-2. The center of the diagram shows what needs to be protected—the information. Because this information is stored on computer hardware, manipulated by software, and transmitted by communications, each of these areas must also be protected. Therefore information security protects the integrity, confidentiality, and availability of information *on the devices that store, manipulate, and transmit the information.*

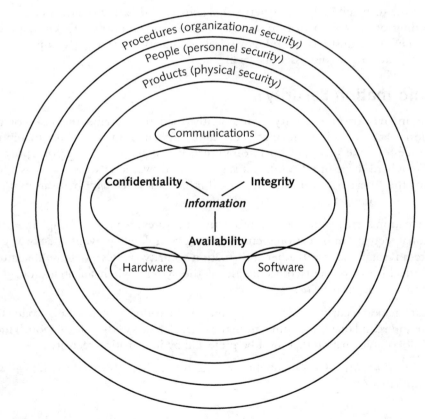

Figure 1-2   Information security components

Finally, information security is achieved through a combination of three entities. As shown in Figure 1-2, information, hardware, software, and communications are protected in three successive layers. The innermost layer consists of the products that provide the necessary security. These products may be as basic as door locks or as complicated as intrusion-detection systems and firewalls. They form the physical security around the data. The next layer is people. Without people implementing and properly using the security products, the data can never be protected. The final layer consists of procedures, which include the plans and policies established by an organization to ensure that people correctly use the products. These three layers interact with each other. The procedures tell the people how to use the products to protect the information. Thus, information security protects the integrity, confidentiality, and availability of information on the devices that store, manipulate, and transmit the information *through products, people, and procedures.*

Difficulties in Defending against Attacks

It is no surprise that attacks on computers, networks, and the information that they contain continue to escalate. According to the Symantec Internet Security Threat Report, during the first six months of 2005:

- More than 10,866 new Microsoft Windows-based (Win32) viruses and worms were released, an increase of 48 percent over the 7,360 documented in the second half of 2004. This is an increase of 142 percent over the 4,496 documented Win32 viruses and worms in the first half of 2004.

- Over 1,862 new vulnerabilities were exposed during this time, and 97 percent were classified as either "moderately" or "highly" severe.

- The time between the disclosure of a vulnerability and the release of an associated exploit was 6.0 days, whereas the average time before a patch was released was 54 days. This means that on average, 48 days transpired between the release of an exploit and the release of an associated patch.

According to the 2005 CSI/FBI Computer Crime and Security Survey, the dollar amount of total losses because of security attacks for 2004 was $130,104,542 for the 639 respondents that were willing and able to estimate their losses. Two areas that showed significant increase were unauthorized access to information, where the average loss per respondent increased from $51,545 in 2004 to $303,234 in 2005, and the theft of proprietary information (average loss per respondent rose from $168,529 in 2004 to $355,552 in 2005).

Security attacks are not isolated against organizations. Spyware and the threat of unwanted programs being secretly loaded onto computers have become serious attack threats to the general public. Over 59 million American adults (43 percent of Internet users) state that they have identified unwanted malicious programs on their home computer, and 68 percent of home Internet users (about 93 million American adults) have experienced at least one computer problem in the past year that is consistent with problems caused by security attacks.

NOTE   Attacks that are specific to WLANs will be covered in Chapters 3 and 4.

The challenge of keeping computers secure has never been greater. A number of factors have converged to make security increasingly difficult. One is the *speed of attacks* that occur today. With modern tools at their disposal, attackers can quickly scan systems to find weaknesses and then launch attacks with unprecedented speed. For example, the Slammer worm infected 75,000 computers in the *first 11 minutes* after it was released, and the number of infections *doubled* every 8.5 seconds. At its peak, Slammer was scanning *55 million computers per second* looking for another computer to infect. Later that same year, the Blaster worm infected 138,000 computers in the *first four hours* and ended up infecting over 1.4 million computers. Many attack tools can now initiate new attacks without any human initiative, therefore increasing the speed at which systems are attacked.

Another factor is the greater *sophistication of attacks.* Security attacks are becoming more complex, making it more difficult to detect and defend against. Attackers now use common Internet tools, such as e-mail and Hypertext Transfer Protocol (HTTP), to send data or commands to attack computers, making it tricky to distinguish an attack from legitimate traffic. Other attack tools vary their behavior, so the same attack appears differently each time, complicating detection.

Because attackers now *detect weaknesses faster*, they can quickly attempt to exploit these vulnerabilities. The number of newly discovered system vulnerabilities doubles annually, making it more difficult for software developers to keep pace by updating their products.

One of the looming fears is the increasing number of zero day attacks. Although most attacks take advantage of vulnerabilities that someone has already uncovered, a **zero day attack** occurs when an attacker discovers and exploits a previously unknown flaw. Providing "zero days" of warning, a zero day attack can be especially crippling to networks and computers because the attack runs rampant while precious time is spent trying to identify the vulnerability.

Another difficulty in computer defense is that instead of attacks coming from only one source, they can be *distributed attacks.* Attackers can now use thousands of computers in an attack against a single computer or network. This "many against one" approach makes it impossible to stop an attack simply by identifying and blocking the source.

The final difficulty in defending against attacks is one that many security experts believe may be the most difficult of all: *user confusion.* Increasingly users are called upon to make difficult security decisions regarding their computer systems, sometimes with little or no information to direct them to the most secure decision.

Why Wireless Security Is Important

Wireless security presents a number of unique challenges. These include:

- *Unauthorized users can access the network*—Because a wireless signal is not confined to the four walls of the building in which the network is located, an unauthorized user may be able to pick up the signal outside the building's security perimeter. It is possible for an intruder lurking in the parking lot with a wireless laptop computer to intercept signals and access the network. Individuals who actively search for wireless signals to pick up, often by simply driving down the street, are participating in an activity known as **wardriving**.

- *Attackers can view transmitted data*—In a wired network an attacker would have to gain access to the cabling infrastructure to attempt to look at the data that is being transmitted across the network or to gain access to a file server. With a wireless network, an attacker only has to pick up an unencrypted wireless signal to see what is being transmitted or gain access to the network.

- *Employees can weaken installed security protections*—An employee who purchases a wireless access point and brings it into the office to provide personal wireless access has installed a **rogue access point**. Typically these rogue access points have no security features implemented. This means that an attacker can pick up the rogue access point's wireless signal and bypass all of the network security that the organization has installed. Rogue access points are illustrated in Figure 1-3.

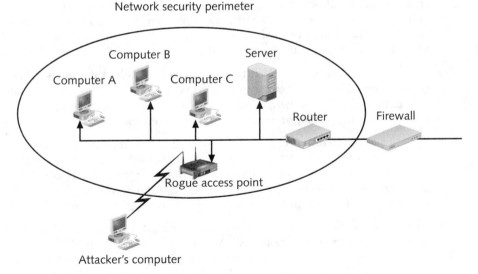

Figure 1-3   Rogue access point

- *Attackers can easily crack existing wireless security*—Early types of wireless LANs had basic security features that could be enabled. However, these features were not properly implemented and turned out to be easy to bypass. Although current products have more robust security features, many older products are still in use with very weak security features. Users are sometimes mistaken in their belief that because the security features are turned on, their computers and data are protected.

Because of the unique security challenges of a WLAN and because the security on early WLANs could be easily defeated, wireless security remains a major issue with organizations and businesses. In many organizations WLANs are deployed only in limited areas or with severe restrictions because of security concerns.

Despite the fact that organizations are concerned about wireless security, users who set up their own personal wireless networks in their homes, apartments, or dorm rooms often don't share this concern. It is common for users to be able to pick up a neighbor's unprotected wireless signal from within their own home or apartment, and often there are multiple unprotected signals from which to choose. These users often express an attitude of, "I don't need to be worried about security on my home computer."

However, that attitude indicates a misunderstanding or underestimation of the serious damage that can result from an unprotected wireless signal on a home wireless network. A wireless attacker can:

- *Steal personal data*—An attacker (or even a curious person) who picks up an unprotected wireless signal can gain access to any folder on a computer with file sharing enabled. Users may typically set file sharing on multiple folders to allow other users in the home or apartment to be able to access documents. Unfortunately, this may leave personal information, financial data, and even treasured digital photographs open to attackers to steal or erase.

- *View wireless transmissions*—With freely available **wireless packet sniffer** software (or sometimes hardware) that can view the contents of wireless packets, an attacker can easily capture usernames, passwords, social security numbers, or any other information that is transmitted in an unprotected form.

- *Inject malware*—**Malware** is a general term used to describe worms, viruses, spyware, or other types of software with a malicious intent. Firewalls are typically used to restrict specific types of malware from entering a network. However, an attacker who can access a home computer through an unprotected wireless signal is behind the firewall and can inject malware onto the computer.

- *Download harmful content*—In several instances, attackers have used an unprotected wireless signal to enter a home WLAN and download harmful Web content, such as child pornography, onto the user's computer. The attackers then contact law enforcement personnel who obtain a search warrant to seize the unsuspecting owner's computer and discover the harmful content. Only with great difficulty have the owners been able to prove they were not the ones responsible for the content.

- *Cause loss of equipment*—Several states have started prosecuting individuals who are caught using a wireless connection without the owner's permission. Although many users applaud this action, it also means that the home network and computers that were compromised must be confiscated as evidence by law enforcement personnel. This means that the innocent owner must wait for several months until they can get their equipment back.

- *Cause violation of an ISP agreement*—A subscriber who pays a monthly fee to an Internet Service Provider (ISP) but then freely shares wireless access with neighbors may consider that he or she is just being friendly. However, almost all ISPs do not share that sentiment. The contracts that a subscriber signs with an ISP usually explicitly state that the broadband access is for personal use only and the subscriber is not permitted to share the network with other people outside of the household and the ISP may sue any customer who shares wireless access with others. In many instances ISPs have sent a cease-and-desist order from their legal department to offenders. Although it is unlikely that an ISP will actively seek out those who are sharing their wireless signal, it's not unusual for a neighbor who has a complaint against another neighbor to turn them in to the ISP.

- *Identify "weak link" users*—A user who is not concerned about security in his or her home wireless network will generally not be concerned about security in the organization in which they work. This employee may be a "weak link" for attackers to exploit. It is important to practice good security habits at home so that these follow the user to the workplace.

NOTE

As one security expert says, "Security begins at home."

Wireless Standards Organizations and Regulatory Agencies

There are three primary standard-setting and regulatory bodies that play a major role in wireless LAN technology. These include the Institute of Electrical and Electronics Engineers (IEEE), the Wi-Fi Alliance, and the U.S. Federal Communications Commission (FCC).

Institute of Electrical and Electronics Engineers (IEEE)

For computer networking and wireless communications the most widely known and influential organization is the **Institute of Electrical and Electronics Engineers (IEEE)**. The IEEE and its predecessor organizations date back to 1884. The IEEE establishes standards for telecommunications. However, the IEEE also covers a wide range of IT standards.

You can find out more about the IEEE and its standards on its Web site, *www.ieee.org*.

NOTE

IEEE is the world's largest technical professional society with members around the globe. Serving the computing, electrical engineering, and electronics professions, the IEEE engages in technical, educational, and professional activities that advance the theory and practice of what they call "electrotechnology." The 37 Societies and Councils of the IEEE routinely publish technically focused journals, magazines, and proceedings, as well as work on over 800 standards. Some of these standards apply to circuits and devices, communication and information technology, control and automation, electromagnetics, geoscience, ocean technology and remote sensing, instrumentation and measurement testing, optics, power and energy, and signal processing.

The IEEE is currently developing standards for rechargeable batteries for laptop computers and electronic voting equipment data exchange, among many other projects.

NOTE

Although the IEEE is one of the leading developers of global standards in a broad range of industries such as energy, biomedical and healthcare, and transportation, it is best known for its work in establishing standards for computer networks. In the early 1980s, the IEEE began work on developing computer network architecture standards. Its work was called **Project 802**. Project 802 quickly expanded into several different categories of network technology, known as 802.1, 802.2, all the way to 802.20. For example, IEEE 802.3 set specifications for Ethernet local area network technology.

The IEEE calls its "major" committees *working groups (WG)*, such as 802.11 (wireless), 802.3 (Ethernet), etc. Within the working groups are subgroups known as *task groups (TG)*, such as 802.11n.

NOTE

As older network technologies have been replaced with newer technologies, the IEEE 802 committees have likewise reflected the changes in technology. Several committees have been retired, while new committees have been formed to address emerging technologies. Table 1-2 lists the current IEEE 802 network committees.

Table 1-2 Current IEEE 802 task groups

Task Group	Description	Comments
802.11a	54 Mbps WLAN at 5 GHz	Ratified 1999, but devices did not appear until 2001
802.11b	11 Mbps WLAN at 2.4 GHz	Ratified 1999, also known as "Wi-Fi"

Table 1-2   Current IEEE 802 task groups (continued)

Task Group	Description	Comments
802.11c	Bridge connections	Moved to 802.1 Working Group
802.11d	Worldwide compliance with regulations for use of wireless signal spectrum	Adds features and restrictions to allow WLANs to operate within the countries that have wireless spectrum conflicts; ratified 2001
802.11e	Quality of Service	Ratified in 2005
802.11F	Inter-Access Point Protocol (IAPP)	Handles the registration and exchange of information between different vendors' access points; ratified 2003
802.11g	54 Mbps WLAN at 2.4 GHz	Ratified 2003
802.11h	Enhanced version of 802.11a	Supplement to the MAC layer to comply with European regulations for 5 GHz WLANs
802.11i	Wireless security	Also known as Robust Security Network, ratified 2004
802.11j	Enhancements to 5 GHz signaling	Proposed addition that incorporates Japanese regulatory extensions to the 802.11a standard
802.11k	Wireless LAN management system	In progress
802.11l	Not used	Omitted to avoid confusion with "802.11i"
802.11m	Maintenance of 802.11 documentation	In progress
802.11n	Future 300+ Mbps WLAN	In progress, anticipated ratification 2007
802.11p	Wireless Access for the Vehicular Environment (WAVE)	WLANs for automobiles
802.11r	Handoffs between mobile clients	As a major support to VoWLANs, it is designed to speed the handoff of wireless phones between wireless networks
802.11s	Mesh wireless network	A mesh network can determine the optimum route for a packet to travel across the WLAN based on the quality required
802.11t	Wireless Performance Prediction (WPP)	Standardized test methods and metrics for WLAN performance
802.11u	Interworking with non-802 networks (e.g., cellular)	Standards for how WLANs connect to external networks such as the Internet or cellular networks

Table 1-2   Current IEEE 802 task groups (continued)

Task Group	Description	Comments
802.11v	Wireless management	Creates efficient mechanisms to simplify wireless network deployment and management
802.11w	Protected Management Frames	Increases security of management frames

NOTE

Project 802 received its name from the fact that the work was begun in 1980 (80) during February, the second month (2).

Wi-Fi Alliance

Shortly after the IEEE released its revised wireless network standards in 1999, there was concern about how this new wireless technology would be accepted in the marketplace. A consortium of wireless equipment manufacturers and software providers was formed to promote wireless network technology. This group was known as the **Wireless Ethernet Compatibility Alliance (WECA)**. The WECA had three goals:

- To encourage wireless manufacturers to use the IEEE 802.11 technologies in their wireless networking products

- To promote and market these technologies to consumers in the home, in small office home office (SOHO) settings, and in large enterprise businesses and organizations

- To test and certify that wireless products adhere to the IEEE 802.11 standards to ensure product interoperability

In October 2002, the WECA organization changed its name to **Wi-Fi (Wireless Fidelity) Alliance**, which reflected the name of the certification that it uses (Wi-Fi) to verify that a product follows IEEE standards (its Web site is *www.wi-fi.org*). Wireless devices are sometimes generically called "Wi-Fi," though in reality only products that have passed Wi-Fi Alliance testing are allowed to be called Wi-Fi Certified, which is a registered trademark shown in Figure 1-4.

Figure 1-4   Wi-Fi Certified seal

A support technician received an e-mail from a department head asking if her staff could get "Y5" accounts. The technician was confused until a colleague read the e-mail aloud and he then realized the person was requesting "Wi-Fi" accounts!

Federal Communications Commission (FCC)

In the United States, the organization that controls and regulates wireless transmissions for use by citizens (as opposed to the federal government) is the **Federal Communications Commission (FCC)**. The FCC serves as the primary regulatory agency for wireless communications in the United States and its territorial possessions. The FCC is an independent government agency that is directly responsible to Congress, established by the Communications Act of 1934 and charged with regulating interstate and international communications by radio, television, wire, satellite, and cable.

To preserve its independence, the FCC is directed by five commissioners who are appointed by the President and confirmed by the Senate for five-year terms. Only three commissioners may be members of the same political party, and none of them can have a financial interest in any FCC-related business.

The FCC's responsibilities are very broad. In addition to developing and implementing regulatory programs, they also process applications for licenses and other filings, analyze complaints, conduct investigations, and take part in congressional hearings. They also represent the United States in negotiations with other nations about telecommunications issues.

The Web site of the FCC is *www.fcc.gov*.

The FCC plays an important role in wireless communications. It regulates radio and television broadcast stations as well as cable and satellite stations. It oversees cellular telephones, pagers, and two-way radios. The FCC regulates the use of radio frequencies to fulfill the communications needs of businesses, local and state governments, public safety service providers, aircraft and ship operators, and individuals.

The FCC is charged with regulating the radio frequency spectrum. The **radio frequency spectrum** is the entire range of all radio frequencies. The spectrum is divided into over 450 different sections or **bands**. Although a license is normally required from the FCC to send and receive on a specific frequency, there is a notable exception. This is known as the **license-exempt spectrum** or **unregulated bands**. Unregulated bands are in effect bands of the radio spectrum that are available nationwide to all users, without requiring a license. Devices that use these bands can be either fixed or mobile. The FCC says that it created the unregulated bands to "foster the development of a broad range of new devices, stimulate the growth of new industries, and promote the ability of U.S. manufacturers to compete globally by enabling them to develop unlicensed digital products for the world market."

NOTE   The FCC, by imposing power limits on devices using the unregulated bands to reduce interference with licensed channels and minimize health risks, in effect reduces their range. This prevents manufacturers of devices such as long-range walkie-talkies from using these frequencies instead of the regulated frequencies intended for these products.

The FCC unregulated bands are summarized in Table 1-3. Two of the bands are used for WLANs. One of these bands is the **Industrial, Scientific and Medical (ISM)** band, which was approved by the FCC in 1985. Another unlicensed band used for WLANs is the **Unlicensed National Information Infrastructure (UNII)** band, approved in 1996. The UNII band is intended for devices that provide short-range, high-speed wireless digital communications. UNII devices may provide a means for educational institutions, libraries, and health care providers to connect to basic and advanced telecommunications services. Educational institutions, for example, could form inexpensive wireless computer networks between classrooms. UNII unlicensed wireless networks could help improve the quality and reduce the cost of medical care by allowing medical staff to obtain on-the-spot patient data, X-rays, and medical charts, and by giving health care workers in remote areas access to telecommunications services. Depending on the type of wireless LAN, it will use either the ISM or the U-NII band.

Table 1-3   Unlicensed bands

Unlicensed Band	Frequency	Total Bandwidth	Common Uses
Industrial, Scientific and Medical (ISM)	902-928 MHz 2.4-2.4835 GHz 5.725-5.85 GHz	234.5 MHz	Cordless phones, WLANs, Wireless Public Branch Exchanges
Unlicensed Personal Communications Systems	1910-1930 MHz 2390-2400 MHz	30 MHz	Wireless Public Branch Exchanges
Unlicensed National Information Infra-structure (UNII)	5.15-5.25 GHz 5.25-5.35 GHz 5.725-5.825 GHz	300 Mhz	WLANs, Wireless Public Branch Exchanges, campus applications, long outdoor links
Millimeter Wave	59-64 GHz	5 GHz	Home networking applications

There are some negative features of the unregulated bands. Because they are not regulated and licensed, devices from different vendors may attempt to use the same frequency. This conflict can cause the signals from different devices to interfere with each other and prevent the devices from functioning properly. Therefore the performance of devices using unregulated bands may be unpredictable.

WIRELESS LAN STANDARDS AND TYPES

Since the late 1990s, the IEEE has approved four standards for wireless LANs (in chronological order): IEEE 802.11, 802.11b, 802.11a, and 802.11g. A new standard, 802.11n, is expected to be approved by 2007. Each of the standards will now be examined in detail.

IEEE 802.11

In 1990, the IEEE organization formed a committee to develop a standard for WLANs operating at 1 and 2 Mbps. Several different proposals were initially recommended before a draft was developed. This draft went through seven revisions that took almost seven years to complete. On June 26, 1997, the IEEE approved the final draft.

The **IEEE 802.11** standard specified that wireless transmissions could take place in one of two ways. The first is through infrared light, and the other type of transmission is by sending radio signals. Because of limitations using infrared light, 802.11 infrared WLAN systems were never widely adopted. Today infrared transmissions are generally used in specialized applications, such as data transfers between laptop computers, digital cameras, handheld data collection devices, PDAs, and other mobile devices.

NOTE WLANs that use infrared transmissions are used in specialized situations in which radio signals would interfere with other equipment, such as in hospital operating rooms, or when security is a concern, such as in secure government buildings.

IEEE 802.11b

The bandwidth of 2 Mbps for the 802.11 standard introduced in 1997 was not sufficient for most network applications. The IEEE body revisited the 802.11 standard shortly after it was released to determine what changes could be made to increase the speed. In September 1999 a new **IEEE 802.11b** amendment was added to the standard, which added two higher speeds (5.5 Mbps and 11 Mbps) to the original 802.11 standard (1 Mbps and 2 Mbps). Like the 802.11 standard, 802.11b uses the ISM band.

The 802.11b standard can support wireless devices that are up to 115 meters (375 feet) apart. However, devices that are that far apart might not be transmitting at 11 Mbps. Radio waves decrease in power over distance, much like the sound of your voice: a person standing 1 meter away from you might hear you very clearly, whereas a person 60 meters away would have difficulty hearing you. Instead of completely dropping the signal if it falls out of range to transmit at 11 Mbps, the 802.11b standard specifies that the devices should drop their transmission speed to the next lower level (5.5, 2, or 1 Mbps). This allows devices to transmit farther apart but at slower speeds.

IEEE 802.11a

At the same time the IEEE created the 802.11b standard, it also issued another standard with even higher speeds. The **IEEE 802.11a** standard specifies a maximum rated speed of 54 Mbps and also supports 48, 36, 24, 18, 12, 9, and 6 Mbps transmissions using the UNII band. Although the 802.11a and 802.11b specifications were published at the same time by IEEE, 802.11b products started to appear almost immediately, whereas 802.11a products did not arrive until late 2001. 802.11a products came to the market later because of technical issues along with the high cost of developing products for the standard. Devices based on the 802.11a standard cannot use complementary metal oxide semiconductor (CMOS) (the semiconductor used in 802.11b WLANs). Instead, they must use a compound such as gallium arsenide (GaAs) or silicon germanium (SiGe). These semiconductors are more expensive and require more capital investment and time to develop and manufacture.

Although the 802.11a standard achieves higher speed, the tradeoff is that devices cannot be as far apart as with the 802.11b standard. A wireless network that follows the 802.11a standard may generally have devices that are no more than 30 meters (100 feet) apart.

IEEE 802.11g

The tremendous success of the IEEE 802.11b standard shortly after its release prompted the IEEE to re-examine the 802.11b and 802.11a standards to determine if a third intermediate standard could be developed. This "best of both worlds" approach would preserve the stable and widely accepted features of 802.11b but increase the data transfer rates to those similar to 802.11a. The IEEE formed an initial task group to explore this possibility. By late 2001 a draft standard was proposed known as **IEEE 802.11g**. The standard was formally ratified in 2003.

The IEEE 802.11g draft was a compromise based on input from several different chip (microprocessor) manufacturers, who had a major stake in the outcome. Although most major commercial wireless networking product vendors will build and sell products based upon whatever standard is approved, the same is not true for the chip manufacturers. These businesses must make huge monetary investments in designing, sampling, and manufacturing the silicon chips used in the wireless network products. They must then try to sell their chips to product vendors that design and build commercial products based on those chips.

The 802.11g standard, which is backward-compatible with 802.11b, specifies that devices operate entirely in the ISM frequency and not the UNII band used by 802.11a. This gives the 802.11g standard the ability to support devices that are farther apart with higher speeds, but it uses the crowded ISM band. Like 802.11b, 802.11g can support devices that are up to 115 meters (375 feet) apart.

Projected IEEE 802.11n

In September 2004, the IEEE started working on a new standard to significantly increase the bandwidth of today's WLANs. This standard, known as **802.11n**, **Multiple-Input, Multiple-Output Enhanced WLAN (MEW)**, or simply **Multiple-Input, Multiple-Output (MIMO)**, will set standards for transmissions expected to exceed 300 Mbps. The 802.11n committee is evaluating over 60 different proposals regarding how to accomplish this. The top speed of the 802.11n standard will be anywhere from 300 Mbps to 600 Mbps, depending on which proposal is approved.

Although the final proposal might not be ratified until the year 2007, devices that follow one of the proposed options will appear much earlier than that. This is because there is a significant time lag between the time the final proposal is published and when it is ultimately ratified by the IEEE. This occurred with the 802.11g standard: devices were marketed and sold months before the standard was finally ratified. A WLAN based on one of the 802.11n proposals appeared in mid-2004 under the name "802.11 pre-N."

NOTE The Wi-Fi Alliance refuses to sanction and certify devices prior to the final release of the standard.

A summary of the different WLAN standards and types is found in Table 1-4.

Table 1-4 Summary of IEEE standards

IEEE Standard	Frequency Band	Bandwidth
802.11	ISM	2 Mbps
802.11b	ISM	11 Mbps
802.11a	UNII	54 Mbps
802.11g	ISM	54 Mbps
802.11n (proposed)	ISM	300+ Mbps

WIRELESS CERTIFICATIONS

As with most networking certifications, wireless certifications can be divided into two categories: vendor-neutral certifications and vendor-specific certifications.

The most well-known wireless certifications are the Certified Wireless Network Professional (CWNP) certifications offered by Planet3 Wireless. There are six different certifications within CWNP:

- *Wireless#*—This certification is an entry-level certification that covers different types of wireless technology standards.

- *Certified Wireless Network Administrator (CWNA)*—The CWNA certification covers the skills to administer a wireless network in an enterprise setting.

- *Certified Wireless Security Professional (CWSP)*—This certification is designed for individuals who will be providing security for a WLAN in an enterprise or SOHO setting.

- *Certified Wireless Analysis Professional (CWAN)*—Troubleshooting, wireless network configuration, and performance enhancing are the primary topics of the CWAN certification.

- *Certified Wireless Network Expert (CWNE)*—This certification is designed for individuals who will be responsible for designing, installing, configuring, and troubleshooting a WLAN.

- *Certified Wireless Network Trainers (CWNT)*—An individual with a CWNT certification is qualified to deliver CWNP training.

The Web site for CWNP is *www.cwnp.com*

NOTE

Another wireless certification is administered by AreTec, which is an organization that promotes standardization in wireless technologies. There are three AreTec certifications: AreTec Certified Wireless Professional (AceWP), AreTec Certified Wireless Developer (AceWD), and AreTec Certified Wireless Expert (AceWE). The basic AceWP is a combination of five career tracks: wireless applications development, analog and digital data communications and multimedia signal processing; wireless carriers, such as providers, networks and satellite communications; wireless networking and security; and wireless embedded systems, which includes circuit designs and protocol interfacing. Training for each of these paths lasts 80 hours, and half of the time is working on hands-on lab projects.

The National Association of Radio and Telecommunications Engineers (NARTE) offers the Wireless System Installers Certification program for professionals who are responsible for the implementation of wireless LANs and other wireless networks. There are two certifications under NARTE program, which are the Wireless Installer Technician and the Wireless Installer Engineer

The best-known vendor-specific certification is offered by Cisco Systems. There are three wireless certifications available. These include the Cisco Wireless LAN Design Specialist, the Cisco Wireless LAN Sales Specialist, and the Cisco Wireless LAN Support Specialist.

1

CHAPTER SUMMARY

- Wireless LAN applications can be found in every industry with employees who need the freedom to conduct business without being confined to a specific location. Businesses use WLANs to provide employees with access to data when they are out of their offices. WLANs have made it possible for businesses to improve services while reducing costs. The travel industry has been a leader in adopting wireless technologies. Airport terminals, trains, ships, and even highway rest stops all have used WLAN technology for a variety of purposes. Educational facilities have also widely implemented WLANs to support instruction as well as to provide students with access to data. The health care industry uses WLANs to help track patient information.

- There are several significant advantages to WLANs. These include mobility, easier and less expensive network installations, increased reliability, and disaster recovery. Disadvantages of WLANS are radio signal interference, health risks, and security.

- The term information security is frequently used to describe the tasks of guarding information that is in a digital format. Information security protects the integrity, confidentiality, and availability of information on the devices that store, manipulate, and transmit the information through products, people, and procedures. Despite the fact that information security is considered very important, there are a number of challenges in defending against attackers, such as the speed of attacks, increased sophistication of attacks, faster detection of weaknesses, distributed attacks, and user confusion.

- Wireless security presents a number of unique challenges, such as unauthorized users accessing the network, attackers viewing transmitted data, employees installing rogue access points, and the weaknesses of older wireless security defenses.

- There are three primary standard-setting and regulatory bodies that play a major role in wireless LAN technology. These include the IEEE, the Wi-Fi Alliance, and the U.S. FCC.

- Since the late 1990s, the IEEE has approved four standards for wireless LANs: IEEE 802.11, 802.11b, 802.11a, and 802.11g. A new standard, 802.11n, is expected to be approved by 2007.

KEY TERMS

bands — Sections of the radio frequency spectrum.

cold site — A disaster recovery option that consists of a remote site that provides office space in the event of a disaster, but the customer must provide and install all the equipment needed to continue operations.

Federal Communications Commission (FCC) — The primary regulatory agency for wireless communications in the United States and its territorial possessions.

hot site — A remote site that contains redundant equipment, supplies, and telecommunications infrastructure for a business in the event of a disaster, so that operations can continue nearly seamlessly.

IEEE 802.11 — A wireless local area network with a bandwidth (maximum throughput) of 2 Mbps.

IEEE 802.11a — A wireless local area network with a bandwidth (maximum throughput) of 54 Mbps and uses the UNII band.

IEEE 802.11b — A wireless local area network with a bandwidth (maximum throughput) of 11 Mbps and uses the ISM band.

IEEE 802.11g — A wireless local area network with a bandwidth (maximum throughput) of 54 Mbps and uses the ISM band.

IEEE 802.11n — A proposed WLAN standard with a bandwidth (maximum throughput) between 300–600 Mbps.

Industrial, Scientific and Medical (ISM) — An unregulated band used for WLAN transmissions.

information security — The tasks of guarding information that is in a digital format, with the objective of protecting the integrity, confidentiality, and availability of that information.

Institute of Electrical and Electronics Engineers (IEEE) — An organization that establishes standards for networks.

license-exempt spectrum — Unregulated bands available nationwide to all users without requiring a license.

malware — A general term used to describe worms, viruses, spyware, or other types of software with a malicious intent.

Multiple-Input, Multiple-Output Enhanced WLAN (MEW) — A proposed WLAN standard with a bandwidth between 300–600 Mbps.

Multiple-Input, Multiple-Output (MIMO) — A proposed WLAN standard with a bandwidth between 300–600 Mbps.

Project 802 — The original effort by the IEEE beginning in 1980 to establish network standards.

radio frequency spectrum — The entire range of all radio frequencies.

rogue access point — A wireless device that is installed without permission.

Unlicensed National Information Infrastructure (UNII) — An unregulated band used for WLAN transmissions.

unregulated bands — Bands of the radio spectrum that are available to all users without requiring a license.

voice over wireless LAN (VoWLAN) — A technology that uses an existing data WLAN for making and receiving telephone calls. Also called wireless voice over IP (wVoIP), voice over IP (VoIP), and VoWi-Fi.

wardriving — Driving through an area with a wireless device searching for an unprotected wireless signal.

Wi-Fi (Wireless Fidelity) Alliance — A consortium of wireless network equipment manufacturers and software providers.

Wireless Ethernet Compatibility Alliance (WECA) — A consortium of wireless equipment manufacturers and software providers that has been superceded by the Wi-Fi Alliance.

wireless packet sniffer — Software or hardware that can be used to view the contents of wireless packets.

zero day attack — An attack based on a previously unknown flaw in software that provides no warning, that is "zero days" of warning.

REVIEW QUESTIONS

1. Each of the following is an advantage that wireless local area networks deliver to businesses except
   a. greater network security
   b. increased productivity
   c. time savings
   d. financial savings

2. Another name for a wireless local area network is
   a. Wi-Fi
   b. Wireless communication system
   c. Radio frequency identification resource
   d. Wireless network adapter system

3. VoWLAN uses a WLAN for
   a. enhanced security transmissions
   b. voice communications
   c. roaming between wired segments
   d. segmentation

4. The primary advantage of wireless technology is
   a. low cost
   b. decreased flexibility
   c. mobility
   d. bandwidth

5. A _____ has all the equipment needed for an organization to continue running, including office space and furniture, telephone jacks, computer equipment, and a live telecommunications link.
   a. hot site
   b. warm site
   c. cold site
   d. distributed remote access location (DRAL)

6. A WLAN can create interference on other wireless devices but cannot itself be inter-fered with because of its high microwatt power distribution. True or False?

7. Currently, no scientific studies have revealed health problems associated with the absorption of low levels of RF energy by the human body. True or False?

8. Many organizations have resisted implementing wireless on a broad scale because of the lack of security in wireless. True or False?

9. A zero day attack occurs when an attacker discovers and exploits a previously unknown flaw in software. True or False?

10. It is not possible for an attacker to use multiple computers to launch an attack. True or False?

11. Individuals who actively search for wireless signals to pick up, often by just driving down the street, are participating in an activity known as _____ .

12. An employee who purchases a wireless access point and brings it into the office to provide personal wireless access has installed a(n) _____ .

13. A(n)_____ is software or hardware that can view the contents of wire-less packets.

14. _____ is a general term used to describe worms, viruses, spyware, or other types of software with a malicious intent.

15. Almost all _____ have clauses in their contracts that prohibit users from sharing a wireless Internet connection with members outside of the household.

16. Explain how information security can be achieved.

17. What is the Wi-Fi organization and what does it do?

18. What is the role of the Federal Communications Commission in relation to WLANs?

19. What are the characteristics of an IEEE 802.11b WLAN?

20. What are the expected features of the IEEE 802.11n standard?

Hands-On Projects

Project 1-1: Identifying Shared Network Files

As noted in a previous section, a wireless attacker (or even a curious person) who picks up an unprotected wireless signal can gain access to any folder on a computer that is set with file sharing enabled. Users may typically set file sharing on multiple folders to allow other users in the home or apartment to be able to access their documents. Unfortunately, this may leave personal information open to attackers. In this project you will download and use a program to identify shared files.

1. Point your Web browser to *www.sysinternals.com/Utilities/ShareEnum.html*.

2. Follow the instructions to download **ShareEnum** onto your desktop.

3. When the download is finished, install the program using the default installation settings.

4. Locate the file **ShareEnum.exe** and double-click on it to launch the application. In the list box, select one at a time each of the domains listed and click the **Refresh** button after each selection. A report similar to that in Figure 1-5 will be displayed.

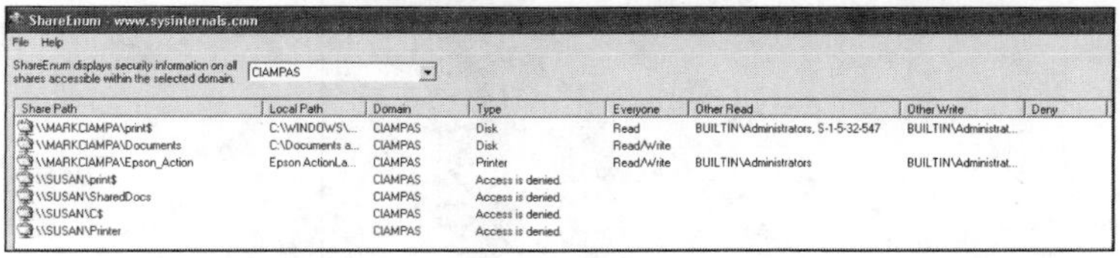

Figure 1-5   Shared folders

5. Each of these shared folders could potentially be accessible to attackers. To close a shared file so it is no longer accessible, click **Start** and **My Computer**.

6. Locate the folder that is being shared. Right-click the shared folder and then click **Sharing and Security** on the shortcut menu. Uncheck the **Share this folder on the network** box. What would happen if someone tried to access this folder now? Click **OK**.

7. To turn sharing back on, right-click the shared folder and then click **Sharing and Security** on the shortcut menu. Check the **Share this folder on the network** box. Click **OK**.

8. Close all windows.

Project 1-2: Locate Area Hotspots Using Yahoo Maps

A hotspot is an area of wireless LAN coverage. There are several Internet-based tools that can be used to locate hotspots. In this project you use Yahoo Maps to find local hotspots.

1. Go to *http://maps.yahoo.com*

2. Under **Address**, enter your street address, city, and state.

3. Click **Get Map**.

4. When the map appears click **SBC FreedomLink Wi-Fi** under **Travel and Transportation** as seen in Figure 1-6.

5. Click on one of the nearest hotspot locations. When the popup menu appears click **WiFi Hotspot Details**.

6. Look at the results that are displayed and see if you can identify any of these locations.

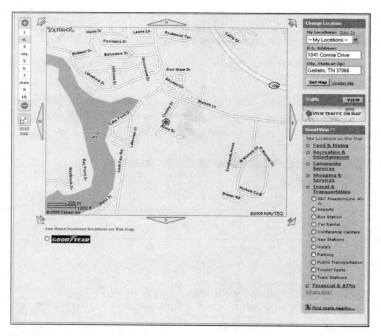

Figure 1-6   Yahoo! Maps Hotspots

7. Close your Web browser.

HANDS-ON
PROJECTS

Project 1-3: Store Passwords in Safe Document

Because of the difficulty in remembering passwords, some users create a document that contains the different passwords that they use. However, if an attacker were to steal this file, then all of the sites could be compromised. In this project, you download and use a Windows utility that encrypts passwords in one document so that even if it is stolen the passwords cannot be viewed.

1. Use your Web browser to go to *http://passwordsafe.sourceforge.net*.

2. Download **pwsafe-x.xx.exe** where "x.xx" is the latest version number to your desktop.

3. When the file is finished downloading, follow the instructions to install this program on your computer using the default settings.

4. Double-click the desktop icon to start PasswordSafe, shown in Figure 1-7.

5. Click **Create new database**.

6. Enter a strong password for **Safe Combination**. The password must have upper- and lowercase letters and at least one digit or character of punctuation. Re-enter it under **Verify**. Click **OK**.

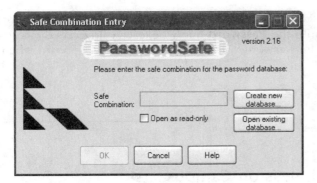

Figure 1-7 PasswordSafe

7. Click **File** and then **Save** and enter the filename **Password** and click the **Save** button.

8. Now you can add your passwords to the database. Click **Edit** and **Add entry**, as shown in Figure 1-8. Fill in the blanks for an account and password you use regularly. Enter **Project 1–3** in the **Title** entry. Note that the password will appear in cleartext (not encrypted) when you enter it. Click **OK**. If you are asked to set a default username name, click **No**.

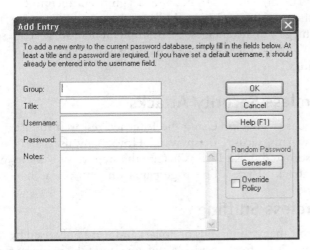

Figure 1-8 Add entry to PasswordSafe

9. Click **File** and then click **Exit**. Be sure to save the file before exiting.

10. Start **PasswordSafe**. Enter your safe combination.

11. Double-click the entry. Your password is now added to the Windows Clipboard. You can paste the password into the **Password** line whenever you access the account to which it corresponds. The password will be cleared from the Clipboard when PasswordSafe is closed.

12. Close PasswordSafe.

CASE PROJECTS

Case Project 1-1: Wireless on Campus

What wireless technology is currently functional on your campus? Prepare a list of questions regarding the type of wireless technology, when it was installed, where it can be accessed, the future upgrade plans, what security is being used, and so on, and present those to the person on campus responsible for wireless technology. You may want to invite this person to a class so that all students can ask questions at one time. What suggestions would you make for the current wireless infrastructure? Write a one-paragraph summary of what you have learned.

Case Project 1-2: VoWLAN Technology

Voice over wireless LAN (VoWLAN) is posed to become a significant technology for both businesses and consumers in the near future. Using the Internet and print sources, research VoWLAN. What are its advantages, disadvantages, costs, implementation strategies, and so on? What would the price have to be for you to purchase for your personal use? Write a one-page paper on your findings.

Case Project 1-3: Wireless Security Attacks

What are the latest wireless security attacks? Using the Internet, research the latest attacks that are occurring. Are they worms, viruses, or spyware? How many users has this attack infected? What has been the estimated dollar loss? What are the steps to prevent it? What are the steps to clean up after an attack? Write a one-page paper on your research.

Case Project 1-4: Wireless Sniffing

Until recently packet sniffers cost many thousands of dollars and were only used by network professionals. However, now sniffers are freely available and are one of the primary tools used by attackers. Is this a good thing? Should sniffers be regulated and licensed? Should they be controlled, and if so, how? Write a one-page paper justifying your opinions.

Case Project 1-5: Sharing a Wireless Connection

What is your opinion regarding sharing a wireless connection? Should ISPs be able to limit the users to only those in a single household? Using the Internet and other resources, research this topic. Locate a subscriber agreement that an ISP uses. What does it say regarding sharing the Internet connection? Do you agree with it? If not, what would you suggest so that the ISP is not deprived of potential revenue from users who are accessing it for free? Write a one-page paper on your findings.

Fairvue Technology Consulting

Fairvue Technology Consulting (FTC) is a local company that offers voice, data, and video consulting services. FTC often hires consultants to assist them with projects, and has recently asked you to help them with a project. A local healthcare clinic, Green Walk-In Care, has expressed an interest in replacing their wired network with a wireless LAN, but the office manager would like to know more about WLANs to make an informed decision.

1. Create a PowerPoint presentation that lists some of the advantages of wireless over wired technology for Green Walk-In Care. Because you are unable to visit the clinic at the present time, you have been asked by FTC to reflect back on the last time you visited your primary care physician and offer suggestions regarding how wireless technology could be used to streamline that process. Your presentation should be 6–8 slides in length.

2. Green Walk-In Care was impressed by your presentation, but is very concerned about the security of patient information. FTC has asked you to create a one-page memo that briefly outlines the concerns regarding wireless security and what your recommendation would be.

Wireless LAN Vulnerabilities

After completing this chapter you should be able to do the following:

➤ Explain the basic IEEE 802.11 security protections

➤ Describe the vulnerabilities of IEEE 802.11 authentication

➤ Tell how address filtering is limited

➤ List the vulnerabilities of WEP

The World of Wireless Security

Automobile accidents continue to pose a serious problem for the over 230 million cars on U.S. roadways. Each year over 6 million accidents result in over 3 million injuries and 42,000 fatalities. It is estimated that these vehicular accidents cost over $260 billion annually. One way to reduce the number of accidents comes from an unlikely source: wireless LANs.

The U.S. Department of Transportation (DOT), along with Daimler-Chrysler, Nissan, and General Motors (GM), is working on a project to enable nationwide wireless communication between cars and roadside facilities with the goal of preventing accidents and relieving traffic congestion. The Vehicle Infrastructure Integration (VII) project is a federally funded effort that aims to build almost one quarter of a million IEEE 802.11a and 802.11p WLAN hotspots along interstate and state highways. Car manufacturers would install special sensors and probes along with antennas, receivers, and transceivers in all new vehicles, while the DOT would install the communication links on the roadside.

Whenever a car passes a VII hotspot it would anonymously transmit on-board sensor data, such as its average speed, recent braking, and other information. This data would be combined with that from other cars that pass the same hotspot and then would be forwarded to a central point that would organize the data by geographic coordinates to paint a picture of traffic conditions and accidents that may have occurred. The data would then be distributed back to all hotspots along that route to warn other drivers of impending congestion or accidents to avoid.

The VII could be used for other purposes as well. Cars could receive maintenance update information and reminders from manufacturers regarding when preventive maintenance is due for a specific car based on the number of miles that have been driven. The car itself could even notify the manufacturer through the VII when a part is wearing out. The cost of the VII is estimated to be up to $10 billion. A prototype system is expected by 2007.

Security will be an important component of VII. As part of the IEEE 802.11p protocol, the three primary areas that will be addressed are anonymity (so individual driver information cannot be traced back to the source), authenticity (so that no fake transmissions can be used), and confidentiality (so that the contents of the transmissions cannot be viewed).

Suppose you purchase a top-of-the-line new lock for your front door, pay to have someone install it, and always lock the door when you leave the house. One day you come home to find that your house has been broken into and your possessions stolen. It turns out the lock had a weakness and could be opened with a small screwdriver, and instructions about how to do this were freely available on the Internet. You had done all that you should have done to protect your possessions, yet a vulnerability beyond your control literally opened the door for the thieves.

That scenario is similar to what early WLAN users faced regarding network security. The original IEEE 802.11 standard contained provisions for security to protect WLANs from attackers and keep information safe, and users were encouraged to implement these provisions. However, shortly after wireless devices began to appear, researchers determined that there were serious flaws in the IEEE 802.11 standards and WLANs that implemented them were not secure. In fact, using the security features was considered even worse than if a user did not turn on security. This is because when the security features were not turned on, the users *knew* that the network was unsecured and could treat it that way by restricting what they did on it. Users who implemented the security features *thought* their transmissions were secure, but in reality they were exposed to attacks.

This chapter looks at the original IEEE 802.11 security provisions in detail and investigates how and why these provisions were vulnerable and did not provide adequate security for wireless transmissions.

NOTE It is important to understand that the security weaknesses covered in this chapter relate only to the *original* IEEE 802.11 standards. More recent standards do contain security technologies that can protect wireless LANs. However, many wireless networks in use today still support only the original IEEE standards. Wireless LAN administrators and users should be aware of these weaknesses and what steps can be taken to mitigate them.

Basic IEEE 802.11 Security Protections

The IEEE 802.11 committee realized that wireless transmissions were vulnerable to attack and interception, and implemented several protections in the original 1997 802.11 standard, while leaving other protections to be applied at the WLAN vendor's discretion. These protections can be divided into three categories: access control, wired equivalent privacy (WEP), and authentication.

Access Control

Access control is defined as a method of restricting access to resources. Access control is intended to guard the *availability* of information by making it accessible only to authorized users. (Recall that availability is one of the three "CIA" characteristics of information security: confidentiality, integrity, and availability.)

Wireless access control is accomplished by limiting a device's access to the **access point (AP)**. An AP contains an antenna and a radio transmitter/receiver to send and receive wireless signals, and an RJ-45 port that allows it to connect by cable to a wired network. An AP acts as the central base station for the wireless network. All of the wireless devices transmit to the AP, which in turn redirects the signal to the other wireless devices. The AP also acts as a bridge between wireless and wired networks, as shown in Figure 2-1. Because of its central location in a WLAN, restricting access to the AP is the ideal access control solution: only authorized devices are able to connect to the AP and become part of the network.

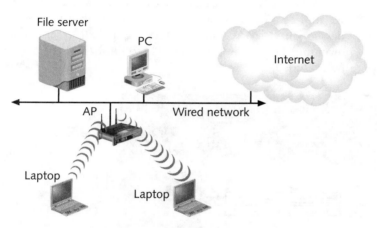

Figure 2-1   Access point as central base station

The IEEE 802.11 standard does not specify how wireless access control is to be implemented. Almost all wireless AP vendors implement access control through **Media Access Control (MAC) address filtering**. The MAC address is a hardware address that uniquely identifies each node of a network. Other names for the MAC address are vendor address, vendor ID, NIC address, Ethernet address, and physical address.

Because a wireless device can only be reliably identified by its MAC address, it was chosen for wireless access control.

NOTE

The MAC address is a unique 48-bit number that is "burned" into the network interface adapter when it is manufactured. This number consists of two parts: a 24-bit organizationally unique identifier (OUI), sometimes called a "company ID," which references the company that produced the adapter, and a 24-bit individual address block (IAB), which uniquely identifies the card itself. A typical MAC address is illustrated in Figure 2-2.

Organizationally Unique   Individual Address
Identifier (OUI)   Block (IAB)

00-50-F2-7C-62-E1

Figure 2-2   MAC address

Access to the wireless network can be restricted by entering the MAC address of a wireless device into the AP (known as a **MAC address filter**). As seen in Figure 2-3, restrictions can generally be implemented in one of two ways: a device can be *permitted* or allowed into the network ("Let this device in") or a device can be *prevented* or blocked from accessing the network ("Keep this device out"). MAC address filtering is usually implemented by permitting instead of preventing, because it is not possible to know the MAC address of all the devices that are to be excluded.

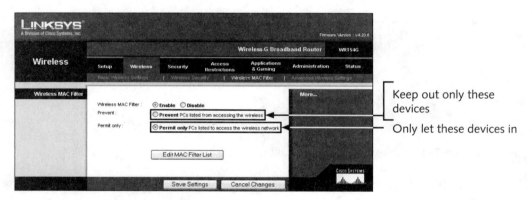

Figure 2-3   MAC address filter

Wireless access control through MAC address filtering should not be confused with **access restrictions**, or restrictions placed on what users can perform *after* they are accepted into the network. Access restrictions can limit a user's access to the Internet—what days and times it can be accessed, which Web sites can be visited, or the type of traffic that passes through the access point based on the protocol—as seen in Figure 2-4.

 NOTE   When restricting traffic based on the protocol, the access point acts like a firewall by closing ports. For example, if you want to disallow Web and FTP traffic, the AP could be configured to reject all HTTP traffic (on TCP/IP Port 80) and FTP traffic (Port 21).

MAC address filtering is considered a basic means of controlling access. One of the drawbacks of MAC address filtering is that it requires pre-approved authentication: the MAC address must first be entered into the MAC address filter on the access point before

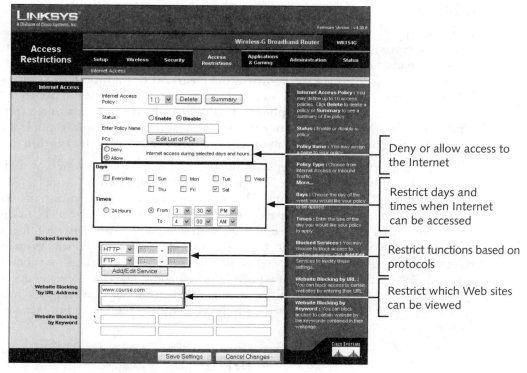

Figure 2-4   Access restrictions

the device can be accepted or rejected. This makes it difficult to provide temporary access for "guest" devices.

Wireless LAN MAC address filtering has serious vulnerabilities. These vulnerabilities are discussed later in this chapter.

NOTE

Wired Equivalent Privacy (WEP)

Wired equivalent privacy (WEP) is intended to guard another of the three CIA characteristics of information, namely *confidentiality*. This ensures that only authorized parties can view the information. WEP accomplishes confidentiality by "scrambling" the wireless data as it is transmitted so that it cannot be viewed by unauthorized parties.

WEP is used in IEEE 802.11 to encrypt wireless transmissions, and was the original cryptography mechanism of that standard. The process of how information can be changed so that it is not viewed and how WEP is implemented is discussed in the following section.

Cryptography

Cryptography comes from two Greek words: *crypto*, meaning hidden, and *graph*, meaning to write. Cryptography is the science of transforming information so that it is secure while it is being transmitted or stored. A simple illustration of cryptography is to begin with the original (unencrypted) message, known as the **cleartext** or **plaintext**, and shift each letter five places "down" in the alphabet, so that an A is replaced by a F, a B is replaced by a G, and so forth, to create an encoded **ciphertext**. Changing the original text to a secret message using cryptography is known as **encryption**, whereas the reverse process (such as replacing an F with an A) to change the message back to cleartext is called **decryption**.

The success of cryptography depends upon the process used to encrypt and decrypt messages. The process is based on a procedure called an **algorithm** (formula). An encryption algorithm is known as a **cipher**. The algorithm is given a value known as a **key** that it uses to encrypt the message. In the example of shifting each letter "down" by five positions, the number 5 is the key, so that the algorithm is taking any letter of the alphabet, determining its position in the alphabet (A=1, B=2, etc.), and adding the key value (5) to the position. Figure 2-5 illustrates the process of cryptography. The cleartext is submitted to an encryption algorithm (cipher) that is provided a key value. The cipher creates the encrypted ciphertext, which is then transmitted to the recipient. When the recipient receives the encrypted text, it must be decrypted with the cipher using the key to produce the original cleartext.

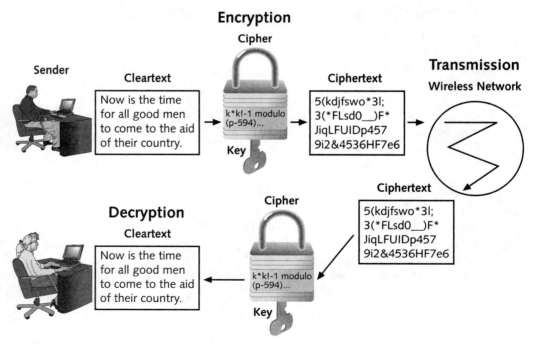

Figure 2-5   Cryptography

The substitution algorithm with a key of 5 is too simple to be used because the key creates a repeating pattern. A key that creates this type of repeating pattern is known as a **weak key**. Attackers could examine a paragraph of ciphertext created with a weak key and quickly determine the key value, which would give them the necessary tools to decrypt the messages. In cryptography, anything that creates a detectable pattern must be avoided.

WEP Implementation

The IEEE 802.11 committee designed WEP to meet the following criteria:

- *Efficient*—The WEP algorithm must be proficient enough to be implemented in either hardware or software.

- *Exportable*—WEP must meet the guidelines set by the U.S. Department of Commerce so that the wireless device using WEP can be exported overseas.

- *Optional*—The implementation of WEP in wireless LANs is an optional feature.

- *Reasonably strong*—The security of the algorithm lies in the difficulty of determining the secret keys through attacks. This in turn is related to the length of the secret key and the frequency of changing keys. WEP was to be "reasonably" strong in resisting attacks.

- *Self-synchronizing*—When using WEP, each packet must be separately encrypted. This is to prevent a single lost packet from making subsequent packets indecipherable.

WEP relies on a secret key shared between a wireless client device and the access point. The same secret key must be installed on both the device and the AP in advance. In addition, the shared secret key is used to encrypt the cleartext as well as decrypt the ciphertext. This process is also called **private key cryptography** or **symmetric encryption**.

IEEE 802.11 WEP shared secret keys must be a minimum of 64 bits in length. Most vendors add an option to use a larger 128-bit shared secret key for added security (a longer key is more difficult to break). Keys are created by the user entering the same string of either ASCII or hexadecimal characters on both the device and the AP. The options for creating keys are:

- 64-bit key—Created by entering 5 ASCII characters (for example *5y7js*) or 10 hexadecimal characters (for example 0x*456789ABCD*) (the 0x preceding the characters indicate it is a hexadecimal number).

- 128-bit key—Created by entering 13 ASCII characters (for example *98jui2wss35u4*) or 26 hexadecimal characters (for example 0x*3344556677889900AABBCCDDEE*).

- Passphrase—Created by entering a specific number of ASCII characters (for example *christmasholiday*), which then generates a hexadecimal key.

NOTE

The advantage of a passphrase is that it is easier to remember than a string of characters. However, different vendors' passphrase generators create different hexadecimal keys, so a passphrase entered on a Linksys AP will not generate the same passphrase on a D-Link AP.

The IEEE standard also specifies that the access points and devices can hold up to four shared secret keys, one of which must be designated as the **default key**. This is the key value that is used to encrypt the cleartext before the transmission is sent, and the receiver will use the identical key to decrypt the ciphertext. Yet the same key does not have to be designated as the default (encryption) key on each device. In Figure 2-6 the access point uses Key 1 as the default key to encrypt so that each receiving device must also use Key 1 to decrypt the ciphertext that is received. Although Key 1 is the default key for the access point, another wireless device can be set to use another key as its default key to encrypt cleartext. The access point must then use that same key to decrypt it. A device will only encrypt based on its default key, but must decrypt based on one of the corresponding four keys. In most instances the same key is used as the default key among all devices and APs.

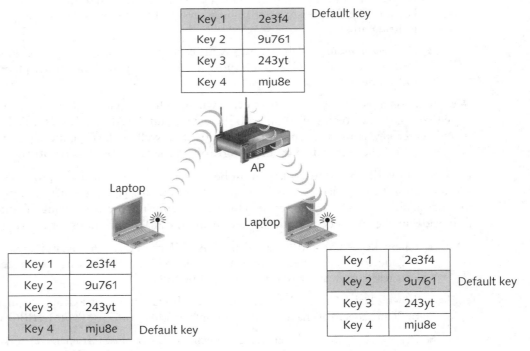

Figure 2-6   Default WEP key

If multiple keys are used, not only must the keys themselves match but also the order of the keys must be the same for all devices and access points.

NOTE

2

The mechanics of how WEP performs encryption is illustrated in Figure 2-7. The steps are as follows:

1. The cleartext has a **cyclic redundancy check (CRC)** value calculated, which is a checksum based on the contents of the text. WEP calls this the **integrity check value (ICV)** and appends it to the end of the text.

2. The shared secret key designated as the default key (used for encryption) is combined with an **initialization vector (IV)**. The IV is a 24-bit value that changes each time a packet is encrypted. The IV and the default key are combined and used as a "seed" for generating a random number in Step 3. If only the default key were used as a seed, then the number generated would be the same each time. Varying the IV for each packet ensures that the random number created from it is indeed random.

3. The default key and IV are then entered as the seed values into a **pseudo-random number generator (PRNG)** that creates a random number. The PRNG is based on the **RC4** cipher algorithm. RC4 is a **stream cipher** that accepts keys up to 128 bits in length. A stream cipher takes one character and replaces it with another character. This output is known as the **keystream**. The keystream is essentially a series of 1's and 0's equal in length to the text plus the ICV.

4. The two values (text plus ICV and the keystream) are then combined through the exclusive OR (XOR) operation to create the ciphertext. The Boolean operation of exclusive OR (XOR) yields the result TRUE (1) when only one of its operands is TRUE (1); otherwise, the result is FALSE (0). The four XOR results are 0 XOR 0 = 0, 0 XOR 1 = 1, 1 XOR 0 = 1, and 1 XOR 1 = 0.

5. The IV is added to the front ("pre-pended") of the ciphertext and the packet is ready for transmission. The pre-pended IV is in cleartext and is not encrypted. The reason the IV is transmitted in cleartext is that the receiving device needs it in this form to decrypt the ciphertext.

Rivest Cipher (RC) is a family of cipher algorithms designed by Ron Rivest. He developed six ciphers, ranging from RC1 to RC6, but did not release RC1 and RC3.

NOTE

The IV and ciphertext are then sent over radio frequency (RF) waves to the receiving device. When it arrives at its destination the receiving device first separates the IV from the ciphertext and then combines the IV with its appropriate secret key to create a keystream. This keystream is XORed with the ciphertext to re-create the cleartext and ICV. The text

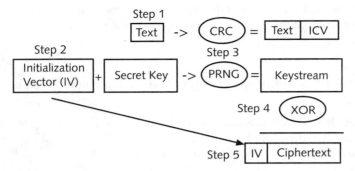

Figure 2-7   WEP encryption process

is finally run through the CRC to ensure that the ICVs match and that nothing was lost in the transmission process. This is illustrated in Figure 2–8.

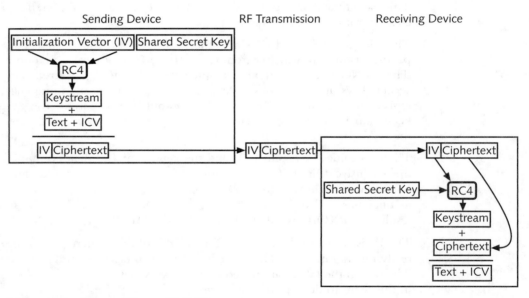

Figure 2-8   Transmitting with WEP

Authentication

In a standard wired LAN, a user sits down at a desktop computer connected to the network by a cable and then logs into the network with a username and password. Because physical access to the wired network can be restricted by walls and locked doors, all devices connected to the network are assumed to be authentic. Only the *user* must be authenticated with a username and password.

However, because wireless LANs cannot limit access to the RF signal by walls or doors, **wireless authentication** requires the *wireless device* (and not the user) to be authenticated prior to being connected to the network. After the wireless device is authenticated, the user may be asked to authenticate by entering a username and password. IEEE 802.11 wireless authentication is a process in which the AP accepts or rejects a wireless device.

There are two types of authentication supported by the 802.11 standard. **Open system authentication** is the default method. A device discovers a wireless network in the vicinity through scanning the radio frequency and sends a frame known as an **association request frame** to the AP. The frame carries information about the data rates that the device can support along with the **Service Set Identifier (SSID)** of the network it wants to join. The SSID serves as the "network name" for the wireless network and can be any alphanumeric string from 2 to 32 characters. After receiving the association request frame, the access point compares the SSID received with the actual SSID of the network. If the two match then the wireless device is authenticated. Open system authentication is illustrated in Figure 2-9.

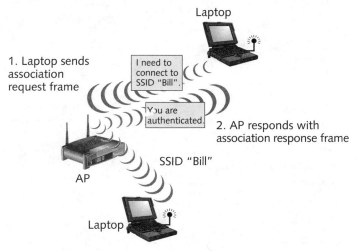

Figure 2-9   Open system authentication

NOTE   The use of the terms "packet" and "frame" is sometimes hotly debated. The term "frame" refers to the packets that are defined by hardware, or Layers 1 and 2 of the OSI model, and these frames sent across the Internet are technically called "datagrams." However, in TCP/IP and in everyday use the generic term "packet" is used to refer to any small unit of data used in networking systems. Although it is technically correct (and more precise) to refer to the packets used on an IEEE 802.11 Ethernet-based WLAN as "Ethernet frames," the more generic word "packet" is becoming more acceptable.

An optional authentication method is **shared key authentication** in which the WEP default key is used. A wireless device sends a frame to the AP and the AP sends back a frame that contains a block of text known as the **challenge text**. The wireless device must encrypt the text with the default key and return it to the AP. The AP will then decrypt what was returned to see if it matches the original challenge text. If it does, the device is authenticated and allowed to become part of the network (known as **association**). Shared key authentication is based upon the fact that only pre-approved wireless devices are given the shared key and is illustrated in Figure 2-10.

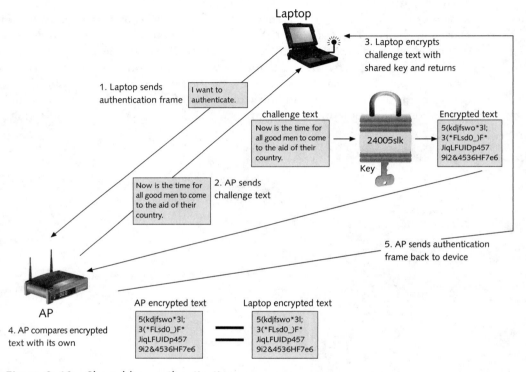

Figure 2-10   Shared key authentication

 When WEP is used for shared key authentication it is serving a dual function of encryption and authentication.

NOTE

VULNERABILITIES OF IEEE 802.11 SECURITY

Despite the fact that the IEEE 802.11 standard contained security mechanisms for wireless networks, these proved to provide a very weak level of security. These security vulnerabilities have exposed wireless networking to a variety of attacks. This section explores the vulnerabilities in the areas of authentication, access control, and WEP.

Authentication

There are security vulnerabilities with both open system authentication and shared key authentication.

Open System Authentication Vulnerabilities

Open system authentication is weak because authentication is based on only one factor: a match of SSIDs. An attacker only has to determine an SSID to be authenticated. There are several ways that SSIDs can be discovered, such as looking at the SSID on a device that is already authenticated. However, the easiest way to discover the SSID is to actually do nothing.

At regular intervals (normally every 100 ms) the AP sends a **beacon frame** to announce its presence and to provide the necessary information for other devices that want to join the network. This process is known as **beaconing** and is an orderly means for wireless devices to establish and maintain communications. Each wireless device is set to look for those beacon frames from the AP. This is known as **scanning**. Although there are two types of scanning, the most common is called **passive scanning**. With passive scanning a wireless device simply listens for a beacon frame for a set period of time. Once a wireless device receives a beacon frame and the SSID it can then attempt to join the network.

By default, beacon frames contain the SSID of the WLAN. Thus there is nothing that the attacker has to do other than roam into the area of the access point, accept the SSID in the beacon frame, and become authenticated.

For a degree of protection, some wireless security sources encourage users to configure their access points to not allow the beacon frame to include the SSID. Instead, the SSID must be entered manually by the user on the wireless device. Although this may seem to provide protection by not advertising the SSID, in reality it does not for several reasons. First, it is not always possible or convenient to turn off beaconing the SSID. Not all access points allow beaconing to be turned off, and even those that do typically discourage users from doing so, as seen in Figure 2-11. Because beaconing the SSID is the default mode in most access points, a user must have specific knowledge regarding how and why to turn it off. Also, the steps to manually enter the SSID on a wireless device that does not receive a beaconed SSID are not always convenient. For example, depending upon the configuration of Microsoft Windows, the following steps may have to be taken to manually enter an SSID:

1. Click Start and Control Panel and Network and Internet Connections.
2. Click Network Connections.
3. Double-click Wireless Network Connection.
4. Click View Wireless Networks.
5. Click Change advanced settings.
6. Click the Wireless Networks tab.

7. Click Add.

8. Click the Association tab.

9. Enter the SSID, as seen in Figure 2-12.

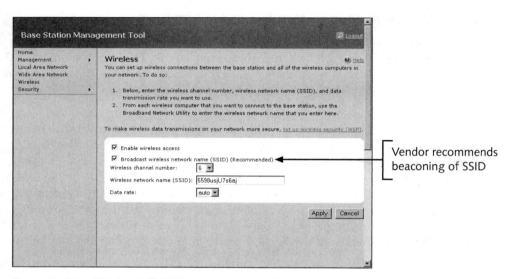

Figure 2-11 Turning off SSID beaconing discouraged

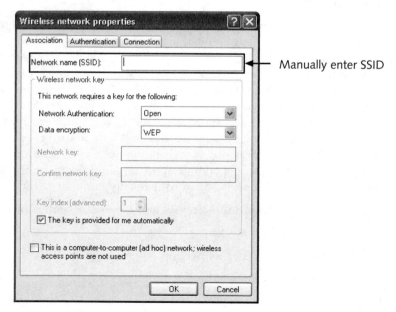

Figure 2-12 Enter SSID

A more important reason turning off the beaconing of the SSID is not appropriate is that problems may arise when the SSID is not beaconed. Turning off SSID beaconing prevents wireless devices from freely roaming from one wireless network to another. To increase the area of coverage of a wireless LAN, multiple access points are installed with areas of overlap, as seen in Figure 2-13, much like cells in a cellular telephone system. The APs can be positioned so that the cells overlap to facilitate movement between cells, known as **roaming**. When a mobile wireless user (perhaps carrying a wireless laptop computer) enters into the range of more than one AP, the wireless device will choose an AP based on signal strength (some also look at packet error rates). Mobile devices constantly survey the radio frequencies at regular intervals to determine if a different AP can provide better service. If it finds one (perhaps because the user has moved closer to it), then the device automatically attempts to associate with the new AP (this process is called a **handoff**).

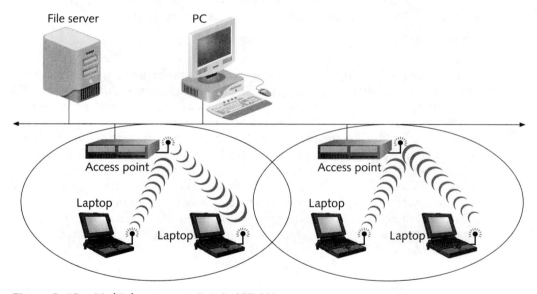

Figure 2-13   Multiple access points in WLAN

 One of the weaknesses of the IEEE 802.11 standard is that it does not specify how a handoff should take place. Because roaming between APs of different vendors can sometimes be a problem, some industry experts recommend that
NOTE   all APs in a WLAN be from the same vendor.

When the SSIDs are beaconed, roaming is seamless because the wireless device never has an interruption of service. However, if SSIDs are not beaconed, a roaming user must know in advance the SSID of each AP, determine which AP is closest, and manually enter the SSID at the correct time, which is often after the signal is completely lost from the original AP and a disruption of service occurs. Because turning off beaconing of SSIDs prevents seamless roaming, many users elect to leave beaconing SSIDs turned on for convenience.

Another problem that may arise when turning off beaconing of SSIDs is that when a wireless device is using Microsoft Windows XP and there are signals from both a wireless network that is broadcasting an SSID and one that is not broadcasting the SSID, the device will always connect to the access point that is broadcasting its SSID. This occurs regardless of the preference order of the networks that are configured on the Preferred networks list. This means that if a device is connected to an access point that is not broadcasting its SSID, and another access point is turned on that is broadcasting its SSID, the device will automatically disconnect from the first AP and connect to the AP that is broadcasting. For example, users who have turned off broadcasting the SSID may never be able to join their own wireless network—no matter how strong the signal strength is—if a user in the apartment above is broadcasting their SSID.

NOTE

Microsoft says that this behavior of connecting to the network that broadcasts the SSID over one that does not broadcast it is "by design."

A final reason restricting SSID beaconing is not appropriate is that the SSID can be easily discovered even when it is not contained in beacon frames. Although the SSID can be suppressed from beacon frames, it still is transmitted in other management frames sent by the AP. Attackers who use wireless tools freely available on the Internet can easily see the SSID being transmitted. Also, the SSID is initially transmitted in cleartext form when the device is negotiating with the access point. An attacker can easily view the SSID when this process is occurring. If an attacker cannot capture an initial negotiation process. it can force one to occur. An attacker can pretend to be an access point and send a disassociation frame to a wireless device. This will cause the device to disassociate from the access point. However, the device will then immediately attempt to reconnect to the AP, at which time the attacker can capture packets and see the SSID transmitted in plaintext. This is illustrated in Figure 2-14.

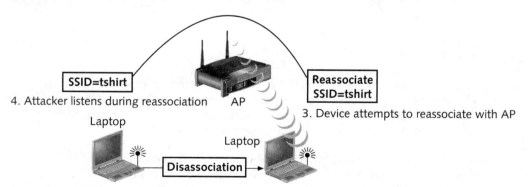

Figure 2-14   Forcing renegotiation

NOTE Many users do not change the default SSID and these are well known. An attacker can simply try default SSIDs until a connection is accepted. A list of default SSIDs can be found by searching for *default SSID* with an Internet search engine. One example of a list is at *www.cirt.net/cgi-bin/ssids.pl*.

Despite misleading claims to the contrary, configuring an access point to not allow the beacon frame to include the SSID provides virtually no protection. Although it may prevent a "casual" unauthorized user using Windows XP from capturing the SSID and entering the network, wireless security should be set at a higher level to restrict any unauthorized user from accessing the WLAN.

Shared Key Authentication Vulnerabilities

The shared key authentication technique, using challenge text, is likewise vulnerable. The first vulnerability is based on the fact that key management can be very difficult when it must support a large number of wireless devices. Because the shared secret key must be entered on each wireless device, an attacker could view the key on an approved device (by stealing a device or "shoulder surfing"—looking over someone's shoulder). Also, because only the default key is used for encryption, the attacker would only need to know that one key.

An attacker who cannot steal the shared secret key may try to "break" the message to determine the key that was used to encrypt it. The first type of attack is a **brute force attack**, in which an attacker attempts to create every possible key combination by using a program to systematically change one character at a time in a possible default key, and then using each newly generated key to decrypt a message. For example, if a key contains five numbers, such as 49833, the brute force attack would start with the combination 00000 and attempt to use that as the password. If it fails, the next attack is 00001, then 00002, and so on until all possible combinations are exhausted. Although it may at first appear that a brute force attack could take a long time, it actually may not. In the 00000 example, if a key consists of five numbers, then there are $10*10*10*10*10$ or 100,000 possible combinations. A standard personal computer can easily create over 1,000,000 possible password combinations per second.

NOTE Brute force password attack programs are readily available on the Internet.

The second type of password guessing is a **dictionary attack**. Unlike a brute force attack in which all possible combinations are used, a dictionary attack takes each word from a dictionary and encodes it in the same way the passphrase was encoded. Attackers then compare the encoded dictionary words against those in the encrypted frame. When attackers find a match, they know which dictionary word made up the passphrase.

NOTE   Research has indicated that 64-bit passphrase generators may contain flaws. Many wireless security experts recommend avoiding passphrase generators altogether.

Besides stealing or breaking the key, there is a third way in which shared key authentication systems can be attacked. With shared key authentication, the AP sends to a device wanting to join the network a block of text known as the challenge text. The wireless device encrypts it with its shared secret key and returns it to the AP. The vulnerability is in the fact that when the AP sends the challenge text it is sent in cleartext. An attacker can capture the challenge text along with the device's response (encrypted text and IV) and have all that is needed to then mathematically derive the keystream.

Open system authentication and shared key authentication are the only two types of wireless authentication available under the 802.11 standard. These are summarized in Table 2-1. Unfortunately, both exhibit serious security vulnerabilities.

Table 2-1   802.11 authentication attacks

Authentication Type	Attack Technique	Description
Open system authentication	View SSID	Look at SSID on authenticated device
Open system authentication	Accept SSID	Receive SSID from passive scanning
Open system authentication	Steal SSID	View plaintext SSID during negotiation phase with AP or force renegotiation
Shared key authentication	View SSID	Steal a device or shoulder surf
Shared key authentication	Brute force attack	Break default key by attempting combinations
Shared key authentication	Dictionary attack	Break default key by using dictionary words
Shared key authentication	Steal challenge text and encrypted text	Use challenge text and encrypted text to mathematically derive keystream

Address Filtering

MAC address filtering also has several vulnerabilities. First, managing a larger number of MAC addresses can pose significant challenges. The sheer number of users makes it difficult to manage all of the MAC addresses and thus creates avenues for attackers. As new users are added to the network and old users leave, MAC address filtering demands constant attention.

In addition, MAC address filtering does not provide a means to temporarily allow a guest user to access the network other than manually entering the user's MAC address into the access point.

A second disadvantage to MAC address filtering is that, like SSIDs, MAC addresses are initially exchanged in plaintext. This means that an attacker can easily see the MAC address of an approved device and use it to join the network. And, like open system authentication, an attacker can send a disassociation frame to force a device to reassociate and send the MAC address so that it can be captured.

A third disadvantage of MAC address filtering is that a MAC address can be "spoofed" or substituted. Some wireless NICs allow for a substitute MAC address to be used. In addition, there are programs available that allow users to spoof a MAC address. This is possible because Microsoft Windows reads the MAC address of the wireless NIC and stores that value in the Windows registry database. A MAC address spoof program changes the setting in the registry.

Much like authentication, address filtering contains several security vulnerabilities, as summarized in Table 2-2. For this reason MAC address filtering is not recommended for enterprise use or in environments where security is essential.

Table 2-2 MAC address attacks

Attack Technique	Description
Key management	Take advantage of difficulty in managing large number of MAC addresses
Steal MAC address	Access MAC address as exchanged in plaintext
Spoof MAC address	Substitute approved MAC address on wireless device

WEP

Although authentication and MAC address filtering have serious security vulnerabilities, the vulnerability that attracted the most attention focuses on WEP. The vulnerabilities are based on how WEP and the RC4 cipher are implemented.

First, to encrypt packets WEP can use only a 64-bit or 128-bit number, which is made up of a 24-bit initialization vector (IV) and a 40-bit or 104-bit default key. The relatively short length of the default key limits its strength, because shorter keys are much easier to break than longer keys.

Second, WEP implementation violates the cardinal rule of cryptography: anything that creates a detectable pattern must be avoided. This is because patterns provide an attacker with valuable information to break the encryption. The implementation of WEP creates a detectable pattern for attackers. IVs are 24-bit numbers, meaning there are 16,777,216 possible values. An AP transmitting at only 11 Mbps can send and receive 700 packets each second. If a different IV were used for each packet, then the IVs would start repeating in fewer than seven hours (a "busy" AP can produce duplicates in fewer than five hours). An attacker who captures packets for this length of time can see the duplication and use it to crack the code.

Yet it does not always require seven hours of capturing packets to see the IV repeat. Some wireless systems always start with the same IV after the system is restarted and then follow the same sequence of incrementing IVs. If 50 devices start in the morning they may all be given the same initial IV and then follow the same sequence of subsequent IVs. This would give an attacker the same IV value that would appear 50 times for each value in the sequence, which would be sufficient data for cracking the code. In addition, some new WEP-cracking tools can make "estimations" of the IV based on capturing as few as 500,000 packets, reducing the time needed for capturing packets from hours to minutes.

NOTE

In April 2005, the Federal Bureau of Investigation (FBI) made headlines when it demonstrated at the Information Systems Security Association meeting that it could break WEP in less than three minutes.

Because of the weaknesses of the implementation of WEP it is possible for an attacker to identify two packets derived from the same IV (called a **collision**). With that information, the attacker can begin a **keystream attack**. A keystream attack is a method of determining the keystream by analyzing two packets that were created from the same IV.

The basis for a keystream attack is as follows: *performing an XOR on two ciphertexts will equal an XOR on the two plaintexts.* This is seen in Figure 2-15. In Operation 1, Plaintext A and Keystream X are XORed together to create Ciphertext A. In Operation 2, Plaintext B and Keystream X are also XORed to create Ciphertext B. Notice that in Operation 3 if Ciphertext A and Ciphertext B are XORed then they create the same result as when Plaintext A and Plaintext B are XORed in Operation 4.

Figure 2-16 illustrates how an attacker can take advantage of this. If the attack captures Packet 1's IV and keystream, and then captures the IV and keystream from Packet 222 that uses the same IV, then the attacker knows two keystreams that were created by the same IV. An XOR of those two keystreams finds the same value as an XOR of the plaintext of Packet 1 and Packet 222. The attacker can now work backward: if even part of the plaintext of Packet 1 can be discovered, then the attacker can derive the plaintext of Packet 222 by doing an XOR operation on the keystream of Ciphertext 1 and Ciphertext 222 (11111110) and Packet 1 (11010011). In fact, once the plaintext of Packet 1 has been discovered, the plaintext of *any* packet that uses that IV can be found.

The question then becomes, "How can the attacker find enough of Plaintext 1 to decrypt Plaintext 222?" There are several ways. Some of the values of the frames are definitely known, such as certain fields in the header. In other fields the value may not be known but the purpose is known (such as the IP address fields have a limited set of possible values in most networks). Also, the body portion of the text often encodes ASCII text, again giving some possible clues. An attacker can collect enough samples of duplicated IVs, guess at substantial portions of the keystream, and then decode more and more. Another approach is

2

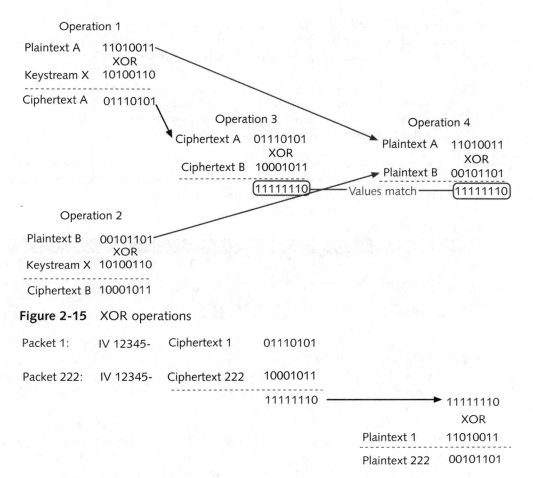

Figure 2-15 XOR operations

Packet 1:   IV 12345-   Ciphertext 1   01110101

Packet 222:   IV 12345-   Ciphertext 222   10001011

                           11111110 ──────────────────▶ 11111110
                                                              XOR
                                          Plaintext 1   11010011

                                          Plaintext 222   00101101

Figure 2-16 Capturing packets

to capture an encrypted packet and, based on its size (28 bytes), know that it's an address resolution protocol (ARP) request. The attacker can then flood the network with the re-injected ARP request, which results in a flood of ARP responses, supplying a wealth of data to use. A third approach uses a computer on the Internet to send traffic from the outside to a device on the wireless network. Because the content of the message is known to the attacker, when the WEP-encrypted version of the message is sent over wireless LAN, the attacker will have all the necessary data to decrypt all packets that use the same initialization vector (IV).

A final weakness of WEP is in RC4. RC4 uses a pseudo random number generator (PRNG) to create the keystream. This PRNG does not create a true random number but what appears to be (pseudo) a random number. Also, difficiencies within RC4 have been identified. For example, the first 256 bytes of the RC4 cipher can be determined by bytes in the key itself. Finally, the RC4 source code (or a derivation of it) has been revealed, allowing attackers to see how the keystream itself is generated. For these reasons the RC4 cipher is no longer considered the most effective cipher for the task.

 NOTE   RC4 It is not a patented algorithm but is protected under federal law as a trade secret. In 1994, an anonymous person posted on the Internet what was labeled as the source code to the RC4 algorithm. Although it is unclear if this was the actual RC4 algorithm, it does produce exactly the same output as RC4.

WEP encryption has serious limitations, as summarized in Table 2-3, and is not recommended in settings where security is essential. Other more robust security mechanisms covered in this book provide a greater degree of protection.

Table 2-3   WEP attacks

Attack Technique	Description
Weak key	WEP default keys are shortened to 40 or 104 bits and make it easier for attackers to break
Keystream	View collisions to derive plaintext values
RC4 pseudo random number	RC4 generates weak keys

The WEP attacks listed in Table 2-3 can be performed through any one of a number of tools that are freely available on the Internet. Some of the best known include AirSnort, Aircrack, ChopChop WEP Cracker, and WEP Crack. However, these tools require a certain degree of computer experience to use. Only certain wireless NIC adapter cards with specific drivers can be used, and almost all of these tools were developed under the Linux operating system and are designed to function under Linux. Although a few of these tools have been ported to the Windows operating system, they require special supporting software packages to properly function. Also, the length of time needed to capture enough packets to break WEP can be several (5 to 7) hours, depending on the volume of traffic.

 CAUTION   These tools should be used *only* to demonstrate and learn about WEP attacks, using equipment that is owned by the user or has been approved by a third-party institution. Under no circumstances should these tools be used to break WEP encryption on another WLAN. Users who violate these conditions may be subject to legal action.

WEP2

In September 1999, the IEEE ratified the 802.11b and 802.11a WLAN standards, which include Wired Equivalent Privacy (WEP) technology for shared key authentication and packet encryption. By early 2001, independent studies from universities and commercial institutions had identified weaknesses in WEP. After the security flaws in WEP were publicized, the IEEE TGi task group (known as *Task Group i*), which was responsible for the implementation of the original WEP, released a new proposed implementation of WEP known as **WEP2** (**WEP Version 2**). WEP2 attempted to overcome the limitations of WEP by adding two new security enhancements. First, the shared secret key was increased to 128 bits from 64 bits to address the weakness of encryption. Second, a different authentication system was used, known as **Kerberos**. Kerberos was developed by the Massachusetts Institute of Technology (MIT) and used to verify the identity of network users. Kerberos is named after a three-headed dog in Greek mythology that guarded the gates of Hades.

Kerberos is typically used when someone on a network attempts to use a network service, and the service wants assurance that the user is an authorized user. The user is provided a ticket that is issued by the Kerberos server, much as a driver's license is issued by the Division of Motor Vehicles. This ticket contains information linking it to the user. The user presents this ticket to the network for a service. The service then examines the ticket to verify the identity of the user. If all checks out, the user is accepted. Kerberos tickets share some of the same characteristics as a driver's license: tickets are difficult to copy (because they are encrypted), they contain specific user information, they restrict what a user can do, and they expire after a few hours or a day.

However, it soon became clear that WEP2 was no more secure than WEP itself. First, increasing the shared secret key to 128 bits did not prevent collisions (two packets derived from the same IV). Second, the inclusion of mandatory Kerberos opened WEP2 to new dictionary-based attacks. It was estimated that up to 10 percent of Kerberos-protected user passwords can be cracked within 24 hours using a dictionary attack mounted by an inexpensive network of computers. Because of these weaknesses WEP2 has rarely been implemented.

Dynamic WEP

In addition to WEP2, another solution was advanced called **dynamic WEP**. Dynamic WEP solves the weak initialization vector (IV) problem by rotating the keys frequently, making it much more difficult to crack the encrypted packet. Dynamic WEP uses different keys for **unicast traffic** (traffic destined for only one address) and **broadcast traffic** (traffic sent to all users on the network). The unicast WEP key, which is unique to each user's session, is dynamically generated and changed frequently. This key is also changed every time the user roams to a new AP or logs out and logs back in. A separate key is used for broadcast traffic. The broadcast WEP key must be the same for all users on a particular subnet and AP because users connecting to the same AP must see the same broadcast information. Keys can be set to change frequently, such as every 15 to 30 minutes. Dynamic WEP is illustrated in Figure 2-17.

A major advantage of using dynamic WEP is its straightforward deployment. Dynamic WEP can be implemented without upgrading device drivers or AP firmware. Deploying dynamic WEP is a no-cost solution with minimal effort.

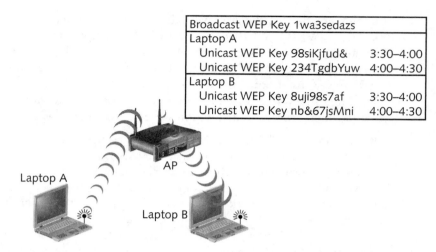

Broadcast WEP Key 1wa3sedazs	
Laptop A	
Unicast WEP Key 98siKjfud&	3:30–4:00
Unicast WEP Key 234TgdbYuw	4:00–4:30
Laptop B	
Unicast WEP Key 8uji98s7af	3:30–4:00
Unicast WEP Key nb&67jsMni	4:00–4:30

Broadcast WEP Key 1wa3sedazs	
Unicast WEP Key 98siKjfud&	3:30–4:00
Unicast WEP Key 234TgdbYuw	4:00–4:30

Broadcast WEP Key 1wa3sedazs	
Unicast WEP Key 8uji98s7af	3:30–4:00
Unicast WEP Key nb&67jsMni	4:00–4:30

Figure 2-17   Dynamic WEP

Although dynamic WEP overcomes the weak IV problem of original WEP, it is still only a partial solution. Dynamic WEP does not protect against certain types of other wireless attacks. Because it only offers a partial security solution, dynamic WEP was never widely implemented.

NOTE   When implementing dynamic WEP with Windows XP client devices and Cisco access points, the client devices will not associate to the AP when dynamic WEP is enabled unless the AP is set to Full Encryption. Setting the AP to Optional Encryption or No Encryption will cause the AP to send out 802.11 beacons with its privacy bit set to 0 (that is, no WEP) and the devices will not associate.

CHAPTER SUMMARY

- Because of the unique nature of a wireless LANs, it was important that basic wireless security protections be built into WLANs.

- The IEEE 802.11 committee implemented several protections in the original 1997 802.11 standard while leaving other protections to be applied at the WLAN vendor's discretion. These protections can be divided into three categories: access control, WEP, and authentication.

❏ Wireless access control is accomplished by limiting a device's access to the AP. The IEEE 802.11 standard does not specify how wireless access control is to be implemented. Almost all wireless AP vendors implement access control through MAC address filtering.

❏ WEP is intended to ensure that only authorized parties can view the information. WEP is used in IEEE 802.11 to encrypt wireless transmissions, and was the original cryptography mechanism of that standard.

❏ Wireless authentication requires the wireless device (and not the user) to be authenticated prior to being connected to the network. There are two types of authentication supported by the 802.11 standard, open system authentication and shared key authentication.

❏ Despite the fact that the IEEE 802.11 standard contained security mechanisms for wireless networks, these proved to provide a very weak level of security. These security vulnerabilities exposed wireless networking to a variety of attacks. Open system authentication is weak because authentication is based on only one factor: a match of SSIDs. There are several ways that SSIDs can be discovered. Restricting the transmission of the SSID provides virtually no security. Shared key authentication likewise has security vulnerabilities. MAC address filtering can easily be circumvented by a variety of different means.

❏ Although authentication and MAC address filtering have serious security vulnerabilities, the vulnerability that attracts the most attention focuses on WEP. WEP implementation violates the cardinal rule of cryptography: anything that creates a detectable pattern must be avoided.

❏ WEP2 and dynamic WEP were both designed to overcome the weaknesses of WEP. However, each proved to have its own limitations and they were never widely implemented.

KEY TERMS

access control — A method of restricting access to resources.

access point (AP) — A device that acts as a base station to receive signals from and transmit signals to wireless network devices, and to connect those devices to a wired network.

access restrictions — Restrictions placed on what a user can perform on a network after being accepted into the network.

algorithm — In cryptography, the underlying process or formula for encrypting and decrypting messages.

association — The process of being accepted into the wireless network.

association request frame — A frame sent from a device to an access point containing information about the device.

beacon frame — A frame from an access point that announces its presence and provides necessary information for other devices to join the network.

beaconing — The process in which an access point announces its presence and provides necessary information for other devices to join the network.

broadcast traffic — Traffic sent to all users on the network.

brute force attack — An attack in which an attacker attempts to create every possible key combination by systematically changing one character at a time.

challenge text — A block of text that must be encrypted by the wireless device in shared key authentication.

cipher — An encryption algorithm.

ciphertext — An encrypted message.

cleartext — The original unencrypted text, also known as plaintext.

collision — In wireless security, two packets that were created from the same initialization vector (IV).

cryptography — The science of transforming information so that it is secure while it is being transmitted or stored.

cyclic redundancy check (CRC) — A checksum value that is based on the contents of the text; used to verify that no bits have been changed or inserted in transmission.

decryption — The process of changing ciphertext into cleartext.

default key — A key value that is used to encrypt wireless data transmissions when they are sent.

dictionary attack — An attack that takes each word from a dictionary and encodes it in the same way a passphrase was encoded.

dynamic WEP — A proposed solution to solve the weak initialization vector problem by rotating keys frequently.

encryption — The process of encoding cleartext into ciphertext.

handoff — The process of switching associations from one access point to another.

initialization vector (IV) — A 24-bit value that changes each time a packet is transmitted.

integrity check value (ICV) — A checksum value that is based on the contents of the text; also known as cyclic redundancy check (CRC).

Kerberos — A technology develop the Massachusetts Institute of Technology used to verify the identity of network users.

key — The value that it algorithm uses to encrypt or decrypt a message.

keystream — The output from a pseudo random number generator (PRNG).

keystream attack — An attack method to determine the keystream by analyzing two packets that were created from the same initialization vector.

MAC address filter — A filtering mechanism on an access point that permits or prevents access based on the media access control number of a client device's wireless adapter.

Media Access Control (MAC) address filtering — An access control method that restricts access based on the media access control address.

open system authentication — An authentication method in which a wireless device sends a request to the access point.

passive scanning — The process of the wireless device listening for a beacon frame.

private key cryptography — Using the same secret key to encrypt and decrypt messages.

pseudo-random number generator (PRNG) — A part of the process for encrypting packages using a shared secret key that generates a keystream.

RC4 — A cipher algorithm used in WEP.

roaming — Movement between WLAN cells.

scanning — The process of a receiving wireless device looking for beacons.

Service Set Identifier (SSID) — A unique number of up to 32 alphanumeric case-sensitive characters in that serves as a WLAN network name.

shared key authentication — An authentication method in which a wireless device must encrypt challenge text before it can be authenticated.

stream cipher — A cipher that takes one character and replaces it with another character.

symmetric encryption — Using the same secret key to both encrypt and decrypt messages.

unicast traffic — Traffic destined for only one address.

weak key — A cryptographic key that creates a repeating pattern.

WEP2 (WEP Version 2) — An updated standard that addressed the limitations of WEP by adding two new security enhancements.

wired equivalent privacy (WEP) — An IEEE 802.11 cryptography mechanism.

wireless authentication — The process of authenticating the wireless device prior to being connected to the network.

REVIEW QUESTIONS

1. Each of the following is a category of security protection that can be implemented using WLANs except

   a. access control

   b. wired equivalent privacy (WEP)

   c. access restrictions

   d. authentication

2. Each of the following is another name for a MAC address except

   a. vendor address

   b. Ethernet address

   c. physical address

   d. Layer 7 address

3. MAC address filtering can be implemented by either permitting or _____ a device.

   a. preventing

   b. configuring

   c. throttling

   d. encrypting

4. Cryptography depends on a process used to encrypt and decrypt messages based on a procedure called a(n)
   a. algorithm
   b. key
   c. cipher
   d. CR4

5. Keys that create a repeating pattern are known as
   a. structure algorithms
   b. cipher abnormalities (CA)
   c. inferior algorithms
   d. weak keys

6. A WEP shared secret key is used to encrypt cleartext but not decrypt ciphertext. True or False?

7. The IEEE standard specifies that the access points and devices can hold up to four shared secret keys, one of which must be designated as the default key. True or False?

8. Another name for the cyclic redundancy check (CRC) is the integrity check value (ICV). True or False?

9. The initialization vector (IV) is a 24-bit value that changes each time a packet is encrypted. True or False?

10. The initialization vector (IV) is part of the shared secret key that must be installed individually on each wireless device. True or False?

11. Wireless authentication requires the _____ and not the user to be authenticated prior to being connected to the network.

12. An optional authentication method known as _____ uses the WEP default key.

13. With _____ scanning a wireless device simply listens for a beacon frame for a set period of time and once a wireless device receives a beacon frame and the SSID it can then attempt to join the network.

14. _____ is the process of transferring a user from being associated from one access point to another.

15. An attacker using a(n) _____ attempts to create every possible key combination by using a program to systematically change one character at a time in a possible default key.

16. Explain how an attacker can still capture the SSID over the airwaves even if it is turned off in beaconing frames.

17. What is a brute force attack?

18. Explain how WEP violates the cardinal rule of cryptography.

19. What is a weakness of RC4?

20. How did WEP2 attempt to address security vulnerabilities?

HANDS-ON PROJECTS

HANDS-ON PROJECTS

Project 2-1: Set a MAC Address Filter on Cisco AP

In this activity you will set the MAC address filter on a Cisco AP.

1. First determine the MAC address of your wireless device. Click **Start** and **Run**.

2. Type **cmd** and press **Enter**.

3. Type **ipconfig/all** and press **Enter**.

4. Locate **Physical Address** and write down this MAC address of your wireless device. Type **Exit** and press **Enter**.

5. Point your browser to the Cisco Aironet AP and enter the username and password.

NOTE

The IP address of the Cisco Aironet along with the username and password should be available from your lab technician or instructor.

6. Click **Security** in the left pane.

7. Click **SSID Manager** to display the SSID Manager properties, as seen in Figure 2-18.

NOTE

Depending on the model of Cisco Aironet you are using, your screen may look slightly different.

8. Under **Current SSID List** select the SSID that is currently being used.

9. Under **Authentication Methods Accepted** check **Open Authentication**.

10. Click **Add** if necessary.

11. Select **with MAC authentication** from the drop-down list.

12. Click **Apply** and then **OK**.

13. In the left pane click **Advanced Security**.

14. Under **New MAC Address:** enter the MAC address of your device.

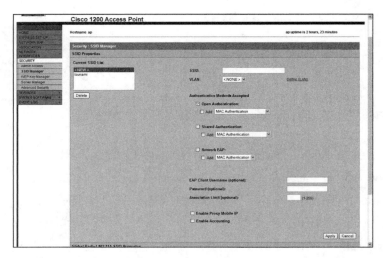

Figure 2-18   SSID Manager Properties screen

NOTE

Although Windows displays your MAC address as aa-bb-cc-dd-ee-ff, you will enter it here in the format aabb.ccdd.eeff.

15. Click **Apply** and then **OK**. The MAC address will appear in the **Local MAC Address List**.

16. Close the browser.

HANDS-ON PROJECTS

Project 2-2: Spoof a MAC Address Using SMAC

A MAC address can easily be spoofed. In this project you will spoof a MAC address to deny service. Although normally a MAC address would be spoofed to gain access, in this activity you will spoof (change) a valid MAC address so that it will not be allowed access. Use the same wireless device as you did for Project 2-1 or follow Steps 1–3 in Project 2-1 to find the MAC address of your wireless device.

1. Go to the SMAC Official Web site at *www.klcconsulting.net/smac*. Locate the link for the current Evaluation Edition version of SMAC and download it to your desktop. Install SMAC using the default installation settings.

2. Double-click the **SMAC** icon on your desktop to start the SMAC and accept the licensing agreement. The main SMAC window opens, as shown in Figure 2-19.

3. Select a wireless NIC adapter on this computer by clicking it in the top pane, if necessary.

4. Click **Update MAC**. A message window opens explaining that the MAC will be changed to the spoofed address when the system is rebooted. Click **OK**.

2

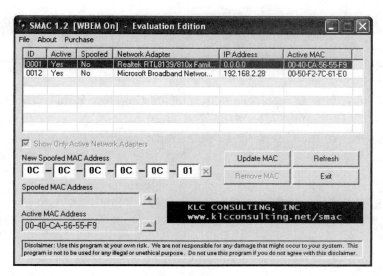

Figure 2-19 SMAC main window

5. In the lower-left corner of the window, note that the spoofed MAC address is different from the active MAC address. Record the spoofed and active MAC addresses.

Depending on your network configuration it may not be advisable to change your MAC address. Ask your network manager or instructor for directions.

NOTE

6. Close SMAC and reboot your computer.

7. Click **Start** and then **Run**. The Run dialog box opens. Type **cmd** and then press **Enter**. A Command Prompt window opens. At the command prompt, type **ipconfig /all** and press **Enter**. What is the current MAC address?

8. Attempt to perform a wireless network operation such as opening your Web browser to a new Internet site. Because this new MAC address is not permitted by the AP you are not associated with the wireless network.

9. Start the SMAC program.

10. If necessary select the wireless NIC adapter. Click **Remove MAC** to restore your original MAC address and then click **Exit**.

11. Reboot your computer.

Project 2-3: Update Linksys Firmware

The firmware on a Linksys access point can be updated from downloading software from the Internet. In this project you will determine if the firmware needs to be updated and, if so, perform the update.

1. On the underside of the Linksys access point identify and record the version number of this product, such as **WRT54G ver. 2**.

2. Point your browser to the Linksys access point and enter the username and password.

The IP address of the Linksys access point, along with the username and password, should be available from your lab technician or instructor or from the Linksys documentation.

NOTE

3. Record the Firmware Version number from the main Setup screen as seen in Figure 2-20.

Figure 2-20   Firmware Version number

4. Minimize the browser that is pointing to the Linksys access point and open another instance of the browser and go to *www.linksys.com*.

5. Navigate to the download area of this Web site.

6. Click the down arrow and select the product that corresponds to the version number that you recorded from the bottom of the AP. For example, if the version number found on the underside of the product is Linksys WRT54G ver. 2 then select **WRT54G V2.0**.

This version number is not necessarily the same as the firmware version number, which may be different based on previous upgrades. Be sure to use the version number found on the underside of the AP.

NOTE

7. Click **Downloads For This Product** and then click **Firmware**. Compare the firmware version number with what you recorded in Step 3 (this is the number found on the Setup screen and not that on the underside of the AP). If the firmware version number on the Web site is higher than the one for your AP then you should complete the remaining steps. If it is not higher, then close all windows and stop.

8. Download the firmware update executable (.exe) file to your desktop.

9. Double-click the executable program to start the firmware update.

10. Follow the instructions to upgrade the firmware. Note that you will need the IP address and the password of the Linksys device, as seen in Figure 2-21.

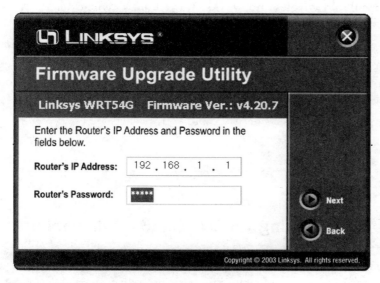

Figure 2-21 Firmware Upgrade screen

11. Do not turn off the power or press any buttons until the firmware upgrade is complete. Click **Upgrade**.

12. When the upgrade is complete close all windows.

Project 2-4: Set WEP on a Linksys AP

In this activity you will set WEP on a Linksys access point.

1. Access the Linksys access point by pointing your browser to its IP address and enter the username and password.

2. Click **Wireless**.

3. Click **Wireless Security**.

4. Under **Security Mode** select **WEP**.

5. Under **Default Transmit Key** click **1**.

6. Under **WEP Encryption** select **128 bits 26 hex digits**.

7. Enter this value under **Key 1: 11223344556677889900aabbccff**.

8. Click **Save Settings**.

9. Close the Linksys browser.

10. Now try to connect to the Linksys AP with a wireless device. Click **Start** and **Connect to** and **Show all connections**.

11. Select the Linksys wireless network connection.

12. Click **View available wireless networks.** If the Linksys wireless LAN is not displayed, click **Refresh network list**.

13. The Linksys wireless network is shown as a **Security-enabled wireless network**. Click on it to join the network. If necessary click **Connect**.

14. When prompted for the WEP key enter **112233445566778899aabbccff**. You will need to enter this key twice. Click **OK**.

15. You are now part of the Linksys network and your packets are encrypted.

16. Close all windows.

CASE PROJECTS

Case Project 2-1: Exposing WLAN Security Vulnerabilities

Vulnerabilities of the original IEEE 802.11 standard were exposed through academic researchers and industry professionals. Using the Internet, record a brief chronology of how these events took place and what vulnerabilities were brought to light. Do you agree with how this was publicized? Should it have been kept secret until the vulnerabilities could be repaired? Give your opinion on how you would have handled it had you been one of the researchers.

Case Project 2-2: RC4

Research how RC4 functions. Be sure to address key scheduling algorithms and the pseudo-random number generator algorithm. Why was RC4 chosen for WEP? Write a one-page paper on your research.

Case Project 2-3: Passphrase Vulnerabilities

Some security professionals maintain that passphrase generators do not produce random keys and should never be used. Using the Internet, research wireless passphrase generators and how they function. Do they produce keys that are random? Do you recommend that they be used?

Case Project 2-4: XOR Truth Table

The Boolean operation exclusive OR (XOR) yields the result TRUE (1) when one and only one but not both of its operands is TRUE (1); otherwise, the result is FALSE (0). The results are often shown in a "truth table" that makes it easier to understand the process. Research truth tables using mathematics textbooks or the Internet and create a truth table for AND, OR, and XOR.

Fairvue Technology Consulting

Fairvue Technology Consulting (FTC), a local company that offers voice, data, and video consulting services, has hired you to help them with a project. A regional delicatessen, Vena's Deli, wants to offer free WLAN service to its customers but is reluctant because of security issues.

1. Create a PowerPoint presentation that lists some of the vulnerabilities of WLAN security covering access control, WEP encryption, and authentication. The audience will include Vena's Deli IT staff so your presentation should be technical in nature. Your presentation should be at least seven slides in length.

2. One of Vena's Deli IT managers has asked about your recommendations regarding turning off the SSID broadcast, because he does this at home and nobody has broken into his network. Create a one-page memo addressing the pros and cons of suppressing broadcast SSIDs along with your recommendation.

PASSIVE WIRELESS DISCOVERY

The World of Wireless Security

Failure to secure your wireless network from attackers is not only dangerous, but it may soon also be against the law, at least in one suburb of New York City. According to a proposal under consideration, any business with an open wireless connection that lacks proper security to fend off attacks would be in violation of a city ordinance.

Officials in Westchester County, New York are debating the adoption of the law that requires businesses with WLANs to use secure wireless access points. Representatives from the county's Information Technology (IT) department drove around downtown White Plains, New York, with laptop computers and wireless software to determine how many wireless network signals they could detect. In less than 30 minutes, 248 WLANs were detected. Over half lacked any security features.

The county ordinance, which would be the first such legislation in the United States to regulate wireless networks, is designed to protect personal data transmitted or accessible through WLANs. The proposal has two parts. First, any wireless "public access Internet," such as those available to patrons at a coffee shop, must have a network gateway server equipped with a firewall. These businesses must also post a sign stating, "You are accessing a network which has been secured with firewall protection. Because such protection does not guarantee the security of your personal information, use your own discretion." Second, any business that stores personal information must install similar security protections, even if the wireless connection is closed to the public and encrypted with WEP or similar security. According to the Westchester County proposal, all businesses with WLANs would be required to register with the county within 90 days. Violations of any part of the law would be punishable with fines of $250 or $500.

However, the ordinance may not apply only to large businesses and organizations. The special assistant to the county's chief information officer said that the law would also apply to home offices as well.

A common question regarding wireless attacks is, "How can I know if someone is monitoring my wireless transmissions?" The idea behind the question is that if I can detect that someone is listening to my radio frequency transmissions, then I can hunt for that suspect or at least turn off my network if I detect that someone is monitoring.

Unfortunately, there is no means to determine if anyone else is listening in on your WLAN, just as a broadcast commercial radio station cannot determine who or how many listeners may have their radio dial tuned to FM 89.5 (and must rely on other means to count the number of listeners). However, knowing how intrusions take place can help you counter and prevent them.

Listening for a WLAN signal is the first and most basic step in any wireless intrusion. Whether it is a neighbor looking for a free signal to check her e-mail or a seasoned attacker hunting for a network to penetrate, listening for the signal, sometimes called passive wireless discovery, must always happen first.

Even though passive wireless discovery cannot be completely prevented, it is still important to be aware of the tools that attackers use. This helps determine what type of defenses can be built, and these defenses will be covered in future chapters. This chapter explores passive wireless discovery. You will learn about wireless discovery tools, which reveal the presence of a WLAN, and also explore packet sniffers, which can quietly reveal the contents of wireless transmissions. First, however, the chapter considers general ways of discovering important information about a network without using software or hardware.

 It is important to remember that the reason for studying passive wireless discovery tools is to be knowledgeable about the tools that attackers use, so you can defend against these kinds of attacks. These tools should never be used to monitor or access a wireless network (which in some states is illegal) unless you have permission from the owner.

GENERAL INFORMATION GATHERING

Sophisticated hardware, special software, and an advanced knowledge of networking and protocols are often viewed as the tools needed for breaking into a network and stealing information. However, there is an entirely different means of collecting information that does not even depend heavily on technology. This general information gathering instead relies on deception, deceit, and digging. This type of general information gathering includes social engineering, phishing, improperly recycled equipment, search engine scanning, and dumpster diving.

Social Engineering

The easiest way to attack a computer system requires no technical ability and is highly successful. **Social engineering** relies on tricking and deceiving someone to access a system. Consider the following examples:

3

- Maria is a customer service representative who receives a telephone call from someone claiming to be a client. This person has a thick accent that makes his speech difficult to understand. Maria asks him to respond to a series of ID authentication questions to ensure that he is an approved client. However, when asked a question, the caller mumbles his response so that Maria cannot understand him. Too embarrassed to keep asking him to repeat his answer, Maria finally provides him with the password.

- The help desk at a large corporation is overwhelmed by the number of telephone calls it receives after a virus attack. Ari is a help desk technician and receives a frantic call from a user who identifies himself as Frank, a company vice president. Frank says that an office assistant has been unable to complete and send him a critical report because of the virus and is now going home sick. Frank must have that office assistant's network password so he can finish the report, which is due by the end of the day. Because Ari is worn out from the virus attack and has more calls coming in, he looks up the password and gives it to Frank. Ari does not know that Frank is not an employee, but an outsider who now can easily access the company's computer system.

- Natalie, a contract programmer at a financial institution, drives past a security guard who recognizes her and waves her into the building. However, the guard does not realize that Natalie's contract was terminated the previous week. Once inside, Natalie pretends that she is performing an audit and questions a new employee, who willingly gives her the information she requests. Natalie then uses that information to transfer more than $10 million to her foreign bank account.

These examples are based on actual incidents and share a common characteristic: no technical skills or abilities were needed to break into the system. Social engineering relies on the friendliness, frustration, or helpfulness of a company employee to reveal the information necessary to access a system. Social engineering is a difficult security weakness to defend against because it relies on human nature ("I just want to be helpful") and not on technology. One of the best defenses against social engineering in an organization is to have a written policy regarding what information should be distributed and to whom, and then strongly enforce the policy among all employees. Social engineering can be used to obtain WLAN SSIDs, passwords, and other information useful to a wireless attacker.

NOTE One of the most celebrated cases of social engineering occurred in 1978, when Stanley Mark Rifkin tricked the Security Pacific National Bank in Los Angeles into sending more than $10 million to his private bank account in Switzerland. He was caught only after he tried to return to the United States with $8 million worth of diamonds that he had purchased. The bank was unaware of the theft until after his arrest.

Phishing

An electronic version of social engineering is known as phishing. **Phishing** (pronounced "fishing") involves sending an e-mail or displaying a Web announcement that falsely claims to be from a legitimate enterprise in an attempt to trick the user into surrendering information. The user is directed to visit a Web site and asked to enter or update information such as passwords, credit card numbers, Social Security numbers, bank account numbers, or other information. However, the Web site is actually a fake and is set up to steal the user's information.

NOTE The word *phishing* is a variation on actual fishing, the idea being that bait is thrown out knowing that whereas most will ignore it some will be tempted into biting it.

One of the problems with phishing is that both the e-mails and the fake Web sites appear to be legitimate. Figures 3-1 through 3-3 illustrate fictitious e-mail messages that were used in phishing. Because these messages contain the actual logos, color schemes, and wording similar to that used by the real site, it is difficult to determine that they are fraudulent.

Because of the difficulty in distinguishing between legitimate and fraudulent messages and Web sites, the number of phishing sites (Web sites that imitate the legitimate Web sites but fraudulently capture a user's information) and successful attacks is increasing at an alarming rate. In July 2005, there were 14,135 phishing Web sites, which represents a 7,000 percent increase in one year (in January 2004, there were only 198 phishing sites, according to data from the Anti-Phishing Working Group). As much as 5 percent of all e-mail is now believed to be phishing attempts, according to Brightmail, a company that tracks spam and scam e-mail.

NOTE Most phishing sites only function for three to five days to prevent law enforcement agencies from tracking the attackers. In that short period, a phishing attack can net over $50,000.

Figure 3-1 e-Bay phishing Web message

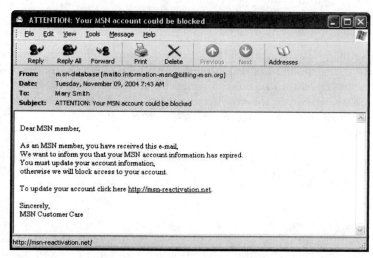

Figure 3-2 MSN phishing e-mail message

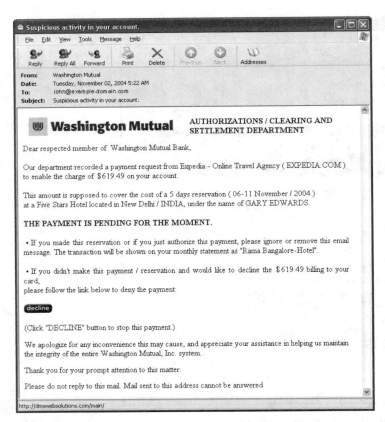

Figure 3-3 Washington Mutual phishing Web message

Following are variations on phishing attacks:

- Spear phishing—Whereas phishing involves sending millions of generic e-mail messages to users, **spear phishing** targets only specific users. The e-mails used in spear phishing are customized to the recipient, including their name and personal information, to make the message appear legitimate. Because the volume of the e-mail in a spear phishing attack is much lower than in a regular phishing attack, spear phishing scams are more difficult to detect.

- Pharming—Instead of asking the user to visit a fraudulent Web site, **pharming** automatically redirects the user to the fake site. This is accomplished by attackers penetrating the servers on the Internet that direct traffic.

- Google phishing—Named after the well-known search engine, **Google phishing** involves phishers setting up their own search engines to direct traffic to illegitimate sites. For example, unsuspecting users who access Google phishing search engines and search for *Amazon* are sent to a fake site that looks like Amazon but is actually a phishing site.

3

Like social engineering, phishing can also be used to trick users out of their usernames, passwords, SSIDs, and other security information. And like social engineering, phishing schemes can be difficult to defend against. Some of the ways to recognize these messages include:

- Deceptive Web links—A link to a Web site embedded in an e-mail should not have an @ sign in the middle of the address. Also, phishers like to use variations of a legitimate address, such as *www.ebay_secure.com, www.e--bay.com,* or *www.e-baynet. com.* Never log on to a Web site from a link in an e-mail; instead, open a new browser window and type the legitimate address.

- E-mails that look like Web sites—Phishers often include the logo of the vendor and otherwise try to make the e-mail look like the vendor's Web site as a way to convince the recipient that the message is genuine.

- Fake sender's address—Because sender addresses can be forged easily, an e-mail message should not be trusted simply because the sender's e-mail address appears to be valid (such as *tech_support@ebay.com*). Also, an @ in the sender's address is a technique used to hide the real address.

- Generic greeting—Many phishing e-mails begin with a general opening such as "Dear e-Bay Member" and do not include a valid account number. If an e-mail from an online vendor does not contain the user's name, it should be considered suspect. However, because spear phishing sends customized e-mail messages, the inclusion of a username does not mean that the e-mail is legitimate.

- Poor grammar, formatting, or misspellings—Phishing e-mails often contain misspelled words, poor grammar and punctuation, and incorrect formatting. Although this is sometimes because the e-mail originated overseas from a phisher with subpar English language skills, often these mistakes are intentional. These errors help the e-mail avoid a spam filter.

- Pop-up boxes and attachments—Legitimate e-mails from vendors never contain a pop-up box or an attachment because these are tools often used by phishers.

- Unsafe Web sites—Any Web site in which the user is asked to enter personal information should start with *https* instead of *http* and should also include a padlock in the browser status bar. (Some phishers insert a fake padlock in the body of the message or Web page; however, for the padlock to be valid it must be in the browser status bar.) Users should not enter data unless they see the https and padlock indicators.

- Urgent request—Many phishing e-mails try to encourage the recipient to act immediately or their account will be deactivated.

Improperly Recycled Equipment

Because of the difficulty in disposing older computers, many organizations and individuals recycle older computers, wireless access points, and other equipment by giving them to schools or charities, or by selling them online. However, information that should have been deleted from the equipment often is still available. For example, data stored on hard drives may still be available on recycled computers. This is because with many operating systems, such as Microsoft Windows, simply deleting a file (and even emptying the Recycle Bin folder) does not necessarily make the information irretrievable. When that file is deleted, only the name is removed from the table; as more files are saved, the disk space that was used by the first file can be reclaimed and used for other files. Therefore, deleting a file means that the filename is removed from the table but the information itself remains on the hard drive until it is overwritten by new files. Data then can be retrieved from a hard drive by an attacker even after its files have been deleted. In addition, wireless access points may contain a password that is used for all APs across the network, or a computer may still have the WEP key installed. Attackers who can secure this information from recycled equipment can then use it to break into functioning WLANs.

NOTE   Sometimes it is easier for data thieves to steal the computer or access point itself. Portable laptop computers are particularly vulnerable to theft. Within a three-month period in 2005, four major universities reported laptop computers containing personal information on over 181,000 students were stolen or misplaced. By some estimates almost 60 percent of all stolen data is the result of laptop computer theft.

Search Engine Scanning

Search engines, such as Google, are important tools for locating information on the Internet. However, attackers now also use these same search tools to locate information that is not intended for the general public. Although most users simply type the word or phrase that they want to search for, Google and other search engines also offer advanced search tools that can narrow criteria for more specific information. For example, entering *site:www.course.com security* would provide every Web page at that site that contains the word *security*. Attackers can use these same techniques to quickly and invisibly scour the Internet for important attack information.

Table 3–1 lists some search engine scanning techniques. These are used by attackers to locate information that can be used in an attack.

Table 3-1   Search engine scanning techniques

Search Operator	Description	Example	Why Used by Attackers
site	Search a specific Web site for a certain term	*site:www.microsoft.com security*	Provides a listing of every Web page on the site that has information about security
filetype	Search for specific types of documents that contain a certain term	*filetype:pdf security*	Returns a listing of documents that contain security-related information

Table 3-1   Search engine scanning techniques (continued)

Search Operator	Description	Example	Why Used by Attackers
intitle	Search Web sites that contain a certain term in the title of the page	*intitle:index of "parent directory"*	Provides a list of files and directories on a Web page that can be used to identify desired information and how the Web server is organized

3

Dumpster Diving

Looking through large (usually outdoor) trash receptacles, known as **dumpster diving**, is used to find useful items like food and clothing. However, these same dumpsters can also be a source of secure information. Files, letters, memos, passwords, and similar sensitive data can be found in dumpsters. Users who dispose of this information by tossing it into a trash can under their desk perhaps never consider that it could be retrieved.

NOTE
Searching through dirty dumpsters is not the only way to find important information. In many instances public records contain useful information, such as the names of business owners and their addresses. Wireless attackers may use that information to determine the names of the owner's spouse and dependents and then try these as passwords for access into wireless networks.

It is reported that dumpster diving was common in the 1980s because of lack of security by businesses that were unaware of what employees were discarding. However, the heightened emphasis on security today has resulted in sensitive documents being shredded, either by personal shredders or professional shredders who collect and shred documents.

NOTE
The legality of dumpster diving depends on where you live. Dumpster diving is considered illegal in parts of the United States because dumpsters are usually located on private property, although in some areas the courts have ruled that there is no "common law expectation" of privacy for anything that was discarded.

Wardriving

If wireless information cannot be gathered through social engineering, phishing, improperly recycled equipment, search engine scanning, or dumpster diving, then scanning the radio frequency airwaves for a signal can identify and map the location of a wireless network. There are several different tools that are used to map WLANs. These tools can be divided into hardware tools and software tools. Once the tools have identified the WLAN, the information can then be recorded in a public mapping site.

What Is Wardriving?

At regular intervals (normally every 100 ms) the wireless access point sends a beacon frame to announce its presence and to provide the necessary information for devices that want to join the network. This process, known as beaconing, is an orderly means for wireless devices to establish and maintain communications. Each wireless device looks for those beacon frames (known as scanning). Once a wireless device receives a beacon frame it can attempt to join the network.

However, because there is no means to limit who receives the signal, unapproved wireless devices can pick up the beaconing RF transmission. **Wireless location mapping** is the formal expression used to refer to this passive wireless discovery, or the process of finding a WLAN signal and recording information about it. The informal expression used more often for searching for a signal is wardriving.

NOTE

Wardriving is derived from the term *wardialing*. In the 1983 movie *War Games*, Matthew Broderick stars as a teen who discovers a back door into a military central computer and he accidentally starts a countdown to begin World War III. He finds it by creating a modem autodialer to randomly dial telephone numbers until a computer "answers" the call. This random process of searching for a connection was called wardialing, so the word for randomly searching for a wireless signal is wardriving.

Wardriving technically involves using an automobile to search for wireless signals over a large area. Yet an automobile is not the only means of movement to find the signal; the same can be accomplished by carrying a laptop computer or PDA while simply walking down the street (still known as wardriving). Airplanes have also been used to locate RF signals (known as **warflying**). The first known instance of warflying occurred in early 2004 when two small airplanes found over 4,500 RF transmissions from access points, of which only 30 percent had encryption turned on.

Passive wireless discovery through wardriving is in itself not an illegal activity. What can be considered illegal in some localities is using that RF signal to connect to the networks without the owner's permission. Many wardrivers refuse to examine the contents of a wireless network, change anything on the network, or use the network's Internet connection; instead, they are only interested in locating and mapping WLAN signals.

NOTE

Because most computers are designed to "autoconnect" whenever they receive a WLAN signal, wardrivers disable all networking protocols (such as TCP/IP, NetBEUI, NetWare, etc.) on the computer, because without a networking protocol in operation, the computer lacks the means to autoconnect. Another reason wardrivers do not autoconnect is that when a connection is made the SSID of the access point is inserted into the wireless device's operating profile. Some wardriving programs have difficulty recognizing another WLAN with a different SSID and may ignore other WLAN signals, therefore overlooking a wireless site.

Some of the techniques used by wardrivers include:

- Driving at slower speeds—The general consensus is that a speed of about 35 MPH is best for wardriving. Some of the software used to pick up the signal requires time to identify and log the transmission. Driving too fast will not allow the signal to be within range for a long enough period of time.

- Using surface streets—On most freeways the road is farther away from buildings than on surface streets. Being closer to the source allows more RF signals to be identified.

- Creating a plan—Many wardrivers start with a street map of the area and block it out into sectors. Starting with the first sector, they drive up and down every street on the map within that sector and record the signal received. This is then repeated for all of the sectors. An added benefit of picking up the same signal from different locations is that it allows for a more precise identification of the source.

- Repeating over time—Defining a route and then wardriving it on a weekly or monthly basis helps to identify new WLANs as they are installed.

NOTE Knowing the techniques of wardrivers is important if you want to limit your exposure. For example, knowing that wardrivers typically repeat their route regularly means that just because your WLAN does not appear today on a public map of wireless hotspots does not mean it won't be found tomorrow.

Wardriving Hardware

There are four types of hardware needed for wardriving: mobile computing devices, wireless NIC adapters, antennas, and handheld global positioning system (GPS) devices.

Mobile Computing Devices

A mobile computing device used for wardriving can be a standard portable computer, of which there are two types. One is a laptop computer, which contains the traditional features of a desktop computer (screen, keyboard, hard drive, etc.) but in a smaller package to allow for mobility. Most laptop computers weigh from 1.8 to 3.6 kilograms (4 to 8 pounds).

NOTE The first portable computers were more "luggable" than they were portable, weighing in at a hefty 11.7 kilograms (26 pounds). As the technology advanced and smaller versions began to appear on the market, advertisers looked for a way to differentiate between them. The word "laptop" was used to designate the large version of the product whereas "notebook" was used to indicate the smaller version. Today laptop and notebook mean essentially the same.

The other type of standard portable computing device is a **tablet computer**. Instead of being simply a smaller version of a desktop computer, a tablet computer is designed for truly mobile computing. The key element of a tablet computer is the ability to navigate and enter data using a stylus instead of a keyboard. There are two types of tablet computers. A *convertible tablet* looks similar to a laptop in that it has a keyboard, but the display swivels and folds flat while facing outward when using a stylus, as seen in Figure 3-4. A *slate tablet* has no attached keyboard and is basically a large screen for viewing and entering data with a stylus, as seen in Figure 3-5.

Figure 3-4   Convertible tablet

Figure 3-5   Slate tablet

Tablet computers have several advantages:

- Users can write rather than type on a keyboard.

- Handwritten notes are immediately digitized, which makes them easier to amend and share with others.

- Drawings, formulas, signatures, and other graphical objects can be more easily used and manipulated on a tablet computer.

NOTE Tablet computers account for only about 3 percent of total laptop computer sales in the United States. This is because they cost significantly more than traditional laptops and usually offer inferior battery life, which is perhaps the most important element of any portable computer.

Even smaller than a laptop or tablet computer is a **handheld PC**. As seen in Figure 3-6, a handheld PC is small enough to be held in a single hand yet has many of the features of a laptop computer. These features include a screen supporting a resolution of greater than 480 × 240, keyboard, a PCMCIA slot, an infrared (IrDA) port, and Universal Serial Bus (USB) connectivity.

Figure 3-6   Handheld PC

The handheld PC was the original hardware design for a portable consumer device running a version of Microsoft Windows known as Windows CE. Billed by Microsoft as a PC Companion Device, the handheld PC was designed to provide the familiar applications from a desktop computer in a mobile format. However, because of its bulky design and small keyboard, handheld PCs were never widely popular.

NOTE   Microsoft has not issued software to support handheld PCs since 2000.

The smallest mobile computing device is a **personal digital assistant (PDA)**, which is a handheld device that was originally designed as a personal organizer but quickly became more sophisticated. Today a standard PDA usually includes a date book, address book, task list, memo pad, clock, and calculator software. A significant advantage of using PDAs is their ability to synchronize data with another computer. PDAs are illustrated in Figure 3-7.

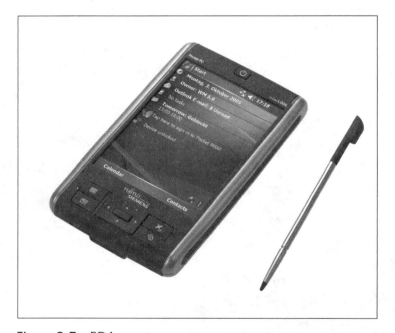

Figure 3-7   PDA

NOTE   The major PDA operating systems currently available are the Palm OS, Windows Mobile, and BlackBerry. In addition, there are several PDA operating systems based on Linux.

Despite its initial appeal, the popularity of PDAs is declining, according to a market study by the Gartner Group. Many of the functions of a PDA are now incorporated into cellular telephones sometimes called **smartphones**. These devices combine personal information management and mobile phone capabilities into a single device, freeing the user from carrying both a cell phone and a PDA.

Table 3-2 lists the advantages and disadvantages of each of these types of mobile computing devices. A common characteristic that they all share is that they can support IEEE 802.11 wireless technology, making them ideal for wardriving.

Table 3-2 Mobile computing devices

Device	Advantages	Disadvantages
Laptop computer	Portable	Limited battery life
Tablet computer	Recognize handwriting	High cost; limited battery life
Handheld PC	Same applications as desktop	Bulky design and small keyboard
Personal digital assistant	Fits in one hand	Replaced by smartphones
Smartphone	Combines several features into single device	High cost

Wireless Network Interface Card

The hardware that allows the mobile computing device to detect a wireless signal is a **wireless network interface card** (or **wireless client network adapter**). Unlike their desktop counterparts, wireless NICs for mobile devices are available in a variety of shapes and styles.

For laptop, tablet, and handheld PCs, an external wireless NIC can plug into the USB port, either as a standalone device (Figure 3-8a) or a key fob (Figure 3-8b). A standalone USB device has an advantage over a key fob because the standalone device can be repositioned to improve reception. In addition, PC card wireless adapters are available in different configurations, such as CardBus, PC Card Type II, or PC Card Type III. Figure 3-9 shows CardBus and Mini PCI cards.

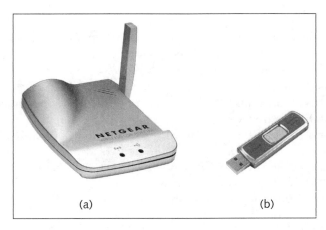

(a)   (b)

Figure 3-8 USB wireless NICs: (a) standalone USB device and (b) USB key fob

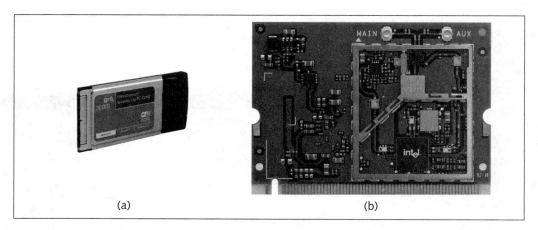

(a)   (b)

Figure 3-9   Wireless NIC PC Card adapters: (a) CardBus card and (b) Mini PCI card

Instead of being a separate device, most laptops and tablets have the wireless NIC built in as a **Mini PCI**. A Mini PCI is a small card that is functionally equivalent to a standard PCI expansion card. It was specifically developed for integrating communications peripherals such as modems and NICs onto a laptop computer. Most laptop computers now come standard with a wireless Mini PCI card installed. Some vendors have enhanced the Mini PCI slot by embedding an antenna in the case of the laptop that surrounds the screen. When a wireless NIC Mini PCI card is used, it automatically activates the antenna to improve the reception of the wireless signal.

Almost 90 percent of laptop and tablet computers today come with a Mini PCI wireless NIC installed as standard equipment.

NOTE

For smaller devices like handheld PCs and PDAs, there are several options for wireless NICs, depending on the manufacturer. Some PDAs will accept a standard CardBus or Type II PC Card wireless NIC like those used in a laptop computer. However, sometimes an external attachment known as a **sled** must be purchased and connected to the PDA. The sled contains a slot for a wireless NIC or similar device. Another option is a CompactFlash (CF) card, as seen in Figure 3-10. **Flash memory** is a type of solid-state (microchip) technology in which there are no moving parts. CF cards consist of a small circuit board that contains flash memory chips and a dedicated controller chip. There are two advantages of CF wireless NICs over PC Cards: they are smaller and they consume less power. Another option is to use a SDIO (Secure Digital I/O) or SDIO NOW! card. SDIO cards provide high-speed data input/output with low power consumption for mobile electronic devices.

3

Figure 3-10   Wireless CompactFlash card

NOTE

Separate wireless NICs could soon be a thing of the past. Some vendors plan to integrate a wireless NIC onto a single chip that could be included on the motherboard, eliminating the need for a separate card. Not all vendors agree with this solution, however. Some manufacturers want to keep radio signals farther from the motherboard, to reduce the likelihood of interference with the audio system. Instead of integrating the components of a wireless NIC on the motherboard of the computer, they integrate a wireless NIC behind the LCD display, therefore keeping radio waves away from the motherboard.

Although wireless NIC adapters may look the same on the outside, on the inside they can be significantly different based on the **chipset**, or the group of integrated circuits that provide the functionality of the wireless NIC. There are several different chipsets (Prism, Hermes, Atheros, and others) that are used by wireless NIC adapter manufacturers. Some chipsets are considered better at capturing wireless data than others.

Not all chipsets support **radio frequency monitoring (RFMON)**. RFMON is a passive method of receiving WLAN signals. A wireless NIC client adapter in RFMON mode can capture all RF signals on the channels to which it is configured to listen. However, while in RFMON mode wireless clients are unable to transmit: they can only receive and capture wireless traffic. On wired networks, a NIC may receive packets for which it is not the intended recipient, but it will ordinarily ignore those packets. A wired NIC can be set to **promiscuous mode**, which turns off the filtering mechanism and allows it to capture all the packets it receives. However, promiscuous mode will not work on a WLAN. First, it would only capture packets of the network that it was currently associated with and not any other wireless network. Also, it only passes the packets as IEEE 802.3/Ethernet-II frames, so no IEEE 802.11 headers or management frames could be seen.

Antennas

Although all wireless NIC adapters have embedded antennas, attaching an external antenna will significantly increase the ability to detect a wireless signal. There are two fundamental characteristics of antennas. First, as the frequency gets higher the wavelength becomes smaller. This means that the size of the antenna is smaller. Consider a cellular telephone: it uses a high frequency so only a small antenna is required. Second, as the gain (positive difference in amplitude between two signals) of an antenna increases, the coverage area narrows. High-gain antennas offer longer coverage areas than low-gain antennas at the same input power level.

There are three basic categories of antennas: omni-directional, semi-directional, and highly directional. The most common type of antenna for a WLAN, whether wardriving or in standard use, is an **omni-directional antenna**, also known as a **dipole antenna**. An omni-directional antenna detects signals from all directions equally.

Unlike an omni-directional antenna that evenly spreads the signal in all directions, a **semi-directional antenna** focuses the energy in one direction. Semi-directional antennas are primarily used for short- and medium-range remote wireless bridge networks. **Highly directional antennas** send a narrowly focused signal beam. Highly directional antennas are generally concave dish-shaped devices. These antennas are used for long-distance, point-to-point wireless links, such as connecting buildings that are up to 42 kilometers (25 miles) apart. Omni-directional antennas are commonly used for WLAN wardriving.

For a review of antennas and radio wave concepts, see *CWNA Guide to Wireless LANs* (ISBN 0-619-21579-8).

NOTE

Global Positioning System (GPS)

The final piece of hardware used for wardriving is a **global positioning system (GPS)** receiver, which is one part of the entire GPS system. The GPS system, which was originally developed by the U.S. military in the late 1970s as a navigation system but was later opened to civilian use, is used to precisely identify the location of the receiver. GPS is composed of 27 earth-orbiting satellites, each of which circles the globe twice each day at a height of 19,300 km (12,000 miles). This configuration, illustrated in Figure 3-11, is designed so that from any location on Earth a minimum of four satellites can be seen at all times.

Of the 27 GPS satellites in space only 24 are in operation. The remaining three are spares in case a satellite fails.

NOTE

3

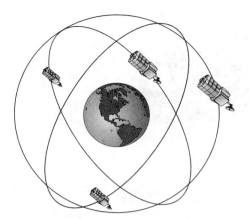

Figure 3-11   Global positioning system (GPS)

Each satellite continually transmits two signals, L1 and L2, to Earth using high-frequency radio signals at 1575.42 MHz and 1227.60 MHz, respectively. Civilian navigation receivers use a code sent on the L1 frequency, although some high-end civilian surveying GPS receivers can utilize the L2 band for more precise measurements. The GPS receiver measures the signals received from the satellites and calculates the time required for the signal to travel from the satellite to the receiver (this can be done by knowing the time that the signal left the satellite and comparing the time it was received based on its internal clock). Once the location of the satellites and the distance from each of those satellites are known, the GPS receiver can deduce its own location based on a mathematical principle called **trilateration**.

NOTE

The degree of accuracy of an L1 GPS receiver is approximately 5 meters (16 feet).

Although using a GPS device is optional when wardriving, the information accumulated is much less useful without the GPS information. A GPS receiver allows the user to precisely record where the WLANs are located. Most GPS receivers have small graphic screens for displaying the current location. However, wardrivers use a GPS receiver that lacks a display but instead has a USB connection, like that seen in Figure 3-12. USB GPS receivers for wardriving typically have a magnetic base so that they can be affixed to the roof of a moving automobile. The entire wardriving hardware configuration of a mobile computer, wireless NIC, antenna, and GPS is illustrated in Figure 3-13.

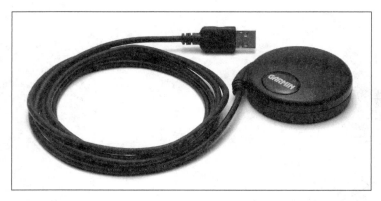

Figure 3-12   USB GPS

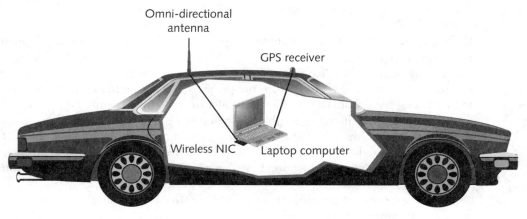

Figure 3-13   Wardriving hardware

Wardriving Software

In addition to wardriving hardware, software is also necessary to detect a WLAN signal. Wardriving software can be divided into three categories: client utilities, integrated operating system tools, and freeware discovery applications.

Client Utilities

When WLANs first appeared, operating systems were not equipped to be aware of their presence. Wireless NIC adapter manufacturers included client software utilities that were used to detect a wireless signal and then connect to that network. These client utilities also provided the ability to adjust client parameters, report statistics, and show signal strength, as seen in Figures 3-14 and 3-15.

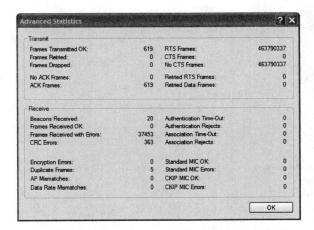

Figure 3-14   Client utility statistics

However, the popularity of client utilities has decreased. Few wireless NIC adapter manufacturers now include client software utilities to accompany their hardware. In addition, some of those that do make the utilities available configure the software not to function unless that vendor's specific wireless NIC is installed and functioning in the computer.

NOTE   Cisco's Aironet Desktop Utility (ADU), one of the more sophisticated client utilities, will not function unless a Cisco wireless NIC card is installed.

Integrated Operating System Tools

One reason why NIC adapter manufacturers stopped distributing client utilities is because operating systems have become wireless aware. This integration of wireless networking into the operating system has made it much easier to use WLANs.

The integrated operating system tool for a Windows-based computer is Microsoft's **Wireless Zero Configuration (WZC)** service. This software, which is tightly integrated with Windows XP Service Pack 2 (SP2) and Windows Server 2003, consists of several components. First, WZC adds a new Wireless Networks tab, which is available from the

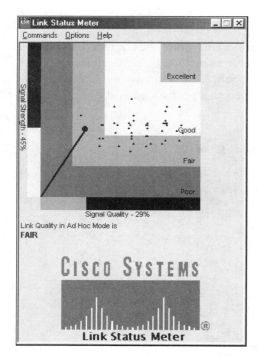

Figure 3-15   Client utility signal strength meter

properties of a wireless adapter connection in Network Connections. As seen in Figure 3-16, WZC supports the following functions:

- Use Windows to configure my wireless network settings—Selecting this check box enables WZC to automatically configure wireless settings. This option is enabled by default. If client utilities or other third-party wireless software is used then this check box should be cleared.

- Available networks—A list of wireless networks that are within range of the wireless NIC adapter can be viewed by clicking View Wireless Networks. This is used by wardrivers to detect a WLAN signal.

- Preferred networks—This lists, by order of preference, the WLANs with which the wireless NIC will attempt to connect. New WLANs that do not appear in the list can be added by clicking Add, whereas a network can be deleted from the list by selecting Remove. The Properties button allows the user to configure the WLAN.

- Advanced—The Advanced button allows the user to configure additional wireless settings that are independent of the wireless networks. For example, the user can specify whether to connect only to infrastructure (through an access point) or ad hoc (peer-to-peer) wireless networks or to automatically connect to wireless networks that are not in the preferred list.

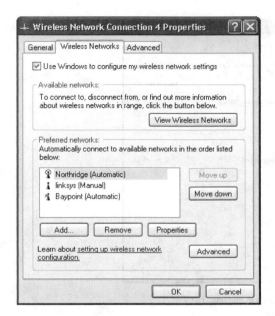

Figure 3-16 Wireless Network Connection Properties window

When you click the View Wireless Networks button under Available networks, the Choose a wireless network dialog box opens, as seen in Figure 3-17. When WZC detects a network that is not a preferred network, a message appears in the Windows Taskbar that indicates "One or more wireless networks are available." Clicking on that message launches the Choose a Wireless Network dialog box and allows the user to select an available network with which to connect. When a successful connection is made for the first time, that network is then automatically added to the top of the list of preferred networks and grouped by type of network (ad hoc or infrastructure mode).

One of the advantages of WZC is that it facilitates roaming between different WLANs without having to reconfigure the network connection settings on the computer for each location. Whenever you move from one location to another, WZC scans for an available WLAN in the new location, configures your network adapter card to match the settings of that WLAN, and attempts to access that WLAN.

Freeware Discovery Applications

Client utilities and integrated operating system tools were designed primarily for the owner of a WLAN to connect to a wireless network, view its configuration, and make minor adjustments. Although this software can be used for wardriving to detect a WLAN signal, other more specialized software is often used. Wardriving software that is specifically

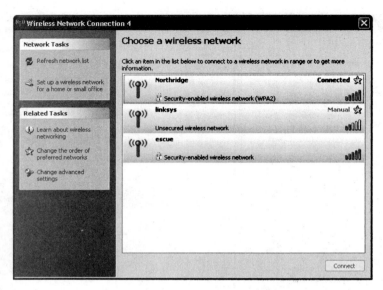

Figure 3-17   Choose a wireless network dialog box

designed to pick up a radio frequency **WLAN** signal is known as a freeware discovery application. These programs, of which there are currently over 50, are readily available over the Internet.

Perhaps the best-known freeware discovery application is **NetStumbler**. NetStumbler was one of the first freeware discovery applications and is probably the most widely used. NetStumbler (and its companion product MiniStumbler, which runs on handheld devices) can check for wireless networks and their signal strength, review which channels are being used, and then compare competing networks to monitor interference. The NetStumbler screen interface is seen in Figure 3-18. It provides a broad wealth of detailed feedback, such as:

- Channels used
- Encryption method (WEP, WPA)
- MAC addresses
- Real-time signal and noise information (**Figure 3-19**)
- Signal strength
- SSID
- Type of network (IEEE 802.11a/b/g/pre-n)

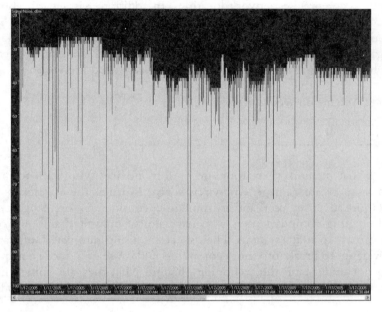

Figure 3-18   NetStumbler main screen

Figure 3-19   NetStumbler signal-to-noise ratio

NOTE   NetStumbler can also determine an access point's location using a GPS device to mark locations. This information can then be imported into products such as Microsoft's MapPoint to create a map of access point locations along with the NetStumbler information.

Although NetStumbler is sometimes criticized for lacking features, in reality NetStumbler is not designed to perform some of these activities. For example, NetStumbler cannot capture and decode wireless packets, monitor utilization, or make automatic connections to networks it discovers because it is not intended to. The major drawback of NetStumbler is that it cannot report all types of encryption, such as **IP Security (IPSec)**. IPSec is a set of protocols developed to support the secure exchange of packets.

The NetStumbler Web site is *www.netstumbler.com*.

Another popular tool is **Kismet**, which runs under the Linux operating system. Kismet can report similar information as NetStumbler, such as the SSID, access point and client MAC addresses, data rates, channel used, and quality, signal, and noise information. Kismet also supports GPS devices for precise network locations. In addition, Kismet can also capture packets and periodically dump them to a file. These files can later be used as input to wireless packet analysis tools. Kismet also recognizes the signatures of popular wireless attacks and can provide alerts regarding a potential intrusion. A similar tool, **KisMAC**, is an application for the Apple MacOS X operating system. It is intended for advanced users.

The Kismet Web site is *www.kismetwireless.net*.

It should be noted that many of these tools are used by novices who want to break into computer networks to create damage. Known as **script kiddies**, these attackers lack the technical skills of more advanced users and are sometimes considered more dangerous. Script kiddies tend to be young computer users who have almost unlimited amounts of leisure time, which they can use to attack systems. Their success in using automated software scripts tends to fuel their desire to break into more computers and cause even more harm. Because script kiddies do not understand the technology behind what they are doing, they often indiscriminately target a wide range of WLANs, causing problems for a large audience.

Public Mapping Sites

The final step in wardriving is to document and then advertise the location of the wireless LANs. Early WLAN users copied a system that hobos used during the Great Depression to indicate friendly locations. Wireless networks were identified by drawing on sidewalks or walls around the area of the network known as **warchalking**. This system relied on a series of symbols, as seen in Figure 3-20.

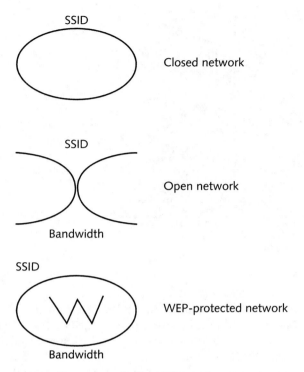

Figure 3-20   Warchalking symbols

However, warchalking today has been largely replaced by public online databases and mapping sites. These sites allow users to enter information they have obtained through wardriving, as seen in Figure 3-21, as well as look up locations of WLAN hotspots, as seen in Figure 3-22.

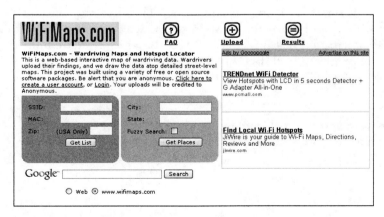

Figure 3-21   Recording WLAN information

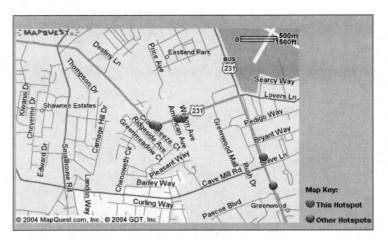

Figure 3-22   WLAN hotspots

WIRELESS PACKET SNIFFERS

Monitoring network traffic is important to determine the health of a network. One of the tools that is used is the **Simple Network Management Protocol (SNMP)**, which is part of the TCP/IP protocol suite. SNMP is an industry-wide standard supported by most network equipment manufacturers. SNMP allows computers and network equipment to gather data about network performance. **Software agents** are loaded onto each network device that will be managed. Each agent monitors network traffic and stores that information in its **management information base (MIB)**. In addition, a computer with the SNMP management software, known as the **SNMP management station**, communicates with the software agents on each network device and collects the data stored in the MIBs. The SNMP management station then combines all of the data and produces statistics about the network, such as transmission or connectivity errors, the number of bytes or data packets sent, and information on IP activity and addressing. The first two versions of SNMP, SNMPv1 and SNMPv2, used **community strings** that acted like a password to allow or deny access to the information that was collected. The Read-Only community string gave permission to the requester to read data whereas the Read-Write community string gave permission to modify data. However, all data transmissions including the community string was sent in cleartext.

Community strings are used only by devices that support SNMPv1 and SNMPv2c protocol. SNMPv3 uses usernames and passwords along with an encryption key.

NOTE

3

Another means of monitoring the network is to use a **packet sniffer**, which captures TCP/IP packets as they are being transmitted. Wired packet sniffers can be either separate devices or software that is installed on a computer and operates in promiscuous mode. There are three categories of packet sniffers based on their functions:

- Counts the number of packets that are being transmitted
- Shows general characteristics of traffic
- Provides a detailed analysis of all protocols

Like their wired counterparts, **wireless packet sniffers** can play an important role in analyzing network traffic and identifying problems. Wireless sniffers can capture not only the data frames but also management frames, such as beacon frames and acknowledgement frames. A wireless packet sniffer can be used to help reveal the following WLAN problems:

- An access point that is advertising its SSID when it is intended to be turned off
- An access point with encryption disabled
- A wireless client that is sending a high rate of low-speed packets
- An access point that is transmitting an excessive number of beacon frames

NOTE

Although there is a long list of wireless sniffer and analyzer software, the most popular tools include Kismet (which also doubles as a freeware discovery tool), Ethereal, AiroPeek NX, and Airmagnet.

Wireless packet sniffers can also be used by attackers to capture unencrypted packets and view their contents. Wireless packet sniffers can reveal usernames and passwords, SNMP community strings, encryption keys, and MAC addresses. The best way to protect against data being viewed by wireless packet sniffers is to encrypt the packets before they are transmitted.

Chapter Summary

- General information gathering relies on deception and digging to obtain information about networks, and includes social engineering, phishing, improperly recycled equipment, search engine scanning, and dumpster diving.
- Social engineering relies on deceiving someone to access a system. Phishing involves sending an e-mail or displaying a Web announcement that falsely claims to be from a legitimate enterprise to trick the user into surrendering information. Improperly recycled equipment often has valuable data stored on it. Search engine scanning is used by attackers to locate information that is not intended for the general public. Dumpster diving involves looking through a trash receptacle for sensitive information.

❏ Wireless location mapping, or wardriving, refers to passive wireless discovery, or the process of finding a WLAN signal and recording information about it. There are four types of hardware needed for wardriving: mobile computing devices, wireless NIC adapters, antennas, and handheld GPS devices.

❏ Wardriving software includes integrated operating system tools that automatically detect and connect to a WLAN, client utilities provided by wireless NIC manufacturers, and freeware discovery applications, such as NetStumbler, Kismet, and KisMAC, that are designed to pick up a WLAN signal by wardriving. Once the sites have been identified they can be recorded into public online databases.

❏ Wireless packet sniffers play an important role in analyzing network traffic and identifying problems because they can capture not only the data frames but also management frames, such as beacon frames and acknowledgment frames. However, wireless packet sniffers can also be used by attackers to capture unencrypted packets and view their contents. The best way to protect data on a WLAN from packet sniffers is to encrypt the packets before they are transmitted.

KEY TERMS

chipset — A group of integrated circuits that provides specific functionality.

community string — An authentication string that functions like a password to allow or deny access to the information that was collected by SNMP (Simple Network Management Protocol).

dipole antenna — An antenna that detects from all directions equally. Also known as an omni-directional antenna.

dumpster diving — Looking through an outdoor trash receptacle as a source of secure information.

flash memory — A type of solid-state (microchip) technology in which there are no moving parts.

global positioning system (GPS) — A navigation system that allows a user to determine his precise location.

Google phishing — A phishing technique in which attackers set up their own search engines to direct traffic to illegitimate sites.

handheld PC — A small computer that can be held in a single hand yet has many of the features of a notebook computer.

highly directional antenna — An antenna that sends a narrowly focused signal beam.

IP Security (IPSec) — A set of protocols developed to support the secure exchange of packets.

KisMAC — A freeware discovery application for the Apple MacOS X operating systems.

Kismet — A freeware discovery application that runs under the Linux operating system.

management information base (MIB) — The location where SNMP network traffic information is stored.

mini PCI — A small card that is functionally equivalent to a standard PCI expansion card.

NetStumbler — The best-known freeware discovery application.

omni-directional antenna — An antenna that detects from all directions equally; also known as a dipole antenna.

packet sniffer — A device or software that captures TCP/IP packets as they are being transmitted.

personal digital assistant (PDA) — A handheld device that was originally designed as a personal organizer.

pharming — A form of phishing that automatically redirects the user to the fake site.

phishing — Sending an e-mail or displaying a Web announcement that falsely claims to be from a legitimate enterprise in an attempt to trick the user into surrendering information.

promiscuous mode — A mode that turns off the filtering mechanism and allows a wired NIC to capture all the packets it receives.

radio frequency monitoring (RFMON) — A passive method of receiving WLAN signals.

script kiddies — Attackers that lack the technical skills of more advanced users and are sometimes considered more dangerous.

semi-directional antenna — An antenna that focuses the energy in one direction.

Simple Network Management Protocol (SNMP) — An industry-wide standard supported by most network equipment manufacturers.

sled — An external attachment for a PDA that can accommodate a wireless NIC or similar device.

smartphone — A cellular telephone that includes many of the functions of a PDA.

SNMP management station — An SNMP device that communicates with the software agents on each network device and collects the data stored in the MIBs.

social engineering — A technique that relies on tricking and deceiving someone to access a system.

software agent — SNMP software that is loaded onto each network device that will be managed.

spear phishing — Phishing that targets specific users.

tablet computer — A computer designed for truly mobile computing. Tablet computers come in two styles: a convertible tablet, with a keyboard and a display that swivels and folds flat to be used with a stylus, and a slate tablet, which has no attached keyboard and is basically a large screen for viewing and entering data with a stylus.

trilateration — The mathematical principle that enables a GPS receiver to deduce its own location from satellite information.

warchalking — The process of identifying wireless networks by drawing on sidewalks or walls around the area of the network.

warflying — Using an airplane to find a WLAN signal.

wireless client network adapter — The hardware that allows a mobile computing device to detect a wireless signal; also called wireless network interface card.

wireless location mapping — The formal expression used to refer to this passive wireless discovery or the process of finding a WLAN signal and recording information about it.

wireless network interface card — The hardware that allows a mobile computing device to detect a wireless signal; also called wireless client network adapter.

wireless packet sniffer — A device or software that captures wireless TCP/IP packets as they are being transmitted.

Wireless Zero Configuration (WZC) — The integrated operating system tool connecting to and configuring wireless networks for Microsoft Windows XP and later Windows-based computers.

REVIEW QUESTIONS

1. _____ involves sending an e-mail or displaying a Web announcement that falsely claims to be from a legitimate enterprise in an attempt to trick the user into surrendering information.

   a. Phishing

   b. Social engineering

   c. Resource allocation (RA)

   d. Web posting

2. Wireless location mapping refers to passive wireless discovery, also known as

   a. wardriving

   b. wireless address allocation (WAA)

   c. spear driving

   d. access point collecting

3. Each of the following is a technique used by wardrivers except

   a. drive at slower speeds

   b. use freeways or interstate highways

   c. repeat over time

   d. divide the area into sectors

4. Each of the following is a necessary piece of hardware for wardriving except

   a. automobile

   b. computing device

   c. antenna

   d. wireless NIC adapter

5. A _____ is a computer that lacks a keyboard.
   a. convertible table
   b. handheld PC
   c. desktop
   d. slate tablet

6. Social engineering relies on tricking and deceiving someone to access a system. True or False?

7. Whereas phishing involves sending millions of generic e-mail messages to users, spear phishing targets only specific users. True or False?

8. Google phishing involves stealing information from the Google Web site that contains personal information. True or False?

9. Attackers use search tools to locate information that is not intended for the general public. True or False?

10. Handheld PCs outsell PDAs by a 2-to-1 margin. True or False?

11. The smallest mobile computing device is a(n) _____ , which is a handheld device that was originally designed strictly as personal organizers but quickly became more sophisticated.

12. For laptop, tablet, and handheld PCs an external wireless NICs can plug into the _____ port, as either as a standalone device or a key fob.

13. A(n) _____ is a small card that is functionally equivalent to a standard PCI expansion card and is used for wireless NIC adapters in laptop computers.

14. Not all chipsets support _____ , which is a passive method of receiving WLAN signals.

15. GPS receivers can deduce their own location based on the mathematical principle of _____ .

16. Describe the two fundamental characteristics of antennas.

17. What are the three types of antennas? What type(s) are commonly used to detect wireless networks?

18. What is a wireless client utility and why were they used?

19. What is warchalking?

20. How are wireless networks vulnerable to wireless packet sniffers, and how do you protect against this vulnerability?

HANDS-ON PROJECTS

Project 3-1: Set SNMP Options on Cisco Aironet Access Point

Monitoring network traffic is important to determine the health of a network, and one of the tools that is commonly used is the Simple Network Management Protocol (SNMP), which is part of the TCP/IP protocol suite. SNMP allows computers and network equipment to gather data about network performance. In this activity you set up the SNMP options on a Cisco access point. If your network is not using SNMP then this data will not be captured. If your network is configured for SNMP, contact your network technician or instructor regarding any changes in these settings before making them.

1. Connect to the Cisco access point and enter the username and password.
2. Click **Services** in the left pane.
3. Click **SNMP**.
4. Under **Simple Network Management Protocol (SNMP):** click **Enabled** if it is not already selected. Click **Apply** and then click **OK**.
5. Under **System Name (optional):** enter **WLAN Monitoring**.
6. Under **System Location (optional):** enter the room number or building name of the access point.
7. Under **System Contact (optional):** enter your name. Click **Apply** and **OK**.
8. Scroll down to **SNMP Trap Community**.
9. Click **Enable Specific Traps**.
10. Click **802.11 Event Traps**.
11. Click **Apply** and then click **OK**.
12. Close your browser.

Project 3-2: Logging using Wireless Zero Configuration

One of the additional features of Windows Wireless Zero Configuration (WZC) is the ability to create and view a log of the actions that WZC is performing that are normally transparent to the user. In this activity you activate and view the two wireless log files. Your computer should have Windows Wireless Zero Configuration enabled to complete this project.

When troubleshooting wireless issues, Microsoft often asks users to submit this WZC log file for analysis.

NOTE

1. To enable logging click **Start** and **Run**.

2. Type **cmd** and press **Enter**.

3. At the command prompt type **netsh ras set tracing * enabled** and press **Enter**. This will enable logging.

4. To understand the information that WZC records you will need to initiate an unusual event, which will be to turn off your wireless adapter. Click **Start**, point to **Connect To**, and click **Show all connections**.

5. Select your wireless network connection and click the right mouse button.

6. Select **Disable** to turn off the wireless adapter. You may receive a notice on the toolbar that you are no longer connected to the wireless network.

7. Now re-enable the wireless adapter. If the Network Connections screen is no longer showing on your system click **Start**, point to **Connect To**, and click **Show all connections**.

8. Select your wireless network connection and click the right mouse button. Select **Enable** to turn on the wireless adapter. All of this activity is now recorded in log files.

9. Using Windows Explorer navigate to the folder that contains your log files (normally it will be C:\WINDOWS\tracing). Locate the file **WZCDLG.LOG** and double-click to open it. If you cannot locate this file in the subdirectory you may need to search for it.

10. This file displays the events that occurred when you first connected with the wireless network, as seen in Figure 3-23.

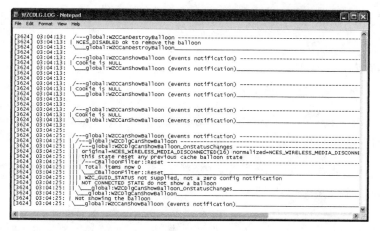

Figure 3-23   WZCDLG.LOG file contents

11. As you scroll down through the file you may note that some of the information is difficult to decipher; however, the information is useful in troubleshooting. Can you find where the wireless NIC adapter was disabled and then re-enabled? What information does it give you?

12. Click **Edit** and then **Find.** Enter **SSID** and press **Enter**. You will be taken to the line that contains the SSID of the access point with which you are currently associated.

13. Close **WZCDLG.LOG**.

14. Open the file **WZCTrace.LOG** as seen in Figure 3-24. The WZCTrace.LOG file contains information that is continuously updated and each event receives a time stamp. The WZCTrace.LOG records the sequence of events in this fashion: the first question that is asked is, "What SSIDs does this adapter know about?" Then the next question that is asked is, "What SSIDs are being heard right now?" From those two lists, the first items are then compared. Whenever a "known about" SSID matches with a "heard" SSID then an association is attempted.

Figure 3-24 WZCTrace.LOG file contents

15. Click **Edit** and then **Find**. Enter **SSID** and press **Enter**. You will be taken to the first line that contain the "SSID." Continue to press **Enter** to see the SSID of all the access points in your area that are detected (this will appear in the format WZCCopySelectedConfigs[0]: SSID=<8:*SSID*> From List).

16. Close this file and wait several minutes.

17. Reopen the file **WZCTrace.LOG** and search again for the **SSID**. Note how frequently information is gathered regarding which access point to associate with.

18. Close the WZCTrace.LOG file.

3

19. To disable tracing type **netsh ras set tracing * disabled** and press **Enter** at a command prompt.

20. Close all windows.

Project 3-3: Download and Use Cisco Wireless Utilities

The Cisco Aironet Client Utility (ACU) is one of the most powerful client utilities available. Although it has been updated to a newer version known as the Cisco Aironet Desktop Utility (ADU), the ACU has a feature that can be used for wardriving known as the Link Status meter. However, it requires that a Cisco Aironet wireless NIC be installed and functioning in the computer. In this project you will download and use the ACU. Note that you will need a Cisco wireless network interface card to perform this project.

1. On a laptop computer point your browser to
   http://rorschach.concordia.ca/neg/remote_access/wireless/general_info/download.html.
   Note that if the software is no longer available at this site it may be necessary to search for "aironet client utility" using a Web browser.

2. Click on **350-Windows-98-2K-Me-XP-Bundle-1.exe**.

3. Save the file to your desktop. Install the ACU by running the file saved to your desktop. Accept the default configuration settings.

4. Click **Start**, point to **All Programs**, and click **Cisco Aironet** and **Aironet Client Utility**.

5. Click on each menu option and notice the functions that the ACU provides.

6. One of the tools of the ACU that is used for wardriving identifies a WLAN signal and its strength. Click **Link Status**.

7. A graph appears showing the signal strength between the computer and the AP to which it is associated. Note the strength based on the current location of the laptop computer.

8. Monitor the strength of the Link Status meter as you move farther away from the AP.

9. If you are in an area with multiple access points your signal could be picked up by another access point as you roam closer to it. Note on your Link Status meter where the signal falls and then suddenly receives an increase in strength. You have moved from one area of coverage to another and are "wardriving."

10. Close all open windows.

Project 3-4: Download and Install NetStumbler

One of the best freeware discovery applications is NetStumbler. In this project you will download and install NetStumbler.

1. In a Web browser enter the address *http://www.netstumbler.com*.

2. Click **Downloads**.

3. Click **NetStumbler x.x.x Installer**, where *x.x.x* indicates the latest version of the product.

4. Download NetStumbler to your desktop. After the download is complete, launch the file to start the installation process and follow the steps to install the program using the default installation settings.

5. Click **Start**, point to **All Programs**, and click **Network Stumbler**. Be aware that NetStumbler first turns off Windows WZC service so that it can manage the wireless signal. It will turn WZC back on when you exit NetStumbler.

6. NetStumbler will pick up all of the WLAN signals in your area. Select the different menu options to view the functionality of the program. How does it compare to the Aironet Client Utility?

7. Expand the items in the left pane by clicking the **+** sign.

8. The column **SNR** gives the strength of the signal divided by the noise level and is measured in decibels. Roam with your computer and observe the fluctuation of this value. You may also pick up other wireless signals that you could not from your original location.

9. Locate the access point that you are connected to in the right page on NetStumble and double-click on it to display a graphic of the SNR.

10. Close NetStumbler. Click **No** and do not save the settings.

Project 3-5: Download and Install Airopeek NX

There are several wireless packet sniffers that are available to monitor wireless TCP/IP packets. In this project you will download and use the demonstration version of Airopeek NX. Note that specific hardware may be required to run Airopeek. Go to *http://www.wildpackets.com/support/product_support/airopeek/hardware* for more information.

The purpose of these tools is strictly to demonstrate the process by using equipment that is owned by the user or has been approved by a third-party institution. Under no circumstances should these tools be used to monitor packets on another WLAN without the owner's express prior approval. Users who violate these conditions may be subject to legal action.

1. In a Web browser enter the address *http://www.wildpackets.com*.

2. Click **Downloads**.

3. Click **Product Demos**.

4. Click **Airopeek NX**. Note that this is a very large download exceeding 30 MB.

5. Enter the requested information and click **Submit**.

6. Follow the instructions to access Airopeek and download it to your desktop. After the download is complete, launch the file to start the installation process and follow the steps to install the program using the default installation settings.

7. Click **Start** and **All Programs** and then **WildPackets AiroPeek NX Demo**.

8. Note the following features of the EtherPeek main screen:

   ❏ Toolbar—This displays the icons for the frequently used tasks in AiroPeek. Selecting **View** and **Toolbar** will toggle off and on the display of this toolbar.

   ❏ Status Bar—The Status Bar shows context-sensitive messages on the left side and the current monitor adapter on the right side.

   ❏ Monitor Options—This allows you to select an adapter for collecting statistics and make other configurations.

   ❏ Network Statistics Gauge—These show network utilization as dials with corresponding digital displays.

9. The first step is to configure the adapter that is being used. Open **Capture Options**.

10. Click **802.11** in the Navigation Bar.

11. Click **Edit Scanning Options**. The **Channel Scanning Options** dialog box will display all of the channels that can be scanned. Be sure that all of the **Enabled** checkboxes are selected. The **Duration (msec)** should be set to **500**.

12. Click **OK**.

13. If WPA or WEP is being used then return to **Capture Options** and click **802.11** in the Navigation Bar.

14. Click **Edit Key Set**.

15. Click **Insert** to display the **Edit Key Set** dialog box.

16. Enter **Project 3–5** for the **Name**.

17. Under **Key type** select the type of security that is being used.

18. Enter the WEP key under **Key 1** or the WPA passphrase. Close any open dialog boxes.

19. To begin monitoring click **Monitor** and then **Monitor Options**.

20. Click the wireless adapter that is being used under **Local machine**.

21. Click **OK**.

22. Click **Monitor** and then **Summary** to view a summary of the statistics that are being captured.

23. To capture packets click **File** and then **New**.

24. Click **Adapter** to select the appropriate wireless adapter to use.

25. Click **OK**.

26. A capture window appears. Click **Start Capture**.

27. Depending on the amount of wireless traffic, you will want to capture packets for about one to two minutes. Click **Stop Capture**.

28. Double-click a packet in the **Packets** window to display its information. Note that at the bottom right of the window the ASCII view of the packet can be read.

29. Close all windows.

CASE PROJECTS

Case Project 3-1: Social Engineering Defenses

Many security experts consider social engineering as one of the greatest threats against data. Using the Internet, research social engineering and locate two incidences of it. Summarize those attacks. Next, write a one-page paper outlining the procedures that an organization should have in place to combat social engineering attacks.

Case Project 3-2: Public Mapping Sites

Locate at least three public mapping sites on the Internet and identify the WLANs in your immediate area. Which sites were you unaware of? Which ones did you know about? What information about them would be helpful to an attacker? If you owned one of the sites listed, would you want its information published? If not, what steps would you take to prevent it from being advertised? Write a one-page paper regarding it.

Case Project 3-3: Client Utilities

Although wardriving client utilities are not as common as they once were, some are still available. Using the Internet locate a client utility that can be used on your computer. Install the utility and observe the information that it can provide. Is it useful? Could it be used for wardriving? Write a one-paragraph summary regarding this tool.

Case Project 3-4: Chipsets

Using the Internet locate information regarding which chipsets are used in different WLAN wireless NIC adapters. Create a table that lists at least six of the most popular adapters and the chips that are used. Be sure to include the adapters used in any wireless computers that you use.

3

Fairvue Technology Consulting

Fairvue Technology Consulting (FTC) has hired you to help them complete a project with Roger and Julie's Backyard Burgers (RJBB), which has several locations in the area. RJBB offers free wireless access to its customers who eat indoors as well as on the patio of their restaurants, but they don't want any others using their WLAN signal. RJBB was alarmed when they recently discovered a public mapping site that contained information about the wireless network in each of their stores. They are afraid that a disgruntled employee may have leaked information about the network.

1. Create a PowerPoint presentation that shows RJBB how this information may have been obtained through wardriving. Include a description of what wardriving is and the tools that can be used. Your presentation should be at least seven slides in length.

2. RJBB would still like to offer WLAN service to its customers but wants to know how they can restrict others from using the service. Research the different methods that a retailer can use to restrict unauthorized access to its WLAN. Write a one-page summary of your findings for RJBB.

ACTIVE WIRELESS ATTACKS

After completing this chapter you should be able to do the following:

➤ Describe the basic vulnerabilities of a WLAN

➤ Tell how malware and spyware can infect wireless networks

➤ List the vulnerabilities involved with implementing unsecured wireless LANs

➤ Explain the different types of wireless infrastructure attacks

The World of Wireless Security

Public utilities have been a key element of local municipal governments in the United States. These utilities supply an essential service, such as water or electrical power, at reasonable prices to anyone who applies for the service. Although public utilities frequently operate as monopolies in their market, this is considered reasonable because the unavailability of the service would negatively impact public health and welfare. The public utilities typically found today include water, gas, sewer, electricity, transportation facilities (subways, bus lines, and railroads), and cable television.

One more public utility is now being added to this list: wireless networks. In early 2006 more than 300 U.S. cities had launched or were preparing to offer wireless broadband networking as a public utility. With monthly costs averaging between $10 and $20, large cities such as Philadelphia (135-square mile citywide network serving 1.5 million users), Minneapolis (59-square mile network for 385,000 citizens), and Lexington, Kentucky (for 275,000 residents) as well as smaller cities like Addison, Texas and Franklin, Tennessee, are rushing to bring affordable wireless Internet access to their citizens. According to these cities, the rationale behind municipal wireless is the same as for municipal water and gas: it provides an essential service to its citizens.

However, municipal wireless is not without its detractors. Some question the need for a city to spend $35 million to install and manage a network in times of tight budgets. Others question whether wireless Internet access is truly an essential service like water or electricity. And some private Internet providers, such as telephone and cable systems, claim this is a tactic to allow other Internet service providers to make deals with local municipalities and squeeze them out. Even the U.S. Congress is now weighing in: the Community Broadband Act of 2005 was proposed in the Senate to amend the Telecommunications Act of 1996 and allow municipalities the right to offer broadband Internet access.

In the debate over municipal wireless, one group is strongly urging citizens to avoid it. That group is a growing chorus of wireless security experts. Many public municipal wireless offerings are "wide open" with no real security protections in place (these protections are omitted to make it easier for the users). Those users who do opt to use a municipal wireless network run the risk of attackers being able to retrieve passwords, credit card numbers, and other personal information as it is transmitted. Many wireless security experts are strongly urging caveat emptor—let the buyer beware!

In the previous chapter you learned about passive wireless discovery, or the tools and techniques used to detect a wireless LAN signal. As noted, there is no means available to monitor RF transmissions sent from a WLAN to determine if anyone else is listening in, nor is it possible to completely prevent intruders from monitoring your WLAN. Detecting the WLAN signal is the first step an attacker takes to penetrate a wireless network.

This chapter turns to the next step in the process, the active wireless attacks themselves. These attacks are based on wireless vulnerabilities that are exploited once a signal is detected. Some of the wireless vulnerabilities and attacks have their counterparts in the wired network world as well, such as weak passwords and denial of service (DoS) attacks. Other wireless vulnerabilities and attacks are unique to WLANs.

Our study of active wireless attacks begins by looking at three types of wireless vulnerabilities that make these attacks possible. Then you will explore the types of attacks that can result based on these vulnerabilities. Chapter 5 begins looking at the ways to defend against active wireless attacks.

It is important to remember that the reason for studying active wireless attacks is to be aware of the tools that attackers use so that defenses can be built to ward off attacks. These tools should never be used to access or monitor a wireless network unless you have permission from the owner.

Security Vulnerabilities

A **security vulnerability** may be defined as a weakness or flaw in an information system that could be exploited to cause harm. Although the weakness is often viewed as a flaw in the hardware or software that is being used, the weakness could also be in the security procedures, controls, or even the physical layout of the network. For example, leaving the network account of an employee who has been terminated accessible is an example of a procedural vulnerability.

In technical terms, security vulnerability describes the points of risk regarding the penetration of a security defense.

Security vulnerabilities for wireless LANs can be divided into three categories:

- Basic vulnerabilities (some of which are shared by wired networks)
- Vulnerabilities when using a public-access WLAN
- Vulnerabilities associated with implementing an unsecured wireless network

Vulnerabilities of the IEEE 802.11 security protections, such as wired equivalent privacy (WEP), are discussed in Chapter 2.

NOTE

Basic Vulnerabilities

There are several basic wireless security vulnerabilities that can be exploited to attack WLAN equipment such as an access point (AP) or wireless gateway. These include default passwords, weak passwords, SNMP community strings, and improper configuration.

Default Passwords

Before users can be given access to a computer and its data, they must in some way prove that they are who they claim to be. That is, users must give proof that they are "genuine" or authentic. This process of providing proof is known as **authentication**. Authentication can be performed based on what you have, what you know, or what you are.

Consider that Greg stops at the health club to exercise in the afternoon. After he locks his car doors, he walks into the club and is greeted by Brian, the clerk at the desk. Brian chats with Greg and allows him to pass on to the locker room. Once in the locker room, Greg opens his locker using a combination lock that requires him to spin a dial to a series of numbers that he has memorized.

Greg has used the three methods of authentication at the health club. First, by locking the doors of his car, its contents are protected by what he *has*, namely the car key. Next, access to the locker room is protected by what Greg *is*. Brian had to recognize Greg's unique characteristics (his hair color, his face, his body type, and his voice) before he could enter the locker room. Those characteristics serve to make Greg who he is. Finally, the contents of Greg's locker are protected by what he *knows*: the lock combination.

A **password** is a secret combination of letters and numbers that serves to validate or authenticate a user by what he knows. Passwords are used with user names to log on to a computer. A user name is a unique identifier, such as *Jbutterfield*, *Traci_Li*, or *Administrator*. Though anyone could type the person's user name, only that person would know the secret password. Passwords are used to prove that the person entering it is authentic and not a "fake."

Wireless access points and other equipment require the user to enter a username and password to access their configuration management features, as seen in Figure 4-1. All access points from a specific vendor are configured with the same standard password (known as the **default password**) that is used to access the AP configuration program. Although it is critical to immediately change a default password once equipment is installed, this is often overlooked. Default passwords are well known and can be easily found on the Internet. Using a default password, an attacker can change any AP configuration and even lock out a network administrator from the access point.

Figure 4-1 AP username and password

NOTE Lists of default passwords are found throughout the Internet by searching for *default passwords* with an Internet search engine. One example of a list is at *http://www.phenoelit.de/dpl/dpl.html*.

Weak Passwords

Although changing the default password on wireless equipment is a critical first step when installing the equipment, it is important that the *right* password be created. However, this is not always done because of the **password paradox**. For a password to remain secure and prevent an attacker from discovering it, passwords should never be written down but instead must be committed to memory. Yet passwords must also be of a sufficient length and complexity so that an attacker cannot easily guess the password. This creates the paradox: although lengthy and complex passwords should be used and never written down, it is very difficult to memorize these types of passwords.

In addition, most users today have an average of 20 or more different computers or accounts that require a password, such as computers at work, school, and home, e-mail accounts, banks, and Internet stores. The sheer number of passwords makes it impossible to remember all of them. Some passwords also expire after a set period of time, such as 60 days, and a new one must be created. Some computer systems even prevent a previously used password from being recycled and used again, forcing the user to memorize an entirely new password again. This makes using passwords more secure but difficult for the user to memorize.

All of these factors cause most computer users to revert to using **weak passwords**, or those that compromise security. Characteristics of weak passwords include:

- *A common word used as a password (such as "Christmas")*—Attackers can use an electronic dictionary of common words to match the password.

- *Not changing passwords unless forced to do so*—An attacker would have unlimited access to the user's account for the foreseeable future.

- *Passwords that are short (such as WXYZ)*—Short passwords are easier to break than long passwords.

- *Personal information in a password (such as the name of a pet)*—These passwords are easy to identify.

- *Using the same password for all accounts*—Once the attacker has one password he can gain access to any computer or account this person uses.

- *Writing the password down*—This serves as an open invitation to break into the account.

Attackers can exploit weak passwords by **password guessing**. Password-guessing attacks can be brute force, in which an attacker attempts to create every possible password combination by systematically changing one character at a time in a password, or a dictionary attack, in which each word from a dictionary is encoded in the same way the computer encodes a user's password for protection. Attackers then compare the encoded dictionary words against those in the encoded password file.

NOTE Brute force and dictionary attacks are covered in Chapter 2.

The following are considered minimum criteria for creating good passwords:

- Password must be at least eight characters long.

- Password contains characters from at least three of the following five categories:
  - English uppercase characters (A–Z)
  - English lowercase characters (a–z)
  - Base 10 digits (0–9)
  - Non–alphanumeric (For example: !, $, #, or %)
  - Extended ASCII characters

- Password does not contain three or more characters from the user's account name.

NOTE Extended ASCII characters (ASCII 128-255) are those that normally would not be used, such as the Greek letter *alpha*. They can be created by holding down the ALT key and typing the corresponding decimal numeric value on the keyboard's number pad, such as ALT + 224 to create the *alpha*. A complete list of these codes can be found by searching the Internet for *extended ascii values*.

Operating systems, such as Windows XP and Windows Server 2003, allow additional settings to be configured that relate to password characteristics. These settings include Enforce password history (determines the number of unique new passwords a user must use before an old password can be reused), Maximum password age (how many days a password can be used before the user is required to change it), Minimum password age (determines how many days a user must keep new passwords before they can change them), and Minimum password length. However, most access points, wireless gateways, and other wireless devices lack the ability to enforce these type of settings. It is recommended that a password policy be created that includes the criteria listed in Table 4-1 for setting passwords on wireless equipment.

In addition to creating strong passwords, using configuration settings that force strong password characteristics, and implementing good password policies, another technique is to use third-party software tools to store passwords from attackers. An example is PasswordSafe, which was covered in Hands-On Project 1-3.

Table 4-1 Password settings for wireless equipment

Password Category	Recommended Setting
Password length	Minimum 8 characters, recommended length 10 characters
Password content	Contains characters from three of the following categories: uppercase, lowercase, digit, non-alphanumeric, extended ASCII
Password history	Must create 12 new passwords before old password can be reused
Maximum password age	Change password every 30 days
Minimum password age	Must keep password at least 7 days

The Minimum password age is the number of days a user must keep a new password before changing it. This is intended to work with the Enforce password history setting so that users cannot quickly reset their passwords the required number of times and then change back to their old password.

SNMP Community Strings

As you learned in Chapter 3, the Simple Network Management Protocol (SNMP) is a popular protocol used to manage networked equipment. These devices include not only core network devices such as switches, routers, hubs, bridges, and wireless APs, but also printers, copiers, fax machines, and even uninterruptible power supplies (UPSs). SNMP was designed in the late 1980s for exchanging management information between networked devices, and enables system administrators to remotely monitor, manage, and configure devices on the network.

SNMP can be used to manage operating systems, cable modems, DSL modems, and even digital cameras and image scanners that are attached to the network.

Each SNMP-managed device must have an agent or a service that "listens" for commands and then executes them. These agents are protected with a password known as a *community string* to prevent unauthorized users from taking control over a device. There are two types of community strings: a read-only string allows information from the agent to be viewed and a read-write string allows settings to be changed.

The use of community strings in the first two versions of SNMP, SNMPv1 and SNMPv2, created several vulnerabilities. First, the default SNMP community strings for read-only and read-write were *public* and *private*, respectively. Administrators who did not change these default strings left open the possibility of an attacker taking control of a network device. Second, many administrators who reset the community strings used weak strings (passwords) for security. Finally, community strings are transmitted in cleartext, meaning that an attacker with a packet sniffer can view the contents of the strings as they are transmitted.

NOTE Using a packet sniffer to view SNMP community strings is discussed in Chapter 3.

There are defenses that can be used against an attacker viewing SNMP community strings over a WLAN. Community strings are used only by devices that support SNMPv1 and SNMPv2 protocol. SNMPv3 uses usernames and passwords along with an encryption key. Wireless devices that use SNMP should use the current version SNMPv3. If SNMPv1 or SNMPv2 must be used, then the default password should be changed and a strong password (community string) should be implemented.

Improper Configuration

A final basic vulnerability is generic and is often found on both wired and wireless equipment. An incorrect configuration of wireless hardware or software can often result in easy access to a system. Although incorrect configuration can cover a wide range of settings, two examples from **wireless gateways** (devices that combine access point, router, and network address translation features) may illustrate the seriousness of this vulnerability.

NOTE Much like passwords, vulnerabilities in incorrect configurations are usually because of implementing weak security to make the network easier to use or not changing the default settings of a device. A list of default settings and their vulnerabilities, like those listed at www.remote-exploit.org/index.php/Wlan_ defaults, can be found by searching the Internet for *wireless default settings*.

One incorrect configuration is to enable **Universal Plug and Play (UPnP)** when it is not necessary. UPnP is similar to the Windows **Plug and Play (PnP)** service. PnP allows the Windows operating system to automatically detect new hardware when it is installed on a computer. For example, if a new mouse is added to a system, PnP allows Windows to detect the hardware device, load the necessary drivers, and begin using it. In a similar fashion UPnP extends this concept to network devices. UPnP is a service that allows devices on a network to discover other devices and determine how to work with them. For example, a networked computer can use UPnP to detect if there are printers present on the network that are available and determine how to use them, instead of manually configuring the printers on each computer.

Not all Windows operating systems fully support UPnP. Table 4-2 lists the operating systems and their UPnP functionality.

Table 4-2   Windows UPnP support

Windows Version	UPnP Support
Windows XP Professional and Home	Native UPnP capability; installed and running by default.
Windows Server 2003	No UPnP support.
Windows ME	Native UPnP capability but is not installed or used by default.
Windows NT 4.0 and Windows 2000	No UPnP support.
Windows 98 and 98SE	No native support; can only be added by installing the client software for Internet Connection Sharing (ICS) provided in Windows XP.

However, there are vulnerabilities associated with UPnP based on the way the UPnP performs device discovery (determining what network devices are available). These vulnerabilities can enable an attacker to either gain complete control over an affected device or to prevent an affected system from performing its intended service. One brand of wireless gateway with UPnP enabled could allow an attacker to read all of the wireless configuration settings without knowing the password to the gateway. (The vulnerability was fixed in a firmware update, illustrating the importance of keeping device firmware updated.)

Figure 4-2 illustrates the UPnP setting on a wireless gateway. It is recommended that UPnP be disabled unless this service is known to be necessary.

NOTE

If you are unsure if UPnP is required on your wireless LAN, you can disable the feature and monitor the network to see if any problems arise. For home and SOHO WLANs, UPnP can generally be disabled with no impact on the network.

A second vulnerability based on an incorrect configuration is seen in Figure 4-2. Remote access allows for the wireless gateway to be configured remotely over the Internet. Entering a URL that contains both the IP address of the wireless gateway as well as the port number, such as *http://72.150.140.144:8080*, allows a remote user to access the configuration settings (after entering the username and password).

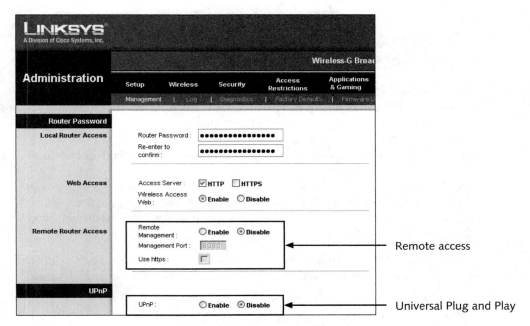

Figure 4-2   UPnP and remote access

NOTE   Almost all APs and wireless gateways have a browser interface for viewing and changing configuration settings. Disabling remote access does not affect accessing this interface through the local network; it only restricts access from remote computers.

An incorrect configuration would enable this setting and allow an attacker to attempt to break into the wireless gateway or access point. Unlike operating system authentication in which it may be possible to provide a limited number of attempts at guessing a password before the account is disabled, a wireless gateway will permit an unlimited number of attempts to break the password.

Vulnerabilities Associated with Using Public WLANs

In addition to packet sniffing, there are two other significant vulnerabilities associated with using an unsecured public WLAN, such as the WLAN in a coffee shop. These vulnerabilities include malware and spyware.

Malware

Malicious software, also called *malware*, is the term used to describe computer programs designed to break into and create havoc on portable or desktop computers. According to the security organization Sandvine, Internet service providers (ISPs) in North America spend more than $245 million annually to combat malware. The most common types of malware are viruses, worms, and logic bombs.

Viruses

A computer **virus** is a program that secretly attaches itself to another document or program and executes when that document or program is opened. Like its biological equivalent, viruses require a host to carry them from one system to another. Although viruses once spread by exchanging infected floppy disks, today viruses spread primarily through CD-ROMs, Web sites, downloaded files, and e-mail attachments. After a computer is infected, the virus then seeks another computer to attack. The number of viruses is staggering. According to Sophos, an antivirus software vendor, more than 95,000 known viruses attack computers, and on average one new virus is written and released every hour.

NOTE   Modern viruses can be programmed to send themselves to all users listed in an e-mail address book. The recipients, seeing they have received a message from a friend or business contact, often unsuspectingly open the attachment, infect their computer, and send the virus to their contacts.

A virus might do something as simple as display an annoying message, similar to the one shown in Figure 4-3. However, some viruses can be much more lethal. Viruses can also:

- Cause a computer to repeatedly crash
- Erase files from a hard drive
- Install hidden programs, such as stolen ("pirated") software, which is then secretly distributed or even sold from the computer
- Make multiple copies of itself and consume all of the free space in a hard drive
- Reduce security settings and allow intruders to remotely access the computer
- Reformat the hard disk drive

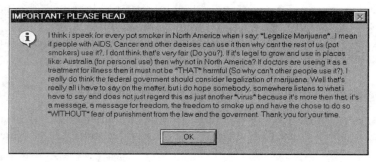

Figure 4-3   Annoying virus message

NOTE   One area in which viruses are attacking at an alarming rate is through instant messaging (IM). Using an IM program, such as MSN Messenger, AOL Instant Messenger, Yahoo Messenger, or others, IM viruses are spread when a user opens an infected file that was sent in an instant message.

The symptoms that indicate a virus has infected a computer may include any of the following:

- A program suddenly disappears from the computer.
- New icons appear on the screen or are not associated with any recently installed programs.
- New programs do not install properly.
- Out-of-memory error messages appear.
- Programs that used to function normally now stop responding.
- The computer sometimes starts normally but at other times it stops responding before it finishes loading.
- Unusual dialog boxes or message boxes appear.
- Sounds or music plays from the speakers unexpectedly.
- The computer runs very slowly and takes a long time to start.
- There is a significant amount of modem activity.
- The computer restarts unexpectedly.
- Error messages appear listing "critical system files" that are missing and the operating system refuses to load.

Worms

Another type of malicious software is a **worm**. Although similar to viruses, worms are different in two regards. First, a virus must attach itself to a computer document, such as an e-mail message, and is spread by traveling along with the document. A worm, on the other hand, does not attach to a document to spread but can travel by itself. Worms are most often distributed via e-mail attachments as separate executable programs. Although the worm does not depend on the e-mail message for its survival like a virus but is self-contained within the separate program, it uses e-mail as a convenient means of distribution.

A second difference between a worm and a virus is that a virus needs the user to perform an action, such as starting a program or reading an e-mail message, to start the infection. A worm does not always require action by the computer user to begin its execution.

NOTE Because worms are self-executing, meaning they do not require any action on the part of the user, many users falsely believe they are safe from infection as long as they have not opened the e-mail message or started the infected program. However, because a worm can start on its own, a user's lack of activity does not affect the process.

Worms usually replicate themselves until they clog all available resources, such as the hard disk drive, computer memory, or the Internet network connection. The typical symptoms that indicate a worm has infected computer are that the computer suddenly runs slowly and sluggishly and may unexpectedly reboot, often several times in a row.

Logic Bombs

Logic bombs are another type of malicious code. A logic bomb is a computer program that lies dormant until it is triggered by a specific logical event, such as a certain date reached on the system calendar or a person's rank in an organization dropped below a previous level. Once triggered, the program can perform any number of malicious activities. An example of a logic bomb is one that was planted in a company's payroll system by an employee. This program was designed so that if the employee's name was removed from the payroll (meaning the employee quit or was fired), after three months the logic bomb would corrupt the entire computerized accounting system.

Logic bombs are extremely difficult to detect before they are triggered. This is because logic bombs are often embedded in large computer programs, some containing tens of thousands of lines. An attacker can easily insert three or four lines of computer code into a long program without anyone detecting the insertion.

Spyware

Spyware is a general term used to describe software that violates a user's personal security. The Anti-Spyware Coalition defines spyware as technologies that are implemented in ways that impair a user's control over the use of system resources, including what programs are installed on their computers; the collection, use, and distribution of personal or otherwise sensitive information; or material changes that affect the user's experience, privacy, or system security. Spyware usually performs one of the following functions on a user's computer:

- Advertising
- Collecting personal information
- Changing computer configurations

NOTE The Anti-Spyware Coalition is composed of anti-spyware software companies, hardware vendors, academic institutions, and consumer groups such as Microsoft, Dell, Symantec, and AOL. Their Web site is *www.antispywarecoalition.org*.

The number of spyware attacks is growing significantly. Recent studies reveal the following statistics:

- The average computer has 25 pieces of spyware installed on the hard drive.
- Computer manufacturer Dell Inc. says that 12 percent of the calls made to its help desk are the result of spyware-infected computers.
- The spyware industry earns over $2 billion annually.
- Over 74 percent of broadband users have some type of spyware on their computer, according to the National Cyber Security Alliance.

Beyond being a nuisance to computer users, spyware is a tool attackers employ to gather personal information about users. After attackers have obtained this personal information, they can perform **identity theft**. Identity theft occurs when an individual uses the personal information of someone else, such as a Social Security number, credit card number, or other identifying information, to impersonate that individual with the intent to commit fraud or other crimes. Identity theft has become a serious crime. People whose identities have been stolen can spend months or even years and thousands of dollars restoring their good name and credit record. In the meantime, the victims may lose job opportunities, be refused loans, education, or housing, or even get arrested for crimes they didn't commit.

One of the characteristics of spyware that makes it even more dangerous than viruses and worms is that the creators of spyware are motivated by money, unlike the creators of viruses who generally focus on gaining personal notoriety through their malicious software. Spyware creators seek to generate income through spyware advertisements or by acquiring personal information that they can sell to others or use to perpetrate identity theft themselves. Because of this heightened motivation, spyware is often more intrusive, harder to detect, and harder to remove than viruses.

One of the spyware tools often used is **adware**. Adware is software that delivers advertising content in a manner or context that is unexpected and unwanted by the user. Adware typically displays advertising banners or pop-up ads and is frequently encountered while visiting Web sites with a browser. Most users frown on adware for the following reasons:

- Unwanted advertisements can be a nuisance.
- Continuous pop-up ads can impair productivity.
- Adware may display objectionable content.
- Advertisements can slow a computer down or cause crashes and the loss of data.

Beyond being a nuisance, adware can also be a security risk. Many adware programs perform a tracking function, which monitors and tracks a user's activities and then sends a log of these activities to third parties without the user's authorization or knowledge. For example, a user who visits online automobile sites to view specific types of cars can be tracked by adware and classified as someone interested in buying a new car. Based on the order of the sites visited and the types of Web sites, the adware can also determine whether the user's behavior suggests they are close to making a purchase or are also looking at competitor's cars. This information is gathered and then sold to automobile advertisers, who send the users pop-up ads about their cars.

One adware company's database had records of more than 1.3 million computer users who recently visited automotive Web sites.

One of the dangers of using an unsecured or public WLAN is that the user may be more vulnerable to malware and spyware. Because many public WLANs are completely open with no protection, any wireless user runs an increased risk of infection.

Vulnerabilities Associated with Implementing Unsecured WLANs

In addition to the vulnerabilities associated with using a public-access WLAN, there are vulnerabilities in implementing and maintaining a wireless network that is not secure. These vulnerabilities include information theft, being a repository for illegal content, and serving as a spam site.

Information Theft

An attacker who picks up an unprotected wireless signal can gain access to any folder on a computer that is set with file sharing enabled. In an enterprise setting this would include sensitive documents on a file server, such as payroll information, proprietary company research, and customer lists, that are not intended to be seen by those outside the company.

Home users likewise run the risk of information theft when they fail to adequately secure their WLANs. Users may typically set file sharing on multiple folders to allow other users in the home or apartment to be able to access their documents. Unfortunately, this may leave personal information, financial data, and treasured digital photographs open to attackers to steal or erase.

Repository for Illegal Content

Just as an attacker can use a WLAN to steal information, he or she can also use the network to store illegal or harmful content. An attacker who breaks into a wireless network can set up storage space on a file server and save pirated software, illegal videos or music, stolen credit cards, and other data without the organization's knowledge. In addition, the attacker may be able to set up his or her own Web server using the organization's hardware and host a Web site that allows other users access to the information.

Home users face similar attacks. In several instances, attackers have used an unprotected wireless signal to enter a home WLAN and download harmful Web content, such as child pornography, onto the user's computer. The attackers then contact law enforcement personnel who obtain a search warrant to seize the unsuspecting owner's computer and discover the harmful content. Only with great difficulty have the owners been able to prove they were not the ones who were responsible for the content.

Spam Site

The amount of **spam**, or unsolicited e-mail, that flows across the Internet is difficult to judge. According to a Pew Memorial Trust survey, of the approximately 30 billion daily e-mail messages, almost half are spam. Spam also reduces work productivity. More than 11 percent of workers receive about 50 spam messages each day and spend more than half an hour deleting them. Nucleus Research reports that spam e-mail, on average, costs U.S. organizations $874 per person annually in lost productivity.

Spammers often build their own lists of e-mail addresses using special software that rapidly generates millions of random e-mail addresses from well-known ISPs, such as Yahoo! and others, and then sends messages to these addresses. Because an invalid e-mail account returns the message to the sender, the software can automatically delete the invalid accounts and are left with a list of valid e-mail addresses to send the actual spam. Spammers often swap or buy lists of valid e-mail addresses from other spammers as well.

The reason so many spam messages advertise drugs, cheap mortgage rates, or items for sale is that sending spam is a lucrative business. The profit from spamming can be significant. If a spammer sent out spam to 6 million users for a product with a sale price of $50 that cost only $5 to make, and if only 0.001 percent of the recipients responded and bought the product (a typical response rate), the spammer would make more than $270,000 in profit. It costs spammers next to nothing to send millions of spam e-mail messages. Consider the following costs involved for spamming:

- Equipment and Internet connection for launching spam—Spammers typically purchase an inexpensive laptop computer ($500) and rent a motel room with a high-speed Internet connection ($85 per day) as a base for launching attacks. Sometimes spammers actually lease time from other attackers to use a network of 10,000 to 100,000 infected computers to launch an attack ($40 per hour).

- E-mail addresses—If a spammer wants to save time by purchasing a list of valid e-mail addresses to spam, the cost is relatively inexpensive ($100 for 10 million addresses).

NOTE

Approximately 60 percent of all spam originates in the United States, according to CipherTrust. South Korea ranks second with 10.4 percent.

Beyond being annoying and disruptive, spam may also be dangerous. Spammers can overwhelm users with offers to buy merchandise or trick them into giving money away. It is not unusual for spammers to pretend to be a legitimate charity, particularly in times of a natural disaster such as a hurricane. Spammers can also distribute viruses and worms through their e-mail messages.

Organizations that implement and maintain unsecured WLANs may not only become spam sites but can also open themselves to serious legal penalties. The U.S. Congress passed a law in 2003 entitled **Controlling the Assault of Non-Solicited Pornography and Marketing Act of 2003 (CAN-SPAM)**. The provisions of that bill are summarized in Table 4-3. An organization that finds itself a spam site because of an unsecured WLAN may be the target of litigation, even if they were unaware that such action was taking place. This is because it may be argued that they "should know" and be responsible for what occurs on their networks.

Table 4-3   CAN-SPAM law

Provisions of Bill	Description
Who is affected	• Spammers and those who procure their services • Organizations or individuals who know (or should know) that the promotion of their services or goods is prohibited
What is legal	• E-mail that contains a transaction or relationship message, such as order processing or product update information • Unsolicited commercial e-mail that contains accurate contact information for the sender
What is illegal	• Fraudulent or deceptive subject lines, headers, or e-mail addresses • Sending e-mail to addresses that have been harvested from Web sites or randomly generated • Sending sexually oriented e-mail without an identifying subject line • Not maintaining a functioning unsubscribe system for at least 30 days from the mailing • Registering for e-mail addresses under a false identity • Not removing an e-mail address in a timely fashion after receiving a request from a recipient
Who may bring litigation	• Federal Trade Commission (FTC) • State Attorneys General • Internet service providers (Individual e-mail recipients are not eligible to bring litigation)
What are the penalties	• State Attorneys General may sue for $250 per spam message, up to $2 million • Internet service providers may sue for $100 per spam message, up to $1 million • Three to five years imprisonment

WIRELESS INFRASTRUCTURE ATTACKS

Because of the security vulnerabilities of WLANs, different types of attacks on the wireless infrastructure can be launched. These attacks include direct attacks and denial-of-service attacks.

Direct Attacks Through Rogue Access Points

Lorraine wants to have wireless access in the employee break room and conference room next to her office. However, the IT department of her employer turns down her request for a wireless network because of the security risks. Lorraine decides to take the matter into her own hands. She purchases an inexpensive access point and secretly brings it into her office and connects it to the wired network, therefore providing wireless access to the employees in her area. Unfortunately, Lorraine has also provided open access to an attacker who is in his car in the parking lot who also picks up the wireless signal. This attacker can then circumvent the security protections of the company's network and launch attacks on all users without any hinderance.

Lorraine has installed what is known as a rogue access point (*rogue* means someone or something that is deceitful or unreliable). As seen in Figure 4-4, a rogue access point bypasses all of the network security and opens the entire network and all users to direct attacks. Although firewalls are typically used to restrict specific attacks from entering a network, an attacker who can access the network through a rogue access point is behind the firewall and can directly attack all devices on the network. Once an attacker's wireless device has entered the network and focused its attacks at other similar devices this is known as a **peer-to-peer attack**.

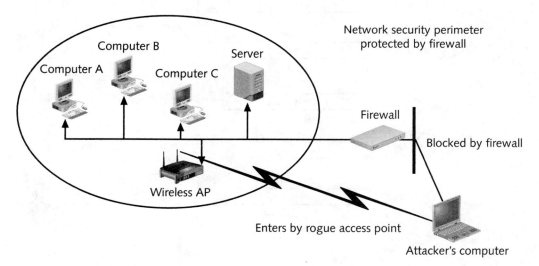

Figure 4-4 Rogue access point

There are technologies available that can detect and even disable rogue access points. These are discussed in Chapter 10.

Denial-of-Service Attack (DoS)

As the name implies, a **denial-of-service (DoS)** attack is designed to prevent a device from performing its intended function. DoS attacks are common against wired network servers. Under normal conditions, a client computer sends a wired network server a request called a SYN. The server responds to the client with an ACK (acknowledgement) and then waits for a reply. To allow for a slow connection, the server might wait several minutes for the reply. When the client replies, the data transfer can begin.

A wired network DoS attack attempts to make the server unavailable by flooding it with requests. Clients send SYN requests to a server. Although the server responds to each request, the clients are programmed not to reply to the server's response. The server will "hold the line open" and continue to wait for a response (which is not coming) while receiving more requests and keeping those lines open for responses. After a short period, the server runs out of resources and can no longer function. Figure 4-5 shows a server waiting for a response during a DoS attack.

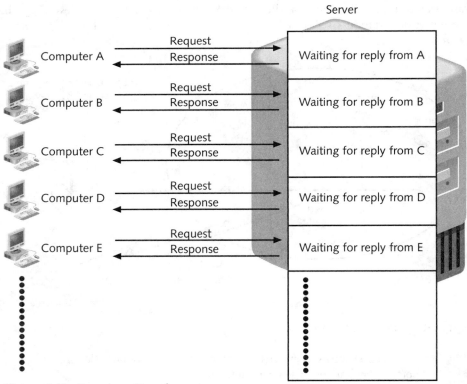

Figure 4-5   Server waiting for response

NOTE Another wired DoS attack tricks clients into responding to a false request. An attacker can send a request to all clients on the network, making it appear a server is asking for a response. Each of the clients then responds to the server, overwhelming it, and causing the server to crash or be unavailable to legitimate users.

Wireless DoS attacks are different than wired network DoS attacks. Instead of denying service to a server, wireless DoS attacks are designed to deny wireless devices access to the access point itself. In addition, the techniques used can vary. Wireless DoS attacks can be divided into two categories, physical layer attacks and MAC layer attacks.

Physical Layer Attacks

Physical layer attacks are those that correspond to the Physical layer of the Open System Interconnection (OSI) network model. Physical layer attacks flood the RF spectrum with enough radiomagnetic interference to prevent a device from effectively communicating with the AP. If a WLAN was set up using Channel 1 in an IEEE 802.11b network, an attacker would flood the 2.412 GHz frequency with enough "noise" to prevent a device from sending or receiving packets. This is illustrated in Figure 4-6.

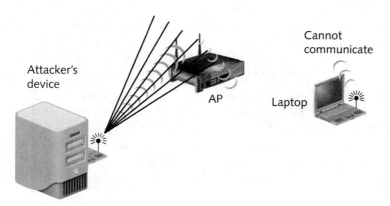

Figure 4-6   Physical layer attack

Physical layer attacks are generally rare because sophisticated and expensive equipment is necessary to flood the RF spectrum with enough interference to impact the network. In addition, because a very powerful transmitter must be used at a relatively close range to execute the attack, it is possible to identify the location of the transmitter and therefore identify the source of the attack.

However, inadvertent interference from other RF devices can sometimes cause DoS. Several different devices share the unlicensed Industrial, Scientific and Medical (ISM) band. These include:

- Cordless telephones
- Microwave ovens
- Baby monitors
- Bluetooth personal area network devices

NOTE   When a wireless LAN begins to experience intermittent or slow transmissions, one of the first troubleshooting steps is to search for inadvertent interference from other RF devices. It may be necessary to turn off these devices or relocate them.

MAC Layer Attacks

Most successful wireless DoS attacks are performed at the Media Access Control (MAC) layer of the OSI model. Because the wireless medium is shared among all devices, there must be rules for cooperation among the wireless devices. The 802.11 standard uses a procedure known as **Carrier Sense Multiple Access with Collision Avoidance (CSMA/CA)**. CSMA/CA attempts to prevent multiple wireless devices from transmitting at the same time. It does this by requiring that all devices wait a random amount of time after a transmission is completed and the medium is clear.

With wireless CSMA/CA the amount of time that a device must wait after the medium is clear is called the **slot time**. Each device must wait a random amount of slot times. For example, the slot time for an 802.11b WLAN is 20 microseconds. If a wireless device's backoff interval is 3 slot times, then it must wait 60 microseconds (20 microseconds × 3 slot times) before attempting to transmit. Because CSMA/CA has all stations wait a random amount of time after the medium is clear, the number of collisions is significantly reduced.

A second way in which CSMA/CA reduces collisions is by using explicit **frame acknowledgment**. An acknowledgment frame (abbreviated ACK) is sent by the receiving device back to the sending device to confirm that the data frame arrived intact. If the ACK frame is not returned to the sending station a problem is assumed to have occurred and the data frame is transmitted again. This explicit ACK mechanism handles interference and other radio-related problems. CSMA/CA and ACK are illustrated in Figure 4-7.

A wireless DoS attack taking advantage of CSMA/CA can occur in one of several different ways. First, an attacker who has already become associated with the WLAN can download an extremely large file from the Internet, such as a video file. This will effectively "tie up" the network and prevent other devices from accessing the network, as seen in Figure 4-8. Another technique is to use a **packet generator** program. This program will create fake packets and flood the wireless network.

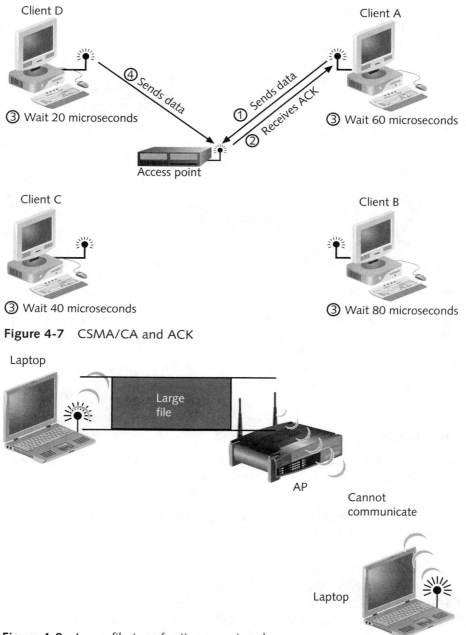

Figure 4-7 CSMA/CA and ACK

Figure 4-8 Large file transfer ties up network

Another MAC layer attack involves an attacker using disassociation frames. An attacker can pretend to be an access point and send a forged disassociation frame to a wireless device. This will cause the device to disassociate from the access point. Sending repeated disassociation frames allows an attacker to continuously prevent any device from communicating with the AP. This is illustrated in Figure 4-9.

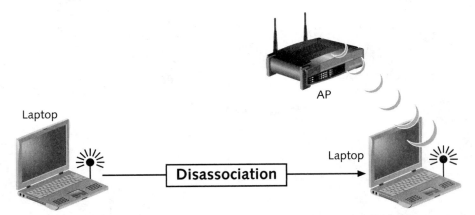

Laptop

AP

Laptop

Disassociation

1. Attacker sends disassocation frame   2. Associated device disassociates from AP

Figure 4-9   DoS using disassociation frames

NOTE   A new security feature of WLANs may inadvertently provide another avenue of wireless DoS attacks. Using this feature, if the AP receives what it thinks is an attack it will automatically disassociate that user from the WLAN for a period of time. An attacker could use this feature to trick the AP into disassociating valid users. This security feature is discussed in Chapter 5.

Chapter Summary

- ❏ Security vulnerabilities for wireless LANs can be divided into three categories: basic vulnerabilities, vulnerabilities associated with using public WLANs, and vulnerabilities associated with implementing unsecured WLANS.

- ❏ Basic vulnerabilities include default passwords, weak passwords, SNMP community strings, and improper configuration.

- ❏ Vulnerabilities when using a public-access WLAN, such as in a coffee shop, include malware and spyware. Malicious software, also called malware, consists of computer programs designed to break into and create havoc on portable or desktop computers. Spyware is a general term for software that violates a user's personal security.

- ❏ There are several vulnerabilities associated with implementing an unsecured WLAN. An attacker can use an improperly configured WLAN to steal information from a network. An attacker can also access an unsecured WLAN and use it to store illegal content. Unprotected WLANs can also be used as a basis for distributing spam.

❏ Direct attacks on the wireless infrastructure can be implemented through rogue access points. Another type of infrastructure attack is a DoS attack. Wireless DoS attacks are different from wired network DoS attacks. Wireless DoS attacks can be physical layer attacks or MAC layer attacks. Physical layer attacks flood the RF spectrum with radiomagnetic noise that prevents another device from communicating. In MAC layer attacks, an attacker can download a large file and deny other users access to the wireless network, or a packet generator program can create fake packets and flood the network. Another technique is to use disassociation frames to disconnect devices from the network.

4

KEY TERMS

adware — A software program that delivers advertising content in a manner or context that is unexpected and unwanted by the user.

authentication — The process of providing proof that a user is "genuine" or authentic.

Carrier Sense Multiple Access with Collision Avoidance (CSMA/CA) — A procedure used by IEEE WLANs to prevent multiple wireless devices from transmitting at the same time.

Controlling the Assault of Non-Solicited Pornography and Marketing Act of 2003 (CAN-SPAM) — A U.S. law passed in 2003 to limit the effect of spam.

default password — A standard password that is configured on all equipment.

denial-of-service (DoS) — An attack designed to prevent a device from performing its intended function.

frame acknowledgment — A method in which CSMA/CA reduces collisions using explicit acknowledgment.

identity theft — The theft of an individual's personal information to impersonate that individual with the intent to commit fraud or other crimes

logic bomb — A computer program that lies dormant until it is triggered by a specific logical event.

packet generator — A program that creates fake packets that flood the wireless network.

password — A secret combination of letters and numbers that serves to validate or authenticate a user by what the user knows.

password guessing — A technique used by attackers to exploit weak passwords.

password paradox — The paradox of needing lengthy and complex passwords, yet such passwords are difficult to memorize.

peer-to-peer attack — Attacks directed at other similar devices.

Plug and Play (PnP) — A service that allows the Windows operating system to automatically detect new hardware when it is installed on a computer.

security vulnerability — A weakness or flaw in an information system that could be exploited to cause harm.

slot time — The amount of time that a device must wait after the medium is clear.

spam — Unsolicited e-mail.

spyware — A general term used to describe software that violates a user's personal security.

Universal Plug and Play (UPnP) — A service that allows devices on a network to discover other devices and determine how to work with them.

virus — A program that secretly attaches itself to another document or program and executes when that document or program is opened.

weak passwords — Passwords that compromise security.

wireless gateways — Devices that combine an access point, router, and network address translation features.

worm — A malicious program that does not attach to a document to spread but can travel by itself.

REVIEW QUESTIONS

1. Authentication is based on each of the following except
   a. What you have
   b. What you purchase
   c. What you know
   d. What you are

2. Each of the following is a characteristic of a weak password except
   a. Using a common word
   b. Changing the password every 30 days
   c. Short passwords
   d. Using the same password for all accounts

3. _____ is a service that allows devices on a network to discover other devices and determine how to work with them.
   a. Plug and Play (PnP)
   b. Transmission Control Protocol (TCP)
   c. Internetworking Protocol Exchange Messaging (IPEM)
   d. Universal Plug and Play (UPnP)

4. A(n) _____ must attach itself to a computer document, such as an e-mail message, and is spread by traveling along with the document.
   a. virus
   b. worm
   c. adware
   d. trojan

5. Each of the following may indicate a virus has infected a wireless laptop except
    a. A program suddenly disappears from the computer
    b. New programs do not install properly
    c. The Service Set Identifier (SSID) changes from uppercase to lowercase
    d. Out-of-memory error messages appear

6. A security weakness can be in the security procedures, controls, or even the physical layout of the network. True or False?

7. The problem with passwords is that lengthy and complex passwords should be used yet they are difficult to memorize. True or False?

8. The Simple Network Management Protocol (SNMP) is a popular protocol used to manage only wireless networked equipment. True or False?

9. The default SNMP community strings for read-only and read-write are *public* and *private*, respectively. True or False?

10. Identity theft occurs when an individual uses the personal information of someone else, such as a Social Security number, credit card number, or other identifying information, to impersonate that individual with the intent to commit fraud or other crimes. True or False?

11. A(n) _____ may be defined as a weakness or flaw in an information system that could be exploited to cause harm.

12. A(n) _____ is a computer program that lies dormant until it is triggered by a specific logical event.

13. _____ is a general term used to describe software that violates a user's personal security.

14. Unsolicited e-mail is known as _____ .

15. A wireless access point that is secretly installed in an office without the employer's permission is known as a(n) _____ .

16. Explain how a disassociation frame DoS attack functions.

17. Explain the weaknesses of SNMP community strings.

18. What are the vulnerabilities of UPnP?

19. Explain how a Physical layer DoS attack can be performed.

20. Explain how CSMA/CA is used with IEEE 802.11 WLANs.

HANDS-ON PROJECTS

The purpose of these projects is strictly to demonstrate wireless vulnerability using equipment that is owned by the user or has been approved by a third-party institution. Under no circumstances should these tools be used to monitor packets on any WLAN without the owner's express prior approval. Users who violate these conditions may be subject to legal action.

Project 4-1: Check Vulnerability of Access Point

Some access points or wireless gateways running older versions of firmware have a vulnerability that allows all of the configuration settings, including administrator passwords, WEP keys, and approved MAC address, to be viewed. In this project you download a software tool that will check the vulnerability of your access point or wireless gateway firmware.

1. Point your browser to *http://mobileaccess.de/wlan/?go=technik*. Although this site is in Germany the software itself is written in English.

2. Locate the download link for the latest version of **Pong.exe**.

3. Click on the link to download it and save the file to your desktop.

4. If the file is in a compressed format follow the instructions to extract the file to your desktop.

5. Although the file can be launched by clicking on it on the desktop more information can be shown when running it from a command line. Click **Start** and **Run**.

6. Enter **cmd** and press **Enter**.

7. Type **CD desktop** and press **Enter**.

8. Now launch the application by typing **pong –r**. You may need to wait up to 30 seconds for the program to find the access point to which you are connected and retrieve the information.

9. If your access point is vulnerable the information will be displayed on the screen. If no information is returned then your firmware cannot be read and is secure from this type of attack.

10. Type **Exit** and press **Enter**.

11. Close all windows.

Project 4-2: Using a Packet Generator

A packet generator will create fake packets and flood the wireless network, causing a DoS. In this project you download a packet generator program.

1. Point your browser to ***www.tamos.com/download/main/*** to download a 30-day copy of the program CommView for WiFi.

> Note that this program may not function with all wireless network adapters. A list will be displayed prior to downloading that shows the adapters under which it will function.
>
> **NOTE**

4

2. Locate the latest version of the program and download it to your desktop.

3. Follow the instructions to install the software on your computer using the default settings.

4. Launch CommView for WiFi if it has not already started. A screen displaying the supported wireless adapters will be displayed. Be sure your adapter is on that list.

5. Scroll to the bottom of the screen and click **Next**. Follow the steps of the driver installation wizard.

6. When completed the main screen will be displayed, as seen in Figure 4-10.

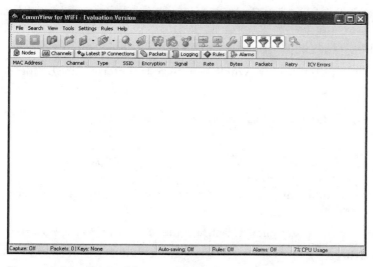

Figure 4-10 CommView main screen

7. Click **File** and **Start Capture**.

8. Click **Tools** and then **Packet Generator**. Increase the **Packet size** to 1500.

9. Increase the **Packets per second** to 500.

10. Make sure the radio button next to **time(s)** is selected and increase this value to **10**.

11. Click **Send**.

12. The access point will be overwhelmed with packets and unable to respond to other requests.

13. Close all windows.

Project 4-3: View Linksys Configuration Settings

Improper configuration settings on wireless equipment can be an open door for attackers to take over total control of the hardware. In this project you view several of these settings and make adjustments as necessary.

1. Point your browser to the Linksys wireless gateway and enter the correct username and password.

2. Click **Administration**.

3. To see how an attacker can attempt to access the equipment over the Internet click **Enable** under **Remote Management** if it is not already selected. Note that if the wireless gateway is still using the default password you will be prompted to change it.

4. Change the **Management Port** number to **8888**.

5. Click **Save Settings**. If you reset the password in Step 3, you will have to enter your username and password before continuing.

6. Now use another computer that is not part of the wireless network.

7. Point your browser to the Linksys wireless gateway by entering the IP address followed by the port number.

Note that this IP address is the one that is viewed from the Internet.

8. Try entering several different passwords. Are you restricted on the number of times you can try passwords?

9. Return to the first computer click **Disable** under **Remote Management**.

10. Click **Save Settings**.

11. Go back to the computer that is not part of the wireless network and try to access the wireless gateway again. What happens now?

12. Return to the first computer click **Disable** under **UPnP**.

13. Click **Save Settings**.

14. Close all windows.

Project 4-4: Testing Antivirus Software

Because antivirus software is so important, one recommended procedure is to test the antivirus software to ensure that it is functioning as intended. In this project, you download a virus test file. This file is not a virus but is designed to appear to an antivirus scanner as if it were a virus. You need to have antivirus software installed on your computer to perform this project.

1. Check the antivirus settings on your computer. Click **Start**, point to **Control Panel**, and then click **Security Center**.

2. The **Virus Protection** setting should be **On**. If it is not, click the **Recommendations** button and indicate that you want Windows to monitor the AV software.

3. Close all windows.

4. Use your Web browser (such as Internet Explorer) to go the eicar – Anti-Virus test file Web site at *www.eicar.org/anti_virus_test_file.htm*. Read the "Anti-Virus test file" information.

5. Click the file **eicar.com**, which contains a fake virus. A dialog box opens that asks if you want to download the file. Wait to see what happens. Your antivirus software should catch the file even before you start to download. Close your antivirus pop-up message and click **Cancel** to stop the download procedure.

6. At the eicar – Anti-Virus test file Web site, click **eicar_com.zip**. This file contains a fake virus inside a compressed (ZIP) file. What happened? Most AV software cannot scan a compressed file for a virus.

7. If your antivirus software did not prevent you from accessing the eicar_com.zip file, click **Save** to save it to your computer.

8. Click **Save** again, and when the download is complete, click **Close**, if necessary.

9. Right-click the **Start** button, and then click **Explore**.

10. In Windows Explorer, navigate to the folder that contains the eicar_com.zip file.

11. Right-click **eicar_com.zip**, and then click **Scan for viruses** on the shortcut menu (your menu command might be slightly different). What happened?

12. Erase **eicar_com.zip** from your hard drive.

13. Close all windows.

Project 4-5: Danger of Weak Passwords

Password guessing is a technique used to break weak passwords and can illustrate the danger of a weak password. In this project you use a password recovery tool to perform different types of password guessing techniques.

1. Start Microsoft Word, and open a new, blank document.

2. Click **Tools** on the menu bar, and then click **Options**. The Options dialog box opens. Click the **Security** tab.

3. In the Password to open text box, type **1234**, and then click **OK**. The Confirm Password dialog box opens so you can verify the password. Type **1234** again and click **OK**.

4. In the new Word document, type **Weak**. Save this document as **Weak** and then close the document.

5. Use your Web browser to go to *www.elcomsoft.com/aopr.html*. Click **Download free trial version of AOPR**. Save the file to the desktop and open it when the download is complete. Follow the instructions to install the software on your computer using the default configurations.

6. If the program does not start automatically, start the program to display the opening window.

7. Be sure that **Dictionary attack (Recommended)** is selected.

8. Click the **Open file** button and select the file **Weak.doc**. AOPR will unlock and display the password under **Word File Opening Password**. Click **OK**.

9. How quickly could an attacker crack any short or simple passwords that you use? How quickly should you change these weak passwords to strong passwords?

10. Close the AOPR program.

CASE PROJECTS

Case Project 4-1: Weak Password Test

Most users assume that they use strong passwords when in reality they do not. Test yourself on the passwords that you have by first creating a set of rules that should be used for creating strong passwords. Next, write down your passwords and give a grade of A-F to each of these passwords. Then, change the passwords that receive a grade of "C" or below. Finally, be sure to shred the paper on which you wrote down your passwords.

Case Project 4-2: Virus Eradication Techniques

Although preventing viruses with anti-virus software is important, it is also good to know how to remove a virus from a computer that may become infected. Using the Web sites of the major anti-virus vendors (Symantec, MacAfee, Sophos, and others) research the different ways in which a virus can be removed from a system. Create a one-page step-by-step instruction sheet that can be used.

Case Project 4-3: DoS Hijacking

Although a DoS attack can be used to make a WLAN inoperable, it can also be used to "hijack" WLANs and force them to associate with an attacker's AP. Using the Internet and other sources, research how this DoS hijacking can be done. What, if any, defenses are available? Write a one-page paper on your findings.

Case Project 4-4: Rogue Access Point Memo

Create a memo for a fictitious organization to all employees that discusses rogue access points. Be sure to cover what they are and why they are a danger to the organization. Because all of your audience may not have a technical background, your memo should not contain too much technical detail. Finally, conclude the memo with realistic penalties for anyone who violates this policy.

Fairvue Technology Consulting

Fairvue Technology Consulting (FTC) has hired you to assist them with a new client, Archway Sporting Goods. The president of Archway wants to add free wireless access to each of its stores in the hopes of attracting more customers. The director of IT is opposed to the idea. FTC has been asked to provide their expertise.

1. Create a PowerPoint presentation that outlines the different vulnerabilities that exist when a customer uses an unsecured WLAN as well as the vulnerabilities for the organization for implementing a WLAN. Include information on the risks that it poses to the wired network infrastructure. Your presentation should be at least 7 slides in length.

2. After viewing your presentation Archway is still at an impasse and has asked for your opinion. The president estimates that sales may increase by 40 percent if a WLAN is available, but others are skeptical of that figure. Using the Internet and other sources, research the additional customer traffic and subsequent increased sales and profit that have been generated by organizations that have added a wireless network for customers. Create a memo to Archway that lists the advantages and disadvantages of the project, and give your opinion regarding what should be done.

WIRELESS SECURITY MODELS

After completing this chapter you should be able to do the following:

➤ Explain the advantages of WPA and WPA2

➤ Explain the technologies that are part of the personal security model

➤ List the features of the transitional security model

➤ Define the enterprise security model

The World of Wireless Security

It would seem that the West Edmonton Mall in Edmonton, Alberta, Canada, already offers everything a customer could possibly want. Covering the equivalent of 48 city blocks, it is much more than just a mall. This shopping, entertainment, and hospitality center, which bills itself as "the greatest indoor show on earth," has 800 retail stores, eight amusement parks, 21 theaters, 110 restaurants, and three hotels. Over 22 million guests visit the West Edmonton Mall annually. Despite all it had to offer, its managers felt one thing was still missing: a WLAN. And now wireless network access has been added to the long list of West Edmonton's features.

When West Edmonton decided to build a wireless LAN for its businesses as well as customers, security was a primary consideration. The goal was to create a WLAN secure enough for the mall's 16,500 employees to remotely access it from home offices, parking lots and even their corporate offices. They also wanted to create different user-access policies and applications to support its wide variety of users.

Today the $300,000 WLAN network, called WEMiSphere, serves the mall's food court, waterpark, and main hotel. Another 70 access points are to be added in 2006, bringing the total to 130. Hotel guests can purchase 24 hours of network access that allows them to wirelessly roam from their room to nearby conference rooms and attractions for only $11. Businesses in the mall, for $35 a month, can use the WLAN for unlimited access to online banking, location-based marketing, and Internet-based services for its customers and employees. The addition of a real-time video surveillance system for the mall's mobile security force is also being considered.

Despite its high installation cost, WEMiSphere has been a big hit. West Edmonton Mall managers credit it with increasing the number of conference attendees who visit the hotels for their conventions and then visit the remaining areas of the mall. The mall expects to recover the initial WLAN investment by 2007. And the mall's parent company is also considering a similar WLAN installation at its giant Mall of America in Bloomington, Minnesota.

In Chapter 2 you saw that the basic security protections of the IEEE 802.11 standards have several significant security deficiencies, making these protocols unacceptable for secure wireless transmissions. Chapter 3 discussed how attackers can also use general information-gathering techniques, wardriving, and wireless packet sniffers as tools to passively discover wireless LAN transmissions and reveal their contents. In Chapter 4 the vulnerabilities and attack techniques used in active infrastructure attacks were explored. It comes then as no surprise that for many users "wireless security" has been viewed as an oxymoron.

However, such is not the case. There are technologies and techniques today that can make a wireless network as secure as its wired counterpart. Beginning with this chapter you explore how to use these techniques and technologies to make a wireless network secure. This chapter begins by looking at the three wireless security solutions that form the foundation of a secure WLAN. Then you will explore the three WLAN security models that are based on these solutions. These models are the transitional security model, personal security model, and enterprise security model.

WIRELESS SECURITY SOLUTIONS

When the IEEE committee ratified the 802.11b and 802.11a WLAN standards in September 1999, it included Wired Equivalent Privacy (WEP) technology for shared key authentication and packet encryption. Yet, soon after its ratification, studies identified serious weaknesses in WEP. These weaknesses revealed that even with WEP enabled, an attacker with the proper tools and some basic technical knowledge could gain unauthorized access to a WLAN.

As a result of these wireless security vulnerabilities, many businesses and organizations were forced to supplement or replace WEP with other wireless security solutions, such as WEP2 and Dynamic WEP. However, these were only "band-aid" fixes and still did not adequately address the two primary weaknesses of wireless security, namely encryption and authentication. A unified approach to WLAN security was needed instead of trying to patch isolated vulnerabilities, so the two leading WLAN organizations, IEEE and the Wi-Fi Alliance, began developing comprehensive security solutions. These solutions, known as IEEE 802.11i, Wi-Fi Protected Access, and Wi-Fi Protected Access 2, quickly became the foundations of wireless security and today serve as the primary wireless defenses against attackers.

WEP2 and Dynamic WEP are covered in Chapter 2.

NOTE

IEEE 802.11i

In March 2001, the IEEE TGi task group voted to split into two separate groups, one of which would be strictly devoted to wireless security. The security group, still designated TGi, started work on new wireless security mechanisms. After three years of work, the **IEEE 802.11i** wireless security standard was ratified in June 2004.

The 802.11i standard addresses the two weaknesses of wireless networks: encryption and authentication. Encryption is accomplished by replacing the RC4 stream cipher algorithm with a **block cipher**. Unlike a stream cipher that only works on one character at a time, a block cipher manipulates an entire block of text at one time. The original cleartext message is divided into separate blocks of 64 to 128 bits, and then each block is encrypted independently of all other blocks.

The block cipher used in 802.11i is the **Advanced Encryption Standard (AES)**. AES was approved by the National Institute of Standards and Technology (NIST) in late 2000 as a replacement for another cryptography algorithm known as Data Encryption Standard (DES). NIST published its requirements for a new encryption algorithm and requested proposals. The requirements stated that the new algorithm had to be fast and function on older computers with 8-bit processors as well as current 32-bit and future 64-bit processors. After a lengthy process that required the cooperation of the U.S. government, industry, and higher educational institutions, five finalists were chosen. The winner was an algorithm known as Rinjdael. Based on the Rinjdael algorithm, AES is now the official encryption standard for the U.S. government.

AES performs three steps on every block (128 bits) of cleartext. Within the second step, multiple iterations (called **rounds**) are performed depending on the key size: 128-bit key performs 9 rounds, a 192-bit key performs 11 rounds, and a 256-bit key uses 13 rounds. And within each round, bits are substituted and rearranged, and then special multiplication is performed based on the new arrangement.

AES is designed to be an encryption technique that is secure from attacks. Table 5-1 illustrates the amount of time it would take to break AES using a brute-force attack with $1 million worth of microcomputers.

Table 5-1 Time needed to break AES

Key Length	Number of Possible Keys	Time Needed to Break with $1 Million Worth of Computers
40 bits	1,099,551,627,776	Less than 1 minute
56 bits	72,057,594,037,927,936	30 minutes
64 bits	18,446,744,073,709,551,616	4 days
80 bits	1.21×10^{24}	800 years
128 bits	3.40×10^{38}	2.20×10^{17} years
192 bits	6.28×10^{57}	10^{36} years
256 bits	1.16×10^{77}	10^{56} years

NOTE

Because AES performs so many rounds and substitutions, legacy WLAN hardware with older processors may not be able to support AES.

IEEE 802.11i authentication and key management is accomplished by the **IEEE 802.1x** standard. This standard, originally developed for wired networks, provides a greater degree of security by implementing **port security**. IEEE 802.1x blocks all traffic on a port-by-port basis until the client is authenticated using credentials stored on an authentication server. Port security prevents an unauthenticated device, either wired or wireless, from receiving *any* network traffic until its identity can be verified. Figure 5-1 illustrates an 802.1x authentication procedure:

- Step 1—The wireless devices requests from the access point permission to join the wireless LAN.
- Step 2—The access point asks the device to verify its identity.
- Step 3—The device sends identity information to the access point which passes it on to an **authentication server**, whose only job is to verify the authentication of devices. The identity information is sent in an encrypted form.
- Step 4—The authentication server verifies or rejects the client's identity and returns the information to the access point.
- Step 5—An approved client can now join the network and transmit data.

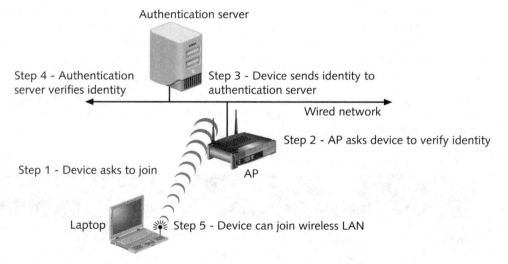

Figure 5-1   IEEE 802.1x

In addition to encryption and authentication, IEEE 802.11i includes **key-caching**, which stores information from a device on the network so if a user roams away from an AP and later returns, he does not need to re-enter all of the credentials. This makes the process transparent to the user. Another feature is **pre-authentication**, which allows a device to become authenticated to an AP before moving into range of the AP. In pre-authentication, the device sends a pre-authentication packet to the AP the user is currently associated with, and the packet is then routed to a remote AP or APs. Pre-authentication allows for faster roaming between access points.

Because wireless security is so critical, the IEEE is considering forming a standing committee that would look at wireless security on an ongoing basis by working with other task groups to ensure that new additions to 802.11 don't introduce their own security vulnerabilities.

NOTE

Wi-Fi Protected Access (WPA)

Although the IEEE TGi worked on the 802.11i standard, the Wi-Fi Alliance grew impatient and decided that security could no longer wait. In October 2003 it introduced **Wi-Fi Protected Access (WPA)**. WPA is actually a subset of 802.11i and addresses both encryption and authentication.

The design goal of WPA was to protect both present and future wireless devices.

NOTE

WPA replaces WEP with an encryption technology called **Temporal Key Integrity Protocol (TKIP)**. WEP uses a 40-bit encryption key and does not change. TKIP has several advantages over WEP. First, it uses a longer 128-bit key. Also, TKIP keys are known as **per-packet keys**. This means that TKIP dynamically generates a new key for each packet that is created. Per-packet keys prevent collisions, which was one of the primary weaknesses of WEP. When coupled with IEEE 802.1x, TKIP provides an even greater level of security. After accepting a device's credentials, the authentication server can use 802.1x to produce a unique master key for that user session. TKIP distributes the key to the wireless device and AP, setting up an automated key hierarchy and management system. TKIP then dynamically generates unique keys to encrypt every data packet that is wirelessly communicated during a session.

Using TKIP, there are 280 trillion possible keys that can be generated for a given data packet.

NOTE

WPA also replaces the Cyclic Redundancy Check (CRC) function in WEP with the **Message Integrity Check (MIC)**, which is designed to prevent an attacker from capturing, altering, and resending data packets. CRC is designed to detect any changes in a packet, whether accidental or intentional. However, CRC does not adequately protect the *integrity* of the packet. An attacker can still modify a packet *and* the CRC, making it appear that the packet contents were the original (because the CRC is correct for that packet). This is illustrated in Figure 5-2. MIC provides a strong mathematical function in which the receiver and the transmitter each independently compute the MIC, and then these values are compared. If they do not match, the data is assumed to have been tampered with and the packet is dropped. There is also an optional MIC countermeasure in which all clients are de-authenticated and new associations are prevented for one minute if an MIC error occurs.

NOTE   WPA operates at the Media Access Control (MAC) layer of the OSI model.

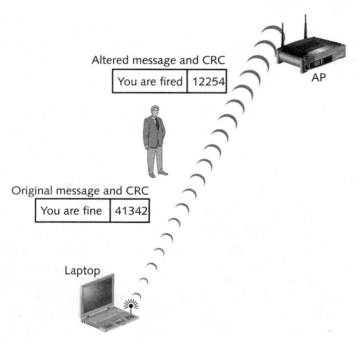

Figure 5-2   Message Integrity Check (MIC)

WPA authentication can be accomplished by using either IEEE 802.1x or **preshared key (PSK)** technology. PSK authentication uses a passphrase to generate the encryption key. Like WEP, the passphrase must be entered on each access point and wireless device in advance. However, unlike WEP the PSK is not used for encryption but instead serves as the starting point (**seed**) for mathematically generating the encryption keys.

A PSK of sufficient length and strength, one that uses a long mix of letters, numbers, and non-alphanumeric characters, is strongly recommended to provide the necessary security.

NOTE

WPA was designed to address WEP vulnerabilities with minimum inconvenience. In many cases WPA can be implemented with a software upgrade on the wireless device and a firmware update on older access points. When properly installed, WPA provides a higher level of assurance that data will remain protected and that only authorized users may access the wireless network.

Wi-Fi Protected Access 2 (WPA2)

In September 2004, the Wi-Fi Alliance introduced **Wi-Fi Protected Access 2 (WPA2)**, which is the second generation of WPA security. WPA2 is based on the final IEEE 802.11i standard ratified in June 2004. WPA2 uses the Advanced Encryption Standard (AES) for data encryption and supports IEEE 802.1x authentication or PSK technology. WPA2 resembles IEEE 802.11i but differs slightly to allow for interoperability concerns with WPA. WPA2 allows both AES and TKIP clients to operate in the same WLAN, whereas IEEE 802.11i only recognizes AES clients.

Just as the term "Wi-Fi" is commonly used when referring to wireless LAN technology (IEEE 802.11a/b/g), "WPA2" is now being used instead of the more technical designation IEEE 802.11i/AES.

NOTE

Table 5-2 summarizes the wireless security solutions presented in this chapter. The two solutions that provide improved levels of security are WPA and WPA2.

Table 5-2 Wireless security solutions

Name	Encryption	Authentication	Security level
WEP	WEP	Shared Key	Low
WPA	TKIP	PSK or 802.11i	Medium
WPA2/IEEE 802.11i	AES	802.1x	High

The Wi-Fi Alliance has created wireless security models based on WPA and WPA2, with subdivisions for personal and enterprise solutions as follows:

- WPA—Personal Security
- WPA—Enterprise Security
- WPA2—Personal Security
- WPA2—Enterprise Security

Each model is intended for a specific setting. Personal security is designed for a small office-home office or consumer use, whereas enterprise security covers business, government, and education. These Wi-Fi security models are outlined in Table 5-3.

Table 5-3   Wi-Fi security models

Wi-Fi Model	Application	WPA	WPA2
Personal	Small office/home office Home use	Authentication: PSK Encryption: TKIP	Authentication: PSK Encryption: AES
Enterprise	Business Education Government	Authentication: 802.1x Encryption: TKIP	Authentication: 802.1x Encryption: AES

In addition to the enterprise and personal models, another model is used as a "bridge" solution in situations where WPA or WPA2 security is not available. The transitional security model is intended as a temporary fix until a stronger solution can be implemented. Each of these models will now be discussed, in order from the least secure to most secure. Authentication and encryption mechanisms are detailed for each model.

TRANSITIONAL SECURITY MODEL

In some situations it may not be possible to use WPA or WPA2 for wireless security because older equipment is being used. For example, a business may decide to reduce IT expenses by not upgrading its access points to support WPA2. They rationalize that, "The older WLAN is still working, so we can get along for another year without the expense of upgrading," without considering the security implications. Or, a non-profit organization may have its funding reduced and cannot afford to replace the APs in its office. In these and similar situations, what type of wireless security should be implemented?

Under these circumstances the answer is to implement the highest level of security possible based upon the equipment in use. Although this is not a secure solution, it is the only practical alternative. It must be recognized, however, that this is only a transitional phase until a migration to software or hardware that supports stronger wireless security is possible. Sometimes called the **transitional security model**, it should *only* be implemented as a temporary solution.

A plan for the purchase and installation of new security equipment should be outlined before the transitional security model is implemented to ensure that upgrading is not forgotten until it is too late.

NOTE

The transitional security model should implement all of the features of the basic IEEE 802.11 WLAN protocol. Although this will not deter a determined attacker, it may serve to ward off a "casual" attack by a novice attacker. It should be clearly understood that these security settings still leave the WLAN vulnerable to attacks.

 The transitional security model should be considered the absolute minimum level of security for a home or an apartment with an older WLAN that does not support WPA or WPA2.

NOTE

5

Authentication

There are four steps that should be taken for authentication under the transitional security model. These are using shared key authentication, turning off SSID beaconing, implementing MAC address filtering, and restricting DHCP distribution of IP addresses.

Shared Key Authentication

When using the transitional security model, shared key authentication should be used instead of open system authentication. Although shared key authentication has security vulnerabilities, it offers a degree of protection over open system authentication, which has virtually no security. Shared key authentication uses WEP keys for authentication. The AP sends to a device wanting to join the network a block of text known as the challenge text. The wireless device encrypts it with its WEP key and returns it to the AP, which then decrypts what was returned to see if it matches the original challenge text. If it does, the device is accepted into the network.

Because the access points and devices can hold up to four WEP keys simultaneously, wireless networks that support multiple devices should use all four keys. A default key will be indicated as the key value that is used to encrypt wireless data transmission when they are sent and the receiver will use the corresponding key to decrypt the data. However, the same key should not be designated as the default key on each device. Instead, it should evenly be divided among the wireless devices. In a network of 12 wireless devices, for example, only three should use the same default key.

SSID Beaconing

As noted in Chapter 2, turning off SSID beaconing provides a limited degree of security. The reasons are as follows:

- Not all access points allow beaconing to be turned off, and even those that do typically discourage users from doing so.
- The steps to manually enter the SSID on a wireless device that does not receive a beaconed SSID are not always convenient.
- Turning off SSID beaconing prevents wireless devices from freely roaming from one wireless network to another.

- When a wireless device is using Microsoft Windows XP, a signal from both a wireless network that is broadcasting an SSID and one that is not broadcasting the SSID, the device will always connect to the access point that is broadcasting its SSID.

- Although the SSID can be suppressed from beacon frames, it still is transmitted in other management frames sent by the AP, and attackers who use wireless tools freely available on the Internet can easily see the SSID being transmitted.

- The SSID is initially transmitted in cleartext form when the device is negotiating with the access point.

- Many users do not change the default SSID and these are well known. An attacker can simply try default SSIDs until a connection is accepted.

Despite the fact that configuring an access point to not allow the beacon frame to include the SSID provides little protection, when implementing the transitional security model, SSID beaconing should be turned off because it provides a limited amount of security. It may prevent a "casual" unauthorized user or novice attacker using Windows XP from capturing the SSID and entering the network. On APs that allow this configuration, SSID beaconing should be turned off and the SSID entered manually on each device.

NOTE

One security expert said that turning off SSID beaconing is like putting a latch on a screen door, in that it will only keep the honest people out!

Although not directly a step in authentication, nevertheless it is a good practice to use a hard-to-guess SSID in a WLAN. An SSID that contains an address like "1906collegeheights" or a name like "robert-escue-wlan" easily identifies the location or owner of the AP and may provide an attacker with additional attack information. Instead, an SSID like "backtoschool" provides no information about the location of the equipment.

NOTE

Default SSIDs should never be used. Using the default SSID also broadcasts the implicit message that, "I don't know anything about security."

MAC Address Filtering

Like turning off SSID beaconing, MAC address filtering has several limitations:

- Managing a large number of MAC addresses is difficult and can create avenues for attackers.

- MAC address filtering does not provide a means to temporarily allow a guest user to access the network other than acquiring the MAC address and entering it manually into the access point.

- WLANs initially exchange MAC addresses in cleartext.
- A MAC address can be "spoofed" or substituted.

Although MAC address filtering contains significant vulnerabilities, like SSID beaconing it provides a small degree of security from "casual" unauthorized users (but not determined attackers). Under the transitional security model, MAC address filtering should be used when possible.

DHCP Restrictions

Almost all wireless gateways and many APs distribute IP addresses to network devices using the **Dynamic Host Configuration Protocol (DHCP)**, part of the TCP/IP protocol suite. DHCP "leases" IP addresses to clients to use while they are connected to the network. Properly configuring these settings can provide a limited degree of protection against wireless attackers. These settings are illustrated in Figure 5-3.

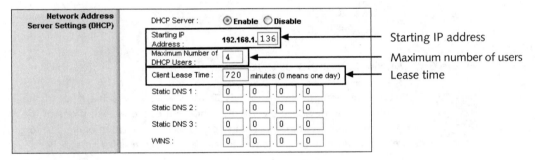

Figure 5-3 DHCP settings

First, DHCP distributes addresses to network devices beginning at a starting address and incrementing by a value of one for each device. That is, if the starting IP address is 192.168.1.2, then the first device will be given the address 192.168.1.2, the next device will be leased 192.168.1.3, and so on. Attackers who attempt to gain unauthorized access to a WLAN sometimes try to determine the IP address of other network devices by taking the starting address of an IP address range (such as 192.168.1.1) and incrementing by a value of one. However, if the starting IP address is set to a higher number, such as 192.168.1.136, it is more difficult for the attacker to guess a device's IP address.

Second, the maximum number of DHCP users (sometimes called DHCP leases) can also be restricted. The maximum number of DHCP users should be limited to the number of authorized devices on the network. That is, if there are four network devices then the maximum number of DHCP users should be set to four. If an attacker is able to breach the wireless security protections and gain access to the network, he would not be leased an IP address because the maximum would have already been distributed. This is illustrated in Figure 5-4. This step, coupled with the first defense of changing the starting IP address, may deter a novice attacker from entering the network.

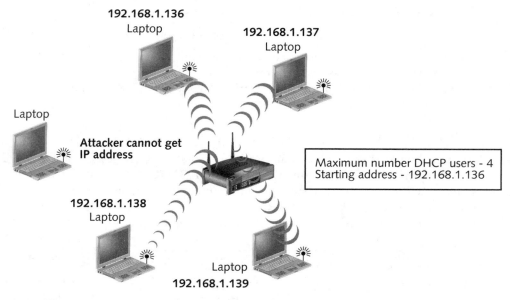

Figure 5-4 Maximum number of DHCP users

NOTE

Setting the maximum number of DHCP users is only valuable if all of the approved network devices are currently connected to the WLAN. If one of the WLAN users is using a notebook computer that is not connected or if a desktop device is turned off, then this leaves an available IP address for an attacker.

The final defense based on DHCP is to set the length of the lease time. The lease time is the length of time that someone can remain connected to the network with their current IP address leased through DHCP. At the end of the lease time, a user would have to reconnect to receive a new IP address. Most wireless gateways or APs allow the lease time to be set in the number of minutes until a lease expires. Setting the lease time so that an attacker who gains access to the network does not have indefinite use of the WLAN may deter an attacker from trying to reconnect once the lease expires.

NOTE

It should be stressed that these DHCP restrictions can be by-passed by determined knowledgeable attackers. They only provide a basic degree of protection from casual unauthorized users.

WEP Encryption

Although WEP has vulnerabilities, it should be turned on if no other options are available for encryption. The longest WEP key available should be used for added security, because a longer key may be more difficult to break. Most vendors have the option of a 128-bit WEP key, which can be created by entering 26 hexadecimal characters (for example

0x3344556677889900AABBCCDDEE). Although some access points support creating a passphrase by entering 13 ASCII characters (for example *AXJANUARY11XA*), this should be discouraged. There is evidence that WEP passphrase generators may create predictable keys.

Although it provides only minimal security, the transitional security model may prevent script kiddies or "casual" eavesdroppers from joining the network. Table 5-4 summarizes the transitional security model.

Table 5-4   Transitional security model

Category	Security mechanism	Security level
Authentication	Shared key authentication	Low
Authentication	Disable SSID beaconing	Low
Authentication	MAC address filtering	Low
Authentication	DHCP restrictions	Low
Encryption	WEP	Low

PERSONAL SECURITY MODEL

A significantly increased level of security can be achieved through using the **personal security model**. The personal security model is designed for single users or small office/home office (SOHO) settings of generally 10 or fewer wireless devices. The personal security model is intended for settings in which an authentication server is unavailable. If an authentication server is available the enterprise security model should be used instead.

The personal security model is divided into two parts, WPA and WPA2. Older equipment may be forced to implement WPA, whereas newer APs and wireless NICs can support WPA2. It is important to implement the highest level of security available within the model. If the equipment can support WPA2, then that should be used instead of WPA.

WPA Personal Security

The personal security model using WPA has enhanced authentication as well as encryption on a wireless LAN compared to the transitional model. The authentication mechanism is PSK and the encryption is TKIP.

PSK Authentication

Although using an authentication server based on IEEE 802.1x is the preferred method for authenticating users, it is recognized that purchasing, installing, and managing an authentication server is costly and may require special technical skills. As an alternative, the IEEE 802.11i provided preshared key (PSK) as an alternative form of authentication.

PSK actually serves two functions. First, it is used to authenticate the user. Second, it plays a role in encryption. PSK itself is not used for encryption. Instead, it serves as the starting seed value for mathematically generating the encryption keys.

The steps for using PSK involve both the access point and wireless client. First, the access point or wireless gateway is configured to support PSK, as seen in Figure 5-5. The settings that pertain to PSK authentication include:

Figure 5-5 Access point settings for PSK

- Security Mode—Depending on the brand of access point and the version of firmware installed, this list may vary. Older access points typically have the option of "WPA-PSK (No Server)." Newer access point will have the options listed by security model, as seen in Figure 5-6.

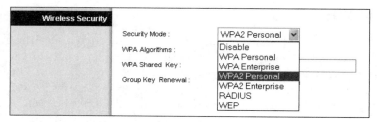

Figure 5-6 Options listed by security model

- WPA Shared Key—The key value is entered here. The value must be between 8 and 63 characters. A passphrase generator then converts this value into a 64-digit hexadecimal number.

After the access point has been configured, each wireless client device must also have the same key value entered to support PSK. As its name implies, a key must be created and entered into both the access point and all wireless devices ("shared") prior to ("pre") the devices communicating with the AP.

When a wireless device attempts to connect to an access point that is using PSK, the user is prompted for the key value.

NOTE

Although PSK is an improvement over the original IEEE 802.11 security protocol, there still are vulnerabilities associated with it. These vulnerabilities center around two areas, namely key management and passphrases. Improper management of the PSK keys can expose a WLAN to attackers. PSK key management weaknesses include the following:

- Like WEP, the distribution and sharing of PSK keys is performed manually without any technology security protections. The keys can be distributed by telephone, e-mail, or a text message (none of which are secure). Any user who obtains the key is assumed to be authentic and approved.

- Unlike WEP, in which four keys can be used, PSK only uses a single key. Should this one PSK key be compromised by an unauthorized attacker the entire WLAN would become vulnerable.

- Standard security practices call for keys to be changed on a regular basis. Changing the PSK key requires reconfiguring the key on every wireless device and on all access points.

- To allow a guest user to have access to a PSK WLAN, the key must be given to that guest. Once the guest departs, this shared secret must be changed on all devices to ensure adequate security for the PSK WLAN.

A second area of PSK vulnerability is the use of passphrases. A PSK is a 64-bit hexadecimal number. The most common way this number is generated is by entering a passphrase (consisting of letters, digits, punctuation, etc.) that is between 8 and 63 characters in length. Although entering a 64-digit hexadecimal number itself would be more secure, most access points do not allow users that option. Instead, a user can *only* enter a passphrase.

Because PSK passphrases are required on most APs, users may be tempted to create a passphrase that is only slightly longer than the minimum length requirements. For example, because a passphrase must be a minimum of 8 characters, a passphrase of double that length (16 characters) would normally be considered secure. However, that is not the case. When developing the IEEE 802.11i security standards, the committee issued this warning:

> A passphrase typically has about 2.5 bits of security per character, so the passphrase of n bytes equates to a key with about 2.5n + 12 bits of security. Hence, it provides a relatively low level of security, with keys generated from short passwords subject to dictionary attack. Use of the key hash is recommended only where it is impractical to make use of a stronger form of user authentication. A key generated from a passphrase of less than about 20 characters is unlikely to deter attacks.

PSK passphrases of fewer than 20 characters can be subject to **offline dictionary attacks**. The original PSK passphrase is mathematically manipulated (known as **hashing**) 4,096 times before it is transmitted. An attacker who captures the passphrase can perform the same hashing on dictionary words seeking a match. If a user created a PSK passphrase of fewer than 20 characters that was a dictionary word then a match can be found and the passphrase broken.

A Pentium IV 3.8 GHz computer can hash approximately 70 dictionary words per second.

Some computer chip manufacturers have attempted to bypass the problem of using weak PSK passphrases by adding an optional method of automatically generating and distributing strong keys through a software and hardware interface. A user pushes a button on the wireless gateway or access point and then launches a program on the wireless device. After a negotiation process of less than a minute a strong PSK key is created and distributed. Linksys's offering, known as SecureEasySetup (SES), also creates a unique SSID in addition to the PSK.

Even though PSK authentication is intended to be used solely for SOHO and consumer networks, a surprising number of large organizations that could implement an authentication server instead use PSK, presumably for its ease of use.

TKIP Encryption

TKIP encryption is an improvement on WEP encryption. However, instead of replacing the WEP engine, TKIP is designed to fit into the existing WEP procedure. Referring back to Figure 5-5, the access point settings that pertain to TKIP include:

- WPA Algorithms—This is the type of encryption that is used.

- Group Key Renewal—The PSK is used as a seed value to generate new keys. The Group Key Renewal is the number of seconds between generating a new key.

The Group Key Renewal should not be set to less than 300 seconds (5 minutes) because there can be up to four 60-second periods between negotiation retries. Changing the key within that time could affect the retries.

How TKIP and MIC perform encryption is illustrated in Figure 5-7 (the parts of the previous WEP procedure that are no longer used are crossed out). The wireless device has two keys, a 128-bit encryption key called the **temporal key** and a 64-bit MIC. The steps are as follows:

- Step 1—Instead of using an initialization vector and secret key as with WEP, the temporal key is XORed with the sender's MAC address to create an intermediate Value 1.

- Step 2—Value 1 is then mixed with a sequence number to produce Value 2, which is the per-packet key. Value 2 is then entered into the Pseudo-Random Number Generator (PRNG), just as with normal WEP.

- Step 3—Instead of sending the text through the CRC generator, the MIC key, sender's MAC address, and receiver's MAC address are all sent through a MIC function. This creates text with the MIC key appended. This value is then XORed with the keystream to create the ciphertext.

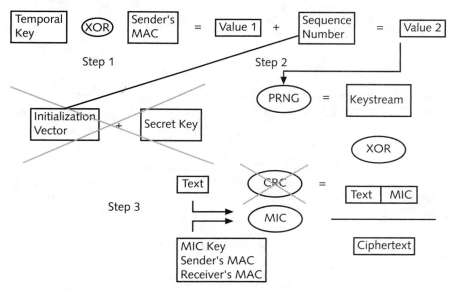

Figure 5-7 TKIP/MIC process

TKIP has three major components to address vulnerabilities:

- *MIC*—MIC protects against forgeries by ensuring that the message has not been tampered with, which CRC under WEP could not do. The original WEP design used a 24-bit initialization vector (IV) along with a secret key to generate a keystream. TKIP creates a different key for each packet.

- *IV sequence*—TKIP reuses the WEP IV field as a sequence number for each packet. Both the transmitter and receiver initialize the packet sequence space to zero whenever new TKIP keys are set, and the transmitter increments the sequence number with each packet it sends. This ensures that an attacker does not record a valid packet and then retransmit it. Also, the length of the sequence number (IV) has been doubled, from 24 bits to 48 bits.

- *TKIP key mixing*—WEP constructs a per-packet RC4 key by concatenating a key and the packet IV. The new per-packet key construction, called the TKIP key mixing function, substitutes a temporary (temporal) key for the WEP base key and constructs a per-packet key that changes with each packet. Temporal keys have a fixed lifetime and are replaced frequently.

TKIP replaces WEP encryption and makes wireless transmissions more secure. Although WEP is optional in IEEE 802.11, TKIP is required in the WPA personal security model. The

TKIP encryption algorithm is stronger than the one used by WEP but works by using the same hardware–based calculation mechanisms WEP uses.

If a wireless device was transmitting 10,000 packets per second with original WEP IV, collisions would occur in 90 minutes; using TKIP, collisions would not occur for over 900 years.

NOTE

WPA2 Personal Security

The personal security model using WPA2 uses PSK as the authentication technology, like WPA. However, WPA2 personal security substitutes AES encryption instead of TKIP.

PSK Authentication

Preshared key (PSK) is intended for personal and small office/home office users who do not have an enterprise authentication server. PSK keys are automatically changed (called **rekeying**) and authenticated between devices after a specified period known as the **rekey interval**.

Some access points rekey after a set number of packets has been transmitted.

NOTE

PSK requires that a key (also called a **shared secret**) be entered in both the access point and the wireless devices. The shared secret is usually entered as a passphrase, which can be between 8 and 63 characters, and can include special characters and spaces.

AES-CCMP Encryption

Encryption under the WPA2 personal security model is accomplished by using the block cipher Advanced Encryption Standard (AES). Specifically, **AES–CCMP** is the encryption protocol in the 802.11i standard. CCMP is based upon the Counter Mode with CBC-MAC (CCM) of the AES encryption algorithm. CCM is the algorithm providing data privacy, whereas the Cipher Block Chaining Message Authentication Code (CBC-MAC) component of CCMP provides data integrity and authentication.

Changing even one bit in an AES-CCMP message produces a different result.

NOTE

The AES algorithm processes blocks of 128 bits, yet the length of the cipher keys and number of rounds can vary, depending on the level of security required. The available key lengths are 128, 192, and 256 bits, and the number of available rounds are 10, 12, and 14. Only the 128-bit key and 128-bit block are mandatory for WPA2.

NOTE

Increasing the key length and number of rounds has an impact on the speed of AES.

It is recommended that AES encryption and decryption be performed in hardware because of the computationally intensive nature of AES. Performing AES encryption in software requires sufficient processing power. If an access point performed AES encryption/decryption in software while serving several devices, the AP would not be able to adequately service the devices, especially if that access point lacked a powerful processor and a large amount of memory.

NOTE

A minimum of the equivalent of a 2.5-GHz Pentium processor is needed to perform AES.

The personal security model, both WPA and WPA2, provides a higher level of security than the transitional security model. WPA2 is preferred over WPA. Table 5-5 summarizes the personal security model.

Table 5-5 Personal security model

Security Model	Category	Security mechanism	Security level
WPA personal security	Authentication	PSK	Low-Medium (depends on length of passphrase)
WPA personal security	Encryption	TKIP	Medium
WPA2 personal security	Authentication	PSK	Medium
WPA2 personal security	Encryption	AES-CCMP	High

ENTERPRISE SECURITY MODEL

The most robust level of security that can be achieved today for wireless LANs is using the **enterprise security model**. The enterprise security model is designed for medium to large-sized organizations such as businesses, government agencies, and universities. The enterprise security model is intended for settings in which an authentication server is available.

NOTE

If an authentication server is not available, the WPA2 personal security model should be used instead.

The enterprise security model, like the personal security model, is divided into two parts, WPA and WPA2. Legacy wireless equipment may be forced to implement WPA, whereas newer hardware can fully support WPA2.

WPA Enterprise Security

The enterprise security model using WPA provides improved authentication and encryption over the personal model on a wireless LAN. The authentication used is IEEE 802.1x and the encryption is TKIP.

IEEE 802.1x Authentication

IEEE 802.1x is an authentication standard that is gaining widespread popularity. 802.1x provides an authentication framework for all IEEE 802-based LANs, including wired Ethernet and Token Ring as well as wireless LANS. It uses port-based authentication mechanisms, meaning that access is denied to any user other than an authorized user attempting to connect to the network through that port. IEEE 802.1x does not perform any encryption; instead, it is intended to authenticate a user and to provide a secure way to exchange keys that can be used for encryption.

A network supporting the 802.1x standard consists of three elements, as shown in Figure 5-8. The **supplicant** is the wireless device that requires secure network access. The supplicant sends the request to an **authenticator** that serves as an intermediary device. The authenticator sends the request from the supplicant to the authentication server. The authentication server accepts or rejects the supplicant's request and sends that information back to the authenticator, which in turn grants or denies access to the supplicant. One of the strengths of the 802.1x protocol is that the supplicant never has direct communication with the authentication server. This minimizes the risk of attack on the authentication server, which contains valuable logon data for all users.

Figure 5-8   IEEE 802.1x process

An authenticator can be an access point on a wireless network or a switch on a wired network.

NOTE

An IEEE 802.1x supplicant, which is required on the wireless device, is software that is installed on the client to implement the IEEE 802.1x protocol framework. Supplicant software may be included in the client operating system, integrated into device drivers, or installed as third-party "stand-alone" software. Some vendors of wireless NICs supply the supplicant with their cards.

All Wi-Fi certified devices are confirmed to work with Microsoft, Funk Software, or a vendor-supplied WPA or WPA2-enabled supplicant. However, a device does not have to possess the supplicant software to be certified.

NOTE

The authentication server in an 802.1x configuration stores the list of the names and credentials of authorized users to verify their authenticity. Typically a **Remote Authentication Dial-In User Service (RADIUS)** server is used. When a user wants to connect to the wireless network, the request is first sent to the authenticator, which relays the information, such as the username and password, type of connection, and other information, to the RADIUS server. The server first determines if the AP itself is permitted to send requests. If so, the RADIUS server attempts to find the user's name in its database. It then applies the password to decide whether access should be granted to this user. Depending on the authentication method used, the server may return a challenge message that carries a random number. The authenticator relays the challenge to the user's computer, which must respond with the correct value to prove its asserted identity. Once the RADIUS server is satisfied that the user is authentic and authorized to use the requested service, it returns an "Accept" message to the AP and the wireless user can then access the network.

RADIUS allows a company to maintain user profiles in a central database that all remote servers can share. Doing so increases security, allowing a company to set up a policy that can be applied at a single administered network point. Having a central service also means that it is easier to track usage for billing and maintaining network statistics. Besides a RADIUS server, wireless user credentials may also be stored in an external database, such as Structured Query Language (SQL), Lightweight Directory Access Protocol (LDAP), or Microsoft Active Directory, that can be accessed by the authentication server. The configuration is not determined by standards and can be specific to each implementation.

Additional information regarding IEEE 802.1x is found in Chapter 8.

NOTE

TKIP Encryption

TKIP was designed to fit into the existing WEP architecture to provide improved encryption by maintaining backward compatibility with existing legacy hardware. As such, TKIP should be considered an interim WPA enterprise security solution. A more robust encryption protocol is AES-CCMP.

WPA2 Enterprise Security

The enterprise security model using WPA2 provides the highest level of secure authentication and encryption on a wireless LAN. The authentication used is IEEE 802.1x and the encryption is AES-CCMP.

IEEE 802.1x Authentication

The strongest type of wireless authentication currently available, IEEE 802.1x authentication, provides the most robust authentication for a WPA2 enterprise model WLAN. The disadvantage of IEEE 802.1x is the high cost involved with purchasing, installing, and maintaining an authentication server.

AES-CCMP Encryption

AES is a block cipher that uses the same key for both encryption and decryption. With AES, bits are encrypted in blocks of plaintext that are calculated independently, rather than a keystream acting across a plaintext data input stream. AES has a block size of 128 bits with three possible key lengths: 128, 192, and 256 bits as specified in the AES standard. For the WPA2/802.11i implementation of AES, a 128-bit key length is used. AES encryption includes four stages that make up one round. Each round is then iterated 10, 12, or 14 times depending on the bit-key size. For the WPA2/802.11i implementation of AES, each round is iterated 10 times.

The enterprise security model of WPA2 provides the highest level of security available and should be implemented whenever an authentication server is available. Table 5-6 summarizes the enterprise security model.

Table 5-6   Enterprise security model

Security Model	Category	Security Mechanism	Security Level
WPA enterprise security	Authentication	802.1x	High
WPA enterprise security	Encryption	TKIP	Medium
WPA2 enterprise security	Authentication	802.1x	High
WPA2 enterprise security	Encryption	AES-CCMP	High

As evidenced by the original IEEE 802.11 security protocol, the vulnerabilities of a security system may not be revealed until after it has been exposed to the public over a period of time. The time needed to react to new vulnerabilities, propose solutions, and finally ratify those proposals can often take years. To address this time lag, the IEEE 802.11i standard also includes a component known as the **Robust Secure Network (RSN)**.

RSN uses dynamic negotiation of authentication and encryption algorithms between access points and wireless devices. This dynamic negotiation of authentication and encryption algorithms lets RSN evolve as vulnerabilities are exposed or improved security is introduced. This allows WLANs to address new threats and continue to provide the security necessary to protect information.

NOTE

Although WPA and WPA2 improve wireless security, RSN is seen as the future of WLAN security for 802.11.

CHAPTER SUMMARY

- ◻ Shortly after the IEEE 802.11 standard was ratified, vulnerabilities were identified in its security mechanisms. Although some "quick fix" solutions were proposed, the IEEE and the Wi-Fi Alliance developed more comprehensive solutions. Those solutions, known as IEEE 802.11i, Wi-Fi Protected Access (WPA), and Wi-Fi Protected Access Version 2 (WPA2) became the foundations of today's wireless security.

- ◻ The IEEE 802.11i standard provided a more solid wireless security model, such as the block cipher Advanced Encryption Standard (AES) and IEEE 802.1x port security.

- ◻ WPA is a subset of 802.11i and addresses both encryption and authentication. WPA replaces WEP with a new encryption technology called Temporal Key Integrity Protocol (TKIP). WPA also includes a Message Integrity Check (MIC) designed to prevent an attacker from capturing, altering, and resending data packets. The MIC replaces the Cyclic Redundancy Check (CRC) function in WEP. Wi-Fi Protected Access 2 (WPA2) is based on the final IEEE 802.11i standard.

- ◻ The transitional security model should be implemented only as a temporary solution for equipment that can not implement WPA or WPA2. This model uses shared key authentication, turning off SSID beaconing, implementing MAC address filtering, and setting DHCP restrictions.

- ◻ The personal security model is designed for single users or small office home office (SOHO) settings of generally 10 or fewer wireless devices and does not include an authentication server. There are two parts to the personal security model, WPA and WPA2.

- ◻ The enterprise security model is designed for medium to large-sized organizations such as businesses, government agencies, and universities. The enterprise security model is intended for settings in which an authentication server is available; if an authentication server is not available, the highest level of the personal security model should be used.

Key Terms

Advanced Encryption Standard (AES) — A block cipher used in IEEE 802.11i.

AES-CCMP — The encryption protocol in the 802.11i standard.

authentication server — A server on an IEEE 802.1x network that verifies the authentication of devices.

authenticator — A device that receives requests and forwards to an authentication server in an 802.1x network.

block cipher — A cipher that manipulates an entire block of cleartext at one time.

Dynamic Host Configuration Protocol (DHCP) — A part of the TCP/IP protocol suite that leases IP address to clients to use while they are connected to the network.

enterprise security model — A wireless security model designed for medium to large-sized organizations such as businesses, government agencies, and universities in which an authentication server is available.

hashing — The process of mathematically manipulating a value to disguise it.

IEEE 802.11i — A wireless security standard intended to replace the original WEP-based standard.

IEEE 802.1x — A standard for authentication and key management that can be used for either wired or wireless networks.

key-caching — A technology that stores information from a device on the network to improve roaming.

Message Integrity Check (MIC) — A technology that replaces the Cyclic Redundancy Check (CRC) that is designed to prevent an attacker from capturing, altering, and resending data packets.

offline dictionary attack — An attack that hashes the encrypted PSK value and compares it with hashed values from a dictionary.

per-packet key — A technology that dynamically generates a new key for each packet and prevents collisions.

personal security model — A model for wireless security designed for single users or small office home office (SOHO) settings of 10 or fewer wireless devices.

port security — An authentication technique that blocks all traffic until the user is approved.

pre-authentication — A technology that allows a device to become authenticated to an AP before moving into its range.

preshared key (PSK) — A technology that uses passphrases for generating encryption keys.

rekey interval — The interval at which PSK keys are changed.

rekeying — The process of automatically changing PSK keys.

Remote Authentication Dial-In User Service (RADIUS) — An authentication server typically used on an IEEE 802.1x network.

Robust Secure Network (RSN) — A protocol that uses dynamic negotiation of authentication and encryption algorithms between access points and wireless devices.

round — An iteration in a block cipher.

seed — The starting point for mathematically generating an encryption key.

shared secret — A passphrase in preshared key (PSK) authentication that must be entered in both the access point and wireless device.

supplicant — The wireless device that requires secure network access in an IEEE 802.1x network.

temporal key — A 128-bit encryption key used in TKIP.

Temporal Key Integrity Protocol (TKIP) — A technology that replaces WEP encryption.

transitional security model — A model for wireless security that should only be implemented as a temporary solution before upgrading to a more secure model, either the personal security model or the enterprise security model.

Wi-Fi Protected Access (WPA) — A subset of 802.11i that addresses encryption and authentication.

Wi-Fi Protected Access 2 (WPA2) — The second generation of WPA security, based on the IEEE 802.11i standard.

REVIEW QUESTIONS

1. The stronger security standard developed by the IEEE committee to address wireless vulnerabilities of the 802.11 standard is
   a. 802.16.2
   b. 802.5
   c. 802.11i
   d. 802.11e

2. The two primary security vulnerabilities of the original 802.11 wireless security mechanism are
   a. speed and data modeling
   b. encryption and authentication
   c. access codes and passwords
   d. tokens and resources

3. The Wi-Fi Alliance was responsible for creating
   a. WPA2
   b. 802.11i
   c. 802.11
   d. AES-CMMPR

4. One step to enhancing encryption was to replace the RC4 stream cipher with a stronger
   a. block cipher
   b. supplicant
   c. authenticator
   d. Dynamic TKIP

5. _____ is the IEEE foundation of future wireless security.
   a. Robust Secure Network (RSN)
   b. Wireless Access Protection 2 (WPA2)
   c. Encryption Model II
   d. Enterprise Standard Security (ESS)

6. Advanced Encryption Standard (AES) is a stream cipher. True or False?

7. The IEEE 802.11 standard enforces port security. True or False?

8. Key-caching stores information from a device on the network and is used when roaming. True or False?

9. Wi-Fi Protected Access (WPA) is a subset of IEEE 802.11i. True or False?

10. TKIP performs encryption by using a per-packet key. True or False?

11. The _____ replaces the Cyclic Redundancy Check (CRC) function.

12. Preshared key (PSK) is primarily used in authentication but also plays a role in encrypting by serving as the _____ for mathematically generating the encryption keys.

13. WPA2 allows both AES and TKIP clients to operate in the same WLAN, yet _____ only recognizes AES.

14. The _____ security model should only be implemented as a temporary solution.

15. Shared key authentication uses _____ keys for authentication.

16. What is the advantage of turning off SSID filtering if it can easily be bypassed?

17. When should the personal security model be implemented?

18. What three DHCP settings should be used in the transitional security model?

19. How does a RADIUS server support IEEE 802.1x?

20. What is the weakness of PSK passphrases?

21. What is the Robust Secure Network (RSN)?

HANDS-ON PROJECTS

Project 5-1: Using the Windows Connect Now Tool

Key management is one of the weaknesses of using PSK. To make key management easier, Windows XP with SP2 supports the Windows Connect Now tool, which automates wireless network configuration. Windows Connect Now is implemented through updates to the wireless client software and a new Wireless Network Setup wizard.

The Windows Connect Now tool was originally known as the Windows Smart Network Key (WSNK).

NOTE

The Wireless Network Setup Wizard steps users through the configuration of wireless network settings, such as a wireless network name, the authentication and encryption method, and a strong PSK, and then writes that configuration as a set of Extensible Markup Language (XML) files to be stored on a Universal Serial Bus (USB) flash drive. The flash drive can then be used to transfer this configuration, which includes keys, to other wireless devices that support Windows Connect Now, which will automatically read the settings from the XML files so the configurations will be identical. In this project you will need access to a computer using Windows XP with SP2 installed and a USB flash drive.

1. Click **Start** and **Control Panel** and **Network and Internet Connections** (in Category view).

2. Click **Wireless Network Setup Wizard** to display the Wireless Network Setup wizard, as seen in Figure 5-9. Click **Next**.

3. Enter the SSID **Roundtable**.

4. Click **Manually assign a network key**.

Because of security and compatibility issues it is recommended that automatic assignment of keys be avoided.

NOTE

5. Click **Use WPA encryption instead of WEP**, as seen in Figure 5-10. Click **Next**.

6. Under **Network key:** enter **0123456789ABCDEF0123456789ABCDEF0123456 789ABCDEF0123456789ABCDEF**.

7. Enter the same key again under **Confirm network key**.

8. Click **Next** to display the **How do you want to set up your network?** window as seen in Figure 5-11.

9. Click **Use a USB flash drive (recommended)**. Click **Next**.

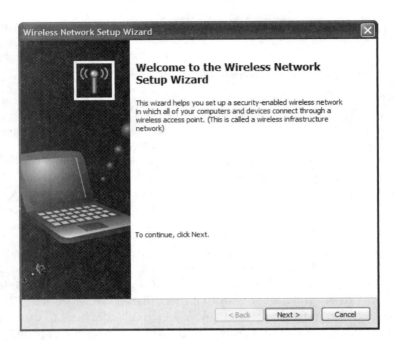

Figure 5-9   Wireless Network Setup wizard

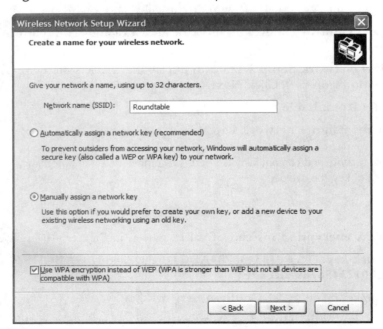

Figure 5-10   Create a name for your wireless network window

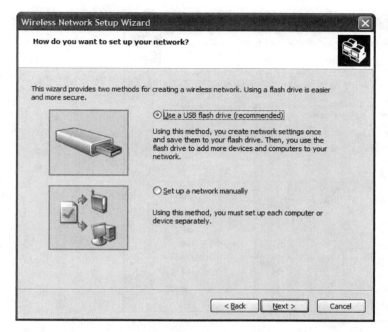

Figure 5-11   How do you want to set up your network? window

10. Plug the flash drive into the USB port. Verify that the drive letter under **Flash drive** is correct. Click **Next**.

11. After the transfer is complete the **Transfer your network settings to your other computers or devices** window appears, as seen in Figure 5-12. Click **Next**.

12. Remove the USB flash drive and click **OK**.

13. Click **Next**.

14. Reinsert the USB flash drive and click **OK**.

15. Click **Next**.

16. You may receive an error information message on the final screen, depending on your network configuration. Click **Finish**.

17. If you were distributing this to other devices, you could now distribute the PSK key more securely using the USB flash drive. This information may not appear by looking at the contents of the key through Windows Explorer.

18. Close all windows.

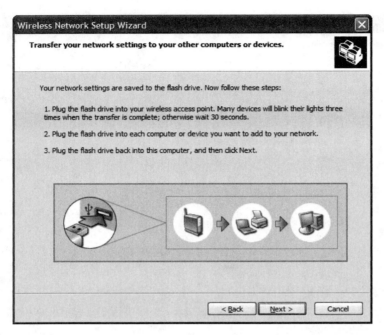

Figure 5-12   Transfer your network settings to your other computers or devices window

Project 5-2: Install Windows Hotfix to Support WPA2

For Windows to support WPA2, a hotfix must be downloaded and installed. In this project you will determine if the hotfix is installed, and, if not, download and install the software.

1. First you should see if the hotfix is already installed. Click **Start**, and then click **Control Panel**.

2. Click **Add or Remove Programs**.

3. If the **Show updates** check box is not selected, click it to turn on this setting.

4. Scroll down to **Windows XP – Software Updates** and locate **Windows XP Hot fix KB 893357**.

5. If the hotfix appears then close all windows and end this project.

6. If the hotfix does not appear, then close all windows and point your browser to *http://support.microsoft.com/?id=893357*.

7. Scroll down to the link under **Download information** and click on it.

8. Follow the instructions to download this hotfix onto your desktop.

9. Double-click on the file to start the installation.

10. Accept the default settings to install this hotfix.

11. You may be asked to restart your computer after the installation is complete.

Project 5-3: Set WPA2 on a Linksys AP

In this activity you set up WPA2 on a Linksys AP.

1. Point your browser to the Linksys AP and enter the username and password.
2. Click the **Wireless** link to display the Wireless settings.
3. Click **Wireless Security**.
4. Under **Security Mode** click the down arrow to reveal the options.
5. Select **WPA2 Personal**.
6. Under **WPA Algorithms:** select **TKIP+AES**.
7. Under **WPA Shared Key:** enter **1234567890abc**.
8. Under **Group Key Renewal** enter **3600.** The key will now change every hour.
9. Click **Save Settings**. A message will appear that says **Settings are successful.** Click **Continue**.
10. On the wireless device click **Start** and **Connect To** and **Show all connections**.
11. Select the wireless connection if necessary and click **View available wireless networks**.
12. Click the SSID of the Linksys network and click **Connect**. It may be necessary to wait 30 to 60 seconds for the connection to be established.
13. Under **Network key** enter **1234567890abc**. Enter it again under **Confirm network key**.
14. Close all windows.

Project 5-4: Setting Cisco Migration Mode

WPA Migration Mode is an access point setting defined by Cisco that enables both WPA and non–WPA clients to associate to an access point using the same SSID. It will enable a "diverse" group of devices to all use the same access point whereas normally they could not. Those devices include:

    □ WPA clients that are capable of TKIP and authenticated key management

    □ IEEE 802.1X clients that are capable of dynamic keying but not TKIP

    □ Static WEP clients that are not capable of TKIP or authenticated key management

In this activity you set up the Cisco Migration Mode.

1. Connect to the Cisco access point and enter the username and password.
2. Click **Security**.
3. Click **Encryption Manager** to display the WEP Key Manager screen.
4. Click the radio button next to **WEP Encryption** to select it.

5. From the pull-down menu select **Optional**.

6. Select **Encryption Key 2** as the **Transmit Key**.

7. Select the **Key Size** as **128 bit**.

8. Enter **abcdef1234567890abcdef1234** as the key value.

9. Click **Apply**.

10. Close all windows.

Project 5-5: Using Linksys SecureEasySetup (SES)

Linksys's SecureEasySetup (SES) is designed to automatically generate SSIDs and secure PSKs for wireless devices. In this project you will use SES. Note that the Linksys access point must have a SES logo and button on the front panel and the Linksys utility software must be installed on the wireless device.

1. On the Linksys wireless gateway locate the SecureEasySetup label. The logo is lit with an orange color when the router powers up in its factory default unsecured state.

2. Press the lighted **Cisco Systems** logo button located next to the SES label. There will be an approximately 8-second delay and then the light will be dark for about 3 seconds, followed by a rapid white flashing backlight that indicates the router is in SES search mode.

3. On the wireless device, launch the Linksys client manager software.

4. Click the **Link Information** tab.

5. Click on the **SecureEasySetup** link.

6. Click **Next**.

7. A **Searching the wireless network** progress will be displayed, which then changes to **Connecting the wireless network**.

8. The SSID and PSK key will be displayed. The PSK key will need to be recorded and entered on any other wireless devices.

9. Close all windows.

CASE PROJECTS

Case Project 5-1: What Is Your Security Model?

Is the wireless network you use as secure as it should be? Examine your wireless network or that of a friend or neighbor to determine which security model it most closely matches. Then, outline the steps it would take to move it to the next highest level. Estimate how much it would cost and how much time it would take to increase the level. Finally, estimate

5

how long it would take you to replace all of the data on your computer if it was corrupted by an attacker, and what you might lose. Write a one-page summary of your work.

Case Project 5-2: Techniques Behind Breaking PSK

What are the techniques that are behind breaking PSK? Using the Internet and other sources, research how PSK can be broken. Be sure to cover such topics as Pairwise Master Key (PMK), PBKDF2 cryptography, sender and recipient MAC addresses, and the 4-Way Handshake. Write a one-page document that outlines these techniques.

Case Project 5-3: Free Linksys RADIUS Server

A firmware upgrade and software is available that turns a Linksys wireless gateway into a RADIUS server. However, there is always a risk in flashing the Linksys gateway with a non-approved Linksys upgrade, which is not recommended except on Linksys equipment that will not result in any loss if the flashing fails and the equipment is rendered inoperable. Go to *www.tinypeap.com* and read the information regarding the RADIUS server. Write a brief summary of how it functions. Based on your research, would you recommend this to anyone?

Case Project 5-4: coWPAtty WPA Cracker

One of the WPA offline dictionary crackers often used to break PSK is known as coWPAtty. Using the Internet, research coWPAtty. What are its strengths? What are its weaknesses? Does it seem to be difficult to use? What other programs must be used in conjunction with it? Write a one-page paper on your findings

Case Project 5-5: Online WPA and WPA2 Password Generators

Because of the difficulty of creating strong passphrases and passwords, several Web sites are available that create these automatically. One such site is Gibson Research Corporation's "Perfect Passwords" at *https://www.grc.com/pass*. Go to this page and read how the passwords are created. Now refresh the site and observe the changes. Would you recommend this site for someone who needs a strong password? Why or why not?

Fairvue Technology Consulting

Remember Me! is a local chain of computer stores that specializes in memory, hard disk drives, flash drives, MP3 players, PDAs, and similar equipment. Remember Me! has provided free wireless Internet access to its customers but was recently the victim of a wireless attack. Now they are debating if they should drop the service or continue by adding more security. Fairvue has asked you to help them with this project.

1. Prepare a PowerPoint presentation that outlines the three models of wireless security and the features included in each model. Also, create a graph of "Most Vulnerable" to

"Least Vulnerable" with each model listed. Identify where Remember Me! would fit on the graph. Your presentation should be about six to eight slides in length.

2. Remember Me! would like to have a RADIUS server for their employees but are unsure what, if any, security they should provide for their customers who use the wireless network. Create a one-page memo that outlines your recommendations for security.

ENTERPRISE WIRELESS HARDWARE SECURITY

After completing this chapter you should be able to do the following:

➤ List and describe the functions of the different types of wireless LAN hardware used in an enterprise

➤ Tell how access control and protocol filtering can protect a WLAN

➤ Describe the functions of Quality of Service, handoffs, and power features in wireless networking hardware

The World of Wireless Security

A controversy is raging over wireless transmissions and security—but it's not what you might think. Manufacturers of garage door openers, which typically use radio frequency (RF) signals like those used by wireless LANs, suddenly started receiving large numbers of complaints that the units did not always work properly. What was particularly puzzling was that the problem only occurred in certain locations in the United States. The same type of device did not function in one city but worked normally in another. After some investigation it was discovered that garage door openers on homes close to U.S. military establishments did not always function properly, which finally revealed the cause of the problem.

Radio frequency garage door openers operate at very low power in an unlicensed band of the RF spectrum (380 MHz to 399.9 MHz). It turns out that since World War II these same frequencies have been reserved for U.S. federal government use for air-to-ground communications systems, but these systems were rarely used. Manufacturers of garage door openers chose the same frequencies for their devices. Within the last few years the U.S. military had started using a new two-way portable radio system at military posts across the country that uses the same RF spectrum as the radio-controlled garage door openers. However, because the military's portable radio system operates at a much higher power level, it caused interference with garage door openers in the surrounding area.

The response to this problem by the U.S. Department of Defense (DoD) centered on security—not wireless security, but homeland security. The DoD maintains that military security needs to override civilian concern with garage door interference. Because of the increased needs for homeland security, the DoD says that it must now make more use of these frequencies to deploy mobile radio systems on and around certain military bases. For security reasons the DoD says that it is not possible to predict which specific users or locations near military bases may experience interference. Under Federal Communication Commission (FCC) rules, the military in this case does not have to take any steps to minimize the interference caused by its new radios. The FCC issued a warning to consumers in early 2005 about the problem, stating that garage door openers near military establishments could have a shorter range or not work at all. However, the doors will not suddenly open or close on their own.

The Government Accountability Office (GAO) was asked by a U.S. congressman to study the problem. Its report, released in December 2005, had only one recommendation: that the DoD should work on "improving their community outreach."

Information security is intended to protect the confidentiality, integrity, and availability of information. Because this information is stored on computer hardware, manipulated by software, and transmitted by communications technology, each of these areas must also be protected. It can be said that information security protects the integrity, confidentiality, and availability of information on the devices that store, manipulate, and transmit the information.

This chapter focuses on the wireless hardware devices and the security that they can provide. Although the wireless gateways discussed in Chapter 5 provide security within the personal security model, these are only intended for SOHO or consumer use. This chapter turns to additional types of wireless hardware that are commonly found in enterprise settings that can provide an even stronger level of security.

First you will explore the different types of WLAN hardware that may be found in an enterprise setting. Then, you will look at the security features of this equipment. Finally, you will look at other features that are found in these types of enterprise wireless hardware. Yet as with any hardware, it is important to remember that these security features must be implemented and properly configured to thwart attackers. Mismanaged or partially implemented security settings on such hardware are an invitation to disaster.

ENTERPRISE WLAN HARDWARE

There are several types of wireless hardware that can be found in an enterprise environment. These devices include access points, remote wireless bridges, wireless routers, wireless gateways, wireless switches, and wireless mesh routers.

Access Point

An access point (AP) consists of three major parts. First, it contains an antenna and a radio transmitter/receiver to send and receive signals. Second, it has an RJ-45 wired network interface that allows it to connect by cable to a standard wired network. Finally, it has special bridging software to interface wireless devices to other devices.

 NOTE It is possible to use a standard PC as an access point. Installing a wireless NIC (which functions as the transmitter/receiver), a standard NIC (which serves as the wired network interface), and special AP control software will allow it to serve as an AP.

An access point has two basic functions. First, the access point acts as the base station for the wireless network. All of the devices that have a wireless NIC can transmit to the AP, which in turn redirects the signal to the other wireless devices. The second function of an AP is to act as a bridge between wireless and wired networks. The AP can be connected to the standard network by a cable, allowing the wireless devices to access the data network through it.

The range of an access point acting as the base station depends on several factors. One factor is the type of wireless network that is supported. Some wireless networks can transmit up to 115 meters (375 feet) whereas other types can only send and receive signals at half that distance. In addition, walls, doors, and other solid objects can reduce the distance the signal may travel. The number of wireless clients that a single access point can support varies as well. In theory, some types of access points can support over 100 wireless clients. However, because the radio signal is shared among users, most industry experts recommend one access point for no more than 50 users if they are performing basic e-mail, light Web surfing, and occasionally transferring medium-sized files. If the users are constantly accessing the network and transferring large files, a preferred ratio is 20 users per AP.

Remote Wireless Bridge

A **bridge** is a device that is used to connect two network segments together, even if those segments use different types of physical media, such as wired and wireless connections. A **remote wireless bridge** is a wireless device designed to connect two or more wired or wireless networks. Remote wireless bridges have the same essential characteristics as an AP with two major exceptions. First, remote wireless bridges transmit at higher power than APs. This enables them to transmit over longer distances.

NOTE An AP usually cannot function as a remote wireless bridge. One exception is the Cisco Aironet 1200, which can perform as either an AP or as a remote wireless bridge.

Second, a remote wireless bridge generally uses a highly directional or semi-directional antenna to focus the transmission in a single direction, whereas a standard AP uses an omni-directional (dipole) antenna that radiates its signal out in all directions. Highly directional antennas are usually concave dish-shaped devices used for long distance, point-to-point wireless links, such as connecting buildings that are up to 40 kilometers (25 miles) apart. A semi-directional antenna focuses the energy in one direction but does not have the high power level of a highly directional antenna. Figure 6-1 illustrates one type of radiation pattern from a semi-directional antenna. Semi-directional antennas are primarily used for short- and medium-range remote wireless bridge networks. Two office buildings that are across the street from one another and need to share a wireless network connection would use remote wireless bridges with semi-directional antennas.

6

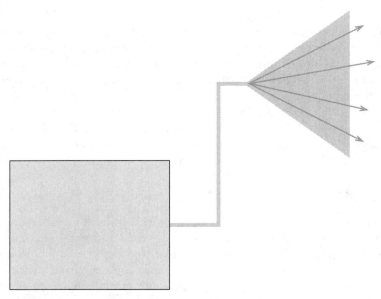

Figure 6-1   Semi-directional antenna pattern

A bridge also contains special software for transmitting and receiving signals. Most bridges have what is known as **delay spread** that minimizes the spread of the signal so that it can reach farther distances.

Bridges also have software that enables them to select the clearest transmission channel to avoid noise and interference.

NOTE

Remote wireless bridges support two types of connections. One type of connection is a **point-to-point** configuration. This configuration is used to connect two LAN segments, as seen in Figure 6-2. These segments can be either wired or wireless. The second configuration is a **point-to-multipoint** configuration. This is used to connect multiple LAN segments, as seen in Figure 6-3.

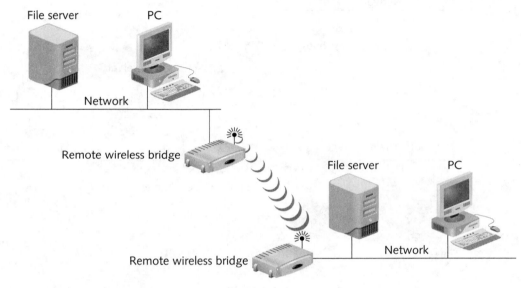

Figure 6-2   Point-to-point remote wireless bridge

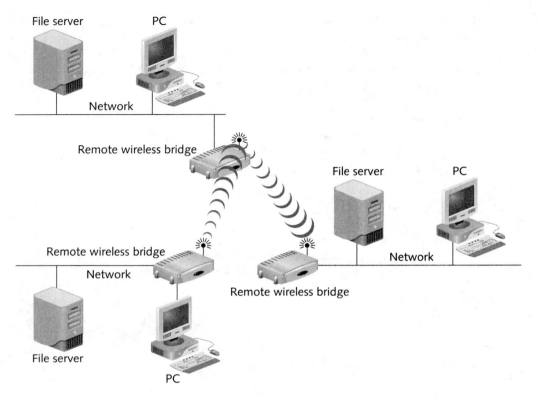

Figure 6-3   Point-to-multipoint remote wireless bridge

A remote wireless bridge can function in one of four different modes:

- If a remote wireless bridge is in **access point mode** it functions as a standard AP only and communicates only with wireless devices like laptop computers and PDAs, not with other remote wireless bridges.

- In **root mode** the bridge, called the **root bridge**, can communicate only with other bridges that are not in root mode. A root bridge, of which there can be only one, cannot communicate with another root bridge or any wireless clients.

- If a remote wireless bridge is set to **non-root mode**, it can transmit only to another bridge in root mode. Some remote wireless bridges can also be configured as an access point. This allows the bridge to simultaneously communicate with a remote wireless root bridge while sending and receiving signals with the wireless clients. This is illustrated in Figure 6-4.

- To extend the distance between LAN segments, another remote wireless bridge may be positioned between two other bridges. This bridge is then in **repeater mode**, as seen in Figure 6-5.

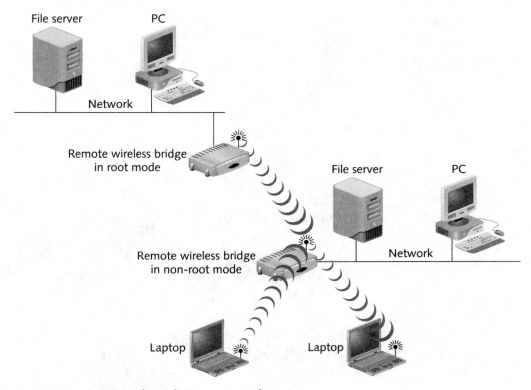

Figure 6-4 Root mode and non-root modes

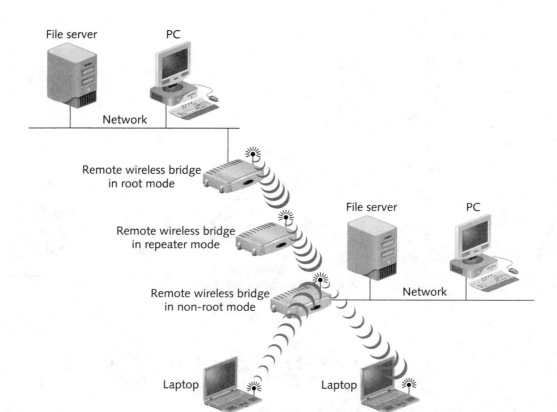

Figure 6-5   Repeater mode

Remote wireless bridges are a cost–effective alternative to expensive leased wired options for connecting remote buildings. Remote wireless bridges can connect sites such as satellite offices, remote campus settings, or temporary office locations when the sites are separated by obstacles such as bodies of water, freeways, or railroads that make using a wired connection impractical or very expensive. The distance between buildings using a remote wireless bridge can be up to 29 kilometers (18 miles) transmitting at 11 Mbps or up to 40 kilometers (25 miles) transmitting at 2 Mbps.

> Even transmitting at the slower 11 Mbps, remote wireless bridges are still seven times faster than a traditional T1 connection.

Wireless Router

A **router** is a network device that transfers packets between networks. A router selects the best link (route) to send packets in order for them to reach closer to their intended destination. Routers use Internet Protocol (IP) packet header information, routing tables, and internal protocols to determine the best path for each packet.

A **wireless router** combines an access point with a router, typically with multiple ports (called a multi-port wireless router). A standard AP only allows wireless devices on the same network segment to communicate. To send packets to another network requires that the AP be connected to a wired router, as seen in Figure 6-6. A wireless router, on the other hand, allows multiple wireless networks to be combined, as seen in Figure 6-7.

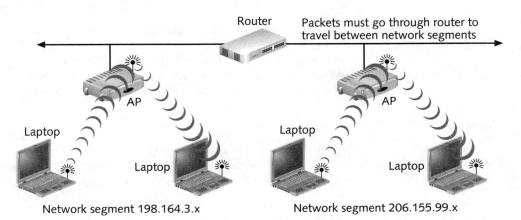

Figure 6-6   Passing packets through a router

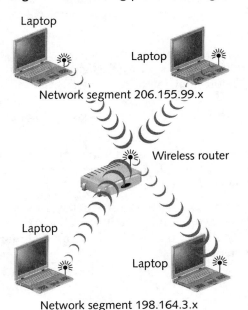

Figure 6-7   Multiple segments connected to a wireless router

Some of the advantages of a wireless router include:

- *Connect multiple networks*—Wireless routers can be used if multiple networks need to be accessible. For instance, an organization may have separate networks on different floors of a building, and employees in a conference room may need access to these different networks and the Internet. A wireless router allows them to access multiple networks wirelessly.

- *Improve network performance*—Because routers only send packets to specific addresses and not to all devices, this reduces traffic and increases bandwidth.

- *Share single IP address*—A wireless router allows users to share a single IP address with multiple wireless users. A cable modem or DSL service gives a single IP address to the wireless router, which in turn provides IP addresses via DHCP to multiple wireless devices on the local wireless network. A wireless router is needed if multiple networked devices on a local network are sharing a single IP address.

Wireless Gateway

A **gateway** is a network device that acts as an entrance to another network. Typically devices that restrict and control traffic within an organization's network or serve as an entry point for a local Internet service provider (ISP) are considered gateways.

A wireless gateway is a device that adds additional functions to a wireless router. It combines an access point, router, network address translation, and other networking features in a single unit. Although wireless gateways are commonly designed for the home consumer market, enterprise wireless gateways add even more features. An enterprise wireless gateway performs the following functions:

- *Authentication*—Instead of using the network operating system's username/password scheme to authenticate wireless users, a wireless gateway ensures that all wireless users are authenticated before allowing them to connect to the network. This provides an additional level of security because unauthorized wireless users will not be able to access the network. Enterprise wireless gateway authentication usually supports such advanced authentication features.

- *Encryption*—An enterprise wireless gateway can use additional encryption features, beyond TKIP and AES-CCMP, so that unauthorized eavesdroppers cannot intercept and interpret the wireless signal.

- *Intrusion detection and malicious program protection*—Most wireless gateways include real-time monitoring of wireless network traffic to detect malicious attacks from wireless users. A wireless gateway enables the wireless network administrator to block intruders and worm penetrations.

- *Bandwidth management*—Because WLAN bandwidth, or the maximum amount of data that can be sent and received, is shared among all users, a few users can monopolize the bandwidth. A wireless gateway allows network traffic to be monitored so that bandwidth can be more evenly allocated among users.

- *Centralized network management*—A wireless gateway can consolidate the management of a WLAN into one device instead of managing each AP individually.

Enterprise wireless gateways provide a single mechanism for managing and monitoring the wireless network. They have proven to be very effective for WLAN security and management in large enterprises.

Wireless Switch

In a wired network a **switch** is a hardware device that joins multiple computers within one local area network (LAN). Network switches often appear to be identical to a network **hub** in that they connect network segments together. However, a switch contains more "intelligence" than a hub. Unlike hubs, network switches are capable of inspecting data packets as they are received, determining the source and destination device of that packet, and forwarding it directly to the recipient. This conserves network bandwidth and gives better performance.

Network switches typically operate at Layer Two, the Data Link Layer, of the OSI model.

NOTE

There are two types of switches. An **unmanaged switch** provides no management capabilities in the operation of the switch. An unmanaged switch only allows the network devices to communicate. Once the unmanaged switch is installed it goes through an automatic configuration process without any intervention from the user. A series of light emitting diode (LED) lights give limited information about the link status of the devices and their activity, but nothing more.

Unmanaged switches are commonly found in WLAN consumer home devices.

NOTE

The other type of switch is a **managed switch**. A managed switch, typically found in an enterprise setting, provides all of the features of an unmanaged switch along with enhanced management features. A managed switch supports both control and monitoring of the network. Control of the network allows the network manager to adjust the communication parameters. For example, in a setting with a large amount of electric noise the data rate can be dropped and certain automatic negotiation features disabled to ensure good transmissions. This can even be done on a port-by-port basis. Monitoring the network is accomplished by using SNMP (Simple Network Management Protocol), which provides information such as the number of bytes transmitted and received, the number of frames transmitted and received, the number of errors, and port status. All of this information can be viewed on a port-by-port basis.

NOTE Some managed switches also make this data available through a Web server so that you can use a standard browser from anywhere there is an Internet connection to view the network status.

One of the challenges of a wireless LAN in an enterprise setting is integrating the management of wired and wireless networks. Integrating wireless LANs into existing wired networks and scaling them to support hundreds or even thousands of mobile users located in remote sites spread over long distances poses significant challenges. Standard network management tools were not designed to handle WLANs, and it has been difficult to port these types of tools and procedures over to wireless networks.

One network management solution introduced by different WLAN vendors is known a **wireless switch**. Whereas the functionality of a WLAN, such as user authentication and encryption, is normally located in the AP itself, these features are removed and instead reside on the wireless switch. The wireless switch, which is often a rack-mounted unit located alongside other network devices, acts like a managed switch. Standard access points in a network using a wireless switch are replaced with simplified radios with a media converter for the wired network. An access point with this limited functionality is known as a **thin access point**, and is illustrated in Figure 6-8.

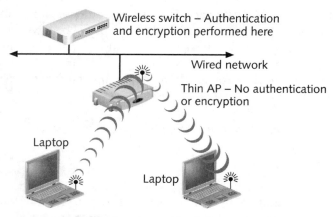

Figure 6-8 Wireless switch and thin access point

Wireless switches and thin APs provide several advantages. First, wireless network management is simplified in that the APs can be managed from one central location (the wireless switch) instead of needing to individually configure each AP scattered across the network.

Second, as wireless client devices move through a WLAN, a lengthy handoff procedure must occur between APs as authentication information is transferred from one AP to another, and the length of time for this procedure can have an adverse affect in WLAN systems using voice over wireless LAN (VoWLAN) communications. However, this handoff procedure is eliminated with thin APs because all authentication is performed in the wireless switch. Also, most wireless switches offer automated site survey tools. These tools can simulate the environment and help predict the best locations for APs. And after deployment, many wireless switching systems can establish the best channel and power settings for the wireless network.

Yet there are disadvantages to the wireless switch/thin AP approach. Today all thin APs and wireless switches are proprietary, so that the switches and APs must be from the same vendor. The Internet Engineering Task Force (IETF) Control and Provisioning of Wireless Access Points (CAPWAP) Working Group is developing a protocol that will allow any vendor's wireless switch to communicate with any thin AP, yet there is no timetable for the new standard and none of the companies involved have yet demonstrated cross-vendor interoperability. The more serious shortcoming of thin APs is that they still do not provide true convergence of the wired and wireless networks but only ease some of the management burdens of WLANs. Many wireless experts maintain that a comprehensive solution that takes full advantage of existing tools, knowledge, resources, and the wired infrastructure to address security, deployment, and control issues is needed.

NOTE

One network management tool that goes beyond wireless switches and thin APs and provides a comprehensive solution to the convergence of wired and wireless networks is the Cisco Structured Wireless-Aware Network (SWAN). SWAN establishes a network framework to integrate and manage wired and wireless networks by extending "wireless awareness" into key elements of the wired network infrastructure. To find more information use a Web browser to search for *Cisco structured wireless-aware network (SWAN)*.

The **IEEE 802.11v** protocol is designed to assist with the management of WLAN devices. This protocol, which is expected to be ratified by 2008, contains the following features:

- *Load balancing*—The 802.11v protocol will force wireless clients to associate with a specific access point if more than one is in the area. Depending on how many devices are already associated with an AP, a device may be directed to an AP with fewer devices to distribute the load more evenly.

- *Automatic configuration*—Instead of forcing the user to select the access point to be associated with, this protocol will enable a network manager to direct a device to a specific AP over the network without the need to manually configure each device.

- *Preserve battery life*—The 802.11v protocol contains schemes that will significantly save battery life on low-powered devices such as telephones using VoWLAN.

Wireless Mesh Routers

There are two significant limitations to the standard WLAN configuration of APs connected to a router via the wired network. First, placement of APs is limited because access points must be connected with a wired RJ-45 Ethernet connection to the existing wired network. An AP can only be placed where a wired connection is available. Second, APs have a limited range. If a client device is too far away from an AP then the signal is lost and the device must find another AP with which to associate.

These two limitations are being addressed through **mesh networks**. Instead of having only a single path through which data can travel, as seen in Figure 6-9, a mesh network provides multiple paths, as illustrated in Figure 6-10. The best example of a mesh network is the Internet, and this was the intent of its original design. In the early 1960s the United States was fearful of a nuclear attack. The government commissioned a study to determine how the military could maintain command and control over its missiles and bombers after an attack occurred. A standard network with only one path for data would not be useful because just one severed connection between the computers scattered across the country would prevent the entire network from functioning. The network that ultimately became the Internet was designed so that each device could receive transmissions through not just one but several data paths.

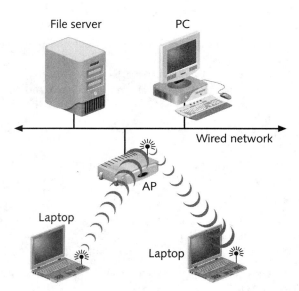

Figure 6-9   Single path for data between devices

NOTE   The interstate highway was likewise designed in response to the threat of a nuclear attack. Instead of just one road that runs between large cities, the interstate system provides multiple ways to travel between cities. If an attack destroyed one route, traffic could still continue through other routes.

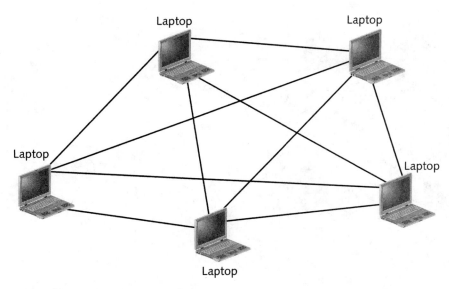

Laptop   Laptop

Laptop

Laptop

Laptop

6

Figure 6-10   Multiple data paths

A **wireless mesh network,** which allows for multiple data paths for wireless transmissions, can be one of two types. An **ad hoc wireless mesh network** is designed to allow wireless devices to be longer distances away from the access point. In this type of network, each client device can act as a relay station for signals to and from the access point. Any device within range of the AP can relay signals to and from other devices, therefore extending the distance from the AP for the other devices. Ad hoc wireless mesh networks are illustrated in Figure 6-11.

NOTE   Ad hoc wireless mesh networks should not be confused with wireless ad hoc networks. An ad hoc WLAN, also called a peer-to-peer WLAN, does not use an AP and therefore the devices only communicate between themselves and have no access to any external networks.

There are several advantages to ad hoc wireless mesh networks. Because each device only needs to transmit to the next closest device, this decentralized network can decrease costs by reducing the number of access points and wired connections that are necessary. These mesh networks can also be reliable: if one device leaves the network or has a hardware failure, the path can switch to a different route. However, in an ad hoc wireless mesh network that has a small number of wireless devices, the loss of one or more devices can have a negative impact on the overall network.

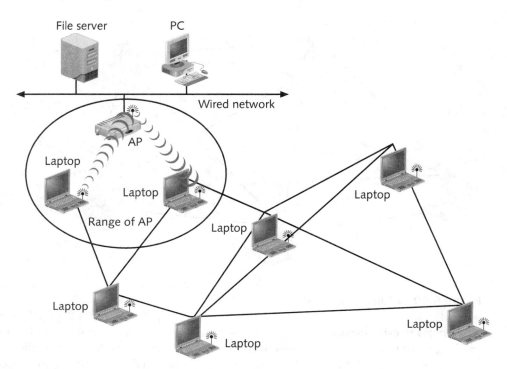

Figure 6-11   Ad hoc wireless mesh network

The second type of wireless mesh network is a **backhaul wireless mesh network**. Instead of connecting wireless devices through a mesh, this type of network connects special access points, known as **wireless mesh routers**, in a mesh configuration. A backhaul wireless mesh network provides alternative data paths for the "backside" connection to the Internet (that is, from the routers to the Internet, called the **backhaul**). Figure 6-12 illustrates a backhaul wireless mesh network. Note that only one of the wireless mesh routers needs to be connected to the wired network.

NOTE   The original IEEE 802.11 standard included an option for a wireless distribution system (WDS) that interconnected two APs wirelessly. However, it was never widely implemented.

Backhaul wireless mesh networks are used extensively in outdoor municipal WLANs. Depending on the amount of foliage or other physical interference and the general topography, between 10 and 20 wireless mesh routers per square mile of coverage are mounted on top of street lights or similar locations. Another advantage to backhaul wireless mesh networks is that they can be quickly deployed in an emergency.

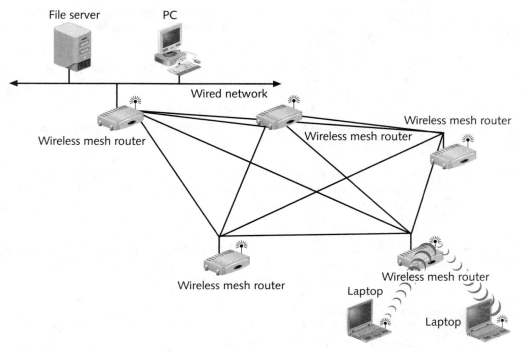

Figure 6-12 Backhaul wireless mesh network

NOTE

Backhaul wireless mesh networks were used extensively in the aftermath of the hurricanes that struck the U.S. coastlines in 2005 to provide communication facilities for rescue personnel.

Currently no standards exist for wireless mesh networks. The **IEEE 802.11s** task group is currently working on standards that may be completed some time in late 2007. In the interim there are over 70 different wireless mesh routing protocols from which to choose when implementing a wireless mesh network. These protocols differ concerning:

- *Algorithm*—The routing used should attempt to ensure that the data takes the most appropriate (fastest) route to its destination.

- *Management data versus transmit data*—Wireless devices in a wireless mesh network receive two types of data from other devices, management data and transmit data. To implement dynamic routing capabilities, each device must constantly communicate its routing information to every device within its area (management data). Devices also continually receive data from other devices that they are to pass on (transmit data). A device that receives data must quickly determine what it should do with it. If it is management data, it must keep it for reference and not pass it on;

if it is transmit data, it should not keep it but pass the data on to its neighbor based on the management data. Different protocols implement these techniques differently.

- *Number of radios*—Unlike IEEE 802.11 WLANs in which only one radio is used, many wireless mesh networks use wireless NIC adapters with multiple radios because a single radio in a wireless mesh network must handle three separate tasks: receive management data, send and receive transmit data, and transmit and receive its own data. When multiple radios are used, these functions are performed on separate radios.

 When using a single radio in a backhaul wireless mesh network, 30 to 50 percent of the access points must be directly connected to the wired network to provide the necessary performance.

NOTE

Wireless mesh networks hold a great deal of potential. Currently, backhaul wireless mesh networks are more common than ad hoc wireless mesh networks, although both types may show significant growth in the near future.

 The Wi-Mesh Alliance (WMA) is an organization of hardware, software, and other wireless vendors that is promoting IEEE 802.11s and wireless mesh networks. Their Web site is *www.wi-mesh.org*.

NOTE

Hardware Security Features

Wireless hardware includes additional security features to make the device and WLAN less vulnerable to attacks. These features include controlling access to hardware and protocol filtering.

Controlling Access to Hardware

Although authentication verifies that the person requesting access is who they claim to be, the task of protection does not stop there. The next logical step is to restrict the user to accessing only the resources essential for the user to do his or her job. This is known as access control. Access control is the mechanism for limiting access to resources based on the users' identity and their membership in various groups. Access control is typically used to control user access to network resources such as servers, directories, files, and printers through the operating system. In a wireless LAN, access control is often performed by enterprise wireless gateways.

To determine what access privileges to assign, one of three different models can be assigned: Mandatory Access Control, Role Based Access Control, or Discretionary Access Control.

Mandatory Access Control

The most restrictive model is known as **mandatory access control (MAC)**. In this model the user is not allowed to give access to another user to use or access anything on the network. Instead, all controls are fixed in place and there is no flexibility. MAC is typically used in military environments where "Secret" and "Top Secret" objects are commonplace.

Role Based Access Control (RBAC)

Handling the permissions for individual users and sometimes even groups can be a time-consuming task. First permissions must be set up, and then they must be adjusted as users take on new responsibilities or assume new job titles. Instead of setting permissions for each user or group, an administrator can assign permissions to a position or "role" and assign users and other objects to that role. The users and objects inherit all of the permissions for the role. This model is known as **role based access control (RBAC)**. For example, instead of creating a user account *Lysa.Berkley* and assigning privileges to that account, the role *Business Manager* can be created based on the privileges a business manager should have. Then, the user Lysa.Berkley can be assigned to that role.

NOTE   Individuals can hold multiple roles in RBAC. For example, Lysa Berkley could be assigned to both Business Manager and Accountant.

In Figure 6-13, roles are created for a variety of job classifications. Users are then assigned to those roles. The flexibility of RBAC makes it easy to establish permissions based on job classification and to enforce those permissions.

Business manager role   Accountant role   Director of finance role

Lysa Berkley   Juan Carlos   Amy Lyons   Jason Williams   Liz Sweeney

Tomas Carter   Paul Tyler

Figure 6-13   Role based access control (RBAC)

Discretionary Access Control

The least restrictive model is known as **discretionary access control (DAC)**. In this setting, the user can adjust the permissions for other users over network devices. Although it gives a degree of freedom to the user, DAC also poses risks in that incorrect permissions may be granted or given to a subject who should not have them.

NOTE   DAC is the type of access that most users associate with their personal computers. For example, in a Windows environment the user selects the file or folder to be shared and then sets the permissions so that other users can access it.

Protocol Filtering

Filtering restricts the traffic on a network based on specific criteria. There are basically three types of filtering:

- *Address filtering*—This restricts access based on the media access control number or IP address.

- *Data filtering*—Data filtering limits a packet based on the contents of what that packet is carrying.

- *Protocol filtering*—This filter restricts specific protocols from being transmitted on the network.

Some access points can be configured to filter unwanted protocols from either entering or leaving the wireless network. An access point that receives an inbound or outbound packet that is using a specific protocol will drop the packet and not allow it to enter or leave the network. Although protocol filtering is difficult for an attacker to circumvent, it can only be used in a few specific situations in which the user's activity is limited to a narrow set of actions that don't require the unwanted protocols.

Because of its limitations, protocol filtering is not widely implemented on wireless hardware. Many access points offer very limited protocol filtering, as seen in Figure 6-14. Those few access points that implement proper protocol filtering tend to be very high-end and expensive devices.

NOTE   If protocol filtering is permitted on an access point, the telnet protocol should be filtered. This prevents an attacker from the outside from breaking into an access point that allows telnet sessions.

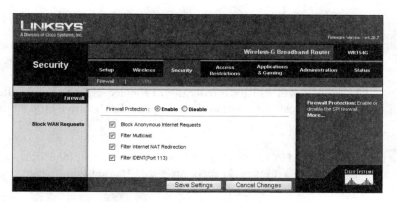

Figure 6-14 Limited protocol filtering

OTHER HARDWARE FEATURES

In addition to security features, wireless hardware also includes other features. These features include quality of service, fast handoff, and power features.

Quality of Service (IEEE 802.11e)

The IEEE 802.11 standard was intended to be a "fair" approach to wireless transmissions in that each wireless device station has an equal opportunity for accessing the medium. Although this works well for data transmissions, the same is not true for real-time traffic that is time dependent. These types of transmissions, like voice or video, depend heavily upon each frame arriving very quickly one after the other (data transmissions are not as sensitive to time). Delays in transmission can result in a video that "freezes" on the screen or a conversation that has gaps of dead space. IEEE 802.11 networks cannot distinguish between voice, video, and data frames to assure that time-sensitive frames have priority.

The capability to prioritize different types of frames is known as **Quality of Service (QoS)**. The **IEEE 802.11e** task group, which has been working on wireless QoS since May 2000, had its final draft approved as a standard in late 2005. The standard has two new modes of operation for the 802.11 MAC layer. The first is known as **Enhanced Distributed Channel Access (EDCA)** which is still contention-based yet supports different "streams" (types) of traffic. These four different streams, called **access categories (AC)**, are differentiated in terms of priority. The ACs ranked from highest priority to lowest are:

- Voice
- Video
- Best effort
- Background

QoS on WLANs has become an increasing area of interest with the widespread adoption of voice over wireless LAN (VoWLAN).

NOTE

With EDCA, wireless devices will still have to contend for access, but the channel access parameters will differ from one AC to another. EDCA provides "relative" QoS but cannot guarantee its service.

One of the weaknesses of EDCA is that any user can request a priority in service, meaning that potentially a user could mark an e-mail transmission as high importance to speed it through the WLAN.

NOTE

The second mode is **Hybrid Coordination Function Controlled Channel Access (HCCA)**, which is based upon polling. It serves as a centralized scheduling mechanism. For example, a transmission would send a resource reservation request to the access point. The access point would then provide an appropriate assignment based on the data rate, frame size, and other parameters.

EDCA is expected to be deployed in enterprise business settings whereas HCCA may find its position in the consumer electronics industry for wireless audiovisual distribution in the home.

NOTE

While the IEEE 802.11e committee was working, the Wi-Fi Alliance released its own QoS specification in 2004 known as **Wi-Fi Multimedia (WMM)**. WMM is modeled after a wired network QoS prioritization scheme and is a subset of IEEE 802.11e. Like 802.11e, WMM specifies four levels of service: voice, video, best effort, and background. During a regular transmission using the IEEE 802.11 Carrier Sense Multiple Access/Collision Avoidance (CSMA/CA) protocol, each wireless device must wait a random amount of time after every transmission. WMM uses different fixed and random wait times for the four categories. Fixed times are known as the **Arbitrary Inter-frame Space Number (AIFSN)** whereas random times are called the **contention window**. The four levels of prioritization and their times are summarized in Table 6-1.

Wait times are measured in "slots." The slot time of an 802.11g and 802.11a device is 9 microseconds; for an 802.11b it is 20 microseconds.

NOTE

Table 6-1   Wi-Fi Multimedia (WMM)

WMM Access Category	Description	AIFSN	Contention Window	Total Wait Time
WMM Voice priority	The highest priority; facilitates multiple high-quality voice calls	2 slots	0–3 slots	2–5 slots
WMM Video priority	Prioritizes video traffic higher than regular data traffic but not as high as voice traffic	2 slots	0–7 slots	2–9 slots
WMM Best Effort priority	Includes traffic from applications that are not time sensitive	3 slots	0–15 slots	3–18 slots
WMM Background priority	Includes low-priority traffic, such as file transfers or print jobs	7 slots	0–15 slots	7–22 slots

NOTE   Several vendors currently support WMM in their products. You will explore WMM using a Linksys device in Hands-On Project 6-5.

Handoffs

Another feature that some types of wireless hardware support is enhanced handoff capabilities. These include the Inter-Access Protocol (IEEE 802.11F) and fast handoff (IEEE 802.11r).

Inter-Access Point Protocol (IEEE 802.11F)

The original 802.11 standard did not specify how communications were to take place between access points to support users roaming from one area of AP coverage to another. Rather than being an oversight, this was intended. The committee wanted to provide flexibility in environments using different distribution systems, such as a wired backbone that may interconnect with an AP. Yet this lack of standardization caused problems. An AP from one vendor handled the handoff in one way whereas that from another vendor implemented a different solution. The result was that access points from different vendors did not always interoperate when a wireless user roamed from one vendor's AP to another vendor's.

To solve this problem, **IEEE 802.11F** recommended practice was created. Using the **Inter-Access Point Protocol (IAPP)**, 802.11F specified information that access points need to exchange to support WLAN roaming. The inclusion of 802.11F in the design of APs has ensured that interoperability exists between different vendors' APs.

This standard was officially withdrawn by IEEE in February 2006 and is now a recommendation instead of an official standard. The use of the capital F instead of lowercase f indicates it is a recommendation.

NOTE

Fast Handoff (IEEE 802.11r)

Although IAPP improved handoffs between access points, it did not address how *quickly* this handoff should occur. With wireless devices sending and receiving data only, this was not an issue. Roaming delays for WLANs average in the hundreds of milliseconds, which is acceptable for data transmissions. However, when wireless clients such as mobile phones are using VoWLAN, they must be able to quickly drop the association from one AP and reconnect to another because a delay longer than 50 milliseconds may degrade the quality of the voice transmission or cause the connection to be lost altogether. Therefore fast handoffs are necessary for wireless networks that are using VoWLAN.

Fifty microseconds is also the smallest interval that can be detected by the human ear.

NOTE

Another issue with the current 802.11 standard when using VoWLAN is that a wireless mobile phone cannot know if QoS is implemented on another AP until after the handoff has taken place. This means that a user cannot know if his telephone conversation can be fully supported until after roaming into a new area of coverage. If the user knew in advance that the new coverage area did not support QoS he could make an informed decision whether to continue a telephone conversation when roaming into a new coverage area or remain in the old area of coverage until the call is completed.

To address these issues a standard is being developed known as **fast handoff** or **IEEE 802.11r.** This standard streamlines the transition process of a mobile client as it roams between APs. The protocol allows a wireless client to determine the QoS (and security) being used at a different AP before making the transition. This "looking ahead" is possible because the wireless device can have its current access point "ask" other access points for their information. This communication can be performed by the AP sending an RF transmission request to another AP or through the wired backhaul.

IEEE 802.11r does not introduce any new security vulnerabilities.

NOTE

The IEEE 802.11r standard, expected to be ratified in 2007, is designed to accelerate the convergence of voice, data, and video transmissions on a WLAN. This will lead to improved functionality and performance for mobile wireless users.

Power Features

Some types of wireless hardware also support enhanced power features. These features include dynamic frequency and power control (IEEE 802.11h) and power over Ethernet (IEEE 802.3af).

Dynamic Frequency and Power Control (IEEE 802.11h)

Because each nation governs the use of its radio frequency spectrum, conflicts can sometimes occur when a WLAN manufactured in one nation for a specific frequency cannot be used in another country because of spectrum restrictions. This was the case with IEEE 802.11a WLANs that use the 5 GHz frequency (known as the UNII band in the United States) yet that same band is reserved in other nations for military use.

The **IEEE 802.11h** standard is designed to enable WLAN devices to share the 5 GHz spectrum with other devices such as military radar systems. There are two primary mechanisms of IEEE 802.11h. The first is **dynamic frequency selection (DFS)**. DFS detects other devices using the same radio channel and then switches the WLAN operation to another channel if necessary. This prevents interference with other devices such as radar systems.

When using DFS, an access point continuously measures channel activity to detect outside radio traffic. If any traffic is detected, the AP sends a measurement request to a wireless device to monitor that specific channel. The measurement request includes the channel to be monitored, the start time of the measurement, and the duration of the measurement. After the device performs the requested measurement of channel activity, it generates data that is then returned to the access point. If the data indicates another outside device is using that channel, the AP initiates a channel switch by sending a frame to all associated devices that identifies the new channel number, the length of time until the channel switch takes effect, and whether transmission is allowed before the channel switch. Stations that receive the channel switch information from the AP change to the new channel after the elapsed time.

Transmit power control (TPC) is also designed to reduce interference to other systems. This is accomplished by reducing the radio transmit power that the WLAN devices use. When a wireless device associates with an AP, the device informs the AP of its transmit power capability. The access point uses this data about the stations associated with it to compute the maximum power needed for the network. If other radio traffic is detected from outside systems, the AP can dynamically reduce the radio signal strength to maintain wireless communications yet not interfere with other systems. Because the AP already knows the power capability of each wireless device, it can adjust signal strength to reduce interference with other devices while still maintaining sufficient power for operation of the wireless network.

As with DFS, with TPC wireless devices can be requested to monitor the signal strength of the wireless network.

Although IEEE 802.11h was designed to ensure cooperation between devices in the 5 GHz band, this standard has additional benefits. DFS and TPC can be used to improve the overall management and operation of IEEE 802.11a networks, which operate in the 5 GHz spectrum.

Power over Ethernet (IEEE 802.3af)

Access points are typically mounted on a ceiling or a similar area high off the ground to reduce interference from surrounding objects. However, electrical power outlets are generally not found in these locations. In these cases **Power over Ethernet (PoE)**, based on the **IEEE 802.3af** standard, has solved the problem. Instead of receiving power directly from an alternating current (AC) electrical outlet, direct current (DC) power is delivered to the AP through the unused wires in a standard unshielded twisted pair (UTP) Ethernet cable that connects the AP to the wired network. This eliminates the need for installing electrical wiring and makes mounting APs more flexible.

The IEEE 802.3af standard defines two types of equipment for sending the power to the AP. The most common is known as an **end-span**. An end-span is an Ethernet switch that has embedded PoE technology. The end-span first must know that a device connected to it needs power. Devices that can support PoE send the end-span an authenticated PoE "signature" indicating that they support this technology, which helps prevent damage to other equipment. Once the end-span knows that the device can accept the power, it sends power along one pair of unused wires in the cable. The total amount of continuous power that can be sent to each device is 12.95 watts. VoWLAN phones and wireless LAN access points typically consume 3.5 to 10 watts.

An end-span can safely support both PoE devices and non-PoE devices.

Another advantage of PoE is that a single uninterruptible power supply (UPS) can be used to protect all devices connected to the end-span instead of requiring one for each separate device. Also, PoE provides remote access and management via SNMP.

However, what would happen if an incident occurs and power to WLAN hardware, such as a remote wireless bridge, is interrupted? If it is critical that the specific device not have any interruption, then **failover support** can be implemented. Failover support is accomplished by having duplicate equipment, known as a **hot standby**, functioning alongside the main equipment. If an event occurs in which the primary device can no longer properly function, failover support will automatically substitute the hot standby in its place.

CHAPTER SUMMARY

❏ Different types of wireless hardware are typically found in an enterprise environment besides an access point. A remote wireless bridge connects two or more wired or wireless networks. A wireless router combines an access point with a router. A wireless gateway is a network device that adds functionality to a wireless router. A wireless switch has the functionality of an access point and is used together with a thin access point. A wireless mesh router allows for multiple data paths for wireless transmissions.

❏ Access control is the mechanism for limiting access to resources based on the users' identity and membership in various groups. There are three types of access control: mandatory access control, role based access control, and discretionary access control.

❏ Some access points can be configured to filter unwanted protocols from entering or leaving the wireless network. An access point that receives an inbound or outbound packet that is using a specific protocol will drop the packet and not allow it to enter or leave the network.

❏ The capability to prioritize different types of frames is known as Quality of Service. The IEEE 802.11e standard and Wi-Fi Multimedia both provide QoS.

❏ The Inter-Access Point Protocol (used in IEEE 802.11F) sets standards for handoffs between access points. Fast handoff is based on the IEEE 802.11r standard.

❏ Two types of power management can be found in enterprise wireless devices. The IEEE 802.11h standard enables 802.11a devices to interoperate in environments in which other devices use the 5 GHz spectrum band. Power over Ethernet (IEEE 802.3af) sends DC power to devices over an unused pair of wires in an Ethernet cable.

KEY TERMS

access categories (AC) — Different streams of traffic under EDCA, prioritized for voice, video, best effort, and background.

access control — The mechanisms for limiting access to resources based on the users' identity and their membership in various groups.

access point mode — A remote wireless bridge configuration in which the device functions as a standard access point only and does not communicate with other remote wireless bridges.

ad hoc wireless mesh network — A wireless network that is designed so that wireless devices can be longer distances away from the access point.

Arbitrary Inter-Frame Space Number (AIFSN) — Fixed slot times of the WMM standard.

backhaul — The wired connection from the access point to the wired Internet connection.

backhaul wireless mesh network — A wireless mesh network that connects wireless mesh routers together.

bridge — Device used to connect two network segments, even if those segments use different types of physical media, such as wired and wireless connections.

contention window — Random slot times of the WMM standard.

delay spread — A technique that minimizes the spread of the signal so that it can reach farther distances.

discretionary access control (DAC) — An access control model in which the user can adjust the permissions for other users over network devices.

dynamic frequency selection (DFS) — A technology that detects other devices using the same radio channel and then switches the WLAN operation to another channel if necessary.

end-span — An Ethernet switch that has embedded Power over Ethernet (PoE) technology.

Enhanced Distributed Channel Access (EDCA) — A mode of IEEE 802.11e QoS that is contention-based yet supports different types of traffic.

failover support — The ability to absorb equipment failures by using redundant equipment.

fast handoff — A standard that streamlines the transition process of a mobile client as it roams between APs. Also known as IEEE 802.11r.

gateway — A network device that acts as an entrance to another network.

hot standby — Equipment that is functioning alongside main equipment to provide failover support.

hub — A network device that joins multiple computers within one local area network (LAN) by sending packets to all attached devices.

Hybrid Coordination Function Controlled Channel Access (HCCA) — A mode of IEEE 802.11e QoS that is based upon polling.

IEEE 802.11e — The standard for wireless Quality of Service (QoS).

IEEE 802.11F — A recommended practice that specifies how roaming between access points should take place.

IEEE 802.11h — A standard that specifies how WLAN devices can share the 5 GHz spectrum with other devices.

IEEE 802.11r — A standard that streamlines the transition process of a mobile client as it roams between APs. Also known as fast handoff.

IEEE 802.11s — A proposed standard for wireless mesh networks.

IEEE 802.11v — A protocol designed to assist with the management of WLAN devices.

IEEE 802.3af — A standard that defines the technology for sending power to devices through the unused wires of an Ethernet cable, also known as Power over Ethernet (PoE).

Inter-Access Point Protocol (IAPP) — A protocol used by IEEE 802.11F that specifies how roaming between access points should take place.

managed switch — A switch that provides all of the features of an unmanaged switch along with enhanced management features.

mandatory access control (MAC) — An access control model in which the user is not allowed to give access to another user to use or access anything on the network.

mesh network — A network that provides multiple data paths.

non-root mode — A remote wireless bridge configuration in which the device can only transmit to another bridge that is in root mode.

point-to-multipoint — A remote wireless bridge configuration that is used to connect multiple LAN segments.

point-to-point — A remote wireless bridge configuration used to connect two LAN segments.

Power over Ethernet (PoE) — A technology that sends power to devices through the unused wires of an Ethernet cable.

Quality of Service (QoS) — The capability to prioritize different types of frames.

remote wireless bridge — Wireless device designed to connect two or more wired or wireless networks together.

repeater mode — A remote wireless bridge configuration in which another remote wireless bridge may be positioned between two other bridges.

role based access control (RBAC) — An access control model in which permissions are assigned to a position or role.

root bridge — A device that cannot communicate with another root bridge or any wireless clients.

root mode — A remote wireless bridge configuration in which the bridge can only communicate with other bridges that are not in root mode.

router — A network device that transfers packets between networks.

switch — A network device that joins multiple computers within one LAN by sending packets to only the intended recipient.

thin access point — An access point with limited functions, used in conjunction with a wireless switch.

transmit power control (TPC) — A technology designed to reduce interference from WLANs to other services by reducing the power level of the network.

unmanaged switch — A switch that provides no management capabilities in the operation of the switch.

Wi-Fi Multimedia (WMM) — The Wi-Fi Alliance QoS specification, released in 2004.

wireless mesh network — A wireless network that allows for multiple data paths for wireless transmissions.

wireless mesh router — A device that provides alternative data paths for the "backside" connection to the Internet.

wireless router — A network device that combines an access point with a router.

wireless switch — A network switch that contains authentication and encryption services for a WLAN.

REVIEW QUESTIONS

1. Each of the following is part of an access point except
   a. antenna
   b. RJ-45 wired network interface
   c. bridging software
   d. delay spectrum (DT)

2. Each of the following are modes of a remote wireless bridge except
   a. access point mode
   b. root mode
   c. node mode
   d. non-root mode

3. The type of antenna used by a remote wireless bridge is a(n)
   a. dipole antenna
   b. omni-directional antenna
   c. highly directional antenna
   d. semi-directional antenna

4. A(n) _____ is a network device that transfers packets between networks.
   a. router
   b. hub
   c. switch
   d. managed switch

5. A(n) _____ assumes the functions of an access point in a wireless network.
   a. wireless switch
   b. wireless hub
   c. gateway
   d. wireless access port (WAP)

6. Thin APs and wireless switches are proprietary, so that a switch must be mated with a specific brand of AP from a single vendor. True or False?

7. Instead of having only two paths through which data may travel, a mesh network provides three paths. True or False?

8. An ad hoc wireless mesh network is designed to provide longer distances for wireless devices to be away from the access point. True or False?

9. Backhaul wireless mesh networks are used extensively in outdoor municipal WLANs. True or False?

10. Access control is the mechanism for limiting access to resources based on the users' identity and membership in various groups. True or False?

11. The capability to prioritize different types of frames is known as _____ *qos* _____ .

12. The highest priority of Enhanced Distributed Channel Access (EDCA) is _____ *voice* _____ .

13. The Wi-Fi Alliance has released its own QoS specification known as _____ *WMM* _____ .

14. The _____ *IAPP* _____ standardizes how APs hand off roaming between devices.

15. _____ *fast handoff* _____ or IEEE 802.11r streamlines the transition process of a mobile client as it roams between APs.

16. Explain how dynamic frequency selection (DFS) functions.

17. Explain how Power over Ethernet (PoE) works.

18. What is a wireless switch and a thin access point? How do they function?

19. What is a backhaul wireless mesh network?

20. What is role based access control (RBAC)?

HANDS-ON PROJECTS

Project 6-1: Set QoS in Cisco WLAN

The Cisco Aironet series of access points supports Quality of Service (QoS) for wireless LANs. In this project you adjust settings on the Cisco AP to support QoS. Note that you will not actually implement these settings for the network in this activity.

1. Access the Cisco AP by pointing your browser to its IP address.

2. Enter the username and password.

3. Click **SERVICES** in the left pane.

4. Click **QoS** to display the **QoS Policies** screen.

5. Enter **VoWLAN** in the **Policy Name** field.

6. In the **IP Precedence:** field click the drop-down menu and select **Routine (0)** if it is not already selected.

The IP Precedence setting can be used to identify packets that contain information in the IP header regarding their precedence.

NOTE

7. In the first **Apply Class of Service** drop-down menu select **Voice < 100ms Latency (5)**. If this class of service is not available, select **Voice < 10ms Latency (6)**. Click **Add**.

8. Click the **Radio0–802.11x Traffic Classes** (where x is the letter of the IEEE 802.11 WLAN for this AP) tab.

9. Notice that you can change the contention window and the slot time for each class of service.

10. Click your browser's **Back** button to return to the QoS Policies screen.

11. Click the **Cancel** button so that these settings are not applied.

12. Close the Web browser.

HANDS-ON PROJECTS

Project 6-2: Modifying AP Transmit Power and Antenna Diversity

The IEEE 802.11h standard will dynamically change frequency and power settings to reduce conflicts between an IEEE 802.11a WLAN and other external devices. Some enterprise access points allow these settings to be changed manually to reduce conflicts. In this project you will adjust the power output of a Cisco AP and its antenna settings, and then note its impact. Be sure to make a written record of any settings before changing them so that they can be set back once the activity is completed.

1. Use a wireless notebook to determine the maximum range of the Cisco AP. If you have the Cisco Aironet Client Utility installed, launch the application and click **Link Status**. If this application is not available, you can use Windows Wireless Zero Configuration instead. Click **Start** and **Control Panel** (in Category View) and **Network and Internet Connections**. Click **Network Connections** then double-click on the wireless network connection of the notebook to display a dialog box with a graph of the signal strength.

2. Monitor the strength of the Link Status meter as you move away from the AP. Note the farthest point in which you can receive a signal.

3. Access the Cisco access point by pointing your browser to its IP address.

4. Enter the username and password.

5. Click **NETWORK INTERFACES** on the menu on the left side.

6. Click **Radio0–802.11x**, where x is the letter of the IEEE standard on which the AP is based. Depending on the IEEE standard your Cisco AP is using your menu may be *Radio0-802.11b, Radio0-802.11a,* or *Radio0-802.11g.*

7. Click the **SETTINGS** tab to display the radio options.

8. Make a written record of the **Transmit Power (mW)**, which is sent from the AP to the wireless devices, and the **Limit Client Power (mW)**.

9. Modify the **Transmit Power** to half of what it was set to. For example, if it was set to 100 mW (or Max) set it to **50 mW.**

10. With a wireless notebook now repeat the same test as in Step 2. How far were you able to roam away from the AP now?

11. Modify the **Transmit Power** to the minimum and roam again with the notebook. What are the differences in range between the original setting on the AP, transmitted at half power, and transmitting at the lowest level of power?

12. Return to the same AP screen and scroll down to see **Receive Antenna** and **Transmit Antenna** and note the settings. Change these settings to **Left** and roam with the wireless notebook. What changes in distance can you see?

13. Now change the **Receive Antenna** and **Transmit Antenna** to **Right** and run the same tests once again, noting any differences.

14. Write a one-paragraph explanation of the impact of changing the power levels and antenna diversity.

15. Adjust the settings in the Cisco AP back to their original state.

16. Close all windows.

Project 6-3: Enable Cisco Management Information Logging

One of the important steps in managing a WLAN is to view the log files of transactions that occur. The Cisco Aironet AP provides utilities that give three sets of information: event logs, wireless transmissions statistics, and wired Ethernet network data. In this project you view all three data sets.

1. Connect to the Cisco access point and enter the username and password.

2. Click **NETWORK INTERFACES** in the left pane.

3. Click **FastEthernet** to view the wired network Ethernet data. Under **Error Statistics** a number of terms are used that may be new, such as "Babbles" and "Late Collisions". Use the Internet or textbooks to define the terms with which you are unfamiliar.

4. Click the **SETTINGS** tab to see the Ethernet settings for the AP.

5. In the left pane click **Radio0–802.11x** where "x" is the type of IEEE standard (a, b or g) on which the access point is based.

6. Click the **RADIO0–802.11X STATUS** tab to see a summary of the wireless information.

7. Click the **DETAILED STATUS** tab to see detailed information. Select two of the statistics with which you are not familiar and find a definition for those terms. What do these statistics reveal about the health of your wireless LAN?

8. Click the **SETTINGS** tab to see the current radio settings for the AP.

9. Click **EVENT LOG** in the left pane to display the Aironet Event Log page.

10. Click the **Previous** button several times to navigate to the beginning of this log file or, if the log file is too large, to at least four or five screens "deep." What type of "Error" messages are displayed? What type of "Notification" messages are found? Would this data be helpful in managing the WLAN?

11. Click **Configuration Options** to display the options.

12. Under **Time Stamp Format for Future Events**, click **Local Time**. This will give the time the event occurred instead of the time relative to when the AP was started.

13. If necessary, increase the **Event Log Size:** and **History Table Size:** to accommodate more data.

14. Click **Apply**. Click **OK** if a warning dialog box appears.

15. Close all windows.

Project 6-4: Enabling Linksys Management Information Logging

Like the enterprise-based Cisco AP, Linksys also has a logging feature. In this activity you turn on and view Linksys logging.

1. Point your browser to the Linksys access point.

2. Enter the username and password.

3. Click **Administration**.

4. Click **Log**.

5. Click **Enable** to start the Linksys logging feature.

6. Click **Incoming Log**. What information do you receive in this log file?

7. Click **Outgoing Log**. What information is contained in this file?

8. Compare these files with the Cisco log above. What are the differences between them? Which file contains more useful information?

9. Close your browser.

Project 6-5: Configuring Linksys Quality of Service

Linksys wireless access points include two types of Quality of Service (QoS) features. The first is known as Wired QoS. This prioritizes packets to wired devices or those that are connected to the AP with a standard Ethernet patch cable. Wireless QoS is used for regulating traffic to wireless devices. In this activity you turn on and view Linksys QoS.

1. Point your browser to the Linksys access point.

2. Enter the username and password.

3. Click **Applications & Gaming**.

4. Click on **QoS**. When the Linksys QoS screen appears, click **Enable**, as seen in Figure 6-15.

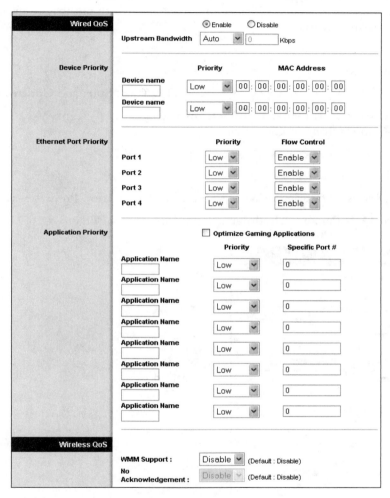

Figure 6-15   Linksys QoS

5. Wired QoS can be set based on either the device, the Ethernet port, or the application. Under **Device Priority** enter **Device1** under the **Device Name**.

6. Change **Priority** to **Highest**.

7. Enter the MAC address of a wired device on the network. If you do not know the MAC address then click **Start** and **Run** and type **cmd** and click **Enter** on that wired device. Enter **ipconfig/all** to display the address.

8. Scroll down to **Wireless QoS**.

9. Under **WMM Support:** change the setting to **Enable**. This will turn on WMM.

10. Change **No Acknowledgement:** to **Enable**. This will configure the AP to not resend data if an error occurs, which can increase bandwidth but may result in a higher number of errors.

11. Click **Save Settings**.

12. Close all windows.

13. On each wireless device you must now turn on QoS. Click **Start** and **Control Panel**.

14. Click **Network and Internet Connections** if you are in Category View or **Network Connections** in Classic view.

15. Click **Network Connections** if you are in Category View.

16. Right-click on your wireless connection.

17. Click **Properties** to display the Wireless Network Connection Properties window.

18. Be sure that **QoS Packet Scheduler** is checked, as seen in Figure 6-16.

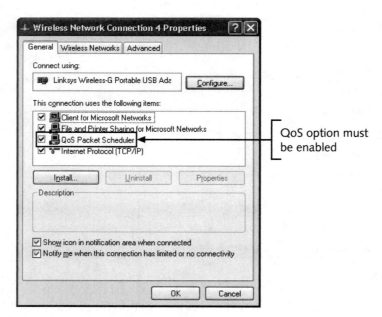

Figure 6-16   QoS Packet Scheduler

19. Close all windows.

CASE PROJECTS

Case Project 6-1: Remote Wireless Bridge Application

Is there an application for a remote wireless bridge at your school or place of business? By talking with your network manager, determine the data transmissions that occur between two locations of the organization that do not exceed about 25 miles. Ask what type of connection is used (such as a T1 line) and find out approximately what the cost is per month. Then contact vendors or use the Internet to price a remote wireless bridge that could be used instead. Estimate the installation costs and then compute how long it would take before the wireless bridge would pay for itself. Would you recommend a switch to a remote wireless bridge? Write a one-page paper regarding your research.

Case Project 6-2: Cost of Wireless Gateways

Using the Internet and other sources, select two wireless gateways for home use and one for enterprise use. Make a list of features that compare the two categories, including cost. What additional features does the enterprise wireless gateway have that the home model does not? Are these features worth the additional cost? Do the additional costs of an enterprise wireless gateway make that hardware the better buy? Write a one-page paper on your results.

Case Project 6-3: Wireless Switches and Thin Access Points

How do wireless switches and thin access points compare to a network that uses standard APs? Design a network on paper that has five access points and 20 users per AP. Using the Internet and other sources, determine what the costs would be for the equipment. Then, estimate what installation costs would be for running a wired Ethernet connection to the five access points (you may have to ask your network administrator for assistance on this cost). Finally, estimate the average hourly costs of a wireless network administrator to manage five access points, assuming that each AP must be individually configured, once each month for 12 months for one hour each (most of this time is spent moving from one AP to another and configuring the changes). Now price a wireless switch and five thin access points. Because thin APs do not require a wired network connection, there will be no installation costs for them. Management costs will be reduced to only one hour per month for all five APs because no travel time is required and all can be set up simultaneously. Based on your estimates, is a wireless network of five standard APs more expensive over a year than for a network with a wireless switch and thin access points? If not, how many access points make this configuration feasible? Write a one-page paper on your findings.

Case Project 6-4: Management Tools

Managing a wireless network is critical. Until the IEEE 802.11v standard is ratified, products like Cisco's SWAN are common for managing a wireless network. What other products are available? Use the Internet to identify other management tools. Create a table that compares features, advantages, disadvantages, and prices. Which product would you recommend?

Case Project 6-5: Wireless Mesh Networks

Using the Internet and other sources, identify five backhaul wireless mesh networks in your state or region. Why was the network developed? Who manages the network? What protocols are they using? How many APs are used in the network? Write a one-page paper on your research.

Fairvue Technology Consulting

Fairvue consulting wants to hire you to help them with a special project. Rosser Road Warriors is a company that is contracted by music bands to set up and tear down the stages used by bands when they travel. Although Rosser has used cell phones for communications between their employees while working at the venue, they are now looking at moving to voice over WLAN (VoWLAN) as an alternative communication infrastructure.

1. Prepare a PowerPoint presentation that outlines the advantages and disadvantages of VoWLAN for this setting. Include technical information regarding how VoWLAN functions. Your presentation should be about 6–8 slides in length.

2. Rosser Road Warriors is impressed with the presentation but is also concerned about roaming. They have asked for research regarding fast handoff and IEEE 802.11r. Use the Internet and other sources to research fast handoff. Write a one-page summary of this technology and how it would impact your proposal.

DESIGNING A SECURE WIRELESS NETWORK

After completing this chapter you should be able to do the following:

➤ Describe the basic principles of security design

➤ Define network segmentation and tell how it can be used for WLANs

➤ List ways in which wireless hardware can be located securely

➤ Describe the steps that can be taken to protect wireless devices

The World of Wireless Security

When the MetroHealth System in Cleveland opened its new Critical Care Pavilion (CCP) in June 2004, the expansion was impressive. A new emergency department, along with 17 new surgical suites, doubled the floor space and tripled the number of monitored beds. MetroHealth serves over 70,000 critical care patients annually and is the only Level 1 trauma center in the upper Ohio region. Though all this is impressive, perhaps even more amazing is that MetroHealth added CCP without hiring any new staff to support it. How could a medical facility dramatically increase its size and still provide top-notch patient care with no additional staffing? According to the vice president of MetroHealth, the answer is simple: wireless.

MetroHealth installed a wireless IEEE 802.11b data network along with a Voice over Wireless LAN (VoWLAN) system to support the CCP. This combination of wireless data and voice has significantly increased the level of patient care. For example, when emergency department nurses come on duty they log their wireless portable phones into the nurse call system along with their patient assignments for the shift. Software automatically links a nurse's phone not only to the phones of her assigned patients but to the cardiac monitors and call buttons in the rooms. No matter where a nurse is in the CCP, she can receive a call on her VoWLAN portable phone as well. Nurses also receive immediate data alerts from monitoring devices over their phones. If a patient's vital signs change, a monitor sends an alert to the patient's nurse through the wireless phone, and if a monitor registers an emergency, all on-duty staffers are immediately notified on their wireless phones. VoWLAN has also made paging doctors more efficient. Instead of emergency department nurses using desk phones to page doctors and then waiting by the phone to receive the return call, a nurse can make the page via her portable VoWLAN phone, and the doctor's return call is received in the same manner.

Although the wireless voice and data system cost over $170,000, savings were recognized immediately. For example, because five staffers did not have to continuously watch patient monitors, MetroHealth saved over $200,000 in its first year. Yet the real benefit, according to the vice president, is the increase in the level of patient care that the wireless system allows them to provide.

Of course, security is key to this system. Because of the confidentiality of patient records required by the Health Insurance Portability and Accountability Act of 1996 (HIPAA), MetroHealth protects the transmissions to prevent unauthorized users from intercepting the information.

Installing the most expensive and up-to-date enterprise wireless hardware and implementing all of the security features available is of limited value in protecting against attackers if the wireless network has not been designed properly. A poorly designed network can leave gaping holes in the security perimeter and provide attackers with numerous entry points that are undetectable by security hardware. Poorly designed networks are one of the major reasons wireless and wired networks are the victims of successful attacks.

Yet it does not have to be this way. A solid network design is a key element in building the security that is needed. This chapter begins by discussing the basics of secure network design and how that design can play an important role in the overall security of the network. Then, you will learn about network segmentation and how to protect remote hardware. Finally, you will learn about security on the wireless devices themselves.

BASIC PRINCIPLES OF SECURITY DESIGN

Consider some of the ways that information on wireless networks can be attacked: weaknesses in the IEEE 802.11 protocol can be exploited, data can be gathered through social engineering, denial of service attacks can be generated by outside attackers, and direct attacks can be launched through rogue access points. Protecting against this wide range of attacks calls for a wide range of defense mechanisms.

Although different defenses are necessary to withstand different types of wireless attacks, these varied defenses are founded upon five key security principles: layering, limiting, diversity, obscurity, and simplicity. This section examines each of these principles, which provide a conceptual foundation for building a secure wireless system.

Layering

At any given time a bank may have tens of thousands of dollars in cash on hand. What security is used to protect the money from theft? There is not a single type of security, such as a front door with a strong lock. Rather, there are several types of security. In addition to a front door with a strong lock, there may also be video cameras, armed guards, motion detectors, and a vault.

Each of these types of bank security is designed to coordinate with the other types of security to create layers of protection around the money. A front door with a strong lock may be the first layer of security, followed by video cameras, motion detectors, armed guards, and finally the vault. The philosophy behind layering security is that an attacker who is able to penetrate one layer (by breaking down the front door) would then face additional layers of security (an armed guard, motion detectors, and a vault) before reaching the money. A layered approach has the advantage of creating a barrier of multiple defenses that can thwart a thief who is able to break through one layer. In addition, layers can prevent a variety of attacks: layers of security at a bank can stop both a midnight break-in as well as a holdup in broad daylight.

Wireless security likewise should be created in layers. Implementing only one or two defense mechanisms, such as using the transitional security model or a hardened wireless switch, may not be sufficient to fend off an attacker. Instead, a wireless security system must be designed with multiple layers, making it unlikely that an attacker possesses the tools and skills to break through all the layers of defenses. Good door locks will keep an attacker (who may have entered the building through social engineering) from accessing a room that contains the wireless switch. Antivirus software can repel virus attacks launched through a rogue access point. Strong passwords will keep at bay attackers who are trying to break into a remote wireless bridge. Because there is no single point of failure, a layered security approach provides the most comprehensive protection and can resist a variety of attacks.

However, one problem with a layered approach is that all the layers must be properly coordinated. If the armed guards who protect the money set off the motion detection alarm as they make their rounds, it is obvious that the layers of security were not properly coordinated. The end result is often that one layer is weakened (by turning off the motion detection system while guards are on duty) so that another layer can function. This approach weakens security by creating holes. It is critical that all of the wireless security tools be properly coordinated to provide a cohesive security perimeter.

Limiting

Consider again protecting the money at a bank. Although a bank may have thousands of dollars on hand, permitting just anyone to touch the money only increases the chances that it will be stolen. Only approved personnel should be authorized to handle the bills. Limiting who can access it reduces the threat against it.

The same is true with wireless security. Limiting access to information reduces the threat against it. Only those who must use data should have access to it. In addition, the amount of access granted to someone should be limited to what that person needs to know. For example, access to the management features of access points should be limited to approved technicians and security personnel. An office worker may be using the wireless LAN provided by the access point, but he should not be able to view or configure the AP settings because he has no job-related need to do so.

Limiting is much more than placing a password on a system to keep unauthorized persons out. Advanced tools are available that restrict what a user is capable of doing on his or her own computer. Security managers can lock down users' systems that not only limit where they can make a wireless connection, but also restrict which application programs they can access and prevent them from copying a file to a USB memory device. These are designed not to cripple the productivity of the user but instead to apply adequate security to protect important information.

NOTE Limiting access to information involves more than only people. Computer programs, for example, should be limited to a security context that allows the program to execute but not perform tasks beyond what it needs to do. If an attacker can compromise a program that is running under the administrative account, the program can access more resources and cause more damage.

What level of access should users have? The answer is the least amount necessary to do their jobs, and no more. There are a number of ways in which access can be limited: some are technology based (such as assigning file permissions so that a user can read but not modify a file) whereas others are procedural (prohibiting an employee from removing a sensitive document from the premises). The key is that access must be restricted to the bare minimum. Although not always a popular approach with employees who may feel they are not being trusted, restricting access is vital in protecting information.

Diversity

Diversity is closely related to layering. Just as it is necessary to protect data with layers of security, so too must the layers be different (diverse), so that if a thief penetrates one layer he cannot use the same techniques to break through all other layers. For example, a thief might be able to foil the security camera in a bank by dressing in black clothes but should not be able to use the same steps to trick the motion detection system.

Using diverse layers of defense means that breaching one wireless security layer does not compromise the entire system. This can be achieved in different ways. It is possible to set a firewall to filter a specific type of traffic, such as all inbound traffic, while a second firewall on the same system filters other traffic types, such as outbound traffic. In addition, using firewalls produced by different vendors creates even greater diversity: an attacker who can get though a Brand A firewall would have more difficulty trying to break through a Brand B firewall because they are different. In wireless networks, diversity in the transitional security model involves implementing both MAC address filtering and DHCP restrictions.

Obscurity

Suppose a thief who wants to break into a bank plans to attack during a shift change of the security guards at night. When the thief observes the guards, however, he finds that the guards do not change shifts at the same time each night. On Monday they rotate shifts at 11:15 P.M., whereas on Tuesday the shift change occurs at 10:50 P.M., and on Wednesday it is at 11:25 P.M. He cannot determine the times of these changes because they are kept secret. The thief, not knowing when a change takes place, cannot detect a clear pattern of times. Because the shift changes are confusing and not well known, an attack becomes more difficult. This technique is sometimes called "security by obscurity." Obscuring what goes on inside a system or organization and avoiding clear patterns of behavior make attacks from the outside much more difficult.

In wireless information security, defending systems through obscurity can be a valuable tool. It is important not to advertise what security is in place, the vendor of the equipment, or any other seemingly harmless information that could be used in an attack. For example, a wireless gateway that transmits the service set identifier (SSID) of "Smith Family" or "ABC Corp" is providing information regarding the location of the WLAN that an attacker may find useful. Another example is user passwords. To predictably alter passwords when they expire (use password SOCCER1 until it expires and then use SOCCER2 until it expires, etc.) is unwise. Obscuring passwords by making each one unrelated to the previous password will provide an additional level of security through obscurity.

NOTE   Through social engineering, attackers often pose as researchers and call a company to inquire about the brand and model of an access point, firewall, or other technology the company uses. Any request for this type of information should be denied.

7

Security by obscurity is sometimes criticized as being too weak. Though it is true that obscurity by itself is a poor type of defense, it can confuse would-be attackers if it is used with other diverse layers of defense.

Simplicity

Because attacks can come from a variety of sources and in many forms, information security is, by its very nature, complex. And the more complex something becomes, the more difficult it is to understand. A security guard who does not understand how motion detectors interact with infrared trip lights may not know what to do when one system alarm shows an intruder but the other does not. In addition, complex systems allow many opportunities for something to go wrong. In short, complex systems can be a thief's ally.

The same is true with information security. Complex security systems can be hard to understand, hard to troubleshoot, and hard to feel secure about. As much as possible, a secure system should be simple enough for those on the inside to understand and use. Complex security schemes are often compromised to make them easier for trusted users to work with, yet this can also make it easier for the attackers as well.

The challenge is to make the system simple from the inside but complex from the outside. For example, a wireless network may be designed so that public access APs are separate from the secure network with multiple firewalls in between, with each firewall performing a somewhat different function. Those on the inside who work closely with security should understand the functionality of the system and know how the various parts interact. The benefit here is that it is much easier to troubleshoot a problem or adjust the configurations if necessary. Yet from the outside the attackers, who do not know the networks are separated and have multiple firewalls, can only guess at the level of complexity. What the attacker does not understand is more difficult to attack. In short, keeping a system simple from the inside but complex on the outside can sometimes be difficult but will reap a large benefit in terms of information security.

Table 7-1 summarizes these basic security principles. Designing a secure wireless network founded upon these five key basic principles of security helps to ensure a secure network.

Table 7-1   Basic security principles

Principle	Description	Example
Layering	Multiple layers of defenses that surround the information	Using antivirus software, strong passwords, and strong door locks
Limiting	Restrict access to information	Limit access to management features of access points
Diversity	Different types of defenses	Use MAC address filtering and DHCP restrictions in the transitional security model
Obscurity	Hide anything that could be useful to attacker	Use a cryptic SSID
Simplicity	Security system must not be confusing to inside security personnel but only to attackers	Use multiple firewalls

NETWORK SEGMENTATION

Another important principle of good network security design is dividing the network into smaller units, a practice known as **segmentation**. A network **segment** is a subset of a larger network. Segmentation was originally used to reduce the amount of traffic on a network. In a standard wired Ethernet network, all devices share the same media and a device can send a packet at any time rather than in a fixed or predictable fashion (known as **non-deterministic** networking). The result is that two devices can transmit simultaneously and create a collision between packets, which slows down network traffic. The area that encompasses all of the network devices that can cause collisions is known as the **collision domain** and is illustrated in Figure 7-1. Dividing the network into segments creates smaller areas in which collisions occur and therefore can increase the speed of the network, as seen in Figure 7-2.

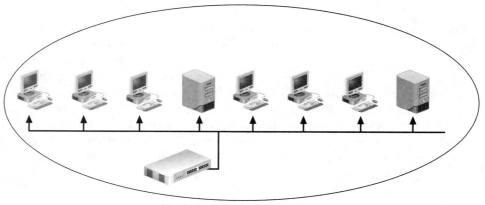

Single large collision domain

Figure 7-1   Collision domain

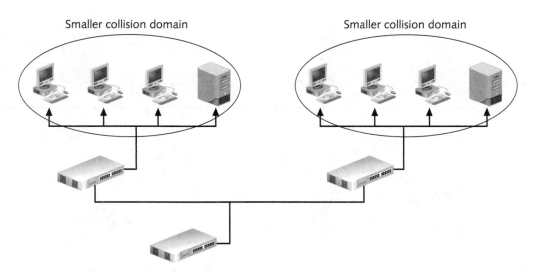

Figure 7-2   Segmentation limits collision domains

Although similar in their purpose, a network segment and a **subnet** are different. Both a segment and a subnet are designed to create a grouping of similar computers. However, a segment is created by connecting equipment to a physical device, whereas a subnet is accomplished through higher-level software configuration. Subnets are usually created by grouping together computers by Internet protocol (IP) addresses.

IEEE 802.11 wireless LANs are similar to Ethernet in that they all share the same media (the wireless channel) and are non-deterministic. A type of wireless segmentation can be accomplished through adding additional access points, as seen in Figure 7-3. However, because each access point is on a different channel, the devices serviced by separate APs are not strictly sharing the same media.

NOTE   IEEE 802.11 WLANs do not have collisions like wired Ethernet networks. WLANs use Carrier Sense Multiple Access/Collision Avoidance (CSMA/CA) instead of Ethernet's Carrier Sense Multiple Access/Collision Detection (CSMA/CD).

Segmentation is still used to reduce collisions and increase the speed of the network. Yet segmentation is also used to create smaller segments for security purposes. Network segments can help isolate computers that may not have the same level of security as other devices, and they may also restrict the impact of an attack on a network. Segmentation can be accomplished through hardware devices and technologies or through creating virtual LANs (VLANs).

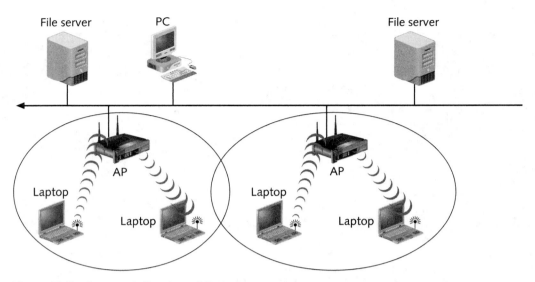

Figure 7-3   Segmentation by adding access points

Segmenting with Devices and Technologies

The boundaries of a network segment can be created by devices that have the capacity to regulate the flow of packets into and out of the segment. In a wired network these devices are generally classified by their relation to the OSI model. Devices that function at Layer 1, the Physical layer, do not filter any packets and instead simply pass them on to all other network devices and therefore cannot perform segmentation. Repeaters and hubs are typically Layer 1 devices. Other devices operate at Layer 2, the Data Link layer, and can perform filtering to create network segments. Bridges, switches, and routers are Layer 2 devices. Routers, which are also Layer 3 (Network layer) devices, can segment networks by directing packets based on their IP number.

In a wireless network, additional networking hardware and technologies are used to create segments. In addition to wireless gateways, wireless routers, and wireless switches, this includes firewalls, demilitarized zones, and devices with network address translation.

Firewalls

A **firewall**, sometimes called a **packet filter**, is designed to prevent malicious packets from entering the network or computer. A firewall can be software based or hardware based. A software firewall runs as a program on a computer to protect it against attacks, whereas hardware firewalls are separate devices that typically protect an entire network. Hardware firewalls usually are located outside the network security perimeter as the first line of defense, as shown in Figure 7-4.

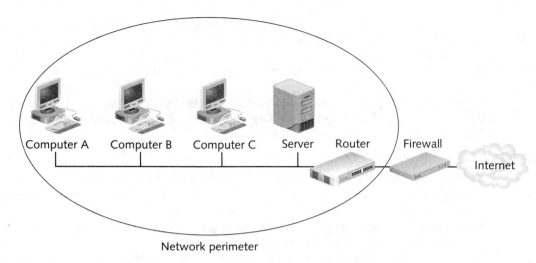

Network perimeter

Figure 7-4   Hardware firewall position in network

The foundation of a firewall is a **rule base**. The rule base establishes what action the firewall should take when it receives a packet. The three typical options are:

- *Allow*—Let the packet pass through and continue on its journey
- *Block*—Prevent the packet from passing to the network and instead destroy it
- *Prompt*—Ask the user what action to take

Packets can be filtered by a firewall in one of two ways. **Stateless packet filtering** looks at the incoming packet and permits or denies it based strictly on the rule base. For example, a user from inside the protected network may send a request to a Web server located on the Internet for a Web page. A rule in the firewall similar to those in Table 7-2 would allow the Web page to be transmitted back to the requesting computer.

Table 7-2   Stateless packet filtering rule

Rule Description	Explanation	Filtering
Source address = any	The source IP address is that of the Web server on the Internet.	Because you cannot know in advance what the IP address of a Web server is, this rule allows a packet coming from anywhere to enter the network.
Destination address = internal IP address	The destination address is the IP address of the computer on the internal network where the packet is being sent.	This rule allows packets directed to this internal computer to pass through but it blocks packets that do not have the correct destination address.
Port = 80	The port indicates what this packet contains, namely an HTML document.	No other types of content besides HTML documents are allowed.

Although a stateless packet filter does provide some degree of protection, attackers can easily bypass the protection. In the previous example, an attacker only has to discover a valid internal IP address of the computer network. Then he can send an attack using that IP address and falsely change the packet to indicate it is an HTML document (port 80).

NOTE Firewalls can filter outgoing traffic as well. For example, an organization can use a firewall to prevent users from viewing an offensive Web page or downloading software.

The second type of firewall provides a greater degree of protection. **Stateful packet filtering** keeps a record of the state of a connection between an internal computer and an external server and then makes decisions based on the connection as well as the rule base. For example, a stateless packet filter firewall might allow a packet to pass through because it is intended for a specific computer on the network. However, a stateful packet filter would not let the packet pass if that internal network computer did not first request the information from the external server. Table 7-3 illustrates stateful packet filtering rules.

Table 7-3 Stateful packet filtering rule

Rule or State Description	Explanation	Filtering
Source address = any	The source IP address is that of the Web server on the Internet	Because you cannot know in advance what the IP address of a Web server is, this rule allows a packet coming from anywhere to enter the network.
Destination address = internal IP address	The destination address is the IP address of the computer on the internal network where the packet is being sent.	This rule allows packets directed to this internal computer to pass through but it blocks packets that do not have the correct destination address
Destination address = internal IP address	Did this computer on the internal network request this information from the Web server?	This state observation prevents those packets from entering that were not first requested by an internal computer.
Port = 80	The port indicates what this packet contains, namely an HTML document.	No other types of content besides HTML documents are allowed.

Firewalls are a critical tool for protecting a wireless network from attacks. Many security experts maintain that because of the vulnerabilities with the original IEEE 802.11 security mechanisms, wireless APs should be treated as "unsecure" and placed outside of the firewall, as seen in Figure 7-5. This leaves only the access point in an unprotected position outside the firewall and external to the secure internal network. An attacker would have little incentive to attack the AP because even if she were to compromise it, she could still not penetrate the network because of the firewall.

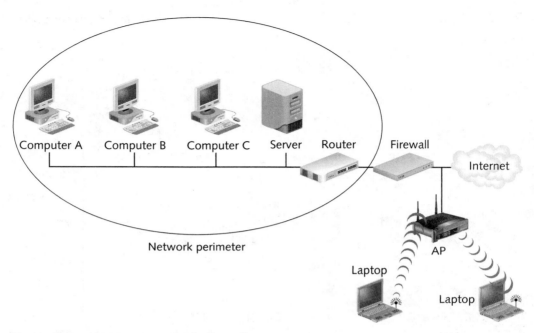

Figure 7-5 Access point outside firewall

 NOTE What happens if an employee wants to connect to a wireless AP outside the firewall yet still needs access to the secure inner network? The answer is to use special software or hardware that allows a secure connection to go through. This is discussed in Chapter 9.

Demilitarized Zone (DMZ)

A **demilitarized zone (DMZ)** is a separate network that sits outside the secure network perimeter and is protected by a firewall. Outside users can access the DMZ but cannot enter the secure network. In Figure 7-6, a DMZ has been set up outside of the secure network perimeter. The DMZ contains a Web server and an e-mail server, two servers that are continuously accessed by outside users. However, outside users never enter the secure network. Placing public-use servers in a DMZ restricts the access of outside users to the secure network.

For small office home office (SOHO) or home users, setting up a formal DMZ may not be practical because it involves purchasing additional equipment. However, many wireless gateways now have built-in firewall features. Many wireless gateways allow users to set up DMZs, as shown in Figure 7-7. The DMZ feature allows one local computer exposed to the Internet to use a special-purpose service such as Internet gaming or videoconferencing. DMZ hosting opens all the ports of that computer, exposing the entire computer so all users on the Internet can see it.

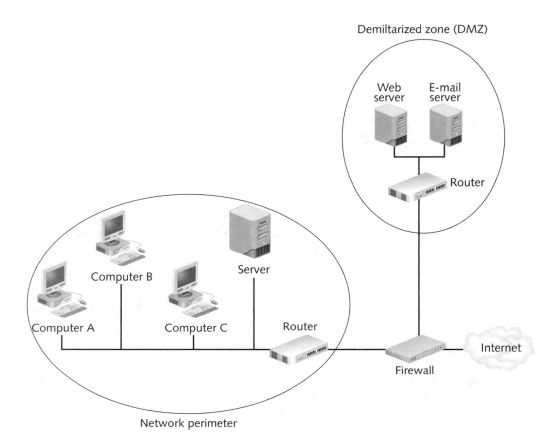

Figure 7-6   Demiltarized zone (DMZ)

Figure 7-7   Setting up a DMZ

NOTE   When using a single wireless gateway for SOHO or home use that has an internal firewall, it is not possible to set up the AP outside the protection of the firewall. This is because the device is designed to have the wireless network protected by the firewall.

Network Address Translation (NAT)

A technology that can be used to segment wireless (as well as wired) networks that also has several other advantages is **network address translation (NAT)**. NAT is not a device; rather it is a technology and can be incorporated into wireless gateways, firewalls, and other network devices. NAT replaces the sender's actual IP address with another IP address. A series of IP addresses known as **private addresses** have been reserved for special use. Private addresses, as listed in Table 7-4, are not issued to any specific user but instead anyone can assign them to a network device without any cost. As the name implies, private addresses are designed to be used only on a private internal network and cannot be used on the Internet.

NOTE   Additional information about IP addresses can be found by searching for *ip address classes* with an Internet search engine. One example of the information is found at *http://www.bergen.org/ATC/Course/InfoTech/Coolip/*.

Table 7-4   Private IP addresses

IP Address Class	Private IP Addresses
Class A	10.0.0.0 – 10.255.255.255
Class B	172.16.0.0 – 172.31.255.255
Class C	192.168.0.0 – 192.168.255.255

When using NAT, a private address is assigned to a network device. As a packet leaves the network, NAT removes the original private IP address from the sender's packet and replaces it with an alias IP address, as shown in Figure 7-8. This alias IP address is a "real" address that can be routed over the Internet and shared by all internal network devices. The NAT software maintains a table of original addresses and corresponding alias addresses. When a packet is returned to the NAT, the process is reversed.

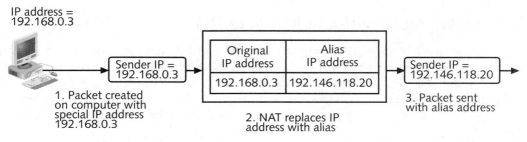

Figure 7-8   Network address translation (NAT)

A variation of NAT is **port address translation (PAT)**. Instead of giving each outgoing packet a different IP address, each packet is given the same IP address but a different port number. This allows a single IP address to be shared by several users. PAT is typically used on home networks that allow multiple users to share one IP address received from an ISP.

NAT technology has several advantages, including:

- *Security*—NAT provides a level of security by hiding the real IP address of computers on the internal network. If the attacker does not know the IP address to attack, then it is more difficult to send a packet past the firewall. An attacker who captures the packet on the Internet can only determine the alias address, not the actual IP address of the sender.

- *Conserves IP addresses*—A single IP address can be used to support over 250 network devices with NAT technology. This not only preserves limited IP addresses but also can be a cost savings. A SOHO or home network can purchase a single Internet connection from an ISP and share it among several to hundreds of computers.

- *Segmentation*—NAT can be used to isolate parts of a network.

NOTE

Another security advantage of NAT is that private IP addresses are not routable and any packet that may reach the Internet is destroyed.

Despite its advantages, NAT has some drawbacks, including:

- *Difficult troubleshooting*—NAT makes troubleshooting more confusing because of the address substitutions.

- *Problems with applications*—Some network applications will not function properly in NAT unless a public IP address is used.

- *Issues with security protocols*—Some security protocols are designed to detect modifications to packets and will send alerts whenever a NAT changes the IP address.

- *Performance impact*—NAT can slow network transmissions because of the translation that must be done to each packet.

Segmenting by Virtual LANs (VLANs)

Another way in which a wireless network can be segmented is through constructing a **virtual local area network (VLAN)**. A VLAN is a logical grouping of network devices within a larger network. VLANs do not require that all of the devices be physically located together. Instead, the devices can be dispersed anywhere throughout the network. Wireless VLANs have proven to be very beneficial in making the network more secure.

How a VLAN Works

When a sending device on a LAN sends a packet that is intended for a single receiving device it is known as a **unicast** transmission. However, there are occasions when a device must send a packet to all network devices. For example, if an Ethernet network device only knows the IP address of the receiving device but needs the MAC address to send the packet, the device will send to all network devices a request asking the owner of a specific IP address to respond with their MAC address. Sending a packet to all network devices is called a **broadcast** transmission. Whereas a collision domain is the area that encompasses all of the Ethernet network devices that can cause a collision, a **broadcast domain** is the area in which a broadcast occurs. A comparison of collision domains and broadcast domains is seen in Figure 7-9.

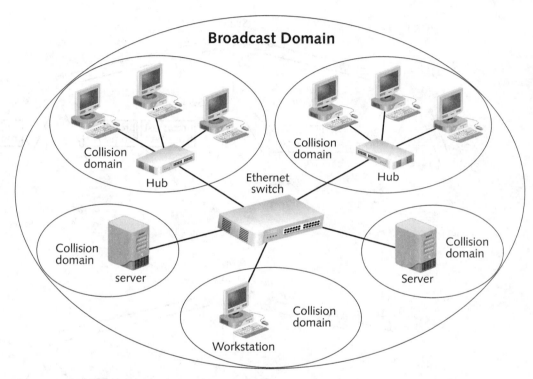

Figure 7-9   Collision domain versus broadcast domain

 A packet in which the 48-bit destination MAC address is all 1's (or 0xFF-FF-FF-FF-FF-FF) is a broadcast packet and is sent to all network devices.

NOTE

In networks with a small number of devices, broadcasts generally do not pose a problem. However, in large networks with many devices, broadcasts can have an impact on network throughput as more devices send more broadcast transmissions. One way to address this problem is to divide the network into separate broadcast domains so that broadcast transmissions will only be sent to a smaller number of devices. This can be accomplished by creating a VLAN.

Figure 7-10 illustrates a regular LAN and a VLAN. With a regular LAN any device that sends a broadcast packet throughout the network will cause the packet to be sent to all other devices. If Device A sends a broadcast packet then Devices B, C, and D, and Servers 1 and 2 all receive it. However, with a VLAN only the devices that are part of the VLAN will receive the broadcast packet. If Device A, Device C, and Server 1 are all part of the same VLAN, then when Device A sends a broadcast packet only those devices in its VLAN will receive it.

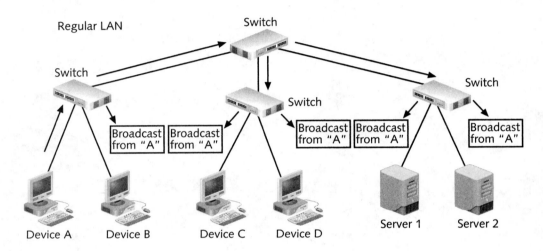

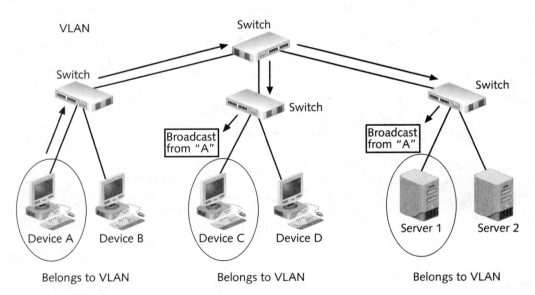

Figure 7-10   Regular LAN versus VLAN

NOTE Because a VLAN can logically group devices (and the employees that use those devices) together, it does not matter where the devices are located on the network. For example, a VLAN group may consist of all the Accounting Department employees even if they are scattered across different floors of an office building or even in different buildings.

The key to VLANs is the ability of the switch to correctly direct packets. Switches allocate an access port for each network device and then keep a record of that device's MAC address with a port number. When a VLAN packet arrives at the switch it can determine which devices are part of that VLAN and only send the packet out to those ports.

Switches are able to send VLAN packets to the correct ports because of the way in which the VLAN packets are identified. One standard for marking VLAN packets is the **IEEE 802.1q** standard that supports **trunking** (trunking means that a single cable is used to support multiple virtual LANs). The 802.1q standard is called an internal tagging mechanism because it inserts a 4–byte "tag" header within the existing Ethernet packet, as seen in Figure 7–11. The tag header is constructed of two fields. Table 7–5 explains the fields in the tag header.

New tag added to packet

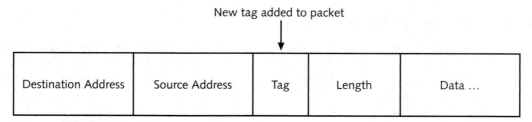

| Destination Address | Source Address | Tag | Length | Data ... |

Figure 7-11 Packet with VLAN tag

Table 7-5 Tag header fields

Field Name	Value	Length	Description
Protocol identifier (TPID)	Fixed value of 0x8100	2 bytes	Indicates that the packet is carrying IEEE 802.1q information
Tag control information (TCI)	VLAN ID	2 bytes	Contains the unique ID of the VLAN

Alternatives to IEEE 802.1q frame tagging are proprietary methods that involve encapsulation. One such proprietary protocol is Cisco Systems' **Inter-Switch Link (ISL)** protocol. ISL "wraps" the original Ethernet packet with 30 bytes of additional information. Table 7-6 explains the field information.

Table 7-6 ISL fields

Field Name	Length	Description
Header field	26 bytes	Embedded within header is a 10-bit VLAN ID
Cyclic redundancy check (CRC) trailer field	4 bytes	An error check in addition to the standard packet checking performed by Ethernet

Although Cisco introduced ISL for trunking multiple VLANs over a single link prior to IEEE 802.1q, today ISL use is in decline because of the IEEE non-proprietary standard. Although it is not recommended that a new network should use ISL, many existing networks continue to use it.

Wireless VLANs

As with wired networks, wireless VLANs can be used to segment traffic. However, the flexibility of a wireless VLAN depends on which device separates the packets and directs them to different networks. In Figure 7-12 separating packets in a wireless VLAN is done by the switch. Each AP is connected to a separate port on the switch and represents a different VLAN. As packets destined for the wireless LAN arrive at the switch, the switch separates the packets and sends them to the appropriate AP (VLAN). However, this configuration has limitations. For example, if a wireless user in the Accounting Department is part of the Accounting VLAN, what happens when the user roams to the Marketing VLAN supported by another access point? The user may no longer have access to the Accounting VLAN and then is unable to use the network resources. Reconfiguring the network to make each VLAN accessible from every access point across the enterprise is not a realistic solution.

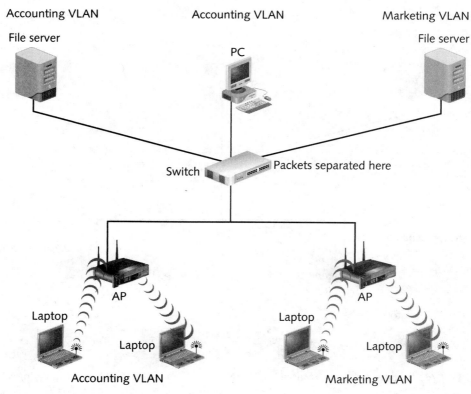

Figure 7-12 Packets separated at switch

A more flexible approach is illustrated in Figure 7-13, where the access point is responsible for separating the packets. Under this configuration a user can roam into different areas of coverage and still be connected to the correct VLAN. The key to this configuration is that *different VLANs are transmitted by the AP on different Service Set Identifiers (SSIDs)*. This enables only the clients associated with a specific VLAN to receive those packets. Many access points that support wireless VLANs can support multiple SSIDs (and therefore multiple VLANs). For example, the Cisco Aironet 1200 can support up to 16 VLANs. Some VLANs can be used for low-security guest Internet access, others for minimum-security enterprise users, and administrators can be put on a high-security VLAN with enhanced firewall permissions. All this can be achieved by using a single AP to emulate multiple wireless infrastructures. The Cisco AP does this by assigning each of the 16 VLANs its own unique SSID.

 If you were to look at a Cisco AP configured for multiple VLANs with NetSumbler, it would appear as 16 different wireless networks.

NOTE

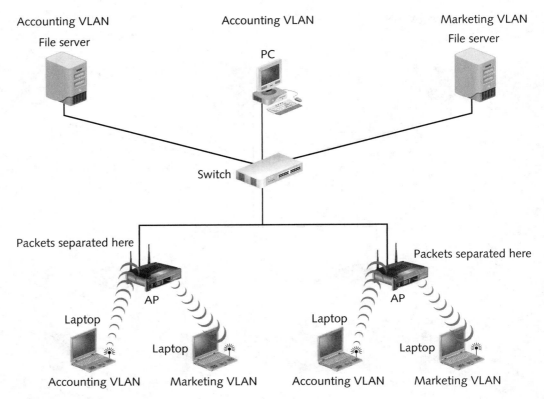

Figure 7-13   Packets separated at access point

Many organizations set up two wireless VLANs. The first is for employee access, in which employees can access the company's files and databases through the network. A second VLAN is for guest access. Guest users can access only the Internet and any external files stored specifically for guests. Employees would configure their wireless network interface client adapters to use the SSID "Employee" whereas guests would use the SSID "Guest," as seen in Table 7-7. When the devices associate to the same access point, they automatically belong to the correct VLAN. And because wired devices attached through the switch can also belong to the same VLAN, wireless VLAN and wired VLAN devices can share subnets or can belong to completely different subnets.

A benefit of using multiple SSIDs and VLANs is that different security features can be configured for each VLAN group.

NOTE

Table 7-7   Wireless VLAN

Access Level	SSID	VLAN ID	Encryption
Employees only	Employee	1	WPA2 Enterprise
Outside guests	Guest	2	None

Wireless VLANs allow a single access point to service both the employees and guests. All employee devices can be protected on a specific VLAN using secure technology such as WPA2, whereas guests can access the Internet through the wireless connection without needing a pre-shared key (PSK). Wireless VLANs keep guests from seeing employee devices, files, or databases even though they are all wirelessly connected to the same access point.

NOTE   Wireless VLANs are also supported by most SOHO and consumer APs, such as the Linksys. Setting up wireless VLANs is an excellent way to prevent an attacker who connects to a wireless network from accessing other computers or files.

HARDWARE PLACEMENT

In addition to logically segmenting a network, placing the hardware in a physically secure location is also important for security. Unlike standard networking equipment that is often secured behind a locked door, access points must often be placed in unprotected public access areas to provide the radio frequency (RF) coverage that is needed. This makes APs tempting devices for thieves.

Access points should be securely fastened to a wall, pole, or similar object to deter thieves. In some instances it may even be necessary to secure the AP with a lock, as seen in Figure 7-14.

In buildings that have a false ceiling (sometimes called a drop or suspended ceiling), there is a temptation to simply remove a ceiling tile, place the access point in the space above the ceiling, and then replace the tile. However, this should not be done unless a special enclosure surrounds the AP and its antennas. The air-handling space above drop ceilings (and sometimes even between the walls and under structural floors) is used to circulate and otherwise handle air in a building. These spaces are called **plenums**. Placing an access point in a plenum can be a hazard because if an electrical short in the access point were to cause a fire, it would generate smoke in the plenum that would be quickly circulated throughout the building. If it is required to place an AP in a plenum, it is important to enclose it within a plenum-rated enclosure to meet fire safety code requirements.

NOTE   There is a temptation to position access points in convenient or easily spotted locations, such as close to an office, to hinder thieves. It is important that access points be placed where they were designed to go. Because access points encounter less interference the higher they are located, most access points are positioned high on interior walls or attached to the ceiling.

Figure 7-14   Access point secured with lock

Wireless Device Security

Just as it is important to design a secure wireless network, the security of the wireless devices themselves (such as laptops or PDAs) should not be overlooked. This includes installing and properly configuring personal firewall, antivirus, antispyware, and patch software. In addition, tools that are used to identify new classes of attacks such as rootkits should be implemented.

Personal Firewall Software

In addition to a hardware firewall that protects the network, each wireless device should have its own software firewall installed, sometimes known as a **personal firewall**. This provides a "double layer" of protection: if malicious software is successful in penetrating the network hardware firewall (often because the firewall was improperly configured), it will be blocked by the personal firewall on the local wireless device.

Firewalls are designed to protect a device's network ports, or endpoints of communication. (Network ports should not be confused with USB and other ports used to connect devices to the computer.) Basic Internet services use specific ports, such as HTTP using port 80 and FTP using port 21. An open port can give attackers an avenue into a wireless device. Personal firewalls close and then hide all unused ports so that attackers cannot even see which ports to attack.

The use of ports is governed by a set of rules. A software firewall may allow outgoing FTP requests but not incoming requests, so that a file can be downloaded from the Internet, but attackers will not be able to download files from the device. Personal firewalls also support outbound monitoring, which allows requests from a Web browser while denying requests from a Trojan, even for the same port. In addition, most personal firewalls use application information along with port information.

NOTE

When an unknown program tries to access the Internet, a software firewall wizard lets you control how much access to grant it.

7

There are several personal firewalls available, including freeware programs and programs for purchase. Microsoft now includes a personal firewall as part of its Windows operating system Service Pack 2, as seen in Figure 7-15.

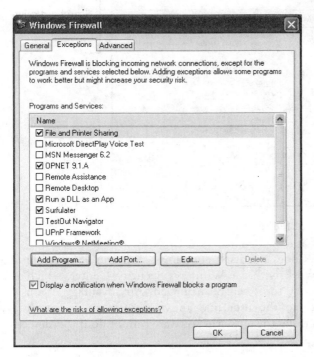

Figure 7-15   Microsoft personal firewall

Antivirus Software

The best defense against viruses is **antivirus (AV) software**. This software can scan a computer for infections and isolate any file that contains a virus, as well as monitor computer activity and scan all new documents, such as e-mail attachments, that might contain a virus.

The drawback of antivirus software is that it must be continuously updated to recognize new viruses. Known as **definition files** or **signature files**, these updates can be downloaded automatically through the Internet to a user's computer.

According to a survey conducted by the National Cyber Security Alliance, 67% of broadband users have no antivirus software or outdated antivirus software on their desktop computers.

Antivirus software is generally configured to constantly monitor for viruses and automatically check for updated signature files. However, the entire hard drive should be scanned for viruses at least once a week. In addition, most antivirus software allows for manual signature updates. These features are illustrated in Figure 7-16.

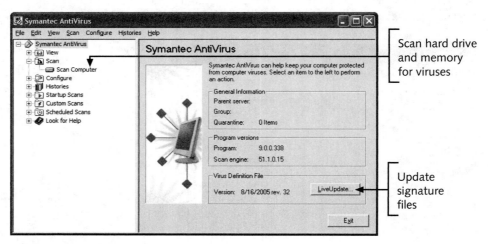

Figure 7-16   Antivirus software features

Although Microsoft Windows does not itself contain an antivirus software product, most antivirus software packages work with the Windows Security Center, which is a central location in which some security tools can be managed. An advantage of this is that the Security Center can indicate to the user that antivirus software is not installed or is improperly functioning, something the antivirus software cannot do if it is defective. This is illustrated in Figure 7-17.

Antispyware

Just as antivirus software is one of the best defenses against viruses, another class of defensive software known as **antispyware** helps prevent computers from becoming infected by different types of spyware. Antivirus software and antispyware share many similarities. First, antispyware must be regularly updated to defend against the most recent spyware attacks.

Figure 7-17   Windows monitoring AV software

Second, antispyware can be set to provide both continuous real-time monitoring and perform a complete scan of the entire computer system at one time. And like antivirus software, antispyware provides good visual tools for the system scan.

Many antispyware products provide the following additional features and tools:

- *Detailed information*—Unlike most antivirus software programs, antispyware often provides detailed information when it locates spyware. The antispyware displays the name of the spyware, a threat level, a description of the spyware, and recommended action regarding how to handle it.

- *System explorers*—These tools expose configuration information that may normally be difficult to access.

- *Tracks eraser*—This tool automatically removes cookies, browser history, a record of which programs have been recently opened, and other information that can help to preserve privacy.

- *Browser restore*—The Browser Restore tool allows the user to restore specific browser settings if spyware infects the Web browser. The tool resets user-defined settings instead of the browser's default settings.

NOTE

The default advice regarding how to handle spyware when detected by antispyware is almost always *Remove*. Other typical options include *Ignore*, *Quarantine*, and *Always Ignore*.

Several good antispyware products are freely available on the Internet along with reasonably priced commercial packages. Some security experts recommend that you install at least two antispyware products on a computer, because one product may not always detect all of the spyware.

Patch Software

Patch software is a general term used to describe software security updates that vendors provide for their application programs and operating systems. Unlike version upgrades that provide enhanced functionality to the program, patch software is generally designed to fix security vulnerabilities. The most frequently distributed patch software is for the Microsoft Windows operating system.

Prior to October 2003, Microsoft released Windows patches whenever a vulnerability was discovered. This often resulted in a new patch canceling out a previous patch or multiple patches being released within a few days. Because of user demand, Microsoft now releases patches to its operating systems on the second Tuesday of every month (sometimes called "Patch Tuesday"). Microsoft typically releases between 5 and 15 software patches for download and installation. Each of the patches is given a unique number, which includes the year of the patch followed by a three-digit number indicating its release order. The first patch of 2005 was designated *MS05-001*, the second patch was *MS05-002*, and so on. The number of the patch corresponds to detailed information in the Microsoft Knowledge Base that explains the vulnerability and what the patch does to correct it, as shown in Figure 7-18.

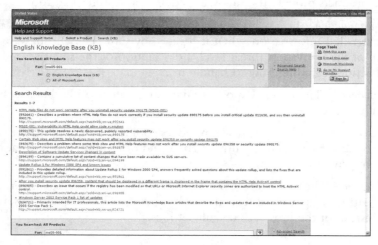

Figure 7-18   Microsoft patch information

The Microsoft Knowledge Base can be accessed at *http://support. microsoft.com*.

Microsoft classifies patches based on level of vulnerability that the patch fixes:

■ *Critical*—A critical vulnerability could freely allow a worm to infect a computer even when other defense mechanisms are in place.

■ *Important*—An important vulnerability could result in the confidentiality, integrity, or availability of data or resources being compromised.

■ *Moderate*—Moderate vulnerabilities are those that are difficult for an attacker to exploit because of current configurations.

■ *Low*—Low vulnerability means that it would be very difficult for an attacker to take advantage of this weakness and the impact would be minimal.

If a critical vulnerability is exposed, Microsoft might also release a special patch prior to Patch Tuesday.

Desktop computers can be configured to automatically receive Windows patches. The four automatic update configuration options are shown in Figure 7-19.

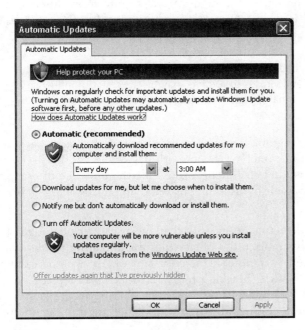

Figure 7-19   Windows automatic update options

- *Automatic*—This option checks the Microsoft Web site every day at a user-designated time and, if there are any patches, Windows automatically downloads and installs them onto the desktop computer.

- *Download*—The Download option automatically downloads the patches but does not install them, allowing the user to review and choose which patches to install.

- *Notify*—This option alerts the user that patches are available but does not download or install them. The user must go to the Microsoft Web site to review and install the patches.

- *Turn off*—The Turn off option disables automatic updates.

Keeping up to date on system patches is one of the most important steps that can be taken to protect a wireless device. After recent enhancements to Microsoft Windows, automatic updates are now easier to manage.

Rootkit Detectors

Security researchers warn that a new generation of powerful attacks that are virtually impossible to detect using current security products could pose a serious risk to corporations and individuals. These are known as rootkits. A **rootkit** is a set of software tools used by an attacker to break into a computer and obtain special operating system privileges in order to both perform unauthorized functions and hide all traces of its existence. Originally, the term "rootkit" referred to a set of modified and recompiled UNIX tools that were designed to hide any trace of an intruder's presence (the highest level administrative user on a UNIX system is known as the "root"). Rootkits are no longer limited to UNIX-based computers but are available for other operating systems, including Microsoft Windows.

 NOTE The increasingly sophisticated rootkits and the speed with which techniques are migrating from spyware and viruses to rootkits may be the result of influence from organized online criminal groups that value stealthy, invasive software, according to one security engineer.

A rootkit often includes several programs designed to monitor traffic, create a back door into the computer, change log files, and attack other network devices. A rootkit itself causes no direct damage to the computer; rather, its function is to hide the presence of other types of malicious software. Rootkits accomplish this hiding by removing traces of log-in records, log entries, and related processes.

The fundamental problem in detecting rootkits is that the user can no longer trust the operating system because rootkits replace the binary files for operating system commands with modified versions designed to ignore its activity and detection. For example, if a command is issued to display all of the files in a folder, a rootkit will replace the original program that performs that function with its own program that never displays any rootkit files in the directory. Other system commands that a rootkit will modify include programs that list processes running on the system (with a similar command that ignores any rootkit processes) and programs that log or record activities (rootkits prevent their activities from being recorded).

Programs are available to help detect the presence of a rootkit. However, disinfecting a computer that has a rootkit can be difficult. This is because removing rootkits involves more than simply detecting and erasing the rootkit programs. Because rootkits have changed the operating system, it may not even be possible to remove the entire rootkit without causing the computer to become unstable. Most security experts say that the only safe and foolproof way to handle a rootkit infection is to reformat the hard drive and reinstall the operating system.

NOTE

One way to detect a rootkit is to turn off the suspect computer and boot from alternative media such as a rescue CD-ROM or a dedicated USB flash drive. Because the rootkit-altered operating system is not running, it cannot hide its presence, and most antivirus programs will be able to detect a change in the operating system files that indicates a rootkit.

Chapter Summary

- Security defenses are based upon five key principles. Layering uses multiple defenses to thwart an attacker instead of a single defense. Limiting restricts access to information to only those who have a need to know. Diversity refers to different approaches in the various layers of security. Hiding the network layout, device configuration, or other information is called obscurity. Simplicity involves making the various defenses simple to understand for those on the inside, but complex for outsiders.

- Segmenting a network has several advantages, one of which is security. Segmenting can be accomplished by using devices such as a firewall (packet filter), a separate network that rests outside the secure network perimeter (a demilitarized zone), or by using network address translation.

- Another technique for segmenting networks is the VLAN. A VLAN is a logical grouping of network devices within a larger network. Most VLANs are based on the IEEE 802.1q standard. Wireless VLANs allow greater flexibility and security for network users.

- Security on wireless devices, such as laptops or PDAs, is also important. A software-based personal firewall serves as a second level of defense against attackers seeking to exploit a system through unprotected ports. Antivirus software can scan a computer for virus infections and isolate a file that contains a virus. Antispyware prevents computers from being infected with spyware. Rootkit detectors can identify a rootkit installed on a computer.

Key Terms

antispyware — Software that helps prevent computers from becoming infected by spyware.

antivirus (AV) software — Software that can scan a computer for virus infections and isolate any file that contains a virus.

broadcast — Sending a packet to all network devices.

broadcast domain — The area in which a broadcast occurs.

collision domain — The area that encompasses all of the network devices that can cause collisions.

definition files — Antivirus software updates; also called signature files.

demilitarized zone (DMZ) — A separate network that sits outside the secure network perimeter and is protected by a firewall.

firewall — Hardware or software that prevents unauthorized access to a network.

IEEE 802.1q — A standard for virtual local area networks (VLANs) that supports trunking.

Inter-Switch Link (ISL) — A Cisco VLAN protocol that "wraps" the original Ethernet packet with 30 bytes of additional information. A proprietary alternative to IEEE 802.1q.

network address translation (NAT) — A technology that replaces the sender's actual IP address with another IP address.

non-deterministic — Network traffic that is not created in a fixed or predictable fashion.

packet filter — Another name for a firewall that is designed to prevent malicious packets from entering the network or computers.

patch software — Software updates provided by vendors to improve operating system and application program security.

personal firewall — A software-based firewall on a local device.

plenum — The air-handling space above drop ceilings (and sometimes even between the walls and under structural floors) in a building.

port address translation (PAT) — A technology similar to NAT, except it gives each packet the same IP address but a different port number.

private addresses — A series of IP addresses reserved for special use on an internal network.

rootkit — A set of software tools used by an attacker to break into a computer and obtain special operating system privileges to both perform unauthorized functions and hide all traces of its existence.

rule base — A set of actions a firewall should take when it receives a packet.

segment — A subset of a larger network that is created by connecting equipment to a physical device.

segmentation — Dividing a network into smaller units.

signature files — Antivirus software updates; also called definition files.

stateful packet filtering — A type of firewall that keeps a record of the state of a connection between an internal computer and an external server and then makes decisions based on the connection as well as the rule base.

stateless packet filtering — A type of firewall that looks at the incoming packet and permits or denies it based strictly on the rule base.

subnet — Computers or other network devices grouped by Internet Protocol address; a "higher-level" software configuration compared to a segment, which is a physical network grouping.

trunking — Using a single cable for multiple virtual LANs.

unicast — When a sending device on a LAN sends a packet that is intended for a single receiving device.

virtual local area network (VLAN) — A smaller logical grouping of network devices.

REVIEW QUESTIONS

1. Each of the following is one of the key principles of security except
   a. layering
   b. limiting
   c. diversity
   d. compatibility

2. Using several different types of security instead of only one is known as
   a. limiting
   b. layering
   c. multi-security levels (MSL)
   d. rootkits

3. Dividing a network into smaller units is called
   a. segmentation
   b. network division
   c. domain restriction
   d. device grouping

4. Networks in which devices can send packets at any time are known as
   a. non-deterministic
   b. deterministic
   c. resource allocation topologies (RAT)
   d. managed

5. A _____ is the area that encompasses all of the network devices that can cause a collision.
   a. collision domain
   b. distribution domain
   c. broadcast domain
   d. response area

6. Segments and subnets are identical. True or False?

7. Another name for a firewall is a packet filter. True or False?

8. A stateless packet filter looks at the incoming packet and permits or denies it based strictly on the rule base. True or False?

9. Stateful packet filtering keeps a record of the state of a connection between an internal computer and an external server and then makes decisions based on the connection as well as the rule base. True or False?

10. A demilitarized zone is the term used for a separate network that sits outside the secure network perimeter and is protected by a firewall. True or False?

11. _____ replaces the sender's actual IP address with another IP address.

12. Instead of giving each outgoing packet a different IP address, _____ assigns the same IP address but a different port number.

13. A packet that is intended for a single receiving device is known as a(n) _____ transmission.

14. A(n) _____ is a smaller logical grouping of network devices.

15. The standard for marking VLAN packets is _____ .

16. Explain the advantages of the access point separating packets in a VLAN.

17. Why shouldn't access points be placed above a suspended ceiling?

18. How does antispyware differ from antivirus software?

19. What is a rootkit and how does it work?

20. Explain how obscurity can be a valuable tool in protecting a wireless network.

HANDS-ON PROJECTS

Project 7-1: Installing Antispyware Software

Antispyware is an important tool for keeping a computer clean from spyware. In this project you will download and use Microsoft Windows Defender antispyware.

1. Point your Web browser to ***http://www.microsoft.com/athome/security/spyware/ software/default.mspx***.

2. Download and install the latest version of Windows Defender by saving the download file on your desktop and then launching it. Accept the default configuration settings.

3. Launch the Windows Defender antispyware program if necessary.

4. Click **Scan** to scan the computer for any antispyware. If any spyware is found it will be listed along with any recommendations regarding what to do. Click **Continue** to follow the recommended actions.

5. Configure Windows Defender for automatically downloading updates. Click **Tools** and **General Settings** to display the configuration window. Click **Check for updated definitions before scanning** if necessary. Click **Save** and then **OK**.

6. Close the antispyware windows (the program will continue running in the background).

HANDS-ON PROJECTS

Project 7-2: Configuring Microsoft Windows Firewall

Microsoft Windows Firewall is a stateful packet filter firewall included in Windows XP Service Pack 2. Although it is not as full-featured as other personal firewalls, it does provide basic protection. In this project, you will configure the firewall.

If you are using a computer in a school's computer lab or a computer at work, talk to your network administrator before performing this project. You may need special permissions before you can change these configuration settings.

1. Click **Start**, click **Control Panel** (if necessary, change to Category View), and then click **Security Center**.

2. Under **Manage security settings for:** click **Windows Firewall**.

3. Click the **Advanced** tab to display the advanced settings. You use the Advanced Settings dialog box to configure the rule base for the firewall. These settings are all for filtering *inbound* traffic; other than checking the source IP address, Windows Firewall does not inspect any outbound packets.

4. Click the **Exceptions** tab and then the **Add Port** button. This will allow you to open a port on your computer to allow packets to enter. Click **Cancel**. Click the **Advanced** tab.

5. Under **Security Logging** click **Settings**. You use this to select the firewall activities you want to log.

6. Check the **Log dropped packets** and **Log successful connections** boxes. Click **OK**.

7. Under **ICMP** click **Settings**. Click **Allow incoming echo request**, if necessary. Click **OK** to close the dialog box, and then click **OK** to close the firewall dialog box.

8. Close all open windows.

Now you can test the firewall connections, which may be difficult because an enterprise firewall should already be protecting the network and suspicious packets would not reach the local Windows firewall. Before performing the following steps, record the IP address of your computer and go to another computer that is connected to the Internet.

1. Click **Start** and then click **Run**. The Run dialog box opens.

2. Type **CMD** and then press **Enter**. The Command Prompt window opens.

3. At the command prompt, type **ping** *ip-address* where *ip-address* is the IP address of the system for which you want to test the ICF connection. Then press **Enter**.

4. Type **Exit** and then press **Enter** to close the Command Prompt window.

5. On the first computer, open and view the ICF log file (default location is C:\Windows\pfirewall.log) to see if a ping was received and dropped.

6. Close all windows.

HANDS-ON PROJECTS

Project 7-3: DMZ and VLAN Settings on Linksys

The Linksys wireless gateway allows you to set a DMZ and VLAN for the wireless network. In this project you will explore those settings.

1. On a separate computer that is part of the network, create a folder and enable file-sharing capabilities. Click **Start** and **My Computer** and open the **Shared Documents** folder and click **File** and **New** and then **Folder.** Name the folder **Shared**.

2. Right-click on the folder **Shared** and click where indicated to answer the question, "If you understand the security risks but want to share files without running the wizard, click here". On the Enable File Sharing dialog box click **Just enable file sharing** and then click **OK**.

3. Click **Share this folder on the network.** Also click **Allow network users to change my files**. Click **OK** in the **Shared Properties** dialog box.

4. Copy any document into the **Shared** folder.

5. On a wireless device other than the computer in which you created the **Shared** folder, open a Web browser and open the Linksys management program by entering the IP address of the Linksys gateway and then enter the username and password.

6. Click **Applications & Gaming**.

7. Click **DMZ**.

8. Enter the IP address of a computer here to place that computer in the DMZ. However, there is serious danger in placing a computer in the DMZ because it is entirely open to any attacks. A better solution is to open specific ports. Click **Port Range Forward**.

9. In this screen, specific ports for applications can be entered to open those ports to the Internet. There is still a danger from attackers from opened port, so neither Port Forwarding or DMZ should be used unless absolutely necessary.

10. Minimize the Linksys management window.

11. Now you will look at the document you put in the **Shared** folder. Right-click on **Start** and then click **Explore**. Navigate in the left pane to the folder **Shared** on the first computer and open it by double-clicking on it. Can you see the file that you copied into it? Close this window.

12. Maximize the Linksys management screen and click **Wireless**.

13. Click **Advanced Wireless Settings**.

14. Change **AP Isolation** to **On**. This creates a separate virtual LAN for all wireless devices. Each device will be in its own virtual network and unable to communicate with another other wireless device. Click **Save Settings**.

15. Now try to locate the **Shared** folder as you did above. What happened? Why?

16. Close all windows.

Project 7-4: Using a Rootkit Discovery Tool

Several programs are available to reveal the presence of a rootkit on a computer. In this project you will use the BlackLight program from F-Secure Corporation. BlackLight examines the system at a deep level to detect any objects that are hidden. If it finds such programs it offers to remove its "cloaking" by renaming the file so that the operating system will display it. However, BlackLight does not remove the rootkit.

1. Open a Web browser and go to *www.f-secure.com/blacklight*.

2. Download the latest version of BlackLight and save it to your desktop. Double-click the file and accept the license agreement.

3. The program will start and display the opening screen, as seen in Figure 7-20.

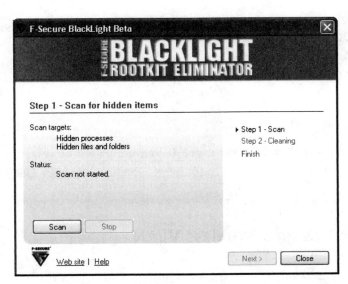

Figure 7-20 BlackLight opening screen

4. Click **Scan** to being scanning for rootkits on the computer.

5. If any rootkits are found, they will be displayed. Click **Next**.

6. If any rootkits were discovered, follow the instructions for renaming them.

7. Click **Exit**.

CASE PROJECTS

Case Project 7-1: Comparing Antivirus Software

Antivirus software is available as both a commercial product that is purchased as well as freeware offerings. Select one brand of antivirus software, either the commercial product or freeware. What features does it have that are different than other vendor's products? What are its strengths? What are its weaknesses? How much does it cost to be able to update the signature files? If it is a commercial product, how expensive is it compared to competing products? Would you recommend this product to others? Write a one-page summary of your findings.

Case Project 7-2: Your Network Defenses

Using the five key principles of security (layering, limiting, diversity, obscurity, and simplicity) create a table that lists each area and how your network uses these. Then add another column that describes how your network could improve its security by enhancing each of these areas.

Case Project 7-3: Comparing Personal Firewalls

How do personal software firewalls compare? Using the Internet and other sources, compare three different personal firewalls. What are their strengths? What are their weaknesses? Which would you recommend to someone looking for a personal firewall? Why?

Case Project 7-4: Rootkits

In late 2005 it was revealed that when Sony music CDs were played on a computer they installed a rootkit. What did this program do? Why was it installed? Was Sony right in doing this? What did they do wrong? How could they have handled this incident better? What if any penalties should be assessed against them? Write a one-page paper on your findings.

Case Project 7-5: Design a Wireless VLAN

Would a wireless VLAN be useful to you? Create a map of the current wireless LAN at your school or organization. Next, redesign the network using VLANs. Identify at least three different VLANs that could be implemented. Finally, determine the cost of access points or switches and estimate the total cost for installing wireless VLANs. Would you recommend a wireless VLAN for this network? Why?

Fairvue Technology Consulting

Hearts and Flowers is a regional florist with several retail shops and a single distribution center. Hearts and Flowers wants to expand their wireless LAN but is concerned about the best way to design their new wireless network. The first network was pieced together over time with different equipment and did not have a cohesive design. Fairvue Technology Consulting asks you to help them.

1. Prepare a PowerPoint presentation that explains the principles of good wireless network design and then briefly describes the technologies and devices that can be used to secure a WLAN. Your presentation should be about 6–8 slides in length.

2. Hearts and Flowers is still unsure about what action to take. Create a memo to the company that lists the five steps you would recommend, in order of importance, in creating their wireless LAN. Include a brief summary of each item describing why you think it is important for the company to implement it.

7

SECURE WIRELESS AUTHENTICATION

After completing this chapter you should be able to do the following:

➤ Define wireless authentication
➤ List and describe the different types of authentication servers

➤ Explain the differences between various extended authentication protocols
➤ Describe IEEE 802.11i authentication and key management

The World of Wireless Security

"Wireless security" is an expression generally used to describe defenses against attackers stealing information from wireless transmissions or penetrating a WLAN. However, there is a new element in "wireless security" that must now be defended against: wireless stalking.

Ben Goldacre, a journalist in Great Britain, decided to investigate a Web site that advertised it could track the location of any cell phone, at any time of day or night, to within 150 yards. There were only three simple conditions that had to be met to use the service. First, the cell phone had to be on in order for it to be tracked. Second, the phone's global positioning system (GPS) had to be set to "Location On" (all cell phones are required to have a GPS transmitter, although it can be configured to be either always on or on only when 911 is dialed). The third condition required that the phone be registered through the Web site.

After first receiving the approval of his girlfriend to participate in the test, Ben borrowed her phone one evening and sat down at his computer. He went to the Web site and paid for the service (about $3). Immediately the cell phone vibrated with a new text message that said, "Ben Goldacre has requested to add you to their Buddy List! To accept, simply reply to this message with 'LOCATE'." Ben sent the requested reply. The phone vibrated again with a message that read, "WARNING: [this service] allows other people to know where you are. For your own safety make sure that you know who is locating you." Ben then deleted both messages and returned the phone to his girlfriend.

After his girlfriend left his apartment, Ben returned to the Web site and clicked Locate. A map appeared of the immediate area with a person-shaped figure shown moving away. When it was being tracked, the cell phone did not ring or send any messages. Ben set up the Web site to track her movement at regular intervals and take a snapshot of her location every three minutes. After she arrived at home it produced a map of her trip.

You do not have to travel to Europe to track a person carrying a cell phone. There are several Web services available in the United States that will track a specific cell phone. Some sites even offer tracking as a free service.

In early 2006, Orange PLC & Quocirca Limited surveyed more than 2,000 IT professionals and asked how they keep unauthorized users from accessing corporate data through employees' mobile devices. The results were sobering. One in five businesses that had widely deployed mobile devices did not have any security policies or procedures in place for the devices. And more than 60 percent of those organizations that did have security policies did not actively enforce them. Among those surveyed, almost 80 percent said their biggest threat to mobile security was from employees not being vigilant in protecting company data.

One of the most important keys in keeping unauthorized users from accessing confidential data through an employee's mobile device that uses a wireless LAN is authentication. If unapproved users are not allowed to enter the WLAN without first authenticating themselves, this goes a long way to protecting the network.

This chapter explores wireless authentication and ways to make it secure. First, you look at what authentication is and the different models that are used for authenticating users. Next, you will explore the various types of servers that are used for authentication. Finally, you will learn about authentication using Extended Authentication Protocols with the IEEE 802.1x standard and how authentication and key management are used in the IEEE 802.11i security standard.

DEFINING AUTHENTICATION

Because authentication plays such a key role in wireless security, it is important to understand exactly what it is and the types of credentials that are used to authenticate users.

What Is Wireless Authentication?

Before users can be given access to a computer and its data, they must prove that they are who they claim to be. That is, users must give proof that they are "genuine" or authentic. This process of providing proof is known as authentication. In a wired local area network a user sits down at a desktop computer that is connected to the network by a cable and then logs in to the network with a username and password. Because physical access to the wired network is restricted by walls and doors, all devices connected to the network are assumed to be authentic. The *user* must be authenticated with a username and password.

However, because wireless LANs cannot limit access to the RF signal by walls or doors, wireless authentication first requires the *wireless device*—not the user—to be authenticated before being connected to the WLAN. Once the wireless device is authenticated, the user may be asked to authenticate through a username and password. In short, wireless authentication is a process in which the wireless device and user are accepted or rejected from being part of the WLAN.

There are two types of device authentication supported by the IEEE 802.11 standard. Open system authentication, the default method, uses the Service Set Identifier (SSID) to authenticate a device. After receiving an association request frame from a wireless device that wants to join the WLAN, the access point compares the SSID received with the actual SSID of the network. If the two match then the wireless device is authenticated. An optional authentication method is shared key authentication, in which the Wired Equivalent Privacy (WEP) default key is used. A wireless device sends a frame to the AP and the AP sends back a frame that contains a block of text known as the challenge text. The wireless device must encrypt the text with the default key and return it to the AP. The AP will then decrypt what was returned to see if it matches the original challenge text. If it does, the device is authenticated and allowed to become part of the network.

NOTE Both open system authorization and shared key authentication have security vulnerabilities. These are discussed in Chapter 2.

Authentication, Authorization, and Accounting (AAA)

Authentication, although an important part of network security, is only one of three key elements: authentication, authorization, and accounting, known as "triple A" or **AAA** for short. AAA makes it possible to determine who the user is (authentication), what the user can do (authorization), and what the user did (accounting). These three elements help control access to network resources, enforce security policies, and audit usage.

NOTE Although AAA forms a strong wireless network defense, all three elements are not always implemented together. You can use authentication alone or with authorization and accounting. However, authorization always requires that a user is authenticated first. You can use accounting alone, or with authentication and authorization.

Authentication provides a way of identifying a user, typically by having them enter a valid username and password before granting access. The process of authentication is based on each user having a unique set of criteria for accessing the network. These authentication credentials are then compared with the credentials stored in a database and access is granted or denied based on whether the two sets of credentials match. Authentication controls access by requiring valid user credentials.

Once authenticated, a user must be given approval or authorization to carry out specific network tasks, such as accessing a server or using a printer. **Authorization** is the process that determines whether the user has the authority to carry out certain tasks. Authorization is often defined as the process of enforcing policies; that is, it determines what types or qualities of activities, resources, or services a user is permitted. Authorization controls access per user after users authenticate.

NOTE Authorization controls the services and commands available to each authenticated user. If authorization was not enabled, authentication alone would provide the same access to services for all authenticated users.

Controlling access to network resources by authorization can be accomplished by configuring a broad authentication rule and then having a detailed authorization configuration. For example, a wireless user on an internal network may want to access a server on the external network. That user's device must first be configured to be authenticated to the entire internal network (broad authentication). Then the user must be authorized to gain access to specific servers.

The third element is **accounting**. Accounting measures the resources a user consumes during each network session. Accounting tracks the traffic that passes through a specific network appliance and enables a record of user activity to be recorded. Accounting information may include when a session begins and ends, the username, the number of bytes that pass through the network appliance for the session, the service that is being used, and the duration of each session. The information can then be used in a variety of ways:

- *To find evidence of problems*—If there is a problem (such as an attempt by an attacker to breach the system), the account data provides a valuable log file of what actions occurred.

- *For billing*—In situations for which users are charged for network access, accounting data can capture the amount of system time used or the amount of data a user sent or received during a session.

- *For planning*—Data gathered by logging session statistics and usage information can be used for trend analysis, resource utilization, and capacity planning activities.

AAA servers (servers dedicated to performing the AAA functions) can provide significant advantages in a wireless LAN. For example, when using role-based access control (RBAC), the roles themselves can be stored on the servers and retrieved as needed.

Authentication Credentials

There are three categories of credentials used to verify authentication:

- Something the user knows
- Something the user is
- Something the user has

Passwords

Credentials that fall into the category of something the user knows are typically passwords, which are a secret combination of letters and numbers that validates (authenticates) a user by what he or she knows. Passwords are used with usernames to log on to a computer and prove that the person entering the password is authentic.

Biometrics

As an alternative to passwords, **biometrics** can be used. Biometrics uses the unique human characteristics of a person for authentication (something the user is). Some human characteristics that can be used for biometric identification include fingerprints and unique characteristics of the face, hand, iris, retina, or voice.

The most common biometric device is a fingerprint scanner, shown in Figure 8-1. Although the cost of biometric devices once made them prohibitive except for within the most secure environments, today the cost of a desktop fingerprint scanner has dropped to less than $40, and some laptops come with built-in fingerprint scanners. Companies have found that the cost of using biometric devices is more than offset by the reduced number of telephone calls to the help desk about passwords that have been forgotten or must be reset.

Figure 8-1   Fingerprint scanner

 CAUTION   Most inexpensive desktop fingerprint scanners allow you to use the fingerprint scanners for several different applications or Web sites that use a password. You can enter your username and password, and it is then associated with your fingerprint, so any time your password is required, all you do is touch the scanner with your finger. However, in some products these passwords are not saved in a secure format. This means that an attacker could steal this file and have a list of all of your passwords.

According to the firm Frost and Sullivan, the market for biometric devices in the United States is expected to more than double from $527 million in 2004 to $1.4 billion by 2008. However, biometrics does have its weaknesses. Many high-end scanners are still relatively expensive, can be difficult to use, and can reject authorized users while accepting unauthorized users. These errors are mainly because of the many facial or hand characteristics that must be scanned and then compared. Also, it is possible to "steal" someone's characteristics by lifting a fingerprint from a glass, photographing an iris, or recording a voice and then using these images to trick the scanner.

Digital Certificates

The original IEEE 802.11 Wired Equivalent Privacy (WEP) relies on a secret key shared between a wireless client device and the access point. The same secret key must be installed on both the device and the AP in advance. In addition, the shared secret key is used to encrypt the cleartext as well as decrypt the ciphertext. This process is also called private key cryptography or symmetric encryption. In symmetric encryption, identical keys are used to both encrypt and decrypt the message.

NOTE

Symmetric encryption is covered in Chapter 2.

Because of the difficulties associated with key management in symmetric encryption, an alternative, known as **asymmetric encryption**, or **public key cryptography**, was designed. With asymmetric encryption, two keys are used instead of one. One of the keys, known as the **private key**, encrypts the message. The second key, called the **public key**, decrypts the message. Asymmetric encryption is illustrated in Figure 8-2. The two keys, public and private, are mathematically related. One key (private) is used to encrypt the data, while the other key (public) decrypts. The reverse also holds true. If the public key is used to encrypt the plaintext, then only the private key will decrypt it.

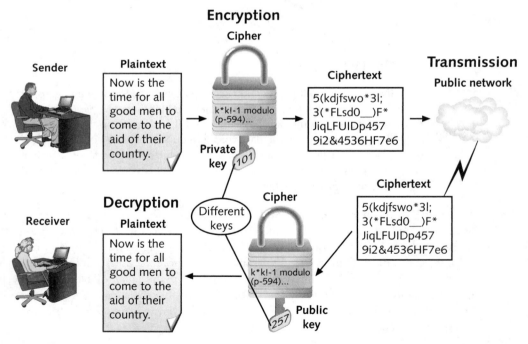

Figure 8-2 Asymmetric encryption

NOTE Asymmetric algorithms can greatly improve cryptography security, convenience, and flexibility. Public keys can be distributed freely. The primary disadvantage of public key cryptography is that it is computing intensive. The process for encrypting and decrypting can be lengthy, especially for large amounts of data.

Digital certificates are electronic files that the user has and are used to uniquely identify users and resources over networks. Much like a passport provides a universal way to establish identity and gain entry into a foreign country, digital certificates provide identification in the electronic world. Certificates are issued by a trusted third party called a **certification authority (CA)**. Similar to the role of the passport office, the CA validates the certificate holders' identity and "signs" the certificate electronically so that it cannot be forged or tampered with. Once a CA has signed a certificate, the holder can present the certificate to the network (as well as to other users and Web sites) to prove their identity and establish encrypted, confidential communications.

Although a CA may be a third party, it does not have to be. The functions that a CA performs, such as authenticating users, can be done locally instead of going to a third party. Some organizations set up a subordinate server, called a **registration authority (RA)**, to handle some CA tasks such as processing certificate requests and authenticating users. Using an RA is acceptable, as long as the user trusts both the CA and the RA.

A certificate typically includes information pertaining to its owner and to the CA that issued it, such as:

- A serial number
- The holder's public key
- The name of the certification authority that issued the certificate
- The name of the holder and other identification information required to uniquely identify the holder, such as the URL of the Web server using the certificate or an e-mail address
- The start and stop date in which the certificate is valid

NOTE The CA's signature on the certificate is much like a tamper-detection seal on a bottle of pills. Any electronic tampering with the contents can be detected.

Digital certificates can be used for authentication in a wireless LAN. In addition, digital certificates can also be used to provide encryption between the wireless device and the access point. Because the digital certificate contains the public key, it can be used (along with the corresponding private key maintained by the owner) to encrypt and decrypt transmissions.

The system of using digital certificates, CAs, and other registration authorities that verify and authenticate the validity of each party involved in a transaction over a public network is known as **public key infrastructure (PKI)**. Because PKIs continue to evolve, there currently is no single standard for using a PKI. However, PKIs play a key role in different types of authentication, particularly in Internet transactions such as electronic commerce (e-commerce).

AUTHENTICATION SERVERS

Authentication, authorization, and accounting services are often provided on a network by a dedicated AAA server. (If the server performs only authentication, it is just called an authentication server.) The most common types of authentication and AAA servers are RADIUS, Kerberos, TACACS+, or generic servers built on the Lightweight Directory Access Protocol (LDAP). Based on the type of server used, there are different network design models that can be deployed.

RADIUS

RADIUS, or Remote Authentication Dial-In User Service, was developed in 1992 and quickly became the industry standard with widespread support across nearly all vendors of networking equipment. RADIUS is suitable for "high volume service control applications" such as dial-in access to a corporate network. With the development of 802.1x port security for both wired and wireless LANs, RADIUS has recently seen even greater usage. The word "Remote" in RADIUS's name is now almost a misnomer because RADIUS authentication is used for more than just dial-in networks.

NOTE RADIUS servers are introduced in Chapter 5 as a type of authentication commonly used in the Wired Protected Access (WPA) enterprise security model.

A RADIUS client is not the wireless device requesting authentication, such as a notebook computer or PDA. Instead, a RADIUS client is typically a device such as a dial-up server or wireless access point that is responsible for sending user credentials and connection parameters in the form of a RADIUS message to a RADIUS server. The RADIUS server authenticates and authorizes the RADIUS client request, and sends back a RADIUS message response. RADIUS clients also send RADIUS accounting messages to RADIUS servers. The key with RADIUS is that messages are never directly sent between the wireless device and the RADIUS server. This prevents an attacker from penetrating the RADIUS server and compromising security.

The RADIUS standards also support the use of what RADIUS proxies. A RADIUS proxy is a computer that forwards RADIUS messages between RADIUS clients, RADIUS servers, and other RADIUS proxies.

The steps for RADIUS authentication are illustrated in Figure 8-3:

1. A wireless device sends a frame to an access point requesting permission to join the WLAN. The AP prompts the user for the user ID and password.

2. The AP creates a data packet from this information called the authentication request. This packet includes information such as identifying the specific AP that is sending the authentication request and the username and password. For protection from eavesdropping the AP (acting as a RADIUS client) encrypts the password using a shared secret key before it is sent to the RADIUS server. The authentication request is sent over the network from the AP to the RADIUS server. This communication can be done over either a local area network or a wide area network. This allows the RADIUS clients to be remotely located from the RADIUS server. If the RADIUS server cannot be reached, the AP can usually route the request to an alternate server.

3. When an authentication request is received, the RADIUS server validates that the request is from an approved AP and then decrypts the data packet to access the username and password information. This information is passed on to the appropriate security user database. This could be a text file, UNIX password file, a commercially available security system, or a custom database.

4. If the username and password are correct, the RADIUS server sends an authentication acknowledgment that includes information on the user's network system and service requirements. For example, the RADIUS server may tell the AP that the user needs TCP/IP. The acknowledgment can even contain filtering information to limit a user's access to specific resources on the network. If the username and password are not correct, the RADIUS server sends an authentication reject message to the AP and the user is denied access to the network. To ensure that requests are not responded to by unauthorized persons or devices on the network, the RADIUS server sends an authentication key, or signature, identifying itself to the RADIUS client.

5. If accounting is also supported by the RADIUS server, then an entry is started in the accounting database.

6. Once the server information is received and verified by the AP, it enables the necessary configuration to deliver the wireless services to the user.

8

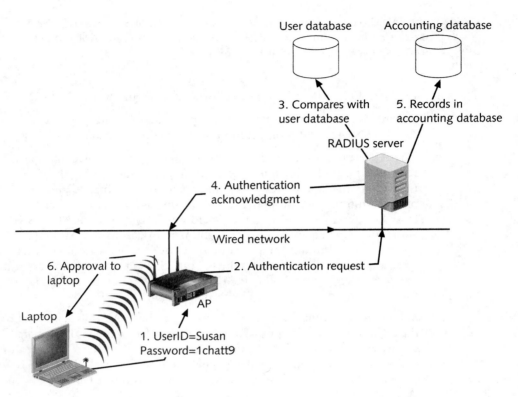

Figure 8-3   RADIUS authentication

NOTE

RADIUS messages are sent as User Datagram Protocol (UDP) messages. Generally, UDP port 1812 is used for RADIUS authentication messages and UDP port 1813 is used for RADIUS accounting messages, though some APs may use UDP port 1645 for RADIUS authentication messages and UDP port 1646 for RADIUS accounting messages. Only one RADIUS message is included in the UDP payload of each RADIUS packet.

RADIUS servers can also be used in conjunction with VLAN tagging for additional security. An access point can apply a specific VLAN tag on a per-user basis by extracting the tag from the authorization response it receives from the RADIUS server. Because the correct VLAN tag is automatically applied independent of the virtual WLAN, it eliminates the need to assign a SSID to a specific functional group or work team. It also enhances user mobility by enabling a WLAN client to remain with the same VLAN when moving between SSIDs.

NOTE

VLANs are introduced in Chapter 7.

RADIUS allows a company to maintain user profiles in a central database that all remote servers can share. Doing so increases security, allowing a company to set up a policy that can be applied at a single administered network point. Having a central service also means that it is easier to track usage for billing and for keeping network statistics.

Kerberos

Kerberos is an authentication system developed by the Massachusetts Institute of Technology (MIT) and is used to verify the identity of networked users. Named after a three-headed dog in Greek mythology that guarded the gates of Hades, Kerberos uses encryption and authentication for security. Kerberos functions under Windows Server 2003, Apple Mac OS, and Linux. It is most often used by universities and government agencies.

NOTE

Kerberos is also covered in Chapter 2.

Kerberos has often been compared to using a driver's license to cash a check. A state agency, such as the Department of Motor Vehicles (DMV), issues a driver's license that has these characteristics:

- It is difficult to copy
- It contains specific information (name, address, height, etc.)
- It lists restrictions (must wear corrective lenses, etc.)
- It will expire at some future date

Kerberos works in a similar fashion. Kerberos is typically used when someone on a network attempts to use a network service, and the service wants assurance that the user is who he says he is. The user is provided a **ticket** that is issued by the Kerberos authentication server, much like a driver's license is issued by the DMV. This ticket contains information linking it to the user. The user presents this ticket to the network for a service. The service then examines the ticket to verify the identity of the user. If all information is confirmed, the user is accepted. Kerberos tickets share some of the same characteristics as a driver's license: tickets are difficult to copy (because they are encrypted), they contain specific user information, they restrict what a user can do, and they expire after a few hours or a day.

NOTE

Issuing and submitting tickets in a Kerberos system is handled internally and is transparent to the user.

Kerberos is considered a very secure authentication system. It is available for free from the MIT Web site.

Terminal Access Control Access Control System (TACACS+)

Similar to RADIUS, **Terminal Access Control Access Control System (TACACS+)** is an industry standard protocol specification that forwards username and password information to a centralized server. The centralized server can either be a TACACS+ database or a database such as a Linux or UNIX password file with TACACS+ protocol support. TACACS+ (as well as other remote access security protocols such as RADIUS) is designed to support thousands of remote connections. In a large network, the user database is usually large, and is best kept on a centralized server. This saves memory in all the access devices and eliminates the need to update every access server when new users are added, or when passwords are modified or changed. TACACS+ supports authentication, authorization, and auditing.

 TACACS+ uses TCP port 49 for communication.

NOTE

Lightweight Directory Access Protocol (LDAP)

A **directory service** is a database stored on the network that contains information about users and network devices. A directory service contains information such as the user's name, telephone extension, e-mail address, logon name, and other facts. The directory service also keeps track of all of the resources on the network and a user's privileges to those resources, and grants or denies access based on the directory service information. Directory services make it much easier to grant privileges or permissions to network users.

The International Organization for Standardization (ISO) created a standard for directory services known as **X.500**. The purpose of the X.500 standard was to standardize how the data was stored so that any computer system could access these directories. It provides the capability to look up information by name (a **white-pages service**) and to browse and search for information by category (a **yellow-pages service**).

The information is held in a **directory information base (DIB)**. Entries in the DIB are arranged in a tree structure called the **directory information tree (DIT)**. Each entry is a named object and consists of a set of attributes. Each attribute has a defined attribute type and one or more values. The directory defines the mandatory and optional attributes for each class of object. Each named object may have one or more object classes associated with it.

The X.500 standard itself does not define any representation for the data stored, such as usernames. What is defined is the structural form of names. Systems that are based on the X.500, such as the DCE Directory, Novell's NDS, and Microsoft's Active Directory, each define their own representation.

The X.500 standard defines a protocol for a client application to access an X.500 directory called the **Directory Access Protocol (DAP)**. However, the DAP is too large to run on a personal computer. The **Lightweight Directory Access Protocol (LDAP)**, sometimes called X.500 Lite, is a simpler subset of DAP. The primary differences between DAP and LDAP are:

- Unlike X.500 DAP, LDAP was designed to run over TCP/IP, making it ideal for Internet and intranet applications. X.500 DAP requires special software to access the network.

- LDAP has simpler functions, making it easier and less expensive to implement.

- LDAP encodes its protocol elements in a less complex way than X.500 that enables it to streamline requests.

If the information requested is not contained in the directory, DAP only returns an error to the client requesting the information, which must then issue a new search request. By contrast, LDAP servers return only results, making the distributed X.500 servers appear as a single logical directory.

 NOTE LDAP was developed by Netscape Communications and the University of Michigan in 1996.

LDAP makes it possible for almost any application running on virtually any computer platform to obtain directory information. Because LDAP is an open protocol, applications need not worry about the type of server hosting the directory. Today many LDAP servers are implemented using standard relational database management systems as the engine, and communicate via eXtensible Markup Language (XML) documents served over HTTP.

LDAP is often used in a wireless LAN in two different ways. First, an authentication server can use LDAP for retrieving user information when authentications are requested. Second, many RADIUS servers support interfacing with an LDAP database. This gives the added security of using RADIUS's secure protocol with the simplicity of an LDAP database.

Authentication Design Models

There are four design models for deploying a RADIUS authentication server and LDAP or other types of databases. Those authentication design models are single site deployment, distributed autonomous sites, distributed sites with centralized authentication and security, and distributed sites and security with centralized authentication.

Single Site Deployment

Single site deployment is the simplest type authentication model. As illustrated in Figure 8-4, it consists of one or more RADIUS servers accessing a centralized authentication database. This model is used when all WLAN users are located at a single site. Single site deployment has the advantage of only one authentication database that must be supported. Another advantage is that it is fairly easy to increase the capacity of the single site deployment model by adding additional RADIUS servers. However, single site deployment can be more difficult to scale as more users are added.

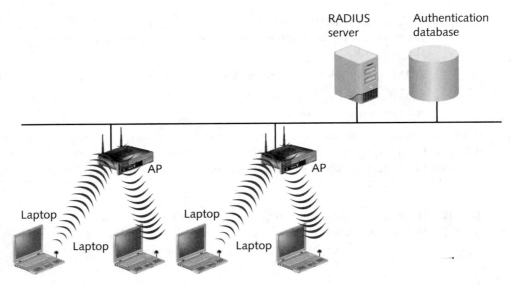

Figure 8-4   Single site deployment

Distributed Autonomous Sites

In an environment in which several different sites support WLAN services, authentication can be performed either locally or remotely. A **distributed autonomous site deployment** uses local authentication with one or more RADIUS servers at each site. However, the authentication database is replicated from one central site to each local site. The local RADIUS servers actually perform the authentication and any accounting activity.

The distributed autonomous site deployment has two advantages. First, because authentication is performed locally it does not rely on a remote network connection to perform this function. This means that if the remote connection is not properly functioning, then authentication can not properly occur. Second, additional RADIUS servers can be added to the remote site to handle any increase in the number of users. This is because not all authentication databases can be easily replicated. However, a disadvantage is that it may not be appropriate for authentication systems other than LDAP or Microsoft Active Directory that are not easily replicated. A distributed autonomous site deployment is illustrated in Figure 8-5.

Distributed Sites with Centralized Authentication and Security

The opposite of distributed autonomous sites, in which the local RADIUS servers perform authentication functions, is **distributed sites with centralized authentication and security deployment**. The distributed sites with centralized authentication and security

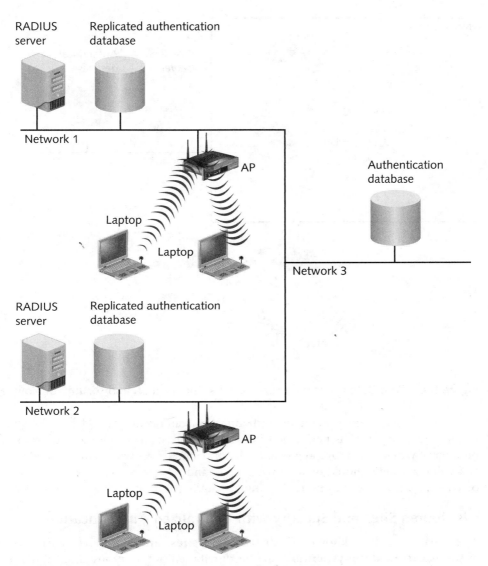

Figure 8-5 Distributed autonomous site deployment

deployment model, as seen in Figure 8-6, relies on remote RADIUS servers to perform authentication. This has a management advantage in that the RADIUS server or servers and authentication database are all centrally located and can be more easily maintained and made more secure.

However, there are significant disadvantages of distributed sites with centralized authentication and security deployment. First, authentication is dependent on the reliability of the network connection between the remote sites and the RADIUS server and authentication

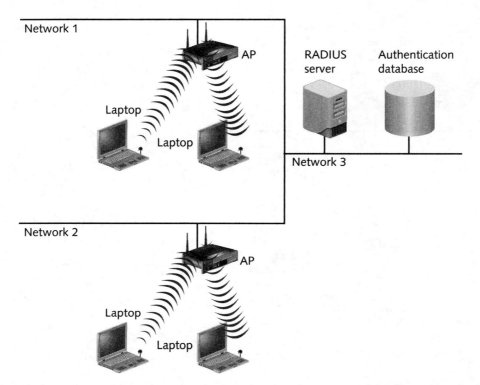

Figure 8-6   Distributed sites with centralized authentication and security deployment

database. If the link goes down, no authentication can occur. Second, because all authentication and encryption is performed in one location, it may cause a bottleneck if a large number of wireless users are supported. The distributed sites with centralized authentication and security model should be used when a fast and reliable network connection is available or when, for security reasons, replicating the authentication database is not desirable.

Distributed Sites and Security with Centralized Authentication

The final model is known as **distributed sites and security with centralized authentication deployment**. As in the distributed autonomous sites model, RADIUS servers are located at each site to perform authentication. However, instead of the authentication database being replicated to each site, it is centrally located. The distributed sites and security with centralized authentication deployment model is illustrated in Figure 8-7.

The advantage of the distributed sites and security with centralized authentication deployment is that it mitigates the bottleneck problem with the distributed sites with centralized authentication and security deployment. The processing load is distributed between the different local RADIUS servers. However, this model still is dependent on a reliable and fast network connection.

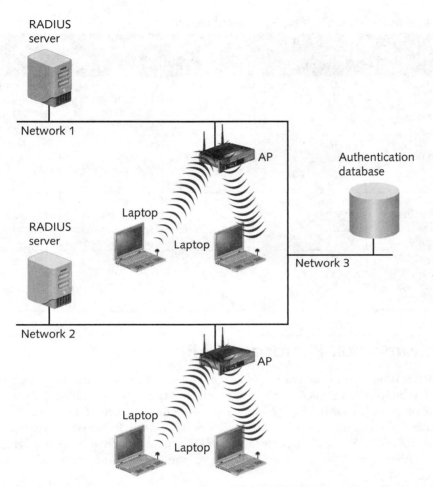

Figure 8-7 Distributed sites and security with centralized authentication deployment

The four authentication design models—single site deployment, distributed autonomous sites, distributed sites with centralized authentication and security, and distributed sites and security with centralized authentication—are summarized in Table 8-1. Each model has its advantages and disadvantages, and careful consideration should be given prior to implementing any of them.

Table 8-1   Authentication design deployment models

Model	Location of RADIUS servers	Location of authentication database	Advantages	Disadvantages
Single site	Local	Local	Only one authentication database to support	May be difficult to scale if large number of users added
Distributed autonomous sites	Local	Remote	Does not rely on remote network connection	Not all authentication databases can be easily replicated
Distributed sites with centralized authentication and security	Remote	Remote	Authentication database more secure because not replicated	Dependent on reliable network link
Distributed sites and security with centralized authentication	Local	Remote	Reduces "bottleneck" processing	Dependent on reliable network link

EXTENDED AUTHENTICATION PROTOCOLS (EAP)

The authentication server in an IEEE 802.1x configuration that stores the list of the names and credentials of authorized users to verify their authenticity is typically a RADIUS server. The management protocol of IEEE 802.1x that governs the interaction between the wireless device, access point, and RADIUS server is known as the **Extensible Authentication Protocol (EAP)**. EAP is an "envelope" that can carry many different kinds of exchange data used for authentication, such as a challenge/response, one-time passwords, and digital certificates.

NOTE   EAP was originally defined for dial-up access but is now used for both wired and wireless access.

Figure 8-8 illustrates how EAP is used in IEEE 802.1x. After the initial association request is set by the wireless device (supplicant) to the access point (authenticator), EAP is then used to begin a "dialog" between the AP and the device. Once the AP sends the information to the RADIUS server (authentication server), EAP continues to be used for sending request, response, and acceptance frames between the AP and the device. Once the device has been authenticated by RADIUS, a final handshake takes place with the keys to be used by Wi-Fi Protected Access 2 (WPA2).

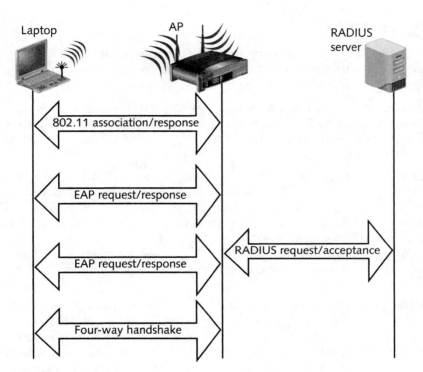

Figure 8-8   EAP in IEEE 802.1x

 Handshakes are discussed later in the chapter.

EAP was designed with flexibility in mind, so that different protocols could be used—even some that had not yet been designed—to support different authentication methods and associated network security policies.

Several of the EAP protocols use **hashing**, also called a **one-way hash**, which creates a ciphertext from cleartext. However, the encrypted text is never intended to be decrypted. Instead, it is used in a comparison for identification purposes. Hash algorithms verify the accuracy of a value without transmitting the value itself, subjecting it to attacks.

 Hashing is covered in more detail in *Security+ Guide to Network Security Fundamentals 2nd ed* (0-619-21566-6).

The EAP protocols that exist today can be divided into three categories: EAP legacy protocols, EAP weak protocols, and EAP strong protocols.

EAP Legacy Protocols

EAP legacy protocols are those that are no longer extensively used for wireless (or wired) authentication. This is because stronger and more flexible protocols have since been created that have supplanted older protocols. Three EAP legacy protocols include:

- **Password Authentication Protocol (PAP)**—PAP was one of the earliest EAP protocols. It is a basic authentication protocol that was used to authenticate a user to a remote access server or to an ISP. PAP transmits unencrypted passwords in cleartext. It is considered a very insecure protocol.

- **Challenge-Handshake Authentication Protocol (CHAP)**—The foundation of CHAP is a three-way handshake, which is accomplished during the initial authentication and may be repeated any time after the link has been established. Both the device and the authenticator share a secret key. The authenticator sends a "challenge" message to the device, which responds with a value calculated using a one-way hash function. The authenticator then compares that response against its own calculation of the expected hash value. If the values match, the authentication is acknowledged.

- **Microsoft Challenge-Handshake Authentication Protocol (MS-CHAP)**—MS-CHAP is the Microsoft implementation of CHAP. There are two versions of MS-CHAP: MS-CHAPv1, and MS-CHAPv2, the first of which was introduced with Windows 2000. MS-CHAP has some additional features, such as providing a method for changing passwords and retrying in the event of a failure.

EAP Weak Protocols

Two EAP protocols are still used but have security vulnerabilities with wireless networks. These EAP weak protocols include:

- **Extended Authentication Protocol–MD 5 (EAP-MD5)**—EAP-MD5 allows a RADIUS server to authenticate wireless devices stations by verifying a hash known as MD5 of each user's password. When used in a wired LAN, EAP-MD5 is considered a basic (and reasonable) choice if there is low risk of attackers sniffing packets or launching an active attack. However, EAP-MD5 is not suitable for wireless LANs because outsiders can easily determine the identities of wireless devices by sniffing packets and password hashes. Or, an attacker can set up fake access points to trick stations into authenticating with the imposter instead of the actual AP.

- **Cisco's Lightweight EAP (LEAP)**—LEAP is considered a step above EAP-MD5. It requires mutual authentication and delivering keys used for WLAN encryption using Cisco clients. However, LEAP is vulnerable to dictionary attack tools.

NOTE

Cisco now recommends that users migrate to a more secure EAP than LEAP.

EAP Strong Protocols

When using EAP for WLANs there are several protocols that are considered strong. These EAP protocols include:

- **EAP with Transport Layer Security (EAP-TLS)**—EAP-TLS requires that the wireless device and RADIUS server prove their identities to each other by using public key cryptography such as digital certificates. The exchange between devices is secured by an encrypted tunnel based on the Transport layer. This makes EAP-TLS resistant to dictionary and other types of attacks. EAP-TLS is generally found in large organizations that use only Windows-based computers (Windows XP, 2000, and 2003) with digital certificates.

- **EAP with Tunneled TLS (EAP-TTLS)** and **Protected EAP (PEAP)**—These EAPs are designed to simplify the deployment of 802.1x. Instead of issuing digital certificates to all users, EAP-TTLS and PEAP (both PEAPv0 and PEAPv1) use Windows logins and passwords. PEAP is a more flexible scheme than EAP-TLS because it creates an encrypted channel between the client and the authentication server, and the channel then protects the subsequent user authentication exchange. To create this channel the PEAP client first authenticates the PEAP authentication server using digital certificate authentication. RADIUS servers that support EAP-TTLS and PEAP can check access requests with Windows Domain Controllers, Active Directories, and other existing user databases. However, EAP-TTLS and PEAP passwords are vulnerable to theft from social engineering whereas a digital certificate is not.

IEEE 802.11 AUTHENTICATION AND KEY MANAGEMENT

Once a user's device is authenticated the next step is to enable encryption. Encryption is based on using a series of interrelated keys. The hierarchy between these keys is illustrated in Figure 8-9.

Master Key (MK)

If authentication is performed by IEEE 802.1x (as described earlier) using the WPA or WPA2 Enterprise model, the distribution of the **master key (MK)**, from which all other keys are formed, is done by the authentication server. An MK is sent from the authentication server (usually a RADIUS server) to the authenticator (access point) as part of an acceptance packet. The MK, which is tied to that specific authentication session, is encrypted within an EAP packet. The access point forwards this packet directly to the wireless device without seeing its contents.

8

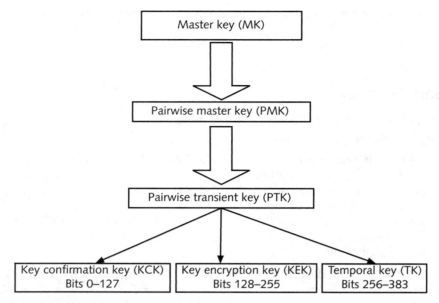

Figure 8-9 Key hierarchy

Pairwise Master Key (PMK)

The second key is derived from the MK and is called the **pairwise master key (PMK)**. The IEEE standard defines two ways in which wireless devices and APs can retrieve a PMK. The difference depends on the security model that is being used. If the Wi-Fi Protected Access (WPA) Personal security model or WPA2 Personal security model is being used, then a preshared key (PSK) is entered by a user into both the access point and the wireless device (usually as a passphrase, which can be between 8 and 63 characters). This PSK is then used in conjunction with the service set identifier (SSID) to form the mathematical basis of the PMK on the wireless device as well as on the access point.

If authentication is performed using the WPA or WPA2 Enterprise security model, the PMK is generated by the RADIUS server and sent to the access point. The wireless device, which has already received the PM from the authentication server, will use it to generate its own PMK.

Pairwise Transient Key (PTK)

Once the device and the access point each have the same PMK, they can create their own **pairwise transient key (PTK)**. The PTK is generated by combining the PMK with four pieces of data:

- The supplicant's (wireless device) MAC address
- The authenticator's (access point) MAC address

- A randomly chosen value called a **nonce** that is created by supplicant (and sent to the authenticator)

- A nonce created by the authenticator (and sent to the supplicant)

The PTK is itself divided into three keys. The first key is the **key confirmation key (KCK)**. The KCK is used by the EAP key exchanges to provide data origin authenticity. The second key is the **key encryption key (KEK)**. The KEK is used by the EAP key exchanges to provide confidentiality. The third key is the **temporal key**. This key is used by the data–confidentiality protocols.

Figure 8-10 illustrates the process of the creation of MK, PMK, and PTK keys in a WPA or WPA2 Enterprise security model. The creation of keys in a WPA or WPA2 Personal security model, using a PSK, is seen in Figure 8-11.

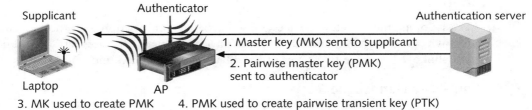

3. MK used to create PMK   4. PMK used to create pairwise transient key (PTK)

5. PMK used to create pairwise transient key (PTK)

Figure 8-10   Key creation in WPA or WPA2 Enterprise security model

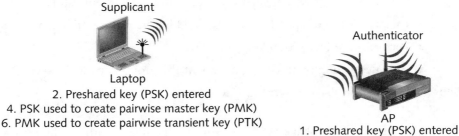

Figure 8-11   Key creation in WPA or WPA2 Personal security model

Group Keys

The MKs are used for access point to wireless device transmissions, or unicast transmissions. When an AP sends the same packet to all wireless devices, known as a broadcast, MKs are not used. Instead, **group keys (GK)** are used. The hierarchy of GKs is seen in Figure 8-12. The starting point of the group key hierarchy is the **group master key (GMK)**. The GMK is simply a random number. A pseudorandom function uses the GMK, the authenticator's

MAC address, and a nonce from the authenticator to create a **group temporal key (GTK)**. The GTK is the value that the wireless devices use to decrypt broadcast messages from APs.

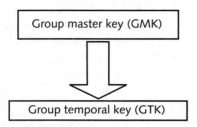

Figure 8-12   Group key hierarchy

Handshakes

Access points and wireless devices must exchange information in order to create and acknowledge the MKs and the GKs. This exchange of information is known as **handshakes.** There are two types of handshakes, one for MKs and one for GKs.

Four-Way Handshake

The exchange of information for the MK is based on a **four-way handshake**. The four-way handshake accomplishes the following tasks:

- Authenticates the security parameters that were negotiated
- Confirms the PMK between the supplicant and authenticator
- Establishes the temporal keys to be used by the data-confidentiality protocol
- Performs the first group key handshake
- Provides keying material to implement the group key handshake

The four-way handshake exchanges four packets between the supplicant and the authenticator:

- Four-Way Handshake Packet 1—In the first message, the authenticator sends the supplicant a random value called a nonce (known as the **ANonce**). The supplicant then creates its nonce known as the **SNonce**. At this point the supplicant can now calculate the PTK (the authenticator has already received its PTK from the RADIUS server).

- Four-Way Handshake Packet 2—The supplicant sends the SNonce to the authenticator and the security parameters that it used during association. The entire message gets an authentication check using the KCK from the pairwise key hierarchy. The authenticator can then verify that all the information, including the security parameters sent at association, are valid.

- Four-Way Handshake Packet 3—The authenticator sends the supplicant the security parameters that it is using when sending out its beacons and probe responses (multicast messages). The authenticator also sends the GTK encrypted using the KEK. Again, the entire message gets an authentication check, which allows the supplicant to verify that the information, such as the authenticator's security parameters, is valid.

- Four-Way Handshake Packet 4—The fourth message is an acknowledgment. This acknowledgement indicates the temporal keys are now in place to be used by the data-confidentiality protocols.

The four-way handshake exchange is seen in Figure 8-13.

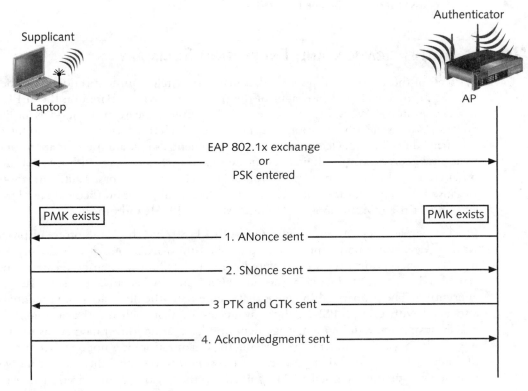

Figure 8-13 Four-way handshake

Group Key Handshake

The purpose of the group key handshake is to authenticate the GTK. The group key handshake is preceded by the four-way handshake, because Packets 3 and 4 include a group key.

- Group Key Handshake Packet 1—The authenticator sends the supplicant the GTK that was encrypted using the KEK. In addition, the entire message gets an authentication verification.

- Group Key Handshake Packet 2—The second message indicates that the temporal keys are now in place and ready to be used by the data confidentiality protocol.

NOTE As wireless devices roam back and forth between APs they must constantly be re-authenticated. This can have a negative effect on system performance or if Voice over WLAN (VoWLAN) is being used. Key caching allows a device and AP to retain a security association when a device roams away from an access point. When the device roams back to the area of that access point, the security association can then be restarted.

WIRELESS AUTHENTICATION AND ENCRYPTION SUMMARY

With all of the various components that make up wireless authentication it can be easy to get lost in the details and lose sight of the process as a whole. Based on the IEEE 802.11i security protocol, WPA Enterprise and WPA2 Enterprise security models utilize IEEE 802.1x port-based authentication. The port over which the device connects to the network is restricted until the device is approved. The credentials that are used for approval can be a username and password, a digital certificate signed by a certificate authority, biometrics, or other credentials. The management protocol that controls port-based authentication is EAP. Because EAP messages are sent as cleartext by default, different protocols are used to encrypt and protect the transmissions, including EAP-TLS, PEAP, and others.

Once a wireless device is authenticated by IEEE 802.1x, this same protocol provides the wireless device a unique encryption key called the MK. From this single key all of the necessary encryption keys for encrypted communication can then be created. These keys can also be changed during a session. There are several advantages to IEEE 802.1x encryption. The primary advantage is that it eliminates the difficulties and potential dangers associated with using a PSK. Other advantages are that each user has a unique key, keys remain strong and require no management, and if a user no longer has permission to use the wireless LAN (such as an employee leaving the organization) it is not necessary to change all of the keys. In addition, adding additional access points to extend the size of a network only requires that the newly installed APs connect to the existing authentication server.

There are a variety of products that support IEEE 802.1x authentication and encryption. On the wireless device, built-in support for supplicants first appeared in Windows XP Service Pack 1 (SP1), Windows 2000 SP4, and Mac OS X 10.3. An open-source project known as Open1X is available for Linux devices. For the authentication server, free products are available, such as FreeRADIUS and add-on support to various devices such as Linksys. Microsoft Windows Server 2003 supports 802.1x, as do several commercial products.

IEEE 802.11i WPA Enterprise and WPA2 Enterprise security using IEEE 802.1x addresses both authentication and encryption for wireless LANs. This provides a secure environment that protects the wireless LAN from attacks.

CHAPTER SUMMARY

❑ Wireless authentication is the process of a device proving that it is "genuine" and not an imposter. Authentication is one part of three key elements, the others being authorization, or determining whether the user has the authority to carry out tasks, and accounting, which measures the resources used during a session. These three are known as "AAA." Authentication can be based on something the user knows, something the user is, or something the user has.

❑ Authentication servers are used to authenticate users in a WLAN. The most common type is a RADIUS server, which can be used as part of the IEEE 802.1x protocol. There are four basic models for deploying a RADIUS server. Kerberos is an authentication system named after a three-headed dog in Greek mythology that guarded the gates of Hades. Kerberos uses encryption and authentication for security. TACACS+ is an industry standard that is designed to support large numbers of connections. LDAP is an open protocol that allows almost any application to obtain directory information.

❑ The management protocol of IEEE 802.1x that governs the interaction between the wireless device, access point, and RADIUS server is known as the EAP. EAP is an "envelope" that can carry many different kinds of exchange data used for authentication, such as a challenge/response, one-time passwords, and digital certificates. EAP was designed with flexibility in mind, so that different protocols could be used—even some that had not yet been designed—to support different authentication methods and associated network security policies.

❑ IEEE 802.11 authentication and key management is based on a key hierarchy. If authentication is performed by IEEE 802.1x using the WPA or WPA2 Enterprise security model, the distribution of the MK, from which all other keys are formed, is sent by the authentication server to the supplicant, from which the PMK is then created. The authentication server directly creates the PMK and sends it to the authenticator. If the WPA or WPA2 Personal security model is used, a PSK is entered into all devices and this is used to create the PMK. PMKs are then used to create the PTK, which is made up of three parts.

❑ When an AP sends a broadcast packet to all wireless devices, GKs are used. The starting point of the group key hierarchy is the GMK, which is a random number that is used along with the authenticator's MAC address and a nonce to create a GTK. This becomes the value that the wireless devices use to decrypt broadcast messages from APs. The exchange of information between the APs and devices is known as a handshake, of which are there two types, one for the MK and one for the GK.

KEY TERMS

AAA — The combination of authentication, authorization, and accounting.

AAA server — A network device that performs authentication, authorization, and accounting services.

accounting — The process of measuring the resources a user consumes during a network session.

ANonce — A nonce sent from the authenticator to the supplicant.

asymmetric encryption — Encryption in which two mathematically related keys are used instead of one. Also known as public key cryptography.

authorization — The process that determines whether the user has the authority to carry out such tasks.

biometrics — Authentication based on the unique human characteristics of a person, such as a fingerprint.

certification authority (CA) — A trusted third party that issues digital certificates.

Challenge-Handshake Authentication Protocol (CHAP) — An older three-way authentication handshake that is accomplished during the initial authentication and may be repeated any time after the link has been established.

digital certificates — Electronic files that are used to uniquely identify users and resources over networks.

Directory Access Protocol (DAP) — The X.500 standard that defines a protocol for a client application to access the X.500 directory.

directory information base (DIB) — The repository in which X.500 information is held.

directory information tree (DIT) — The tree structure of a directory information base.

directory service — A database stored on the network itself that contains information about users and network devices.

distributed autonomous site deployment — An authentication model that uses local authentication with one or more RADIUS servers at each site, but the authentication database is replicated from one central site to each local site.

distributed sites and security with centralized authentication deployment — A deployment model in which RADIUS servers are located at each site to perform authentication. Instead of the authentication database being replicated to each site, it is centrally located.

distributed sites with centralized authentication and security deployment — A deployment model in which the distributed sites with centralized authentication and security deployment rely on remote RADIUS servers to perform authentication.

EAP with Transport Layer Security (EAP-TLS) — An authentication protocol that requires that the wireless device and RADIUS server both prove their identities to each other by using public key cryptography such as digital certificates.

EAP with Tunneled TLS (EAP-TTLS) — An authentication protocol that uses Windows logins and passwords instead of issuing digital certificates.

Extended Authentication Protocol-MD 5 (EAP-MD5) — An authentication protocol that allows a RADIUS server to authenticate wireless devices by verifying a hash of each user's password.

Extensible Authentication Protocol (EAP) — An "envelope" that can carry many different kinds of exchange data used for authentication, such as a challenge/response, one-time passwords, and digital certificates.

four-way handshake — An exchange of information for the master key that authenticates the security parameters that were negotiated, confirms the PNK, establishes temporal keys, performs the first group key handshake, and provides keying material to implement the group key handshake.

group keys (GK) — Keys that are used in the master key model when an AP sends the same packet to all wireless devices.

group master key (GMK) — A random number that becomes the starting point of the group key hierarchy in the master key model.

group temporal key (GTK) — A key created by a pseudorandom function that uses the GMK, the authenticator's MAC address and a nonce from the authenticator in the master key model.

handshake — An electronic exchange of information between two devices that typically contains acknowledgments of the receipt of the information.

hashing — A process of creating a ciphertext that is never intended to be decrypted but instead used in a comparison for identification purposes.

Kerberos — An authentication system developed by the Massachusetts Institute of Technology (MIT) that is used to verify the identity of networked users.

key confirmation key (KCK) — A part of the pairwise transient key that is used by the EAP key exchanges to provide data origin authenticity.

key encryption key (KEK) — A part of the pairwise transient key that is used by the EAP key exchanges to provide confidentiality.

Lightweight Directory Access Protocol (LDAP) — A simpler subset of the Directory Access Protocol (DAP).

Lightweight EAP (LEAP) — An authentication protocol that requires mutual authentication and delivering keys used for WLAN encryption.

master key (MK) — A key from which all other keys are formed when using IEEE 802.1x authentication.

Microsoft Challenge-Handshake Authentication Protocol (MS-CHAP) — The Microsoft implementation of CHAP as an Extensible Authentication Protocol (EAP).

nonce — A random value used in cryptography to prevent different types of attacks.

one-way hash — A process of creating a ciphertext that is never intended to be decrypted but instead is used in a comparison for identification purposes.

pairwise master key (PMK) — A secondary key is derived from the master key.

pairwise transient key (PTK) — A key created by the wireless device and the access point after each device has its PMK.

Password Authentication Protocol (PAP) — An older authentication protocol that was used to authenticate a user to a remote access server or to an ISP.

private key — One key of asymmetric encryption that encrypts the message.

Protected EAP (PEAP) — An authentication protocol that uses Windows logins and passwords instead of issuing digital certificates.

public key — One key of asymmetric encryption that decrypts the message.

public key cryptography — Encryption in which two mathematically related keys are used instead of one.

public key infrastructure (PKI) — The use of digital certificates, CAs, and other registration authorities that validate each party of a transaction over a public network.

registration authority (RA) — A subordinate certification authority server.

single site deployment — The simplest type of authentication model that consists of one or more RADIUS servers accessing a centralized authentication database.

SNonce — A nonce sent from the supplicant to the authenticator.

temporal key — A part of the pairwise transient key that is used by the data-confidentiality protocols.

Terminal Access Control Access Control System (TACACS+) — An industry standard protocol specification that forwards username and password information to a centralized server.

ticket — A token that is issued by a Kerberos authentication server.

X.500 — The International Standards Organization (ISO) standard for directory services.

white-pages service — An X.500 service that provides the capability to look up information by name.

yellow-pages service — An X.500 service that provides the capability to browse and search for information by category.

REVIEW QUESTIONS

1. A wireless LAN requires that the _____ must be authenticated first.
   a. supplicant
   b. authenticator
   c. authentication server
   d. user

2. Each of the following make up the AAA elements in network security *except*
   a. determining user need (analyzing)
   b. controlling access to network resources (authentication)
   c. enforcing security policies (authorization)
   d. auditing usage (accounting)

3. Each of the following is a category of credentials that is used to verify authentication except
   a. something the user knows
   b. something the user purchases
   c. something the user is
   d. something the user has

4. Each of the following human characteristics can be used for biometric identification except
   a. fingerprint
   b. face
   c. iris
   d. weight

5. Asymmetric encryption uses _____ keys.
   a. two
   b. three
   c. four
   d. five

6. Digital signatures are electronic files that are used to uniquely identify users and resources over networks. True or False?

7. Some organizations set up a subordinate server, called a registration authority (RA), to handle some certification authority (CA) tasks, such as processing certificate requests and authenticating users. True or False?

8. The most common type of server used with IEEE 802.1x is a RADIUS server. True or False?

9. A directory service is a database stored on the network and contains all the information about users and network devices. True or False?

10. A disadvantage of the Lightweight Directory Access Protocol (LDAP) is that it can only be used on Windows-based computers. True or False?

11. A(n) _____ uses local authentication with one or more RADIUS servers at each site, yet the authentication database is replicated from one central site to each local site.

12. The _____ is an "envelope" that can carry many different kinds of exchange data used for authentication, such as a challenge/response, one-time passwords, and digital certificates.

13. _____ is considered an acceptable protocol for use in a wired network but not for a WLAN because outsiders can easily determine the identities of wireless devices by sniffing packets and password hashes.

8

14. _____ requires that the wireless device and RADIUS server prove their identities to each other by using public key cryptography such as digital certificates.

15. Instead of issuing digital certificates to all users, _____ and PEAP use Windows logins and passwords.

16. Explain how a pairwise master key is created in an access point and wireless device in a WPA2 Enterprise security model network.

17. What are the three keys that make up the pairwise transient key (PTK)?

18. What is the difference between group keys (GK) and master keys (MK)?

19. Describe the four-way handshake.

20. How does authorization differ from authentication?

HANDS-ON PROJECTS

HANDS-ON PROJECTS

Project 8-1: Viewing a Digital Certificate in Windows XP

A digital certificate is a means of showing that the source of a file is from a trusted user. Windows XP has several digital certificates installed that have been issued by certificate authorities (CAs). This means that Windows XP can download, install, and use software from one of these agencies without asking for permission from you because they are from a trusted source. In this project, you will view the settings of a certificate.

If you are using a computer in a school's computer lab or a computer at work, talk to your network administrator before performing this project. You may need special permissions set before you can change these configuration settings.

1. On a Windows XP computer, click **Start** and then click **Run**. The Run dialog box opens.

2. Type **MMC** in the Open text box, and then click **OK**. The Console1 window opens.

3. Click **File** on the menu bar, and then click **Add/Remove Snap-in** to display the Add/Remove Snap-in dialog box.

4. Click **Add** to display the Add Standalone Snap-in dialog box, as shown in Figure 8-14.

5. Click **Certificates** in the Snap-in list, and then click **Add**. The Certificates snap-in dialog box opens.

6. Click **My user account** if it is not already selected, and then click **Finish**.

7. Click **Close** in the Add Standalone Snap-in dialog box.

8. In the Add/Remove Snap-in dialog box, Certificates – Current User is displayed as a snap-in. Click **OK**.

Figure 8-14   Add Standalone Snap-in dialog box

9. The Console1 dialog box now lists certificates for the current user. In the left pane, click the **+ (plus sign)** next to **Certificates – Current User** to display the certificates issued to the current user.

10. Click the **+ (plus sign)** next to **Trusted Root Certification Authorities**, and then click **Certificates**. The certificates that have been issued are listed in the right pane, as shown in Figure 8-15.

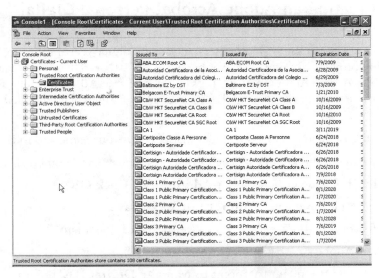

Figure 8-15   Windows XP certificates

11. Scroll down the right pane and double-click **Microsoft Root Authority** to display the Certificate dialog box.

12. Click the **Details** tab.

13. In the top pane, scroll down and click **Public key** to view the key in the bottom pane.

14. Click **OK** to close the Certificate dialog box.

15. Now view the Certificate Revocation Lists (CRL) and see any untrusted certificates on your computer. In the Console1 dialog click the **+ (plus sign)** next to **Intermediate Certification Authorities**, and then click **Certification Revocation List**.

16. Double-click one of the revoked certificates. Read the information about it and click fields for more detail if necessary. Why do you think this certificate has been revoked? Close the Certificate Revocation List by clicking the **OK** button.

17. Click the **+ (plus sign)** next to **Untrusted Certificates**, and then click **Certificates**. The certificates that are no longer trusted are listed in the right pane.

18. Double-click one of the untrusted certificates. Read the information about it and click fields for more detail if necessary. Why do you think this certificate is no longer trusted?

19. Click **OK** to close the Certificate dialog box.

20. To close the Console1 dialog box, click **File** on the menu bar and then click **Exit**. Click **No** when asked if you want to save the settings to Console1. This does not affect using the certificates but only how they are displayed through the snap-in.

HANDS-ON PROJECTS

Project 8-2: Creating an Adobe Acrobat Personal Digital Certificate

A variety of application packages allow users to create digital certificates to validate documents. In this project you will use Adobe Acrobat 7.0 or 6.0 to create a digital certificate. Note that Adobe Acrobat is not the same as the free Adobe Reader software. Before you begin these steps, verify that Adobe Acrobat 6.0 or 7.0 has been installed on your computer.

1. Open Microsoft Word and create a document that contains your name and today's date.

2. To create a PDF file of this document, click **File** on the menu bar and then click **Print**.

3. From the **Print** drop-down menu select **Adobe PDF**. Click **OK**.

4. When asked for a filename enter **Adobe1.pdf**. Click **Save**.

5. Exit Microsoft Word. It is not necessary to save the Word document.

6. If necessary start Adobe Acrobat and open **Adobe1.pdf**.

7. Click **Advanced** on the menu bar, point to **Manage Digital IDs**, point to **My Digital ID Files**, and then click **Select My Digital ID File**.

8. Click **New Digital ID File**, and then click **Continue**. The Create Self-Signed Digital ID dialog box appears as seen in Figure 8-16. Here you can create a Web of trust model digital certificate that does not require a CA.

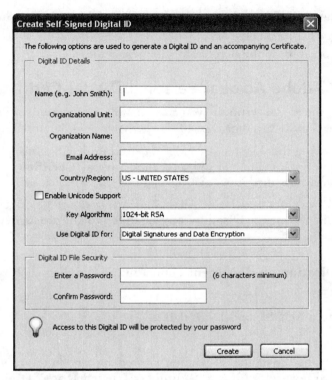

Figure 8-16   Create Self-Signed Digital ID dialog box

9. Enter suitable information in the text boxes. Note that the Key Algorithm can be either 1024-bit or 2048-bit RSA. You can select either one. Be sure to record your password. Click **Create**.

10. The New Self-Sign Digital ID File dialog box opens. Save this file (that is, the certificate) on your computer in a folder of your choice.

11. You will now send your digital certificate to the recipient of this document. Click **Advanced** on the menu bar, point to **Manage Digital IDs**, point to **My Digital ID Files**, and then click **My Digital ID File Settings**. The Digital ID File Settings dialog box opens.

12. Click **Export**. The Data Exchange File – Export Options dialog box opens.

13. Select **Save the data to a file** option button. This is your public key.

14. Click **Next**. The Export Data As dialog box opens.

15. Use the default filename, select a folder on your computer, a floppy disk, or a USB memory stick, and then click **Save**.

16. The Certificate Security — Alert dialog box opens. Click **OK**.

17. You return to the Digital ID File Settings dialog box. Click **Close** to close this dialog box.

18. Leave the document open in Adobe Acrobat for the next project.

HANDS-ON
PROJECTS

Project 8-3: Using Adobe Acrobat Personal Digital Certificates

In this project you will use the digital certificate you created using Adobe Acrobat 7.0 or 6.0 in Project 8-2. You will also make this digital certificate available to other applications.

1. You need to start by saving the document you left open in Project 8-2, using your private key. Click **File** on the menu bar, and then click **Save as Certified Document**. The Save as Certified Document dialog box opens. Click **OK**.

2. The Save as Certified Document – Choose Allowable Actions dialog box opens. In the Allowed Actions list box, select **Disallow any changes to the document** and then click **Next**.

3. The Save as Certified Document – Select Visibility dialog box opens. Select the **Do not show Certification on document** option button and then click **Next**.

4. Click **Add Digital ID**.

5. Click the icon **Create a Self-Signed Digital ID**.

6. Click **Continue**.

7. The information regarding the digital ID you just created appears on the screen. Be sure the box is checked next to **Add as a "Windows Trusted Root" Digital ID**. This makes the certificate available to other applications. Click **Create**.

8. If you receive a security warning about installing this certificate, click **Yes**. If you are asked **Do you want to ADD the following certificate to the Root Store?**, click **Yes**.

9. Select the digital ID you created and click **OK**.

10. Click **View Digital ID** to see the settings. Click **Advanced Windows Details** to see how Windows looks at this digital ID. Click **OK**.

11. Click **Close**.

12. Click **Sign and Save As**.

13. Save the file as **Adobe2**. Click **OK**.

14. Reopen Adobe2. What information does Acrobat provide about this document? Do you think it is sufficient warning?

15. Close all windows.

CASE PROJECTS

Case Project 8-1: Weaknesses of Lightweight EAP (LEAP)

Using the Internet and other sources, research how an attacker can exploit the vulnerabilities of Cisco's Lightweight EAP. Where is LEAP predominately used? How can attacks occur using this vulnerability? What interim solutions are available for protecting LEAP? Write a one-page summary of your findings.

Case Project 8-2: Biometric Debates

Research biometric devices, how they are used, and what their limitations are. Do you agree that biometrics are weak security measures, or are they strong enough to be used? What about two-factor authentication, or using them in conjunction with another type of authentication? Does this solve the problem? What would you recommend?

Case Project 8-3: Asymmetric Encryption

How does asymmetric encryption work? What is the mathematical model behind it? Who first developed it? How is it being used today? Use the Internet and other sources to research asymmetric encryption and write a one-page paper on your research.

Case Project 8-4: Freeware Authentication Servers

Until recently, RADIUS servers could only be found in large organizations. However, now freeware authentication servers are available that run on Linux. Also, modifications are available to change the firmware of wireless gateways such as the Linksys that make it serve as an authentication server. Research freeware authentication servers using the Internet and other sources. Which of these would you recommend? Why?

Case Project 8-5: Designing an Authentication Model

Using a WLAN at a school or a business that currently does not support an authentication server, create a design for one of the four authentication models. Include a sketch that shows the location of the authentication server and database. Would you recommend adding an authentication server for this network? Why?

Fairvue Technology Consulting

As part of their community service outreach, Fairvue Technology Consulting encourages its technicians and engineers to participate in information seminars about technology. Winstead University has asked for a speaker to address the topic of IEEE 802.11 authentication and key management to its Advanced Wireless Networking students. Fairvue has asked you to participate.

1. Prepare a PowerPoint presentation that explains how IEEE 802.11 authentication and key management function. Include slides that illustrate the process of the transfer of keys, how they are created, and the key hierarchy. Because this is an advanced technology course, your presentation should be detailed. The presentation should be at least 8 slides in length.

2. After the presentation one of the students asked you about using Kerberos as an authentication server. Because of time limitations you could not answer that question in detail so you volunteered to write a summary paper about the strengths and weaknesses of Kerberos. Create a one-page paper about Kerberos as an authentication server. Be sure to include its vulnerabilities in a WLAN setting.

CHAPTER NINE

SECURE WIRELESS TRANSMISSIONS

After completing this chapter you should be able to do the following:

➤ Explain how documents to be transmitted wirelessly can be encrypted

➤ List and describe the secure management interfaces for encryption

➤ Tell the features of a virtual private network and how they are used to secure wireless transmissions

The World of Wireless Security

In several U.S. cities, wireless technology has become a tool for helping the homeless. San Francisco, Chicago, and New York all use wireless networks to assist homeless and low-income individuals by linking them to critical services. The San Francisco Department of Human Services (DHS) invites the homeless to a one-day event twice each month that it calls Project Homeless Connect. The DHS sets up a wireless LAN at the Bill Graham Civic Auditorium and provides representatives from about 30 government agencies and private organizations. Approximately 1,000 homeless individuals attend the event to receive wireless network access to a variety of services such as low-cost housing, substance abuse and mental health counseling, legal aid, and food stamps. Because confidential data is being transmitted, it is essential that the transmissions be secure. In order to achieve this, a virtual private network (VPN) is used to protect the confidentiality of the information.

In Chicago, the Center for Neighborhood Technology (CNT) provides wireless Internet access to families in low-income neighborhoods. Known as the Wireless Community Network, CNT has created a rooftop mesh network of wireless repeater nodes for over 800 households scattered throughout four neighborhoods. The Wireless Community Network is a tool to provide citizens with better information, especially those who do not have Internet access. These households generally cannot afford to pay for digital subscriber line (DSL) or cable modem broadband service.

With money provided through both public and private programs, the CNT began providing Internet access in late 2003. If the resident does not have a computer, CNT asks corporations and individuals to donate older computers to the organization that will then distribute them. Residents are using Internet connectivity for online coursework, grocery shopping, and to access medical benefit information. Other uses include filling out online job applications, finding job training, and attending virtual English as a Second Language courses.

In New York, Mount Hope Housing has a similar program for 40,000 residents living within its more than 30 properties in the Bronx. Mount Hope Housing is setting up a network of wireless access points to offer residents access to critical life-improving resources through low-cost wireless Internet access. Wireless devices transport a signal from one building to the next. Within each building, residents can hook into an Ethernet backbone. Residents can access the Internet and information on health services, education, and other opportunities available to low-income families. The primary goal of this network is to provide information regarding services that may be of help to them.

The number of wireless LAN hotspots continues to grow exponentially. Whether these are free to customers (such as in select airports, restaurants, or hotels) or fee-based, they provide users with wireless access to the Internet. However, a serious problem regarding hotspots is that they do not normally support WEP, WPA, or WPA2 encryption of transmissions. Because of the constant addition of new users (such as airport passengers in a terminal) attempting to use a RADIUS server for authentication and encryption would be impossible. Likewise, distributing preshared keys (PSKs) to all wireless users so that they can configure their client devices is not practical (and by distributing the keys you would be providing an attacker with the tools needed to decrypt transmissions sent by others). Because of these drawbacks encrypting transmissions in public hotspots is not considered feasible, and therefore all transmissions by users are open to anyone with a wireless packet sniffer.

However, even though the owner of the hotspot may not provide encryption to its users, that does not mean that encrypting hotspot transmissions is out of the question. Users can implement their own encryption in order to protect wireless transmissions from prying eyes. There are a variety of techniques and protocols that can be used besides WPA or WPA2 to ensure that wireless transmissions are safe.

This chapter explores wireless encryption techniques beyond WPA and WPA2. First, you will look at encrypting individual documents prior to wireless transmission and safely transmitting encrypted documents. Next, you will explore encryption techniques for managing secure network interfaces. And finally, you will learn about authentication using virtual private network (VPN) technology to provide total end-to-end encryption for all transmissions.

ENCRYPTION FOR TRANSMITTING DOCUMENTS

On occasion a user may access an open (unencrypted) hotspot simply to send or receive a single document. For example, a salesperson may need to download a last-minute bid proposal on her meeting with the customer, and may use an open hotspot at a coffee shop around the corner from the customer's building to receive the file. However, because the document contains proprietary information and confidentiality must be ensured, the salesperson would like to encrypt its contents. In settings like these, using encryption to protect one or a small number of documents is important but may not be convenient. There are two ways in which encryption for transmitting documents can be accomplished. One method is using private key cryptography, and the other is using public key cryptography.

Private Key Cryptography

Private key (symmetric) cryptography, which is also the basis of PSK in WPA and WPA2, uses a single key to both encrypt and decrypt the document. Most software packages today that create documents provide an option for encrypting that document. Figure 9-1 illustrates the options for encrypting a Microsoft Word document. In addition, there are a variety of third-party encryption programs available that can be used to encrypt any file or an entire folder.

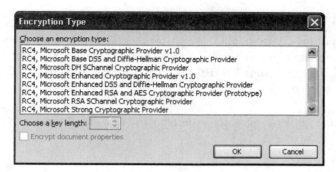

Figure 9-1   Microsoft Word encryption options

Although enabling encryption in this way may be considered a simple solution, in reality it provides a weak degree of protection. This is primarily because of the problems associated with managing the keys. If the salesperson must download an encrypted file, then there must be a means for her to get the key to decrypt it. Sending the key in a separate e-mail message retrieved through the open hotspot would defeat the entire process. Even if she were to use her cell phone to call the office for the key, someone might hear the conversation or watch as she writes it down. Encrypting single documents using private key cryptography is a weak means of protection.

Public Key Cryptography

Because of the difficulties associated with key management in symmetric encryption, asymmetric encryption, or public key cryptography, should be used instead. With public key cryptography two mathematically related keys are used instead of just one: the private key encrypts the message while the public key decrypts the message (or vice versa). Public key cryptography can improve security as well as convenience and flexibility because public keys can be distributed freely.

Public key cryptography is covered in Chapter 8.

NOTE

There are a variety of tools that use public key cryptography for encrypting files and e-mail messages. Some of the most common include Pretty Good Privacy (PGP) and GNU Privacy Guard (GPG), Linux Cryptographic File System (CFS), Secure File Transfer Protocol (SFTP), and Secure Copy (SCP).

Pretty Good Privacy (PGP) and GNU Privacy Guard (GPG)

The most widely used public cryptography system for encrypting e-mail messages on Windows systems is a commercial product called **Pretty Good Privacy (PGP)**. A similar program known as **GNU Privacy Guard (GPG)** is a free product and runs on Windows, UNIX, and Linux operating systems.

NOTE   Messages encrypted by PGP can generally be decrypted by GPG and vice versa.

Both PGP and GPG use both public and private key cryptography. PGP/GPG generates a random private (symmetric) key and uses it to encrypt the message. The private key is then encrypted using the receiver's public key and sent along with the message. When the recipient gets the message, the PGP/GPG software first decrypts the private key with the private key that belongs to the recipient. The decrypted private key is then used to decrypt the rest of the message.

NOTE   PGP/GPG uses symmetric cryptography because it is faster than asymmetric cryptography.

Although PGP was initially embroiled in a fight with the U.S. government regarding exporting its encryption technology to foreign nations, today it is used worldwide for encrypting e-mail messages. As a free alternative, GPG is proving to be very popular.

NOTE   Microsoft's Encrypting File System (EFS) is an encryption scheme for Windows 2000, Windows XP Professional, and Windows 2003 Server operating systems that use the NTFS file system. Because EFS is integrated into the NTFS, file encryption and decryption are transparent. When a user opens a file it is automatically decrypted by EFS as data is read from disk and encrypted when the file is saved. Therefore, EFS cannot be used for sending encrypted files.

Linux Cryptographic File System (CFS)

The Linux operating system does not come with a native cryptography system installed. Users can create a hidden directory named ~/.*private* and set the mode to 0700 so only the user can read the files in that directory. However, this technique is not considered secure.

Linux users can add one of several cryptographic systems to encrypt files. One of the most common is the **Cryptographic File System (CFS)**. CFS can encrypt all files or selected directories and files on a Linux system. Like Microsoft's EFS, it is not used for sending encrypted files.

Secure File Transfer Protocol (SFTP)

Prior to the development of the World Wide Web and Hypertext Transfer Protocol (HTTP), the Internet was primarily used for transferring files from one device to another. Transferring files was most commonly performed by using the **File Transfer Protocol (FTP)**, which is part of the TCP/IP suite. The FTP protocol is used to connect to an FTP server, in much the same way that the HTTP protocol links to a Web server. FTP is still frequently used by both wireless and wired users for transmitting files.

There are three ways in which a user can access FTP:

- *Through a Web browser*—Most Web browsers support the FTP protocol. Instead of prefacing a Web address by entering the protocol *http://*, the FTP protocol is entered instead (*ftp://*) followed by the address of the FTP server, such as *ftp://ftp3.course.com*.

- *Using an FTP client*—Instead of using a Web browser a separate FTP client can be used instead, as shown in Figure 9-2.

- *From the command line*—Commands can be entered at an operating system prompt, as shown in Figure 9-3, instead of clicking icons or buttons. Common FTP commands that are used include *ls* (list files), *get* (retrieve a file from the server), and *put* (transfer a file to the server).

Figure 9-2   FTP client

 NOTE   FTP servers can be configured to allow unauthenticated users to transfer files. Known as "anonymous FTP," any user can enter the account name *anonymous*, which then allows them access to the server.

Several vulnerabilities are associated with using FTP. First, FTP does not use encryption, so that any usernames, passwords, and files being transferred are in cleartext and can be accessed by attackers with sniffers. Also, files being transferred by FTP are vulnerable to man-in-the-middle attacks where data is intercepted and then altered before sending it on its way. Although FTP can transfer binary files, these files are actually converted to cleartext before they are transmitted.

```
C:\WINDOWS\System32\cmd.exe - ftp ftp3.course.com                    _ □ ×

C:\Documents and Settings\Windows XP>ftp ftp3.course.com
Connected to ftp3.course.com.
220 ftp3 Microsoft FTP Service (Version 4.0).
User (ftp3.course.com:(none)): mciampa
331 Password required for mciampa.
Password:
230-Welcome to FTP3!
230-
230-Unauthorized use will be prosecuted
230-to the full extent allowed by law.
230-
230-All connections are logged.
230 User mciampa logged in.
ftp>
```

Figure 9-3   Command-line FTP

NOTE

FTP man-in-the-middle attacks have been one of the primary means by which Web sites are defaced because many Webmasters use unsecured FTP to update Web pages. An attacker determines the IP address of the Web site and then sets up a sniffer to capture packets. As soon as the Webmaster logs on to update the site, the attacker obtains the password and logon information. Using this information, attackers can then download the site's Web pages onto their local computers, edit the pages with fraudulent information, and then use FTP to post the altered pages back on the Web site.

One of the ways to reduce the risk of attack is to use **Secure FTP (SFTP)**. SFTP can be based on one of two underlying protocols. The first protocol is known as Secure Socket Layer (SSL) and performs the encryption. **Secure Sockets Layer (SSL)** is a protocol developed by Netscape for securely transmitting documents over the Internet. SSL uses a private key to encrypt data that is transferred over the SSL connection. **Transport Layer Security (TLS)** is a protocol that guarantees privacy and data integrity between applications communicating over the Internet. TLS is an extension of SSL, and they are often referred to as either SSL/TLS or TLS/SSL.

The SSL/TLS protocol is made up of two layers. The **TLS Handshake Protocol** allows authentication between the server and the client and the negotiation of an encryption algorithm and cryptographic keys before any actual data is transmitted. The **TLS Record Protocol** is layered on top of a reliable transport protocol, such as TCP. It ensures that a connection is private by using data encryption; it also ensures that the connection is reliable. The TLS Record Protocol also is used to encapsulate higher-level protocols, such as the TLS Handshake Protocol.

Using SSL/TLS, SFTP (sometimes known as SFTP/SSL) provides protection from man-in-the-middle attacks because the server is authenticated with the client. In addition, it protects against packet sniffing during transmission because the data is encrypted. SSL/TLS is not only used for SFTP; it can also be used for securing e-mail transmissions, as seen in Figure 9-4.

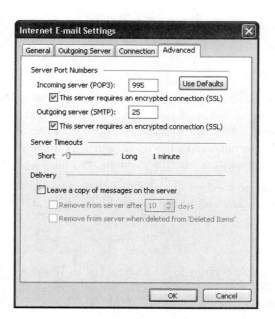

Figure 9-4   E-mail using SSL/TLS

 NOTE A disadvantage of some SFTP products is that they can only be used within a particular FTP client. As an alternative, some vendors offer a Java applet that runs within the Web browser and encrypts and decrypts transmissions with SSL.

A second protocol that can be used with SFTP is **Secure Shell (SSH)** and is called SFTP/SSH. SSH is a UNIX-based command interface and protocol for securely accessing a remote computer. SSH is actually a suite of three utilities—slogin, ssh, and scp—that are secure versions of the unsecure UNIX counterpart utilities. These commands are summarized in Table 9-1. Both the client and server ends of the connection are authenticated using a digital certificate, and passwords are protected by being encrypted. SSH can even be used as a tool for secure network backups.

Table 9-1   UNIX commands for remote security

UNIX Command Name	Description	Syntax	Secure Command Replacement
rlogin	Log on to remote computer	rlogin *remotecomputer*	Slogin
rcp	Copy files between remote computers	rcp [*options*] *localfile remotecomputer:filename*	Scp
rsh	Executing commands on a remote host without logging on	rsh *remotecomputer command*	Ssh

SSH is widely used by network administrators to remotely control UNIX-based
Web servers.

NOTE

The first version of SSH (SSH-1) was released in 1995 by a researcher at the Helsinki University of Technology after his university was the victim of a password-sniffing attack. This tool rapidly gained wide acceptance and was followed in 1996 with a revised version of the protocol, SSH-2. In 2006, SSH-2 became a proposed Internet standard. SSH-2, which is incompatible with SSH-1, contains significant security improvements over the previous version.

Both SFTP/SSL and SFTP/SSH can be used to encrypt files for transport across open wireless networks. Several programs are available that support SFTP/SSH and to a lesser degree SFTP/SSL.

Secure Copy (SCP)

Secure Copy (SCP) is a facility for transferring files securely. Just as Telnet can refer to either the protocol that supports remote computer access or the actual program that provides that function, SCP can refer to either the SCP protocol or the client program that implements the SCP protocol.

The SCP protocol encrypts data during transfer. However, SCP does not perform authentication or other means of security. Instead, SCP relies upon the underlying SSH protocol to perform this function. When uploading files from the client to the server, the SCP protocol connects to the remote device using SSH and then executes the SCP server (the SCP server program is typically the same program as the SCP client). For downloads the client sends a request for files or directories to be transmitted.

The most widely used SCP client is the command-line program *scp*, which is provided in many implementations of SSH. Because the SCP protocol performs file transfers only, SCP clients that contain a graphical user interface (GUI) are rare because this requires additional functionality such as providing a means of listing all files. Hybrid GUI SCP clients are typically not "pure" SCP clients, as they must use other means to implement the additional functionality, which makes them platform-dependent upon the underlying operating system.

Because of its limited functionality SCP is considered not as robust as SFTP. As such, SCP is not as widely used.

ENCRYPTION FOR SECURE MANAGEMENT INTERFACES

Because of the remote location and large number of wireless devices that make up a WLAN, such as access points, remote wireless bridges, wireless routers, wireless gateways, wireless switches, and wireless mesh routers, managing these devices remotely is essential. It is even more important that encryption be used when managing these devices because usernames, passwords, and PSKs may be transmitted wirelessly. The technologies used for encryption in these settings include SSH port forwarding, HTTPS, and SNMPv3.

SSH Port Forwarding

An enhanced feature of SSH is known as **port forwarding**, also called **tunneling**. Port forwarding can be used to provide secure access to other services that do not normally encrypt data during transmission. A TCP/IP connection to an external application that is not secure can be redirected to the SSH program (either the SSH client or server), which then forwards it to the other SSH party (server or client). This party forwards the connection to the desired destination host. The forwarded connection is encrypted and protected on the path between the SSH client and server. For example, most e-mail programs use the unencrypted POP3 protocol to connect to a mailserver that is using TCP/IP port 110. If the client device can first connect via SSH to the mailserver and the SSH session can be configured to "forward" port 110 through the encrypted SSH link, the local e-mail client can access port 110 on the local computer and will be connecting to the remote mailserver while the incoming e-mail will be sent over the encrypted SSH link.

SSH port forwarding is widely used for accessing database servers, e-mail servers, and Windows Remote Desktop.

NOTE

SSH port forwarding can be used to set up a secure management interface over a wireless network to prevent attackers from viewing the contents of the transmissions. SSH port forwarding is often used when a wireless device is managed through Telnet. It can also be used to access an e-mail account or other applications by non-management users across a WLAN.

Secure Hypertext Transport Protocol (HTTPS)

One common use of SSL is to secure Web HTTP communication between a browser and a Web server. This secure version is "plain" HTTP sent over SSL/TLS and is named **HTTPS (Secure Hypertext Transport Protocol)**. Whereas TLS/SSL creates a secure connection between a client and a server over which any amount of data can be sent securely, HTTPS is designed to transmit individual messages securely. SSL and HTTPS are complementary rather than competing technologies.

Besides using TLS/SSL, HTTPS uses port 443 instead of port 80 as with HTTP. Users must enter URLs with HTTPS:// instead of HTTP://. A lock icon appears in the browser's status bar to indicate the transmission is secure.

NOTE

Most wireless devices, such as access points, are managed through a Web interface. These devices typically provide several different HTTPS options, as seen in Figure 9-5. The Web Access options allow management through the Web interface to be entirely disabled or accessed through HTTP or the more secure HTTPS. The Remote Router Access options allow management of the AP from a remote location through the Internet. In addition, the

TCP/IP port to be used can be designated. To remotely manage the AP, the address *http://xxx.xxx.xxx.xxx:8080* where the *x*'s represent the access point's IP address and 8080 represents the specified port is entered in a Web browser's address field.

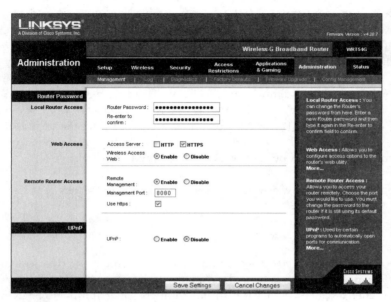

Figure 9-5   Web interface options

The Remote Management feature should be enabled only if it is necessary to manage the AP from somewhere other than the local network. Enabling Remote Management can open the device to attacks.

NOTE

SNMPv3

The **Simple Network Management Protocol (SNMP)** is a protocol used to manage networked equipment. These devices include not only core network devices such as switches, routers, hubs, bridges, and wireless APs, but also printers, copiers, fax machines, and even uninterruptible power supplies (UPSs). Each SNMP-managed device must have an agent or a service that "listens" for commands and then executes them. These agents are protected with a password known as a *community string* in order to prevent unauthorized users from taking control over a device. There are two types of community strings: a read-only string will allow information from the agent to be viewed, and a read–write string allows settings to be changed.

The use of community strings in the two early versions of SNMP (SNMPv1 and SNMPv2) had several vulnerabilities. First, the default SNMP community strings for read-only and read-write were *public* and *private* and these were widely known. Also, community strings were transmitted in cleartext, so an attacker could view the contents of the strings as they are being transmitted.

However, with the introduction of SNMPv3, community strings were replaced with usernames and passwords along with an encryption key. Wireless devices that use SNMP should use the current version SNMPv3.

ENCRYPTION FOR VIRTUAL PRIVATE NETWORKS (VPNs)

9

Although public key and private key encryption for transmitting documents does provide a higher degree of security, it still has drawbacks. First, the user must consciously perform a separate action (such as encrypt a Word document) or use specific software (such as PGP or SCP) in order to transmit a secure document. The time and effort required to do so, albeit small, may discourage users from protecting their documents when in a hurry or simply tired of the additional steps that are required. A second drawback is that these actions only protect *documents* that are transmitted. Other communications performed over a wireless LAN, such as accessing corporate databases or sending and receiving e-mail messages, are not secure. Finally, if the server to which the device is connected over the WLAN does not support SSH or HTTPS, then even document transmissions cannot be easily encrypted.

The solution is a technology known as a virtual private network (VPN). VPNs have become essential tools for corporate "road warriors" who regularly must access secure information over a wireless or unsecured network. In addition, VPNs have grown in popularity for SOHO and home users. This section discusses what a VPN is; the protocols, software, and hardware that are used; and the advantages and disadvantages of a VPN.

What Is a Virtual Private Network?

A **virtual private network (VPN)** uses an unsecured public network, such as a hotspot WLAN or the Internet, as if it were a secure private network. Prior to VPNs, organizations were forced to lease expensive data connections from private carriers so their employees could remotely connect to the organization's network if more than dial-up modem speed was required. When the Internet's explosive growth took place in the mid-1990s, organizations searched for ways to use this public but unsecured network for their employees.

VPNs allow a public network to be used privately. There are two common types of VPNs. A **remote-access VPN** or **virtual private dial-up network (VPDN)** is a user-to-LAN connection used by remote users. The second type is a **site-to-site VPN**, in which multiple sites can connect to other sites over the Internet.

VPNs function in a similar way to SSH port forwarding that can be used to provide secure access to other services that do not normally encrypt data during transmission. A nonsecure TCP/IP connection of an external application is redirected to the SSH program (either client or server), which then forwards it to the other SSH party (server or client), which in turn forwards the connection to the desired destination host. The forwarded connection is encrypted on the path between the SSH client and server only. A VPN is roughly equivalent to an SSH session where everything is being forwarded over a single secure channel.

VPN Tunneling Protocols

There are several "tunneling" protocols (when a packet is enclosed within another packet) that can be used for VPN transmissions. Besides using SSH, the Point-to-Point Tunneling Protocol (PPTP), Layer 2 Tunneling Protocol (L2TP), and IP Security (IPSec) are commonly used with VPNs.

Point-to-Point Tunneling Protocol (PPTP)

Point-to-Point Tunneling Protocol (PPTP) is the most widely deployed tunneling protocol. Not only is it part of the Microsoft Windows operating system, it is also supported on devices from Cisco, Nortel, and other manufacturers. PPTP also supports other protocols besides TCP/IP. PPTP allows IP traffic to be encrypted and then encapsulated in an IP header to be sent across a wireless or public IP network such as the Internet.

NOTE   PPTP was developed by a consortium known as the PPTP Forum. The forum consists of the following organizations: Ascend Communications, Microsoft, 3Com, ECI Telematics, and U.S. Robotics.

PPTP is illustrated in Figure 9-6. This connection is based on the **Point-to-Point Protocol (PPP)**, which is a widely used protocol for establishing connections over a serial line or dial-up connection between two points. The client connects to a **network access server (NAS)** to initiate the connection. NASs are typically maintained by Internet service providers (ISPs). After the connection to the NAS is established, another connection is created between the NAS and a PPTP server through the Internet or unsecured network. This connection acts as the tunnel (using TCP port 1723) through which communications between the client and the PPTP server can occur. PPTP uses the PPP protocol for encryption. An extension to PPTP is the **Link Control Protocol (LCP),** which establishes, configures, and automatically tests the connection.

Another variation of PPP that is used by broadband Internet providers (with DSL or cable modem connections) is **Point-to-Point Protocol over Ethernet (PPPoE)**. PPPoE is software that works with a computer's network interface card adapter to simulate a dial-up session and can assign IP addresses as necessary. PPPoE makes an Ethernet local area network appear like a point-to-point serial link.

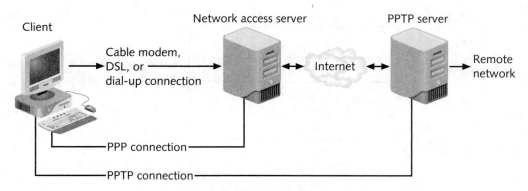

Figure 9-6 Point-to-Point Tunneling Protocol (PPTP)

PPTP became a popular tunneling protocol because it was relatively easy to configure and it was the first VPN protocol that was supported by Microsoft Dial-up Networking. All versions of Microsoft Windows since Windows 95 are bundled with a PPTP client. Linux and Mac OS X also now include a PPTP client.

Layer 2 Tunneling Protocol (L2TP)

Layer 2 Tunneling Protocol (L2TP) represents a merging of the features of PPTP with Cisco's Layer 2 Forwarding Protocol (L2F), which itself was originally designed to address some of the weaknesses of PPTP. L2TP is not limited to working with TCP/IP-based networks, but it supports a wide array of protocols. Unlike PPTP, which is primarily implemented as software on a client computer, L2TP can also be found on devices such as routers.

L2TP is an industry-standard tunneling protocol that allows IP traffic to be encrypted and then transmitted over any medium that supports point-to-point delivery (like IP). L2TP, which uses UDP port 1701, also can support more advanced encryption methods for a higher degree of security. The L2TP standard is being updated with the L2TPv3 (L2TP version 3). L2TP is only supported by Windows 2000 versions and higher.

IP Security (IPsec)

Different security tools function at different layers of the Open System Interconnection (OSI) model. Figure 9-7 illustrates some of the tools at different layers of the OSI model. Tools such as Pretty Good Privacy (PGP) operate at the Application layer, whereas Kerberos functions at the Session layer. The advantages of having security tools function at the higher layers like the Application layer is that they can be designed to protect specific applications.

Kerberos is covered in Chapter 8.

NOTE

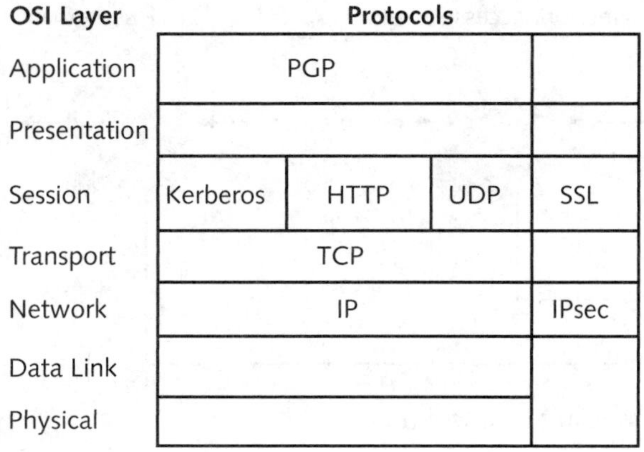

OSI Layer   **Protocols**

Application	PGP			
Presentation				
Session	Kerberos	HTTP	UDP	SSL
Transport	TCP			
Network	IP			IPsec
Data Link				
Physical				

Figure 9-7   Security tools and the OSI model

However, protecting at higher layers may require multiple security tools, even as many as one per application. Secure Socket Layers (SSL)/Transport Layer Security (TLS) operates at the Session layer. The advantage of operating at this lower level is that more applications can be protected, but minor modifications may have to be made to the application.

Improved functionality can be achieved if the protection is even lower in the OSI layers. If the protection is at the Network layer, it can protect a wide range of applications with no modifications needed. Even applications that are ignorant of security, such as a legacy MS-DOS application, can still be protected.

IPsec (an abbreviation of **IP security**) is a set of protocols developed to support the secure exchange of packets. Because it operates at a low level in the OSI model, IPsec is considered a transparent security protocol. It is transparent to the following entities:

- *Applications*—Programs do not have to be modified to run under IPsec.

- *Users*—Unlike some security tools, users do not need to be trained on specific security procedures (such as encrypting with PGP).

- *Software*—Because IPsec is implemented in a device such as a firewall or router, no software changes must be made on the local client.

Unlike SSL, which is implemented as a part of the user application, IPsec is located in the operating system or the communication hardware. IPsec implementation is more likely to operate at a faster speed, because it can cooperate closely with other system programs and the hardware.

IPsec provides three areas of protection that correspond to three IPsec protocols:

- *Authentication*—IPsec authenticates that packets received were sent from the source that is identified in the header of the packet and no man-in-the-middle attacks or replay attacks took place to alter the contents of the packet. This is accomplished by the **Authentication Header (AH)** protocol.

- *Confidentiality*—By encrypting the packets, IPsec ensures that no other parties were able to view the contents. Confidentiality is achieved through the **Encapsulating Security Payload (ESP)** protocol. ESP supports authentication of the sender and encryption of data.

- *Key management*—IPsec manages the keys to ensure that they are not intercepted or used by unauthorized parties. For IPsec to work, the sending and receiving devices must share a key. This is accomplished through a protocol known as **Internet Security Association and Key Management Protocol/Oakley (ISAKMP/Oakley),** which generates the key and authenticates the user using techniques such as digital certificates.

IPsec supports two encryption modes: transport and tunnel. **Transport mode** encrypts only the data portion (payload) of each packet yet leaves the header unencrypted. The more secure **tunnel mode** encrypts both the header and the data portion. IPsec accomplishes transport and tunnel modes by adding new headers to the IP packet. The entire original packet (header and payload) is then treated as the data portion of the new packet. This is illustrated in Figure 9-8. Because tunnel mode protects the entire packet, it is generally used in a network gateway-to-gateway communication. Transport mode is used when a device must see the source and destination addresses to route the packet. For example, a packet sent from a client computer to the local IPsec-enabled firewall would be sent in transport mode so the packet can be transported through the local network. Once it reached the firewall, it would be changed to tunnel mode before being sent onto the Internet. The receiving firewall would then extract, decrypt, and authenticate the original packet before it is routed to the final destination computer.

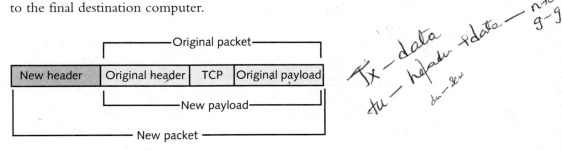

Figure 9-8   New IPsec packet

Both AH and ESP can be used with transport or tunnel mode, creating four possible transport mechanisms:

- *AH in transport mode*—This is used to authenticate (verify that it came from the sender) the packet data and part of the header information. AH in transport mode is illustrated in Figure 9-9.

- *AH in tunnel mode*—In AH in tunnel mode, the entire contents of the packet, both original header and payload, are encrypted, as shown in Figure 9-10.

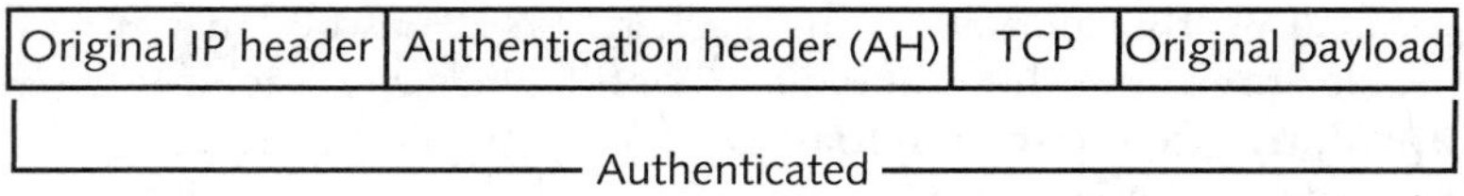

Original IP header	Authentication header (AH)	TCP	Original payload

———————— Authenticated ————————

auth sender

Figure 9-9   AH in transport mode

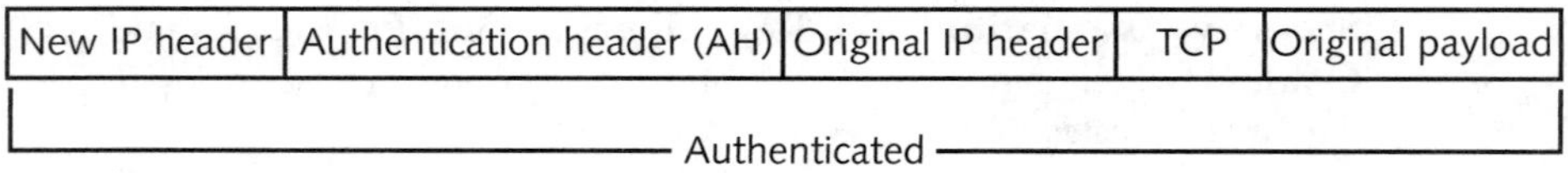

New IP header	Authentication header (AH)	Original IP header	TCP	Original payload

———————————— Authenticated ————————————

Figure 9-10   AH in tunnel mode

- *ESP in transport mode*—ESP in transport mode encrypts and authenticates the payload of the original packet, as shown in Figure 9-11.   *auth & encrypts*

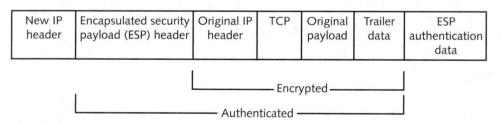

Original IP header	Encapsulated security payload (ESP) header	TCP	Original payload	Trailer data	ESP authentication data

—————— Encrypted ——————

———————— Authenticated ————————

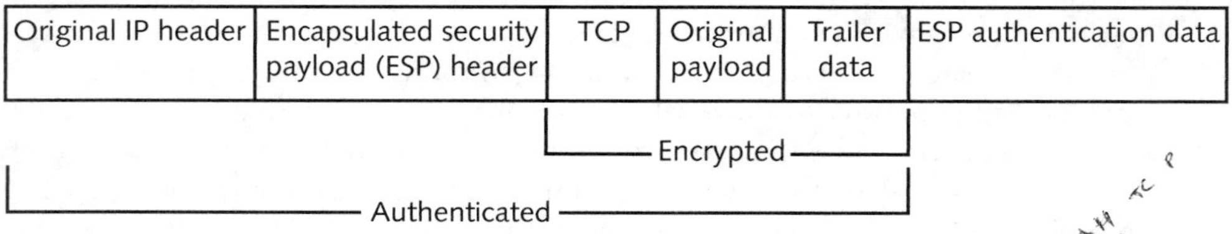

Figure 9-11   ESP in transport mode

- *ESP in tunnel mode*—The entire packet is encrypted and authenticated in ESP in tunnel mode, as shown in Figure 9-12.

New IP header	Encapsulated security payload (ESP) header	Original IP header	TCP	Original payload	Trailer data	ESP authentication data

—————— Encrypted ——————

———————— Authenticated ————————

Figure 9-12   ESP in tunnel mode

NOTE   IPsec is an optional protocol with the current version of TCP/IP, known as IPv4, and was not part of the original specifications. Under the newest version of TCP/IP, IPv6, IPsec is integrated into the IP protocol and is native on all packets. However, its use is still optional.

Table 9-2 compares IPSec, L2TP, and PPTP and when they should be used.

Table 9-2   Tunneling protocol comparisons

Protocol	Security Level	When It Should Be Used
PPTP	Moderate	Connecting to Windows server
L2TP	High	Connecting to Windows server
IPsec	High	Connecting to non-Windows server

VPN Hardware and Software

VPN transmissions are achieved through communicating with endpoints. An **endpoint** is the end of the tunnel between VPN devices. An endpoint can be software on a local computer, a dedicated hardware device such as a **VPN concentrator** (which aggregates hundreds or thousands of multiple connections together), or integrated into another networking device such as a firewall.

NOTE

As with any remote access it is important that a policy for acceptable VPN usage be established and enforced. Wireless security policies are covered in detail in Chapter 11.

Client Software

Depending upon the type of endpoint that is being used, client software may be required on the wireless devices that are connecting to the VPN. Endpoints that provide **passthrough VPN** capability require that a separate VPN client application be installed on each device that connects to a VPN server. This client application handles setting up the connection with the remote VPN server and takes care of the special data handling required to send and receive data through the VPN tunnel. The endpoint simply passes the special VPN encapsulated and encrypted packets through to the client, which then will decode the transmission. Hardware devices that have a **built-in VPN** endpoint handle all the VPN tunnel setup, encapsulation, and encryption in the endpoint. Wireless client devices are not required to run any special software, and the entire VPN process is transparent to them.

NOTE

The client software must be installed on a device with the version of the operating system that fully supports the tunneling protocol that is being used.

There are several different types of VPN client software:

- *Operating system*—Apple Macintosh, Linux, and Microsoft Windows now include a built-in VPN client. For example, Windows includes a VPN client for PPTP tunneling, as seen in Figure 9-13.

- *Freeware*—Free client software is available to support VPNs. Generally this software is bundled together with a personal software firewall.

- *VPN vendors*—Most VPN vendors either sell their client software as a separate product or include it with a VPN hardware device.

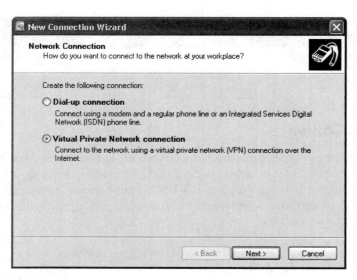

Figure 9-13   Microsoft Windows VPN client

Software-Based VPNs

Software-based VPNs, in which the VPN endpoint is actually software running on the wireless device itself, are preferred in certain situations. For example, with a VPN in which both endpoints are not controlled by the same organization, such as for remote client support or a business partnership, a software-based VPN is preferable. Other situations may include when different firewalls and routers are being used (even within the same organization) a software-based VPN may be better at providing VPN connectivity.

Software-based VPNs offer the most flexibility in how the network traffic is managed. Hardware-based VPNs generally tunnel all traffic they handle regardless of protocol. However, many software-based products allow traffic to be tunneled based on either the protocol or the IP address. Tunneling specific types of network traffic can be an advantage in settings in which different types of network traffic may be found, such as at a remote office that needs to access the corporate database via VPN but does not require VPN for Web surfing. Software-based VPNs are also more desirable for "road warriors" who do not want to carry an additional hardware device with them while traveling. Software-based VPNs are good options where performance requirements are modest, such as when users are connecting over dial-up links.

However, there are disadvantages to software-based VPNs. Generally, software-based VPNs do not have as good performance or security as a hardware-based VPN. Software-based systems are considered harder to manage than hardware endpoints. This is because they require more familiarity with the operating system, the application that is being used, and security mechanisms. Also, some software VPN products require changes to routing tables and network addressing schemes in order to function properly. Not all Internet routers allow for software-based VPN tunnels so a VPN tunnel cannot even be established.

Several excellent open-source VPN software-based products are freely available for wireless users.

NOTE

Hardware-Based VPNs

Hardware-based VPNs are more secure, have better performance, and can offer more flexibility than software-based VPNs. This is because only the network devices, serving as passthrough VPNs, manage the VPN functions and relieve the wireless device from performing any VPN activities. In addition, a hardware-based VPN can protect all wireless devices behind it, so any device that is connected to the WLAN will be secure. Hardware-based VPNs are generally used for connecting two LANs together through the VPN tunnel.

There are two disadvantages to hardware-based VPNs. First, enterprise hardware-based VPNs can be expensive. Also, it is necessary to match vendor VPN endpoints. That is, a Cisco VPN hardware-based endpoint at the corporate office must have a matching Cisco VPN endpoint at the remote site.

9

Cisco is probably the best-known hardware-based VPN and many of their routers are designed specifically for VPNs.

NOTE

The support for a hardware-based WLAN VPN may either be a separate VPN appliance, like that used with a wired LAN, or integrated into existing networking equipment. However, a separate VPN may only protect transmissions that are using the public Internet and not protect wireless transmissions, as seen in Figure 9-14. Enterprise-level access points may have built-in VPN functionality to fully protect wireless transmissions from devices. SOHO and home wireless gateways usually support passthrough VPN for devices that are using software-based VPNs, as seen in Figure 9-15. Wireless routers and switches may also serve as endpoint VPNs.

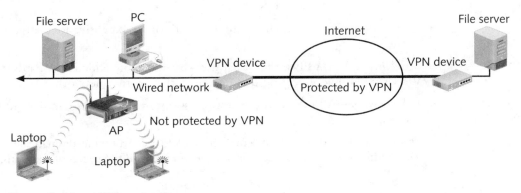

Figure 9-14   VPN protection

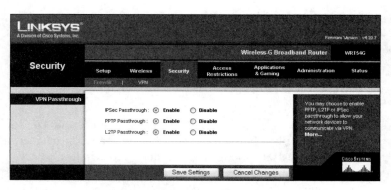

Figure 9-15   Access point passthrough VPN

The VPN encryption provided by wireless hardware such as access points, wireless gateways, wireless switches, and wireless routers all function at Layers 2 and 3 of the OSI model because they support IPSec, PPTP, or L2TP (encryption by WEP, WPA, and WPA2 function at Layer 2). However, traditional routing based on connection-level information at Layers 2 and 3 often cannot keep pace with the data volumes and demands of today's applications. A new breed of devices, sometimes called **Layer 4-7 devices**, can provide intelligent traffic and bandwidth management based on the content of a session and not just on network connections. Layer 4-7 devices, which can make routing decisions based on information unknown to Layer 2-3 switches and routers, can help deliver enhanced capabilities required for application-aware IP networks. These include more intelligent traffic management capabilities, local and global server load balancing, content-aware routing and access control, and content-based bandwidth management. Security will become inherent in these Layer 4-7 applications and services. High-performance, multilayer security will protect data integrity and privacy across all environments, including mobility, without compromising performance. Routing will be transformed by building VPN and firewall security into routing devices.

VPN Advantages and Disadvantages

There are several advantages of VPN technology. These include:

- *Cost savings*—VPNs can eliminate the need for an expensive long-distance leased connection.

- *Scalability*—With VPNs, additional users can be easily added to a hardware-based VPN simply by connecting that device to the existing network.

- *Full protection*—VPN encrypts all transmissions from the client and not just certain applications.

- *Speed*—Compared to dial-up connections, VPN can provide dramatically increased bandwidth. VPN can also compress data and increase the speed of the transmission.

- *Transparency*—Once a VPN is set up it is basically invisible to the user.

- *Authentication*—VPN can ensure that only authorized users have access to information.

- *Industry standards*—VPNs can take advantage of industry-wide protocol standards such as IPsec.

There are also disadvantages to VPN technology:

- *Management*—VPNs require an in-depth understanding of public network security issues and taking proper precautions in their deployment.

- *Availability and performance*—The availability and performance of a VPN over the public networks like the Internet depends on factors largely outside of the control of the organization.

- *Interoperability*—VPN technologies from different vendors may not work well together.

- *Additional protocols*—VPNs need to accommodate protocols other than IP.

- *Performance impact*—Although small, there is a negative performance impact when using software-based VPNs.

- *Expense*—Hardware-based VPNs for multiple users can be expensive.

9

CHAPTER SUMMARY

- ❑ Wireless encryption at an open (unprotected) hotspot and for secure management interfaces is considered critically important to protect the content of transmissions. When transmitting individual documents, a private key cryptography system, such as those included within the application that creates the document or a third-party system, provides a limited degree of security. This is because of the difficulty with key management. Public key cryptography systems provide a higher degree of security. Some of the most common include PGP, GPG, CFS, SFTP, and SCP.

- ❑ Different tools are available for encrypting secure management interfaces in WLANs. SSH port forwarding provides secure access to services that normally would not be encrypted by using the SSH server and client software. HTTPS, which uses TLS/SSL, creates a secure tunnel through which HTTP transmissions can be sent and received. SNMPv3, unlike SNMPv1 of SNMPv2, provides authentication with a username and password instead of community strings and should be used with wireless transmissions.

- ❑ A VPN uses an unsecured public network—like a WLAN hotspot or the Internet—to send and receive private messages by using encryption. VPNs can be either user-to-LAN or site-to-site in their configuration. Besides using SSH, the protocols PPTP, L2TP, and IPsec are commonly used with VPNs.

❑ VPN transmissions are achieved through communicating with endpoints, which are the end of the tunnel between VPN devices. An endpoint can be software on a local computer (in which case the network devices must support passthrough VPN), a dedicated hardware device, or integrated into another networking device such as a firewall. Software-based VPNs, which require that the software be run locally on the system, are preferred in settings in which additional hardware equipment may not be easily accessible. Hardware-based VPNs are generally considered more secure and have better performance than software-based VPNs.

Key Terms

Authentication Header (AH) — An IPsec protocol that authenticates that packets received were sent from the source identified in the header of the packet.

built-in VPN — A type of VPN endpoint that handles all the VPN tunnel setup, encapsulation, and encryption so that wireless client devices are not required to run any special software.

Cryptographic File System (CFS) — A Linux file encryption system.

Encapsulating Security Payload (ESP) — An IPsec protocol through which confidentiality is achieved by encryption.

endpoint — The end of the tunnel between virtual private network (VPN) devices.

File Transfer Protocol (FTP) — A protocol of the TCP/IP suite used to transfer files that is considered unsecure.

GNU Privacy Guard (GPG) — A free product for encrypting e-mail messages that runs on Windows, UNIX, and Linux operating systems.

Secure Hypertext Transport Protocol (HTTPS) — A version of HTTP that incorporates secure transmission standards between clients and servers.

Internet Security Association and Key Management Protocol/Oakley (ISAKMP/Oakley) — An IPsec protocol that allows the receiver to obtain a key and authenticate the sender using digital certificates.

IP security (IPsec) — A set of protocols developed to support the secure exchange of packets.

Layer 2 Tunneling Protocol (L2TP) — A tunneling protocol that merges the features of the Point-to-Point Tunneling Protocol (PPTP) with Layer 2 Forwarding Protocol (L2F).

Layer 4–7 devices — Network devices that can provide intelligent traffic and bandwidth management based on the content of a session and not just on network connections.

Link Control Protocol (LCP) — An extension to the point-to-point tunneling protocol that establishes, configures, and automatically tests the connection.

network access server (NAS) — A server in a point-to-point tunneling protocol configuration.

passthrough VPN — A type of VPN in which a separate VPN client application installed on the local device handles setting up the connection with the remote VPN server, and takes care of the special data handling required to send and receive data through the VPN tunnel.

point-to-point protocol (PPP) — A widely used protocol for establishing connections over a serial line or dial-up connection between two points.

Point-to-Point Protocol over Ethernet (PPPoE) — A variation of PPP that is used by broadband Internet providers (with DSL or cable modem connections).

Point-to-Point Tunneling Protocol (PPTP) — The most widely deployed tunneling protocol.

port forwarding — An enhanced feature of SSH that can be used to provide secure access to other services that do not normally encrypt data during transmission; also known as tunneling.

Pretty Good Privacy (PGP) — A program that encrypts e-mail messages using public and private keys.

remote-access VPN — A virtual private network (VPN) from a single user to a LAN.

Secure Copy (SCP) — A protocol or client program based on the protocol that encrypts data by relying upon an underlying protocol such as SSH.

Secure FTP (SFTP) — An alternative to the unsecure File Transfer Protocol (FTP) for transmitting files.

Secure Hypertext Transport Protocol (HTTPS) — A protocol designed to transmit individual messages securely.

Secure Shell (SSH) — A protocol originally based on a suite of UNIX commands for transmitting documents securely over the Internet but now replaced by a revised version known as SSH-2.

Secure Sockets Layer (SSL) — A protocol developed by Netscape for transmitting documents securely over the Internet.

site-to-site VPN — A virtual private network (VPN) in which multiple sites can connect to other sites over the Internet.

TLS Handshake Protocol — A protocol that allows authentication between the server and the client and the negotiation of an encryption algorithm and cryptographic keys before any data is transmitted.

TLS Record Protocol — A protocol that is layered on top of a reliable transport protocol such as TCP, and ensures that a connection is private by using data encryption.

Transport Layer Security (TLS) — A protocol that guarantees privacy and data integrity between applications communicating over the Internet.

transport mode — An IPsec mode that encrypts only the payload of each packet and leaves the header unencrypted.

tunnel mode — An IPsec mode that encrypts both the header and the data portion of the packet.

tunneling — An enhanced feature of SSH that can be used to provide secure access to other services that do not normally encrypt data during transmission; also known as port forwarding.

virtual private dial-up network (VPDN) — A user-to-LAN connection used by remote dial-up users.

virtual private network (VPN) — A technology that uses an unsecured network as if it were a private network.

VPN concentrator — A device that aggregates hundreds or thousands of virtual private network (VPN) connections.

REVIEW QUESTIONS

1. The weakest type of encryption for sending a single document over a WLAN is
   a. private key cryptography
   b. WPA2
   c. AES
   d. public key cryptography

2. Each of the following are public key cryptography tools used for encrypting files for transmission except
   a. Pretty Good Privacy (PGP)
   b. Secure Copy (SCP)
   c. Cryptographic File System (CFS)
   d. Wired Equivalent Privacy (WEP)

3. The counterpart to the commercial product Pretty Good Privacy (PGP) is a free product that runs on Windows, UNIX, and Linux known as
   a. GNU Privacy Guard (GPG)
   b. File Encryption Security (FES)
   c. Wireless Cryptographic Standard (WCS)
   d. Lock Secure Technology Systems (LSTS)

4. Each of the following are security vulnerabilities of File Transfer Protocol (FTP) except
   a. FTP does not use encryption
   b. Files are vulnerable to man-in-the-middle attacks
   c. Attackers can view the contents of transmitted binary files
   d. FTP only supports SSH

5. _____ is a facility for transmitting files securely yet does not perform authentication or other means of security.
   a. Secure Copy (SCP)
   b. Telnet
   c. SFTP
   d. UPD

6. STP port forwarding can be used to provide secure access to other services that do not normally encrypt data during transmission. True or False?

7. Sending HTTP over TLS/SSL is known as HTTPS (Secure Hypertext Transport Protocol). True or False?

8. SNMPv1 uses usernames and passwords. True or False?

9. A virtual private network (VPN) takes advantage of using an unsecured public network, such as a hotspot WLAN or the Internet, as if it were a secure private network. True or False?

10. A remote-access or virtual private dial-up network (VPDN) is a site-to-site connection used by remote users. True or False?

11. _____ function in a similar way to SSH port forwarding that can be used to provide secure access to other services that do not normally encrypt data during transmission.

12. _____ is the most widely deployed tunneling protocol.

13. A variation of the point-to-point protocol (PPP) that is used by broadband Internet providers (with DSL or cable modem connections) is _____ .

14. _____ is an industry standard and is not limited to working with TCP/IP-based networks, but supports a wide array of protocols.

15. Unlike SSL, which is implemented as a part of the user application, _____ is located in the operating system or the communication hardware.

16. Explain why it may be preferable to have a tunneling protocol operate at a lower layer of the OSI model.

17. List and explain the two encryption modes of IPSec.

18. What is the difference between passthrough VPN and built-in VPN endpoints?

19. When would a software-based VPN be used instead of a hardware-based VPN?

20. What are Layer 4–7 devices?

HANDS-ON PROJECTS

Project 9-1: Installing and using Secure Shell (SSH) Application

Secure Shell (SSH) encrypts remote transmissions to servers. In this project, you download and use an SSH client. To complete all of the steps of this project, you need the address of your mailserver. See your lab manager or instructor for more information.

1. Use a Web browser to go to the PuTTY download site at *www.chiark.greenend.org.uk/~sgtatham/putty/download.html*.

2. Scroll down to the "For Windows 95, 98, ME, NT, 2000 and XP on Intel x86" section. Right-click the **putty.exe** file, and then click **Save Target As** on the shortcut menu.

3. Save this file to your desktop.

4. Open the program by double-clicking the file you saved. The PuTTY program starts and opens the PuTTY Configuration window, shown in Figure 9-16.

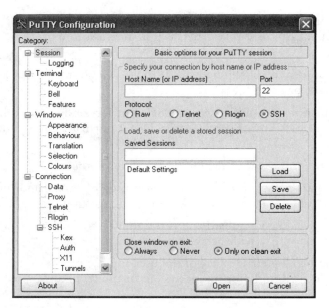

Figure 9-16 PuTTY Configuration window

5. Click **Session** on the left pane. In the **Host Name (or IP address)** text box, enter the address of your mailserver, such as *mailserver.my_isp.com*.

6. Under **Protocol** click **SSH**, if necessary. The **Port** field will automatically change to **22**, which is the normal port that SSH listens on.

7. Click **SSH** in the left pane. Under **Preferred SSH protocol version:** click **2**, if necessary.

8. Click **Tunnels** in the left pane. Under **Add new forwarded port:** enter **110** under **Source port**, the port that e-mail is typically received over.

9. Under **Destination** enter the address and port of e-mail server, such as *smtp_server.my_isp.com:25*.

10. Click **Session** in the left pane. Under **Saved Sessions** enter **Mail**. Click **Save**.

11. Double-click the session **Mail**. You will be connected to your e-mail server and asked to authenticate yourself. You can then read your e-mail over SSH.

12. Close all windows when finished.

Project 9-2: Installing and using Pretty Good Privacy (PGP)

Pretty Good Privacy (PGP) is a public key encryption application that is used to encrypt e-mails and other documents. In this project you will download and install PGP.

1. Go to *www.pgp.com* and click **PGP Desktop 30–Day Trial**. Follow the instructions to download this software. You will receive an e-mail message with a link to click to access the software. Download PGP onto your desktop.

2. Extract the files and launch the installation program. Follow the steps to install PGP onto your computer.

3. Once installation is complete you will be asked to restart your computer. After restarting, an error message may occur that says **PGP cannot open one or both of your default keying files. PGP will create new default keying files for you.** (You may be asked to perform additional steps depending upon your computer's configuration.) Click **OK**.

4. Click **Start** and **All Programs** and **PGP** and finally **PGP Desktop** to launch the application.

5. Launch your e-mail application such as Microsoft Outlook. If a warning message appears that a mailserver has an invalid authentication certificate click **Always Allow for This Site**.

6. A message is displayed that says **Email Account Detected.** Click **Yes, secure this email account.** Click **Next**.

7. Click **New key.** Click **Next**.

8. The **PGP Key Generation Assistant** will help you generate a new key. Click **Next**.

9. Enter your name and your primary e-mail address. Click **Next**.

10. Under **Passphrase** enter a passphrase that is at least 8 characters long and contains alphanumeric characters. Enter it again under **Confirmation** and click **Next**.

11. PGP will generate a key. Click **Next**.

12. Compose an e-mail message for a person in your contact list. Click the PGP **Encrypt** button to encrypt this file before sending it, as seen in Figure 9-17. Close all windows when finished.

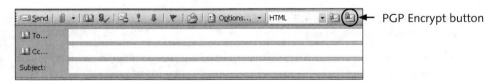

Figure 9-17   PGP Encrypt button

HANDS-ON PROJECTS

Project 9-3 : Creating a Windows XP VPN Server

Microsoft Windows XP can be configured to function as a VPN server to allow other devices to connect to it via the Internet using VPN. In this activity you will configure the Windows XP VPN server. Note that the VPN server must have an IP address that is visible from the Internet. If the wireless gateway is using network address translation (NAT) then the Windows XP computer cannot be seen from the Internet. Possible solutions to this problem include acquiring a static IP address from the Internet service provider that can be assigned to the Windows XP computer and allow requests to "pass through" the gateway, or putting the Windows XP computer in the DMZ.

1. Click **Start** and **Control Panel**. In Classic View, double-click **Network Connections**.

2. Click **Create a new connection** under Network Tasks to display the **New Connection Wizard**. Click **Next**.

3. The **Network Connection Type** dialog box will be displayed, as seen in Figure 9-18. Click **Set up an advanced connection**. Click **Next**.

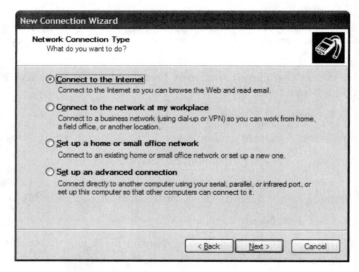

Figure 9-18   Network Connection Type dialog box

4. On the **Advanced Connection Options** screen select **Accept incoming connections**. Click **Next**.

5. The **Devices for Incoming Connections** screen displays devices that can be accessed remotely. Click **Next**.

6. The **Incoming Virtual Private Network (VPN) Connection** screen is displayed. Select **Allow virtual private connections**. Click **Next**.

7. A screen titled **User Permissions** lists the individuals who can connect to this VPN server. Select the individuals for whom permission will be granted. If the person does not already have an account on the computer click the **Add** button to create an account for that person on the computer. Click **Next**.

8. Click **Internet Protocol (TCP/IP)** on the **Networking Software** screen and then click **Properties**.

9. On the **Incoming TCP/IP Properties** screen, the default for assigning IP addresses is **Assign TCP/IP addresses automatically using DHCP**. If the remote device will be part of this existing network and receives its IP address from the DHCP server then this setting cannot be used. Click **Specify TCP/IP addresses** and enter the starting and ending numbers of the range that is different from the range that is being used. If the remote device is on a separate network then select **Allow calling computer to specify its own IP address**. Click **OK**, click **Next**, and then **Finish**.

10. It is also necessary to inform the wireless gateway, that it must pass the VPN packets on to the server. For the Linksys gateway point your browser to the Web management interface and log on. Click **Security** and then **VPN** to display the **VPN Passthrough** screen, as seen in Figure 9-19.

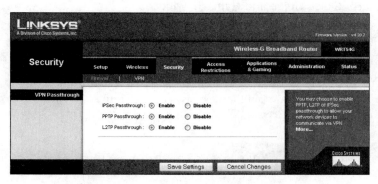

Figure 9-19 VPN Passthrough screen

11. If the correct VPN setting is not enabled (IPSec, PPTP, or L2TP) click **Enable** for that setting. Click **Save Settings**.

12. Close all windows.

Project 9-4: Using VPN Hamachi

Although several software-only VPN solutions are available, almost all require some degree of configuration to the wireless device and the network equipment. One new solution requires almost no configuration and is gaining rapid popularity. Called Hamachi, it is called a "secure mediated peer-to-peer VPN solution." In this project you will install and use Hamachi.

1. Point your Web browser to *www.hamachi.cc*. Click **Download**.

2. Select the latest release of Hamachi for Windows and save it to your desktop. Close all windows and then install the application using the standard default settings.

3. It may be necessary to restart your computer after the installation. Launch Hamachi to display the **Hamachi Quick Guide** and **Hamachi** window, as seen in Figure 9-20. Click **Next** in the **Hamachi Quick Guide**.

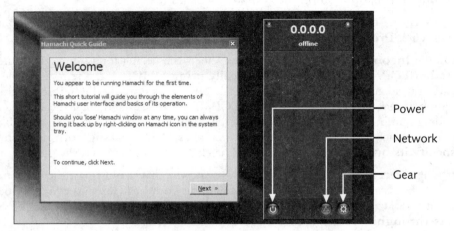

Figure 9-20   Hamachi Quick Guide and Hamachi window

4. Read the information in the **Controls** screen and then click **Next**.

5. Read the information on the **Hamachi Address** screen and then click the **Power** button on the **Hamachi** window.

6. A **Create an account** window will appear, as seen in Figure 9-21. Enter a nickname for yourself and click **Create**.

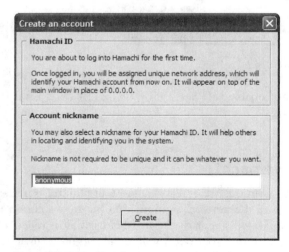

Figure 9-21   Create an account window

7. Hamachi will provide you with a unique IP address that will be used in the communication process. This IP address will not affect your current IP address or that of the remote device. Click **Next**.

8. The **Hamachi Networks** screen appears. Although you can create your own network, for now you will connect to an existing network. Click the **Network** button on the **Hamachi** window. Click **Join existing network**.

9. Under **Network name** enter **test** and under **Network password** enter **secret**. Click **Join**. Click **Next** in the **Hamachi Quick Guide**.

10. Note that the network name **test** appears in the main window along with the current members listed beneath it. A member that appears in white is currently connected whereas a member name in grey means that the person is offline. Click **Next**.

11. The **Network Status** screen explains the status indicators. Double-click **test** to change the status to offline (from white to grey). Click **Next**.

12. The **Peers** screen explains how to change the label of a member. Right-click any member listed under **test** and then click **Set Label**. Click **Address**. Click **Next**.

13. When the **Leaving Network** screen appears, double-click **test** to change its status to online. Then right-click **test** and click **Leave network**. Click **Next**.

14. Click the **Close** button on the **Hamachi Quick Guide.** You can now create your own private network by clicking the **Network** button and then **Create new network**.

15. Close all windows when finished.

Case Projects

Case Project 9-1: Third-Party Private Key Cryptography Tools

Although private key cryptography tools are not considered strong tools for encrypting documents, they do have their place. Using the Internet, locate at least three tools, download them, and use them to encrypt a document. Write a summary that outlines the advantages and disadvantages of each tool, along with the cryptography that it uses. Is this cryptography considered strong or weak? Would you recommend any of these to be used if key management could be safely achieved?

Case Project 9-2: Pretty Good Privacy (PGP)—Too Good?

Since its inception Pretty Good Privacy (PGP), which was developed by Phil Zimmermann, has been under scrutiny because of the strong security that it freely provides. Some individuals maintain that this only allows enemies of the country to correspond in ways that the government cannot monitor. Using the Internet, research the issues that surround PGP and the government's claims against it. Where is it illegal to use PGP? Why? Should there be "back doors" built into all encryption programs in order for the government to view transmissions? Why or why not? Write a one-page paper on your findings.

Case Project 9-3: FTP Warnings

Locate several anonymous FTP sites on the Internet (where anyone can log on without the need for an account) and connect to those FTP servers. Read through the information stored there and look for a warning about transmitting FTP information in cleartext. How many sites contain a warning? Is it sufficient? Now write your own warning that you feel would properly alert users to the risks of FTP.

Case Project 9-4: SSH in Action

Use the Internet and other print media to research SSH. What are its weaknesses? What are its strengths? How is it being used? Next, draw a diagram of how SSH port forwarding functions between a client and a server. Include a one-paragraph description of how it works.

Case Project 9-5: PPTP Vulnerabilities

After PPTP was released, several security vulnerabilities were revealed when using this protocol. Using the Internet, research what these vulnerabilities were. Who discovered them? How were they addressed? What are weaknesses of the current version of PPTP? Would you recommend using it? Why?

Fairvue Technology Consulting

Fairvue Technology Consulting has been hired by a local mortgage company, Premiere Mortgage, to help set up a VPN for its 35 employees to use while at the bank site, a three-story building, to communicate with the branch office downtown. The company also wants to provide VPN solutions to employees at home to access either site through the Internet.

1. Research the costs of VPN solutions for both wireless transmissions as well as wired transmissions through the Internet from both the bank's site and the employee's home. Would you recommend software-based or hardware-based solutions? What type of wireless equipment should be used? Why? What tunneling protocol would you recommend? Prepare a one-page paper that lists the costs and your recommendations.

2. After reading your recommendations, the mortgage company has asked for additional information. They would like a diagram that shows the equipment and software that would be used for the VPNs (wireless, main office, branch office, and home). They also want to see the protection that the VPN would provide. Use Microsoft Paint or a similar program to design the VPN network.

MANAGING THE WIRELESS NETWORK

After completing this chapter you should be able to do the following:

➤ Describe the functions of a WLAN management system

➤ List the different types of probes that are used in monitoring the RF

➤ Explain how a wireless intrusion prevention system differs from a wireless intrusion detection system

➤ List the features of a WIPS

The World of Wireless Security

Detecting wireless intruders is important in the fight to keep a wireless local area network secure. If you can identify and block unauthorized users, the WLAN will be more secure. Detecting wireless intruders is sometimes a costly and imprecise process. However, that may all change very soon.

Intel is currently developing a technology to locate a WLAN user by timing how long it takes for packets to travel from the access point to the user and back. From the length of time it takes the packet to complete its round trip, it can be extrapolated just how far away the user is from the access point. According to Intel, this technology is so precise that it can map a user up to 70 meters (231 feet) away from the access point. It can even determine if the user is on the inside or outside of a wall. For example, an organization may be able to provide wireless access to all of its employees but only within the building. If it is detected that a user is receiving the radio frequency signal outside the outer wall of the building, his or her access can immediately be terminated. This would prevent users outside a house or office from accessing an indoor WLAN.

In addition to limiting a network to authorized users, this system also has other potential uses, according to Intel. Locating a wireless device that can be almost anywhere within the reach of the RF signal often makes troubleshooting difficult. For example, a wireless network interface card adapter that goes "haywire" and starts flooding the wireless network with traffic may require technicians to walk around the entire building or network coverage area trying to find the device. Having the ability to precisely locate a wireless device on the network can be a valuable aid in finding and fixing hardware problems. Also, this technology can be used to inform mobile device users more precisely of areas in which wireless service is available. Another possible use is to allow users to transfer video display information from desktop monitors to mobile devices. For example, if a user is viewing a Web site on a monitor attached to her desktop computer but then carries her wireless notebook computer to a different part of the building, the image on the desktop screen could automatically be displayed on the notebook whenever she moves out of range of the monitor.

Although access points and wireless devices must be modified to support this new technology, Intel indicates that it has great potential for wireless users. Intel plans to present the technology to the IEEE 802.11 group so that it may become part of the 802.11 standard.

Planning, designing, and installing a secure wireless LAN requires a large amount of attention, energy, and money to do the job correctly. When a WLAN has first been installed and is functioning, there is a sense of relief, accomplishment, and pride. Yet in reality, the work has just begun. Any network requires proper management to ensure that it is running adequately and provides the necessary support to all users. However, managing a WLAN actually requires more work than managing a traditional wired network because of the fluid nature of a wireless network. For example, rearranging furniture or placing a large plant in the corner of a room can create "dead spots" of radio frequency coverage that were not there five minutes earlier.

Also, unlike a wired network that limits the number of users by the number of desktop computers connected to the network, a wireless network freely accepts all approved users. This means that the number of users who roam into a hotspot at any given moment may double or even triple and cause throughput to plummet. Therefore a wireless LAN requires constant vigilance to monitor response time and take appropriate action to increase it when necessary.

However, perhaps the most important part of managing a WLAN is ensuring that proper security is maintained. Because an attacker can silently enter a WLAN without any notice, a wireless network must be under constant watch to ensure that all security holes are patched, that no unauthorized users are connected, and that defenses are maintained against the latest wireless attacks.

In this chapter you explore managing a WLAN using two critical tools. The first tool is a WLAN management system. The second is a relatively new technology known as wireless intrusion prevention systems that help provide a higher level of defense.

WLAN MANAGEMENT SYSTEMS

Until recently one of the most important tasks of a network manager was to monitor the network in terms of how it was being used and its performance. This was necessary because the rate of network utilization was growing dramatically every year. In order to continue to provide adequate throughput to all users, new networking equipment, such as hubs, routers, and switches, along with additional network wiring and connections, were needed. Because of the "lead time" needed to make these installations before all network throughput was completely "saturated," network managers constantly monitored network resources to know when to begin planning for the next increase in the network's infrastructure.

In recent years the need for network monitoring has diminished as network equipment has become more powerful, intelligent, significantly less expensive, and even self-monitoring. Some network managers today even question if network monitoring for wired networks is worth the time and money expended.

Even if the need for monitoring wired networks is debated, there is no question that monitoring wireless networks remains critical. Wireless network monitoring enables the network administrator or manager to:

- *Identify security threats*—The need to monitor and manage wireless network resources as a means of proactively detecting security threats continues to be of paramount importance.

- *Verify compliance*—Many organizations use monitoring to document their compliance to federal regulations regarding the protection of data. These regulations include the **Gramm–Leach–Bliley Act (GLBA)**, which gives limited privacy protections against the sale of private financial information and obtaining personal information through false pretenses; the **Sarbanes–Oxley Act**, which covers corporate governance, financial disclosure, and the practice of public accounting; and the **Health Insurance Portability and Accountability Act (HIPAA)**, which governs the privacy of personal health information.

- *Monitor scarce bandwidth*—Because wireless network bandwidth is less than that of a wired network (54 Mbps for an IEEE 802.11g or even 11 Mbps for an 802.11b network versus 100 Mbps or 1,000 Mbps for Fast Ethernet or Gigabit Ethernet), this limited resource must be continually monitored.

- *Administer the shared wireless resource*—Because WLAN bandwidth is a shared resource and not a dedicated resource (like the typical Ethernet switched environment), the number of users and the actions they are performing can have a significant impact on response times.

- *Adjust for unpredictable wireless behavior*—The quality of a WLAN signal can be affected by movement of the wireless device, fading, interference, and even atmospheric conditions. A signal that is satisfactory one minute can become unacceptable the next.

Monitoring a WLAN can be accomplished by using either a standard network management protocol or a system specifically designed for wireless networks. The Simple Network Management Protocol (SNMP) has been the standard network management protocol for wired networks for several years. As part of the TCP/IP protocol, SNMP can also be used for managing wireless LANs.

 SNMP is covered in Chapter 3.

NOTE

SNMP allows computers and network equipment to gather data about network performance. Software agents are loaded onto each network device that will be managed. Each agent monitors network traffic and stores that information in its management information base (MIB). In addition, a computer with the SNMP management software, known as the SNMP management station, communicates with the software agents on each network device and collects the data stored in the MIBs. The SNMP management station then combines all of the data and produces statistics about the network, such as transmission or connectivity errors, the number of bytes or data packets sent, and information on IP activity and addressing. A wireless SNMP network is illustrated in Figure 10-1.

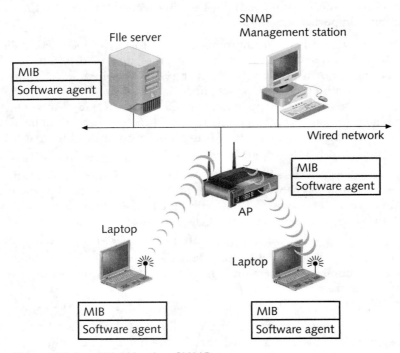

Figure 10-1   WLAN using SNMP

 Hands-On Project 10-1 explores additional information regarding MIBs.

NOTE

Using SNMP for wireless LAN management has several advantages, including the ability to support a variety of different types of devices (called a heterogeneous environment), increased flexibility, the ease of expanding the network, and its widespread popularity. However, SNMP also has several shortcomings, which include wasting bandwidth by sending needless information, complicated encoding rules, and the fact that SNMP may not be quick enough to provide satisfactory support in a WLAN because response time in a WLAN depends heavily upon the quality of the wireless connection.

NOTE   Some studies have indicated that the wireless SNMP response time can vary from several seconds to as much as several minutes depending on the condition of the RF signal, and that SNMP for wireless network management may be completely unusable when there is poor signal quality.

Because of the weaknesses of using SNMP for wireless, alternative dedicated WLAN management systems are available. A WLAN management system, composed of a combination of hardware and software, provides a valuable function in managing the wireless network.

Both SNMP and WLAN management systems contain tools to perform three important management functions: network discovery, monitoring, and configuration.

Discovery

A primary function of any wireless management system is to identify the wireless devices that make up the network itself. Because wireless devices can enter and leave a network at any given time, knowing which devices are part of the network and which are not is important. This discovery can be a performed by using either SNMP or a dedicated WLAN management system. Wireless discovery can be divided into two categories: discovery of wireless devices and discovery of rogue access points.

Wireless Device Discovery

To determine if a wireless device is part of the WLAN, SNMP can send a request similar to a **PING** (**Packet Internet Groper**), which is a diagnostic program that sends a packet to a device and waits for a response to determine if it is properly functioning. When the wireless device receives the SNMP request, software then listens for the response and logs that entry into the MIB. The MIB can then be queried to determine if that wireless device is part of the WLAN.

However, discovery using SNMP is only useful for a wireless device that is *intended* to be part of the network. Unapproved devices, including those used by attackers, would generally not be configured to use SNMP and therefore would not respond to SNMP requests. In order to identify devices that do not respond to SNMP queries, other discovery tools must be used. Dedicated WLAN management systems use discovery tools such as nearest sensor, triangulation, RF fingerprinting, and received signal strength indication.

Nearest Sensor   The **nearest sensor** method, although the simplest method, is also the least precise method. This capacity is supported by almost all wireless LAN network vendors in their management systems. The nearest sensor method first determines the access point to which a wireless device is associated and assumes that this is the sensor that is the closest to that device. Then, it computes how far the RF signal radiates from that access point. For example, an IEEE 802.11g AP may have a signal that radiates 30 meters (100 feet) in all directions. Therefore the nearest sensor method can locate a client to within a 900 meter (10,000 square foot) area. The nearest sensor method is illustrated in Figure 10-2.

10

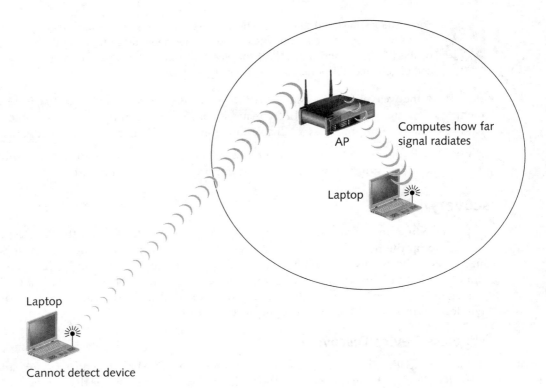

Figure 10-2   Nearest sensor method

The nearest sensor method has two significant limitations. First, locating a wireless device within a large 900-meter area generally is not precise enough except when only a very general location is required. Also, because a device may quickly re-associate with another AP farther away if the nearest AP is overloaded or its signal strength is weakened by objects in its path, the results generated by the nearest sensor method may not be accurate.

Triangulation/Trilateration   Instead of using a single AP to determine the location of a wireless device as with the nearest sensor method, measurements can be combined from multiple APs to pinpoint the location more precisely. **Triangulation** measures the angles between three or more nearby APs; where the measurements intersect this can be used to calculate the location of the device. **Trilateration** measures the distance between three or more APs rather than the angles between them. Trilateration is illustrated in Figure 10-3.

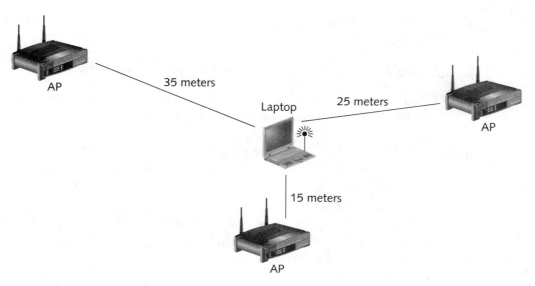

Figure 10-3   Trilateration

RF Fingerprinting   RF fingerprinting uses intelligent algorithms to improve precision by accounting for the environmental effects (such as attenuation, multipath distortion, or physical objects) on the wireless signal itself. A "fingerprint" of the wireless environment is first calculated by conducting a physical "walk-around" using a mobile spectrum analysis device. These measurements are later compared to deviations in the real-time environment to locate the client device.

> Global positioning systems (GPS) are not widely used in 802.11 WLANs because GPS chipsets are expensive and satellite reception within buildings may be difficult to achieve.
>
> **NOTE**

Received Signal Strength Indication (RSSI)   The **Received Signal Strength Indication (RSSI)** is a signal that tells the strength of the incoming (received) signal. The RSSI can be used to measure the RF power loss between transmitter and receiver to calculate the distance from the transmitting device to the receiver.

Rogue Access Point Discovery

The problem of rogue (unauthorized) access points is of increasing concern within organizations. Because of the low cost of home wireless gateways, an unsuspecting employee can bring to her office a device and plug it into an open network connection to provide wireless access for herself and other employees. However, these rogue access points are serious threats to the security of the network because they allow attackers to intercept the RF signal and bypass network security to attack the network or capture sensitive data.

There are several methods to detect a rogue access point. Two of the most common include mobile sniffing audits and wireless probes.

NOTE   Another method for detecting rogue access points is to use a port scanner program and router table entries. Although this approach has significant limitations it may be used if other options are not available. Hands-On Project 10-2 explores how to use a port scanner to detect rogue access points.

Mobile Sniffing Audits   The most basic method for identifying and locating a rogue access point is to "manually" audit the airwaves by using a wireless sniffer such as NetStumbler or AirMagnet. The steps for performing a mobile sniffing audit include:

1. Create a list of approved APs, including the Media Access Control (MAC) addresses, the vendor name, channel number, SSID, and security configurations.

2. Walk through the building or area and capture wireless traffic with the sniffer. When scanning several buildings or a large geographical area this can be extremely time consuming.

3. When an access point is detected by the sniffer, compare it against the list of approved devices. If an access point is discovered by the sniffer but is not listed as being approved it should be considered suspect.

4. Identify the exact location of the rogue AP. Walk in the direction of the signal that causes the RSSI signal strength of the AP to increase. This can be difficult in a building with many offices. It may be necessary to be accompanied by personnel who have keys and the authority to enter locked offices.

NOTE   The success of discovering a rogue access point can be increased if the search occurs at night or on weekends when employees are not present. This is because if an employee sees someone walking through the building looking for a rogue AP she can quickly turn it off and it can no longer be detected.

A mobile sniffing audit has been labeled a "cat and mouse" game for trying to find rogue access points. In most instances it only results in a rogue access point being temporarily turned off while searchers are in the area. Because it is very time consuming and haphazard, most organizations elect to use a more reliable approach.

Wireless Probes   There are two characteristics of a mobile sniffing audit: it only scans the RF frequency and it does this intermittently. A more reliable technique is to continuously monitor the RF airspace. Monitoring the RF frequency requires a special sensor called a **wireless probe**, which is a device that can monitor the airwaves for traffic.

There are four types of wireless probes:

■ *Wireless device probe*—A standard wireless device, such as a portable laptop computer, can be configured to act as a wireless probe. At regular intervals during the normal course of operation, the device can scan and record wireless signals within its range and report this information to a centralized database. This scanning is performed when the device is idle and not receiving any transmissions. When a large number of mobile devices are used as wireless device probes it can provide a high degree of accuracy in identifying rogue access points. However, there are limitations. First, because a wireless device cannot simultaneously listen and send, there can be gaps in the coverage. Also, not all wireless network interface card adapters can act as a wireless device probe.

- *Desktop probe*—Instead of using a mobile wireless device as a probe, a desktop probe utilizes a standard desktop PC. A universal serial bus (USB) wireless network interface card adapter is plugged into the desktop computer and it monitors the RF frequency in the area for transmissions.

- *Access point probe*—Some access point vendors have included in their APs the functionality of detecting neighboring APs, both friendly APs as well as rogue access points. However, this approach is not widely used. The range for a single AP to recognize other APs is limited because access points are typically located so that their signals only overlap in such a way to provide roaming to wireless users. Also, not all vendors support access point probing.

- *Dedicated probe*—A dedicated probe is designed to exclusively monitor the RF frequency for transmissions. Unlike access point probes that serve as both an access point and a probe, dedicated probes only monitor the airwaves. Dedicated probes look similar to standard access points.

These different types of probes are illustrated in Figure 10-4. It is not required that only one type of probe be used; instead, a combination of probe types can provide more extensive coverage over a single probe.

Once a suspicious wireless signal is detected by a wireless probe, that information is sent to a centralized database on which WLAN management system software compares it to a list of approved APs. If the device is not on the list, then it is considered a rogue access point. Returning to Figure 10-4, the managed switch is "aware" of approved access points and the ports to which they are connected. The WLAN management system can cause the switch to disable the port to which the rogue access point is connected, therefore severing its connection to the wired network.

The key to wireless probes is not the probes themselves but the network management tools that establish a network framework to integrate and manage wired and wireless networks by extending "wireless awareness" into key elements of the wired network infrastructure. One well-known comprehensive solution to the convergence of wired and wireless networks is the Cisco Structured Wireless-Aware Network (SWAN). Besides Cisco Aironet WLAN access points and the WLAN client devices, management servers such as the CiscoWorks Wireless LAN Solution Engine (WLSE) detect and suppress rogue APs through switch port shut down and automatically help to protect the radio frequency environment from unauthorized access. Some Cisco switch and router devices now have incorporated wireless capabilities.

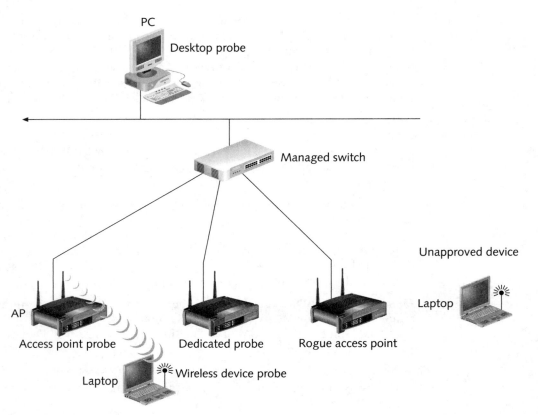

Figure 10-4   Wireless probes

 NOTE   Rogue access points can also be discovered by using SNMP or the Cisco Discovery Protocol (CDP). However, this service must be turned on so that the device will respond to queries. Unapproved devices, including those used by attackers, would not be configured to respond.

Monitoring

In addition to discovering an unauthorized wireless device or rogue access point, the status of the wireless network should also be monitored. If SNMP is being used, monitoring often focuses upon the performance of the network. The bandwidth utilization can be determined by collecting statistics on the amount of data traffic that passes through an access point. In addition, performance monitoring can assess how often and quickly the device responds to a request. This data reported by these monitors can be important to determining the "health" of a wireless LAN: a spike in a network's bandwidth or a decrease in the time to respond to a request are signs that the network is running slowly. These events are known as an **SNMP trap**. There are different actions that can be taken when an SNMP trap occurs. Generally an event alarm is issued and the proper personnel are notified.

SNMP supports different types of notification. An SNMP trap is considered unreliable because the receiver does not send acknowledgments when it receives the trap message and the sender does not know if it was received. An SNMP **inform request** acknowledges the message with an SNMP response. If the sender does not receive a response, the inform request can be re-sent. Although inform requests are more likely to reach their destination, they consume more resources.

Dedicated WLAN management systems also provide similar capabilities. However, these systems are designed to report specific wireless information as well, such as monitoring WLAN devices for send and receive traffic and utilization, data rates, channel usage, and errors rates.

Configuration

Both SNMP and WLAN management systems allow for configuration of the wireless APs through the network without the necessity of "touching" each device. However, SNMP is only capable of a small number of configuration settings. WLAN management systems, on the other hand, offer a very wide range of configuration settings that can be performed remotely through the network. Table 10-1 lists some of the settings that can be manipulated.

Table 10-1   Remote AP configuration settings

Access Point Setting	Description
SSID	Service set identifier for the access point
Allow broadcast SSID	Enable or disable AP to broadcast the SSID
Allow auto channel select	Enable or disable AP to auto select the channel
Channel	Specify the channel number at which the AP transmits
Name	Name of the access point
Use DHCP	Enable or disable DHCP mode
LAN IP	Set IP address of AP
Subnet Mask	Set network mask value
DNS server IP	Set IP address of the DNS server
WEP	Enable or disable WEP data encryption
802.1x	Enables user authentication with RADIUS server
WPA	Enable or disable WPA data encryption and authentication
Beacon period	Set rate for beacon frames
Receive Antenna Left Right Diversity	Set configuration for AP antennas

Remotely accessing APs for configuration is an important labor-saving technique. An equally important technique is to "bulk" configure a group of access points with the same configurations (such as Allow Broadcast SSID) and then adjust a small number of settings for specific access points (such as AP Name).

Some WLAN management systems support template-based configuration. Administrators can select an appropriate template, fill in the values, and then apply the template to select access points.

NOTE

Another aspect of configuration is upgrading the firmware of access points. Firmware upgrade images can be imported and then applied to one AP, all APs, or groups of access points. Grouping APs allow firmware images to be separately distributed based on vendor or model. This allows for upgrades to be performed at night when there is less traffic.

The status of the firmware upgrade and whether it was a success or a failure can also be logged along with a list of APs to which the firmware was applied.

NOTE

WIRELESS INTRUSION PREVENTION SYSTEMS (WIPS)

One of the most important tools for protecting a wireless LAN is rapidly gaining widespread acceptance. Known as a **wireless intrusion prevention system (WIPS)**, its goal is to integrate several layers of protection to detect and prevent malicious attacks.

Intrusion Systems

An **intrusion system** is a security management system that compiles information from a computer network or individual computer and then analyzes it to identify security vulnerabilities and attacks. Although similar in nature to a firewall, an intrusion system differs in that a firewall limits access from external networks by silently filtering packets based on such criteria as the sender's IP address or whether the packet was requested by a device on the protected network. Firewalls do not alert security personnel that a malicious packet has been destroyed. An intrusion system, on the other hand, watches for systematic attacks (instead of just a single malicious packet) and then takes specified action. Intrusion systems can also watch for any attacks that may originate from inside the network as well.

An intrusion system for a wired network is generally a specific module that fits into a rack-mounted device or a stand-alone device.

NOTE

There are two types of intrusion systems for wireless LANs. The first is a wireless intrusion detection system (WIDS) whereas the second is a more sophisticated wireless intrusion prevention system (WIPS). Each of these types use wireless probes to accumulate data.

Wireless Intrusion Detection System (WIDS)

The first generation of intrusion detection systems for wired networks monitored the overall activity of network traffic and focused on detection of attacks. In wireless networks a **wireless intrusion detection system (WIDS)** serves a similar function by constantly monitoring the radio frequency (using wireless probes) for attacks. If an attack is detected, the WIDS sends information about what happened but does not take any action.

There are two technologies for WIDS. The first type is known as **signature detection**. The WIDS analyzes the information it gathers and compares it to large databases of attack signatures (much like how antivirus software detects a virus). A WIDS may use statistical analysis, monitor log files, or search for patterns in the flow of network traffic to detect an attack. If a matching attack signature is found in the database, then it can be determined that an attack is occurring. However, if the signature is not in the database, the system cannot detect an attack. Hence a WIDS is looking for a specific attack that has already been documented. Signature detection WIDS are illustrated in Figure 10-5.

10

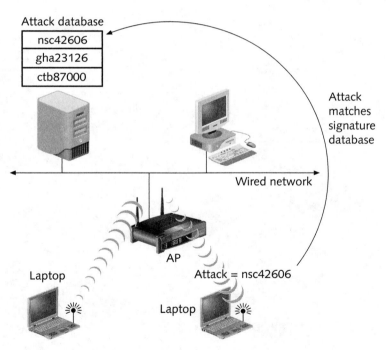

Figure 10-5   Signature detection WIDS

The second type of WIDS is **anomaly detection**. Instead of relying upon a repository of attack signatures, an anomaly detection system monitors the normal activity of the wireless LAN and "learns" its normal characteristics. However, because of the analysis nature of anomaly detection WIDS, a large number of attack alerts that are issued turn out to be false (known as **false positives**).

In a WIDS anomaly detection system the security administrator defines the **baseline** (or normal) state of the network's traffic, such as the protocols used, typical load, average packet size, and so on. When creating baselines it is important to observe the following tasks:

- Measure the performance parameters under normal network conditions and not when there is an unusual amount of traffic, number of users, or other abnormal circumstances.

- Configure the system to recognize all access points in the area as either authorized, monitored, or known.

- Be aware of any common false positives that may exist for a specific network configuration.

The WIDS anomaly detector monitors traffic and compares it to the baseline, looking for variations (anomalies). If an action occurs that is not "normal" then an alarm is triggered. Some WIDS even combine anomaly detection with signature detection. Anomaly detection WIDS are illustrated in Figure 10-6.

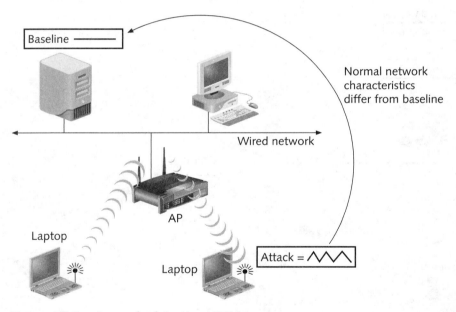

Figure 10-6 Anomaly detection WIDS

 NOTE Some firewalls can also function like anomaly WIDS to filter traffic from entering a network. Instead of creating static rules for filtering traffic, these profile-based firewalls build statistical profiles of user activity and then react to any activity that falls outside those established profiles. A user's profile can contain attributes such as files and servers frequently accessed, time spent logged onto the network, location of the network access, and more.

Although WIDS were highly intelligent devices, they had significant disadvantages:

- *Only issue alert*—Because a WIDS only identifies that an attack has started, it does nothing to prevent the attack from occurring. That would be left up to the system administrator after receiving the WIDS notification.

- *Alert after attack started*—A WIDS only knows that an attack has started after the attack has commenced. By then damage may have already occurred.

- *Dependent upon signatures*—A signature detection WIDS relies entirely upon the database of known attack signatures in order to recognize an attack. If a new attack is launched for which this is no attack signature or if the database is not constantly updated, a signature detection WIDS provides no protection.

- *High number of false positives*—Because of the analytic nature of anomaly detection WIDS, a large number of attack alerts are issued that turn out to be false positives. This creates a tremendous burden on security administrators, especially for WLANs.

NOTE

Because of the limitations of intrusion detection systems, the Gartner Group, a highly respected IT consulting organization, startled the technology community in June 2003 by declaring that IDS will be obsolete by 2005. Gartner said that IDS failed to deliver value relative to its costs and recommended that businesses invest their security dollars on firewalls that block attacks instead of alerting administrators to them. Although the prediction of the demise of IDS did not turn out to be true, it nevertheless highlighted the weaknesses of IDS.

Wireless Intrusion Prevention System (WIPS)

A more proactive approach than intrusion detection is an **intrusion prevention system (IPS)**. An IPS is designed to stop an attack from occurring. Wired networks use IPS devices to protect a network against application-level attacks such as worms, viruses, Trojan horses, denial of service attacks, spyware, and back doors.

NOTE

An IPS performs a total packet inspection (through Layer 7 of the OSI model) to identify attacks.

A **wireless intrusion prevention system (WIPS)** likewise attempts to uncover and prevent an attack before it harms the WLAN. Wireless intrusion detection systems rely on probes to observe and then forward traffic summaries to a central analysis server. WIPS detect categories of attacks using predictable or **deterministic techniques** that may involve a combination of different approaches. Signatures, instead of being used for attack detection, are only used to provide additional details about the attack itself.

WIPS and WIDS are fueling a market that will top $8 billion by 2008, according to In-Stat/MDR. However, the industry trend is for these devices to be integrated into wired protection products and form a more comprehensive security suite that defends against any type of wired or wireless attack.

WIDS/WIPS Probes

Both WIDS and WIPS rely upon a series of probes (sensors) to monitor network traffic and send traffic summaries to a central analysis server for examination. There are two types of probes: integrated and overlay.

Integrated   An **integrated probe** (also called an access point probe or **embedded probe**) uses existing access points to monitor the RF. This approach is generally used to reduce costs by decreasing or eliminating the need for separate sensor probes and infrastructure (wired cabling to connect devices, power connections, etc.). Although an integrated-probe WIDS or WIPS may seem to have several advantages, requiring an AP to perform its normal functions as well as additional RF monitoring has significant drawbacks:

- In an environment in which the AP is supporting a large number of users, the additional time needed to stop its normal functions and perform sensor probe tasks can negatively impact throughput. One vendor reported a drop in throughput of approximately 16 percent when using integrated WIPS sensor probes.

- Because the AP is not dedicated to the task of watching for attacks, an attack can slip through while the AP is performing its normal duties.

- A basic IEEE 802.11b/g AP cannot monitor IEEE 802.11a channels or RF frequencies in the 2.4 GHz band used outside the United States.

- Integrated sensors have less spare time to perform other WIPS functions such as blocking rogue APs.

- Integrated sensors sequentially sample traffic on every available channel, trying to listen long enough and frequently enough to detect an attack. An attack could slip in on Channel 2 while the AP is scanning Channel 5. Also, attacks of short duration and "quiet" rogue devices like wireless bridges are more likely to be missed in scanning.

Wireless vendors such as Aruba, Cisco, and Trapeze use integrated WIPS.

Overlay   An **overlay probe** uses dedicated probes for scanning the RF for attacks. Although this results in higher costs, it does not impact WLAN throughput by placing an additional load on the AP. Also, overlay probes can scan more frequencies, provide broader coverage, and detect more attacks. Another advantage of overlay probes is that they can also be used to troubleshoot WLAN performance issues.

NOTE Wireless vendors such as Network Chemistry, AirDefense, AirMagnet, and AirTight use overlay probes.

There are disadvantages to an overlay probe for WIDS/WIPS. Overlay probes require additional user interfaces, consoles, and databases that must be integrated to avoid duplication. An integrated probe may be more likely to provide a single, integrated management interface for configuring and monitoring the network. Also, some integrated probes may have built-in criteria to differentiate between legitimate APs and rogue APs, whereas an overlay probe must be configured with a list of authorized access points. Another disadvantage of overlay probes is that if a regular AP fails, the dedicated sensor probe cannot be pulled into emergency duty to provide coverage.

WIPS Features

WIPS are good for enforcing the security policies of an organization by mitigating and containing rogue access points and then both reporting and taking action. There are a number of important features or attributes that are found in WIPS. These include AP identification and categorization, device tracking, event action and notification, RF scanning, and protocol analysis.

AP Identification and Categorization

One of the most important features of a WIPS is its ability to learn about the other access points that are in the area and classify those APs. This ability to "pre-classify" all known APs enables the WIPS to recognize rogue access points without delay.

Using probes, the existing APs in the area can be determined. Next the APs can be tagged as to their status. The indicators are usually:

- *Authorized AP*—This is an access point that has been installed and configured by the organization and is part of the WLAN infrastructure.

- *Known AP*—This is a "foreign" yet "friendly" AP (one not owned by the organization) in which the RF signal is detected yet it is not considered as being dangerous. Known APs may be access points that belong to other organizations (such as on another floor of a rented office building that houses multiple businesses).

- *Monitored AP*—A monitored AP may be an access point in which the signal is usually detected when scans are conducted. However, it is not owned by the organization (Authorized AP) or another organization (Known AP) yet it cannot be verified that it is suspect. An access point that is owned by a user in a nearby apartment complex may be tagged as a Monitored AP.

- *Rogue AP*—Any AP that does not fit the profile of the above three types will be designated as a rogue access point.

It is important for a wireless LAN administrator to thoroughly investigate an AP before designating it as a "Known AP" to ensure that it is not a rogue AP masquerading as a known AP.

Once specific parameters are assigned, most WIPSs are able to perform automatic classification and differentiate between authorized, known, monitored, and rogue APs. The ability to perform this type of activity minimizes false positives and unnecessary alarms to security administrators.

Device Tracking

Whereas AP identification is primarily concerned with locating rogue access points, device tracking involves the simultaneous tracking of all wireless devices within the WLAN. Not only can device tracking be used to identify unauthorized device, but it also can be beneficial for other uses such as:

- Asset tracking of wireless equipment that has a high value or that have been stolen or misplaced
- Finding an emergency Voice over WLAN (VoWLAN) telephone caller
- Troubleshooting sources of wireless network interference
- Conducting a site survey
- Determining a wireless user's availability status based on location

Event Action and Notification

A WIPS that identifies an attack must immediately and automatically block any malicious wireless activity that has been detected by its wireless probes. These malicious activities include: wireless denial of service (DoS) attacks, MAC address spoofing, or allowing a device to associate with a rogue AP. In addition, the WIPS must block multiple simultaneous attacks as well as continue to scan the RF looking for new attacks. And, once an attack is detected the WIPS must notify security administrators through cell phone, e-mail alert, or pager.

Not only must WIPS stop all types of attacks, it must do so while not disrupting legitimate wireless users or disturbing another WLAN.

RF Scanning

It is important that all of the radio frequency spectrum be scanned for potential attacks. This means that all channels in the 2.4 GHz range (which supports both IEEE 802.11b and 802.11g) and the 5 GHz (802.11a) must be scanned.

Some WIPS also scan other frequencies to detect attacks on other types of wireless devices.

Protocol Analysis

Just as an attacker can use a packet sniffer to detect what an authorized user is doing, so can a WIPS do the same to attackers. Several WIPS products offer remote packet capture and decode capabilities. The WIPS can view WLAN network traffic to determine exactly what is happening on the network and help determine what actions need to be taken.

The features of a WIPS are summarized in Table 10-2.

Table 10-2 Features of WIPS

Attribute	Description
AP identification and categorization	All access points should be detected and automatically classified.
Device tracking	WIPS must provides tracking of all wireless devices that are associated with the WLAN.
Event actions and notification	An attack must automatically be stopped and security personnel notified immediately.
RF scanning	The entire spectrum (2.4 GHz for IEEE 802.11b/g and 5 GHz for 802.11a) should be scanned by probes.
Protocol analysis	An integrated packet sniffer and decoder can reveal what is happening on the WLAN.

WIPS security is expensive. The cost for installing a WIPS in 20 different buildings on a campus, each with five APs and only four probes per building, can cost almost $130,000.

Chapter Summary

- Wireless LAN management systems are important tools for maintaining wireless networks. The SNMP can be used for WLAN management, although a dedicated WLAN management system can often provide more flexibility. Both perform three important management functions: discovery, monitoring, and configuration. Discovery involves determining the existence and location of both wireless devices and rogue access points through using a series of probes. Monitoring focuses on observing the performance of the network. Configuration allows the settings of the access point to be changed.

❑ A WIDS constantly monitors the radio frequency (using wireless probes) for attacks. If an attack is detected, the WIDS will send information about what happened but will not take any action to stop the attack. A WIDS uses either signature detection or anomaly detection to identify attacks.

❑ A WIPS attempts to uncover and prevent an attack before it harms the WLAN. Both WIDS and WIPS rely on probes to observe and then forward traffic summaries to a central analysis server. There are two types of probes that are commonly used: integrated probes or overlay probes. The features of a WIPS include AP identification and categorization, device tracking, event action and notification, RF scanning, and protocol analysis.

KEY TERMS

anomaly detection — A type of wireless intrusion detection system (WIDS) that monitors the normal activity of the wireless LAN and "learns" its normal characteristics.

baseline — The normal state of a network's traffic.

deterministic techniques — Predictable techniques that are used by wireless intrusion detection systems to detect attacks.

embedded probe — A probe integrated into an existing access point, used for monitoring the RF.

false positive — Attack alert that turns out to be false.

Gramm-Leach-Bliley Act (GLBA) — A 1999 U.S. federal regulation that gives limited privacy protections against the sale of private financial information and obtaining personal information through false pretenses.

Health Insurance Portability and Accountability Act (HIPAA) — A 1996 U.S. federal regulation that governs the privacy of personal health information.

inform request — A Simple Network Management Protocol (SNMP) feature that acknowledges the receipt of a message indicating an abnormal event with an SNMP response.

integrated probe — A probe integrated into an existing access point, used for monitoring the RF.

intrusion prevention system (IPS) — A security system that is designed to stop an attack from occurring.

intrusion detection system (IDS) — A security management system that compiles information from a computer network or individual computer and then analyzes it to identify security vulnerabilities and attacks. The first generation of IDSs were for wired networks and focused on the detection of attacks.

nearest sensor — A method for determining the location of a wireless device that identifies the access point to which a wireless device is associated and computes how far the RF signal radiates from that access point.

overlay probe — A dedicated probe that monitors the RF and scans for attacks.

PING (Packet Internet Groper) — A diagnostic program that sends a packet to a device and waits for a response to determine if it is properly functioning.

Received Signal Strength Indication (RSSI) — A method for determining the location of a wireless device that measures the RF power loss between transmitter and receiver to calculate the distance to the device.

RF fingerprinting — A method for determining the location of a wireless device that creates an image of the wireless environment and then compares it to deviations in the real-time environment to locate the device.

Sarbanes-Oxley Act — A 2002 U.S. federal regulation that covers corporate governance, financial disclosure, and the practice of public accounting.

signature detection — A type of wireless intrusion detection system that analyzes the information it gathers and compares it to large databases of attack signatures.

SNMP trap — An abnormal event that is monitored on a network using the Simple Network Management Protocol (SNMP).

triangulation — A method for determining the location of a wireless device that measures the angles between three or more nearby access points to determine the intersection.

trilateration — A method for determining the location of a wireless device that measures the distance between three or more access points.

wireless intrusion detection system (WIDS) — The first generation of security management systems for wireless networks that focused on the detection of attacks by constantly monitoring the radio frequency.

wireless intrusion prevention system (WIPS) — A newer generation of security systems that attempts to uncover and prevent an attack before it harms the WLAN.

wireless probe — A special sensor that can monitor the airwaves for traffic.

10

REVIEW QUESTIONS

1. Each of the following is a reason to monitor a wireless network *except*

    a. predict when an attack may occur

    b. identify security threats

    c. verify compliance with federal regulations

    d. monitor scarce wireless bandwidth

2. Managing a WLAN can be accomplished by using either a system specifically designed for wireless networks or

    a. Simple Network Management Protocol (SNMP)

    b. File Transfer Protocol (FTP)

    c. Wireless Management Protocol (WMP)

    d. Wired Equivalent Protocol (WEP)

3. Each of the following is a U.S. federal regulation that wireless monitoring can be used to verify compliance *except*
    a. Gramm–Leach–Bliley Act (GLBA)
    b. Sarbanes–Oxley Act
    c. Health Insurance Portability and Accountability Act (HIPAA)
    d. Federal Wireless Security Act

4. Each of the following is a WLAN discovery tool to locate a wireless device *except*
    a. farthest sensor
    b. triangulation
    c. RF fingerprinting
    d. Received signal strength indication

5. The disadvantage of a mobile sniffing audit is
    a. sniffing software is hard to locate
    b. rogue access points do not send RF signals
    c. it is very time consuming
    d. only the network administrator can perform the function

6. Only a laptop computer and not a desktop computer can be used as a wireless probe. True or False?

7. Dedicated probes resemble standard access points. True or False?

8. An SNMP inform request acknowledges the message with an SNMP response. True or False?

9. An intrusion detection system is identical to a firewall. True or False?

10. A signature detection WIDS is susceptible to attacks if the matching attack signature is not in the database. True or False?

11. A(n) _____ detection WIDS monitors the normal activity of the wireless LAN and "learns" its normal characteristics to create a baseline.

12. A(n) _____ is an attack alert that turns out to be false.

13. A(n) _____ attempts to uncover and prevent an attack before it harms the WLAN.

14. A WIPS that uses an existing access point to monitor the RF is known as a(n) _____ probe.

15. One of the most important features of a WIPS is its ability to learn about the other _____ that are in the area and classify them.

16. Explain the difference between triangulation and trilateration.

17. How does RF fingerprinting work?

18. What is a desktop probe?

19. Describe an SNMP trap.

20. How can a WLAN management system be used to upgrade access point firmware?

HANDS-ON PROJECTS

Project 10-1: View SNMP MIBs

The contents of an SNMP MIB illustrate the type of data that it can gather. In this activity you will view MIBs for Linksys and Cisco wireless devices.

1. Use a Web browser to go to the mibDepot site at *www.mibdepot.com.*

2. Click **MIBs** in the left pane.

3. Scroll down and click **Linksys** in the right pane. This will display the Linksys MIBs summary information, as seen in Figure 10-7. (Your summary information may differ.)

10

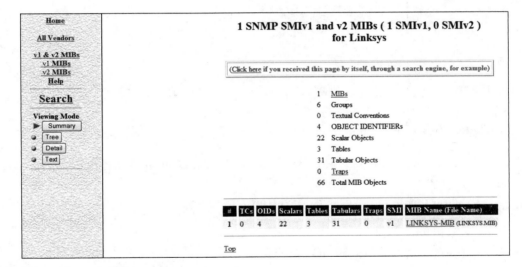

Figure 10-7 Linksys MIB summary data

4. In the left pane, click **v1 & v2 MIBs** to select the SNMP Version 1 and Version 2 MIBs.

5. In the right pane, click **LINKSYS-MIB** under **MIB Name (File Name)**. This will display a list of the Linksys MIBs.

6. Click **Tree** under **Viewing Mode** in the left pane. The MIBs are now categorized by Object Identifier (OID). Each object in a MIB file has an OID associated with it, which is a series of numbers separated by dots that represent where on the MIB "tree" the object is located.

7. Click **Text** in the left pane to display textual information about the Linksys MIBs, as seen in Figure 10-8. Scroll through the Linksys MIBs and read several of the descriptions. How could this information be useful in troubleshooting?

Figure 10-8   Description of Linksys MIBs

8. Now look at the Cisco MIBs. Click **All Vendors** in the left pane to return to a vendor list.

9. Scroll down and click **Cisco Systems** in the right pane. The total number of Linksys MIBs was fewer than 75. How many total Cisco MIB objects listed? Why is there a difference?

10. In the right pane click the link **Traps**.

11. Scroll down to Trap **1081**, which begins the list of Cisco wireless traps. Notice the descriptive names assigned to the wireless traps.

12. Now scroll down to Trap **1094** and click the name **crwTrapInitFailure**. Read the description for this SNMP trap. When would it be invoked? Click the browser's **Back** button to return to the listing.

13. Scroll through the wireless traps (1098–1116) and click on the name to view the description. Identify three traps that you think may be useful in your WLAN.

14. Close all windows when finished.

Project 10-2: Detecting Rogue Access Points

Detecting rogue access points can be a difficult procedure using the mobile sniffing audit technique, and some organizations simply cannot afford to purchase and install probes. Another approach is to use a Transmission Control Protocol (TCP) port scanner program on the wired network that identifies enabled TCP ports from devices connected to the network. Because almost all access point management systems use a Web interface, the port scanner can reveal all access points using the HTTP (Port 80) interfaces on the network. The access point generally will respond to the port scanner's PING by providing the vendor name and its Internet Protocol (IP) address. With this information you may be able to identify if this access point is approved or is a rogue access point. Determining the location of any uncovered rogue access points will require that router table entries be examined. Note that this technique is not foolproof but it may be a good first step.

1. In your Web browser, go to *www.foundstone.com* and click **Resources**.

2. Click **FREE TOOLS**.

3. Scroll down and click **Scanning Tools**.

4. Under **SuperScan v4.0** click **Download this Tool Now**. Follow the instructions to download this software to your desktop.

5. Extract the files and launch **SuperScan4.exe**. The opening screen appears as seen in Figure 10-9.

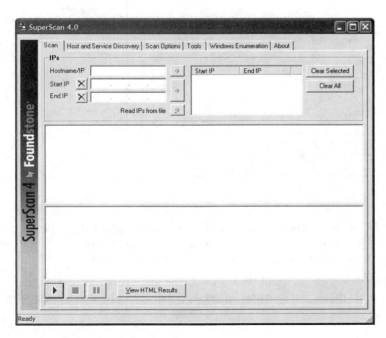

Figure 10-9 SuperScan4

6. Under **Host/IP** enter the IP address of your computer.

NOTE

If you do not know the IP address of your computer click Start and Run and enter cmd and press Enter to reach a command prompt. Enter ipconfig/all and press Enter. Record the number listed under IP address.

7. Under **Start IP** enter the lowest IP address of your network. Enter the highest IP address of your network under **End IP**. Click the right arrow so that these IP addresses appear in the window under **Start IP** and **End IP**.

8. Click the blue **Run** button at the bottom of the screen.

9. When the scan is completed the results will appear like those seen in Figure 10-10.

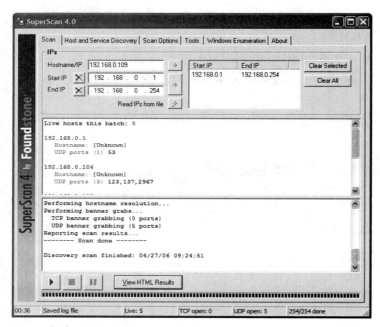

Figure 10-10   Scan results

10. Click **View HTML Results**. This lists all devices that responded to the request. Look under the **Vendor** name for the names of any vendors of access points that are not knowingly installed. If one is detected record the IP address.

11. Open a Web browser and enter that IP address. If the login management screen of an access point appears that is not knowingly installed that could be a rogue access point.

12. Close all windows.

Project 10-3: Basic Intrusion Detection Program

An intrusion detection system monitors the network for activity and reports when an attack occurs. The basic function of an IDS can be illustrated by a TCP/UDP port "listening" program. After providing a list of ports on which to listen, the program notifies you when a connection is made to your computer or data arrives at the port, much like an IDS. In this project you will install a port listening program and watch for activity. Note that depending upon the network security the results of this activity may vary.

1. In your Web browser, go to *www.foundstone.com* and click **Resources**.

2. Click **FREE TOOLS**.

3. Scroll down and click **Intrusion Detection Tools**.

4. Under **Attacker v3.0** click **Download this Tool Now**. Follow the instructions to download this software to your desktop.

5. Extract the files and launch **Attacker.exe**.

6. Click **Ports** to see a list of the TCP and UDP ports that Attacker is listening on. Click **OK**.

7. Click **Start** to begin listening for incoming requests or data. How secure is it to know that this program will only respond after an attack begins?

8. Close all windows when finished.

Project 10-4: Using a Wireless LAN Management Program

The ManageEngine WiFi Manager is a wireless LAN management program for centralized management and security of Wireless LANs. It can detect almost all major wireless threats including rogue attacks, intrusions, sniffers, DoS attacks, and other vulnerabilities. In this activity you will download and use ManageEngine WiFi Manager.

1. Point your Web browser to *http://manageengine.adventnet.com/products/wifi-manager/index.html* and read through the features of the product.

2. Under **Download** click **Free Edition**.

3. The Free Edition allows you manage three access points and 10 devices. Download WiFi Manager onto your desktop and install the software by accepting all standard defaults.

4. Launch the WiFi Manager program. The **Discovery Wizard** will help you configure the software. Accept all standard defaults except enter **A** as the **Community String** under **SNMP Parameters**.

5. When prompted, enter **admin** as the **Username** and **admin** as the **Password**.

6. The WiFi Manager 4 Home screen will appear, as seen in Figure 10-11. Depending upon the number of access points, wireless gateways, and other devices that it detects your screen may differ.

10

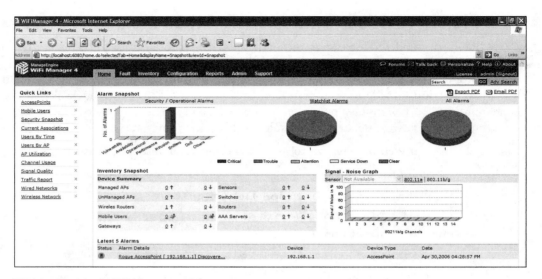

Figure 10-11 WiFi Manager 4 home screen

7. Click the **Inventory** tab.

8. Under **Networks** in the left pane select **Network** to display the wireless networks that are detected.

9. Click the IP address of the network to display a list of devices that are part of that network.

10. Under **Devices** in the left pane select either **Access Points** or **Wireless Routers**, depending upon which is being used in your WLAN.

11. The device will appear as a "Rogue" device because it is not yet recognized as trusted, as seen in Figure 10-12. Under **Name** click the address of the device.

12. You will receive a warning that it cannot receive more inventory details because of improper credentials. Click the **Admin** tab and then click **Credentials** in the left pane.

13. Under **User's Name and Password**, enter or verify the username and password for accessing the Web-based management feature of the access point or wireless router. Click **Save**.

14. Click the **Inventory** tab.

15. Under **Devices** in the left pane, click either **Wireless Routers** or **Access Points**.

16. Select the device by clicking on the IP address. Click **Update Status**. After the status has been updated click **Rediscover**.

17. Close all windows.

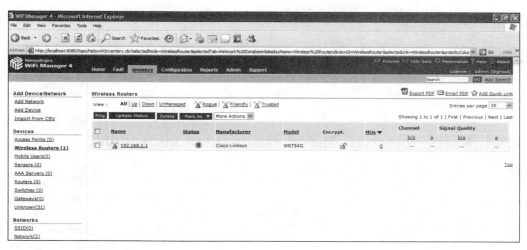

Figure 10-12 Inventory screen

CASE PROJECTS

Case Project 10-1: The Debate Over IDS

The Gartner Group report in 2003 claimed that intrusion detection systems had very limited value sparked a serious debate in the IT community. Using the Internet, research this report and the reactions to it. What is your opinion regarding IDS? Should any organization invest in an IDS today? Or should that investment go toward an IPS? Perform "on-the-spot" Internet research and then use the information as the basis for a discussion with other students.

Case Project 10-2: Probe Costs

What is the difference in costs between the different types of probes? Use the Internet to research the costs for the four different types of probes (wireless device probe, desktop probe, access point probe, and dedicated probe). Which would you recommend? Why? Write a one-page paper on your findings.

Case Project 10-3: IDS and Firewalls

Some security experts predict that the role of the IDS will soon be incorporated into firewalls. Research the differences between IDS and firewalls. Do you think their functionality can be incorporated? Why or why not? What are the disadvantages of combining the two technologies? Write a one- to two-paragraph explanation and include your predictions.

Case Project 10-4: Wireless Management System Features

Using the ManageEngine WiFi Manager (*http://manageengine.adventnet.com/products/ wifi-manager/index.html*) as an example, list the features found in a wireless management system. Classify these features by "Most Desirable," "Good But Not Essential," and "Least Desirable." Within these classifications assign a value of how easy they would be to use. How much would you be willing to pay for this type of software?

Case Project 10-5: Federal Regulations and WIPS

Recent U.S. federal regulations have spurred the requirement of protection of data and full disclosure of certain types of information, fueling the growth of WIPS as a vehicle to show compliance. Using the Internet, research these federal regulations (Sarbanes-Oxley, HIPPA, GLBA, etc.). What types of reporting must be provided for each regulation? How could WIPS help with this reporting? Write a one-page paper on your findings.

Fairvue Technology Consulting

Beautiful Vacations has asked Fairvue Technology Consulting to assist them with implementing a WIDS in three locations that support only 3–5 wireless users each. Fairvue wants you to work on this project.

1. Create a one-page memo for Beautiful Vacations that outlines your preferences for either WIDS or WIPS. Be sure to list the advantages and disadvantages of each. Conclude your memo with your recommendation.

2. After reading your recommendations, Beautiful Vacations wants a price comparison using one dedicated probe at each location. Use the Internet to create an estimated cost for all three locations.

WIRELESS SECURITY POLICY

After completing this chapter you should be able to do the following:

➤ Define security policy

➤ List the elements of the security policy cycle

➤ Describe several types of wireless security policies

The World of Wireless Security

Organizations have widely embraced wireless local area networks as essential tools to give their employees access to network resources throughout the organization's campus. Yet the risk of attackers intercepting wireless transmissions or using a WLAN to attempt to break into the secure wired network is still very real. All security experts agree that a written policy that governs how a wireless network can be used by employees and how the WLAN should be secured is absolutely essential. Without such a policy no employee would know what practices are acceptable, nor would security technicians be able to implement wireless security to protect the organization's assets. With the widespread penetration of wireless technologies across all elements of the economy, it may be assumed that all organizations except a small handful would have wireless policies firmly in place.

However, this is not the case. A recent survey was conducted by the consulting group Orange and Quocirca of 2,035 IT professionals in the United Kingdom in organizations that have widely deployed mobile devices. The survey addressed protecting corporate wireless networks from unauthorized users rather than protection against viruses or other types of malware. The results were surprising. Almost all IT departments reported that they have tools that can be used to help keep wireless devices secure. Yet over 20 percent of the organizations have no policies in place for mobile security. And of those organizations that do have mobile security policies, over 60 percent admit that the policy on the books is not enforced. Almost four out of five organizations surveyed said that their employees are the main threat to security.

According to a report based on the survey, one type of policy that is lacking even among those organizations that have security policies is a policy that deals with what happens when a wireless device is lost or stolen. Policies should be enacted to ensure that data transferred from the organization's database to the wireless device is protected. Technology is available to implement a "remote wipe" that deletes data or makes the devices unusable if they are lost or stolen. This policy should also cover the legal aspects if sensitive data is stolen, in addition to any financial vulnerability.

It is easy to think that the most important element of securing a wireless local area network is the technology. Wireless intrusion detection systems, virtual private networks, RADIUS servers, and other hardware and software are certainly critical in keeping a WLAN safe from attackers. Yet the most important element of a secure WLAN is not the technology itself. Instead, it is the procedures, including the plans and policies, that make a WLAN secure. Without a policy that clearly outlines what needs to be protected, how it should be protected, and what users can and cannot do in support of the policy, there is no wireless security. Many studies have consistently shown that organizations that have a strong and comprehensive security policy have strong security; conversely, those organizations with weak security have a poor security policy or none at all. A security policy is a critical element in wireless security.

In this chapter you will explore the policies for wireless security. First, you will look at exactly what a security policy is. Next, the security policy development cycle is explained. Finally, several types of WLAN security policies are described.

What Is a Security Policy?

One of the most important assets any organization possesses is its data. Although the data will vary between different types of economic sectors (a research hospital's important data may be data collected in the latest clinical trial, whereas a magazine's prime data is a list of its current subscribers), it is the lifeblood of an organization. Without it, the organization is unable to function. Unfortunately, the importance of data is generally underestimated. Data should be considered as vital as all other assets, such as buildings, cash, and personnel.

Some management experts state that employees should be assigned responsibility over data. Just as a controller creates and enforces the acquisition and spending of financial resources, employees should be assigned responsibility for the quality and processing of data.

The goal of information security is to protect the integrity, confidentiality, and availability of data on the devices that store, manipulate, and transmit the information. This is achieved through a combination of three entities in three successive layers. The innermost layer consists of the products that provide the necessary security. These products, which may include intrusion-detection systems or traffic filtering devices, form the physical security around the data. The next layer is people, because without people implementing and properly using the security products, the data can never be protected. The final layer consists of procedures, which include the plans and policies established by an organization to ensure that people correctly use the products. These three layers interact with each other: the procedures tell the people how to use the products to protect the information.

How information security relates to protecting a WLAN is covered in Chapter 1.

One of the most important elements of the procedure layer is a security policy. A **security policy** is a document or series of documents that clearly defines the defense mechanisms an organization will employ to keep information secure. It also outlines how the organization will respond to attacks and the duties and responsibilities of its employees for information security. In short, a security policy is a document that outlines the specific rules that must be met in order to keep the WLAN secure.

The worst approach to creating a security policy is for a member of the IT staff to create the document in one or two days with no input from other individuals. Such an instrument rarely provides reasonable procedures that can be followed by all employees to protect the organization's assets. This type of policy is destined to be placed on a shelf and ignored.

The proper development of a security policy is accomplished through what is called the **security policy cycle**. This cycle defines the overall process involved with developing a security policy. There are three parts to the security policy cycle: risk identification, security policy design and development, and compliance monitoring and evaluation. The security policy cycle is a never-ending process of identifying what needs to be protected, determining how to protect it, and evaluating the adequacy of the protection. The security policy cycle is illustrated in Figure 11-1.

11

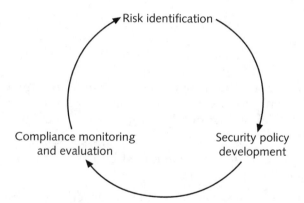

Figure 11-1 Security policy cycle

Risk Identification

The first part of the cycle is **risk identification**. Risk identification seeks to determine the risks that an organization faces against its information assets. That information then becomes the basis of developing the security policy itself. Risk identification in the security policy cycle is illustrated in Figure 11-2.

Figure 11-2   Risk identification elements

Risk identification involves the following steps:

1. Asset identification

2. Threat identification

3. Vulnerability appraisal

4. Risk assessment

Asset Identification

The first step in risk identification is to determine the assets that need to be protected. An **asset** is defined as any item that has a positive economic value, and **asset management** is the process of tracking the assets. An organization has many types of assets, which can be classified as follows:

- *Data*—This involves all data used and transmitted by the organization, such as employee databases and inventory records.

- *Hardware*—Wireless access points, computers, PDAs, networking equipment, and telecommunications connections are included in this category.

- *Personnel*—Personnel assets include employees, customers, business partners, contractors, and vendors.

- *Physical assets*—Physical assets include buildings, automobiles, and other non-computer equipment.

- *Software*—Application programs, operating systems, and security software are examples of software assets.

Asset identification is a lengthy and complicated process. However, identifying assets is one of the most critical steps in risk identification: if you don't know what needs to be protected, how can you protect it? Along with the assets, the attributes of the assets need to be compiled. Samples of the types of attributes for hardware and software assets are listed in Table 11-1.

Table 11-1   Hardware and software attributes

Attribute Name	Description
Equipment name	The name of the device commonly used, such as ACCESS POINT HALLWAY G228
Equipment type	Type of equipment, such as access point or wireless intrusion detection device
Manufacturer	The name of the manufacturer
Model and part number	The identification numbers used by the manufacturer
Manufacturer serial number	The unique serial number assigned by the manufacturer
Inventory tag number	The number assigned by the organization to the item; this is useful as a cross-reference to the order inventory, which contains additional information such as the date purchased, the vendor's name, and the cost
Software or firmware version	The version of the software or firmware, including all updates and service packs installed
Location	The building and room number where the equipment is installed
Addresses	The Media Access Control (MAC) and the IP address of the hardware or the hardware on which the software resides
Unit	The name of the organizational unit responsible for the asset
Function	A description of what the equipment does

After an inventory of the assets has been created and their attributes identified, the next step is to determine each item's relative value. Some assets are of critical value, whereas other assets are of lesser importance. Some organizations assign a numeric value (such as 5 being extremely valuable and 1 being the least valuable) to each asset. Factors that should be considered in determining the relative value are:

- How critical is this asset to the goals of the organization?

- How difficult would it be to replace it?

- How much does it cost to protect it?

- How much revenue does it generate?

- How quickly can it be replaced?

- What is the cost to replace it?

- What is the impact to the organization if this asset is unavailable?

- What is the security implication if this asset is unavailable?

11

As an example, a wireless intrusion prevention system (WIPS) may be considered a critical asset because it prevents malicious attacks from penetrating the WLAN. The WIPS may be assigned a value of a 5, because if it were not functioning it could open the network to attacks. However, a wireless laptop used by an employee may have a lesser value because its loss may not negatively impact the daily workflow of the organization, nor will it seriously prove to be a security risk. It may be assigned a relatively low value of a 2.

NOTE The relative value of an asset may differ widely among organizations. Whereas some organizations may be able to function adequately for a short period of time if an access point stopped functioning, with other organizations the loss could be catastrophic. Each organization must seriously look at the service the asset provides and determine its relative worth.

Threat Identification

After the assets have been inventoried and given a relative value, the next step is to determine the threats from threat agents. A **threat agent** is any threat that exists against an asset. A threat agent is not limited to those from attackers, but also includes acts of God, such as fire or severe weather. Common threat agents are listed in Table 11-2.

Table 11-2 Common threat agents

Category of threat	Example
Acts of God	Fire, flood, earthquake
Compromise of intellectual property	Software piracy or copyright infringement
Espionage	Spy steals production schedule
Extortion	Mail clerk is blackmailed into intercepting letters
Hardware failure or errors	WIPS blocks all traffic
Human error	Employee drops wireless network interface adapter into lake
Sabotage or vandalism	Attacker implants worm that erases files
Software attacks	Virus, worm, denial of service
Software failure or errors	Bug prevents program from properly loading
Technical obsolescence	Program does not function under new version of operating system
Theft	Access point is stolen from hallway
Utility interruption	Electrical power is cut off

Determining the threats to the assets can be a complicated process. One way to approach this task is through a process known as **threat modeling**. Threat modeling constructs scenarios of the types of threats that assets can face. The goal of threat modeling is to better understand who the attackers are, why they attack, and what types of attacks may occur.

A valuable tool used in threat modeling is the construction of an **attack tree**. An attack tree provides a visual image of the attacks that may occur against an asset. Drawn as an inverted tree structure, an attack tree shows the goal of the attack, the types of attacks that may occur, and the techniques used in the attacks.

A partial attack tree for protecting a car stereo system from theft is illustrated in Figure 11-3. At the top of the tree (Level 1) is the goal of the attack, "Steal car stereo." The next level, Level 2, lists the ways an attack may occur: someone could break the glass out of a car window and steal the stereo, someone could steal the keys to the car to get to the stereo, or someone could "hotwire" the ignition to steal the entire car and later remove the stereo. To steal the keys (Level 3), a purse snatcher might grab the keys, or someone might make a copy of them, such as the parking lot attendant. The attendant might copy the keys because of pressure in the form of threats, blackmail, or bribes (Level 4). The attack tree in Figure 11-3 presents a picture of the threats against an asset.

11

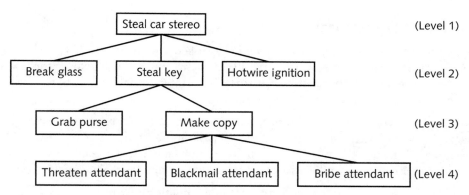

Figure 11-3 Attack tree for stealing car stereo

Creating an attack tree for protecting data that may be accessed by a WLAN can follow the same approach. Figure 11-4 shows a partial attack tree for the research and development database in an organization. Someone may attempt to exploit a WLAN that is using weak security techniques such as Wired Equivalent Privacy (WEP) or may search for a rogue access point. Other techniques do not involve strictly wireless technology, such as stealing a password (Level 2) by looking for one that is written down and stored under a mouse pad in an office or by "shoulder surfing" (Level 3). An alternative approach may be to find a computer that is logged on to the system but left unattended (Level 2). Attack trees help list the types of attacks that that can occur and help trace how and from where the attacks may originate.

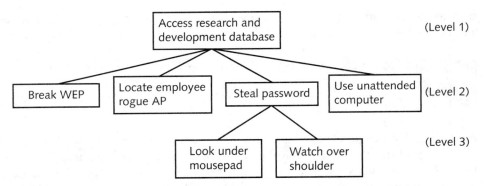

Figure 11-4   Attack tree for accessing a research and development database

 These abbreviated examples of attack trees are not intended to show every possible threat as an actual attack tree would.

Vulnerability Appraisal

After the assets have been inventoried and prioritized, and the threats have been determined, the next natural question is, What current security weaknesses may expose the assets to these threats? Known as **vulnerability appraisal**, this in effect takes a current snapshot of the security of the organization as it now stands.

Revealing the vulnerabilities of an asset is not always as easy as it may seem. Every asset must be viewed in light of each threat; it is not sufficient to limit the assessment to only one or two threats against an asset. Each threat may reveal multiple vulnerabilities. For example, when considering the human error threat to the asset of an access point, the vulnerabilities could be:

- Incorrect configuration stops AP from functioning properly
- Network administrator provides AP administrator access to unauthorized user
- Firmware is improperly installed and prevents wireless users from associating to AP

Determining vulnerabilities often depends on the background and experience of the assessor. It is recommended that teams composed of diverse members be responsible for listing vulnerabilities instead of only one person.

 To assist with determining the vulnerabilities of hardware and software assets, you can use a category of tools known as vulnerability scanners. These tools, available as both free Internet downloads and as commercial products, can compare the asset against a database of known vulnerabilities and can produce a discovery report that exposes the vulnerability and assesses its severity.

Risk Assessment

The final step in identifying risks is to perform a **risk assessment**. A risk assessment involves determining the damage that would result from an attack and the likelihood that a vulnerability is a risk to the organization.

Determining the damage from an attack first requires a realistic look at several types of attacks that may occur, such as denial of service, wireless packet sniffing, access to unsecured WLAN management interfaces, and even social engineering. Then, based on the vulnerabilities recognized in the vulnerability appraisal, an analysis of the impact can be determined. Not all vulnerabilities pose a significant risk; with some vulnerabilities the risk may be minor. One way to determine the severity of a risk is to gauge the impact the vulnerability may have on the organization if it is exploited. Each of the vulnerabilities can be ranked by the scale in Table 11–3.

Table 11-3 Vulnerability impact scale

Impact	Description
No impact	This vulnerability would not affect the organization. For example, the theft of a mouse attached to a wireless laptop computer would not affect the operations of the organization.
Small impact	Small impact vulnerabilities would produce limited periods of inconvenience and may result in changes to a procedure. A wireless network interface adapter card that fails may require that a spare card be made available and that all cards are periodically tested.
Significant	A vulnerability that results in a loss of employee productivity because of downtime or causes a capital outlay to alleviate it may be considered significant. Malware that is injected into the network through an unprotected access point could be classified as a significant vulnerability.
Major	Major vulnerabilities are those that have a significant negative impact on revenue. The theft of the latest product research and development data through a rogue access point could be considered major.
Catastrophic	Vulnerabilities that are ranked as catastrophic are events that would cause the organization to cease functioning or be seriously crippled in its capacity to perform. A tornado that destroys the office building could be a catastrophic vulnerability.

11

NOTE

It is important to perform a risk assessment from the global perspective of the entire organization. Although some risks may seem damaging from the IT perspective, they may not carry the same actual impact on the organization as a whole. For example, the loss of a wireless LAN in the employee cafeteria may seem very serious to the IT staff because of the number of employees who call to complain about it, whereas in reality it may only be an inconvenience to employees and may not impact critical business processes.

Calculating the anticipated losses can be helpful in determining the impact of a vulnerability. Two formulas are commonly used to calculate expected losses. The **Single Loss Expectancy (SLE)** is the expected monetary loss every time a risk occurs. The SLE is computed by multiplying the value of the asset (Asset Value or AV) by the **Exposure Factor (EF)**, or SLE = AV * EF. The Exposure Factor is the proportion of an asset's value that is likely to be destroyed by a particular risk (expressed as a percentage). For example, if the value of a building would be reduced from $10,000,000 to $2,500,000 by a flood, the exposure factor for the risk to the building is 75 percent. The **Annualized Loss Expectancy (ALE)** is the expected monetary loss that can be expected for an asset because of a risk over a one-year period. It is calculated by multiplying the SLE by the **Annualized Rate of Occurrence (ARO)**, or ALE = SLE * ARO. The Annualized Rate of Occurrence (ARO) is the probability that a risk will occur in a particular year. If flood insurance data suggests that a serious flood is likely to occur once in 100 years, then the annualized rate of occurrence is 1/100 or 0.01.

NOTE

Calculating losses should be considered in terms of lost revenue, increased expenses, and penalties or fees for noncompliance.

The next step is to estimate the probability that the vulnerability will actually occur. Some organizations use advanced statistical models for predictions, whereas other organizations use a "best guess" approach and create a ranking system based on observation and past history. These vulnerabilities are ranked on a scale from 1 to 10, with 10 being "Very Likely" and 1 "Unlikely." For example, the risk of a hurricane would be a 10 in South Florida but a 1 in Missouri.

Once the risks are determined and ranked, the final step is to determine what to do about the risks. It is important to recognize that wireless security weaknesses can never be entirely eliminated; it would cost too much and would take too long. Rather, some degree of risk must always be assumed. The questions to ask are, "How much risk is acceptable?" and "Are we willing to tolerate it?"

An organization has three options when confronted with a risk:

- *Accept the risk*—This is accomplished by doing nothing and leaving everything as is. The assumption is that an attack will occur some time in the future, but a decision has already been made to do nothing to protect against it.

- *Diminish the risk*—To diminish or reduce the risk, additional hardware, software, or procedures are implemented.

- *Transfer the risk*—This option makes someone else responsible for the risk.

NOTE Consider protecting a new car stereo. The owner cannot keep the car locked in a garage protected by armed guards 24 hours a day. She could accept the risk and continue her daily routine, knowing that there is a chance of her stereo being stolen. Or she could diminish the risk by parking the car in a locked garage when possible and not letting anyone borrow her car keys. A third option is to transfer the risk to someone else by purchasing additional car insurance and letting the insurance company absorb the loss and reimburse her if the stereo is stolen.

When developing a security policy, the organization must make decisions about risks. Although it is desirable to diminish all risks to some degree, if this is not possible, the risks for the most important assets should be reduced first.

Table 11-4 summarizes the steps in performing risk identification.

11

Table 11-4   Risk identification steps

Risk Identification Action	Steps
A. Asset identification	1. Inventory the assets 2. Record asset attributes 3. Determine the asset's relative value
B. Threat identification	1. Classify threats by category 2. Design attack tree
C. Vulnerability appraisal	1. Determine current weaknesses in assets 2. Use vulnerability scanners on hardware and software
D. Risk assessment	1. Estimate impact of vulnerability on organization 2. Calculate loss expectancy 3. Estimate probability the vulnerability will occur 4. Decide what to do with the risk

Designing the Security Policy

Designing a security policy is the logical next step in the security policy cycle. After the risks are clearly identified, a policy is needed to mitigate what the organization decides are the most important risks. It is important to understand what a policy is, how to balance trust and control in a policy, and the process for designing the policy.

Definition of a Policy

A **policy** is a document that outlines specific requirements or rules that must be met. Although there are a variety of types of policies, most policies have one or more of these characteristics:

- Policies define what appropriate behavior for users is.

- Policies identify what tools and procedures are needed.

- Policies provide a foundation for action in response to inappropriate behavior.
- Policies may be helpful in the event that it is necessary to prosecute violators.
- Policies communicate a consensus of judgment.

A policy is the correct means by which an organization can establish standards for wireless security. Unlike a policy, a **standard** is a collection of requirements specific to the system or procedure that must be met by everyone. For example, a standard may describe how a wireless user must configure her wireless network adapter interface card to connect to the network. Users must follow this standard exactly if they want to be able to connect. On the other extreme, a **guideline** is a collection of suggestions that should be implemented. These are not requirements to be met but are strongly recommended. Although a policy is the correct vehicle for establishing wireless security, usually security policies make references to the standards and guidelines of an organization.

A security policy is a formal document outlining the protections that should be enacted to ensure assets face minimal risks. A security policy is usually not a single large document, but a series of specific security documents that address a single asset or procedure, such as Password Management Policy or Router Security Policy.

Attitudes Toward a Security Policy

Because wireless policies will include the procedures that employees must carry out, it is critical to have users "buy in" to the policy and willingly follow it. The degree to which this is accomplished often hinges upon the employees attitude toward the security policy.

Unfortunately, not all users have positive attitudes about security policies. Users sometimes view security policies as a barrier to their productivity, as requirements that will be difficult to follow, or as a way for management to control their behavior. This is particularly true if policies did not exist in the past or were loosely enforced and now strict policies are established. Part of the reason for these negative attitudes may actually be the result of how users think of security itself. Table 11-5 summarizes how different groups may react to security in an organization.

Table 11-5 Attitudes towards security

User Group	Attitude toward security
Users	Want to be able to get their work done without restrictive security controls.
System support personnel	Concerned about the ease of managing systems under tight security controls.
Management	Concerned about cost of security protection for attacks that may not materialize.

NOTE Most organizations require employees to read the security policy and sign a document indicating they understand the policy and will abide by it.

Overcoming pessimistic attitudes about a security policy is sometimes the greatest challenge with a policy. Getting all sides to agree about all parts of a policy may not always be achievable. Instead, reaching a reasonable consensus may be the best philosophy.

Balancing Control and Trust

To create an effective security policy that will generate a positive attitude, two elements must be carefully balanced. The first is *trust*. There are three models of trust:

- *Trust everyone all of the time*—With this model, all employees are completely trusted to perform the correct actions, and therefore everyone is given full access and control over all information technology resources. This is the easiest model to enforce because there are no restrictions: everyone is "on their honor" to do the right thing. However, this is impractical.

- *Trust some people some of the time*—This approach exercises caution in the amount of trust given. Access is provided as needed with technical controls to ensure the trust is not violated.

- *Trust no one at any time*—This model is the most restrictive and fully protects all information technology resources. However, it is impractical. Few people would work for an organization in which they were not given at least some degree of trust.

A security policy attempts to provide the right amount of trust by balancing no trust and too much trust. It does this by trusting some of the people some of the time and by building trust over time. Deciding on the level of trust may be delicate: too much trust may lead to eventual security problems, whereas too little trust may make it difficult to find and keep good employees.

The second balancing act deals with *control*. One of the major goals of a wireless security policy is to implement control. Deciding on the level of control for a specific policy is not always clear. The security needs and the culture of the organization will play a major role when deciding what level of control is appropriate. If policies are too restrictive or too hard to implement and comply with, they will either be ignored or people will find a way to circumvent the controls in the policies. Management must commit to the proper level of control that a security policy should address.

Elements of a Security Policy

Because security policies are formal documents that outline acceptable and unacceptable employee behavior, legal elements are often included in these documents. The three most common elements are due care, separation of duties, and need to know, as illustrated in Figure 11-5.

Figure 11-5   Security policy elements

Due Care   The term **due care** is used frequently in legal and business settings. It is defined as the obligations that are imposed on owners and operators of assets to exercise reasonable care of the assets and take necessary precautions to protect them. Due care is the care that a reasonable person would exercise under the circumstances.

For information security policies, due care is often used to indicate the reasonable treatment that an employee would exercise when using computer equipment. Some examples of due care may include:

- Technicians will exercise due care when installing a new operating system on an existing wireless device (a reasonable person would not set up a "Guest" account or leave the new password written down and affixed to the laptop).

- Students will exercise due care when using wireless devices in the campus commons area (a reasonable person would be aware that many students in a crowded area could see a password that is entered).

- Employees will exercise due care in opening attachments received from unknown sources (a reasonable person should not open an attachment from an unknown source because it may contain a virus or worm).

Because the standard of "reasonable treatment" in a due care clause is open to interpretation, many security policies include clear and explicit statements regarding conduct and state that due care covers implicit measures that are not enumerated (sometimes called a "catch all" statement).

Separation of Duties   **Separation of duties** means that one person's work serves as a complementary check on another person's actions. Implied in this definition is the concept that no single person should have total control from initialization to completion. For example, a person who receives payments from customers for a business should not be the same person who makes deposits, writes the checks, and reconciles the checkbook from the bank statement each month.

An information security policy should address separation of duties as well. It requires the segregation of administrative, development, security, and user functions to provide security checks and balances. Some examples include:

- An individual should not have access to more than one critical task as identified by management. Personnel should only perform those duties specified in their job descriptions; therefore, programming and operations functions should be performed by different people.

- Programmers should not be able to execute any jobs in a production mode, perform database administration functions, perform application security functions, or have access to production databases.

- Operators should not be able to make changes to production applications or system software libraries, and database changes should be administered by database administration personnel only.

- Security responsibilities should be clearly separated from processing operations functions. Security functions (i.e., authority, access to data, restricting functions) should be performed by security personnel.

Need to Know   One of the best methods to keep information confidential is to restrict who has access to that information. Only that employee whose job function depends on knowing the information is provided access. This is called **need to know**. Access to data should always be on a need-to-know basis.

An information security policy should clearly outline that all information is provided on a strictly need-to-know basis. Need-to-know decisions should be conducted at the management level of the organization and not by individual users.

Policy Creation

When designing a security policy, a starting point is to consider a standard set of principles. These can be divided into what a policy *must* do and what a policy *should* do, and are summarized in Table 11-6.

Table 11-6   Policy *must* and *should* statements

Security Policy Must	Security Policy Should
Be implementable and enforceable	State reasons why the policy is necessary
Be concise and easy to understand	Describe what is covered by the policy
Balance protection with productivity	Outline how violations will be handled

Security policy design should be the work of a team and not one or two technicians. A security policy development team should be formed to handle the task. The team should be charged with developing the initial draft of the policy, determining which groups are required to review the policy, completing the required approval process, and finally determining how the policy will be implemented. The size of the security policy development team depends on the size and scope of the policy. Small-scale policies may only require a few participants, whereas larger policies may require a team of 10. Ideally the team should have the following types of representatives:

- Senior-level administrator
- Member of management who can enforce the policy
- Member of the legal staff
- Representative from the user community

The reason for having administrators and members of management on the team is to ensure management buy-in to the policy.

NOTE

The team should first decide on the scope and goals of the policy. The scope should be a statement about who is covered by the policy, whereas the goals outline what the policy attempts to achieve. The team must also decide on how specific to make the policy. A security policy is not meant to be a detailed plan regarding how to implement the policy. Also, facts that change frequently, such as the number of employees or the size of the organization, should not be included.

The goal at Cisco Corporation is to limit all policies to two or fewer pages.

NOTE

Some points to consider when creating a security policy include:

- Communication is essential. Notify users in advance that a new security policy is being developed and explain why the policy is needed.
- Provide a sample of people affected by the policy with an opportunity to review and comment.
- Prior to deployment, give all users at least two weeks to review and comment.
- The team should clearly define and document all procedures.
- Allow users given responsibility in a policy the authority to carry out their responsibilities.

Some organizations designate a person who served on the development team to serve as the official policy interpreter in case questions arise later.

NOTE

Compliance Monitoring and Evaluation

The final process in the security policy cycle is compliance monitoring and evaluation. After the security policies have been created and approved, it is necessary to ensure that they are consistently implemented and followed properly, often through a centralized management process. At the same time, it is important to evaluate the policies. Compliance monitoring involves the proactive validation that internal controls are in place and functioning as expected.

There are several principles that are involved for good compliance monitoring and evaluation:

- *Clear definition of the controls*—A proper understanding of exactly what the controls are, why they are in place, and how they are to properly function is important. Without this understanding, it will not be possible to determine the validity of the controls.

- *Continual oversight*—Compliance monitoring is a continual process and not just an occasional check on the status of equipment. A process of ongoing risk and control assessment is necessary to see the continued operation of controls. This often involves continual cooperation among different business units within the organization.

- *Validation by an external unit*—Determining if compliance is being achieved should not be performed by the individuals or business units that designed, installed, or manage the controls. There will be too much temptation to approve the controls and not rigorously test the controls if the persons responsible for the controls are also evaluating them. In a large organization, the internal audit department should perform this function.

- *Use of scanning tools* – Whenever possible, tools should be used to scan systems for control implementation. If this is not possible, the controls can be evaluated through manually tracking the workflow.

It may be necessary to fine-tune the policies because of changes in the organization or the emergence of new threats against the wireless LAN. Managing the process of implementing changes is known as **change management**. This then becomes information for the next round of security policy evaluation, starting with the risk analysis.

 Developing and maintaining a WLAN security checklist helps to keep track of new threats and how they should be addressed in the next security policy cycle.

NOTE

Some of the most valuable analysis occurs when an attack penetrates the security defenses. A team must then respond to the initial attack and reexamine the security policies that address the vulnerability to determine what changes need to be made to prevent its reoccurrence.

11

Two elements of compliance monitoring and evaluation are incident response and codes of ethics, which are illustrated in Figure 11-6.

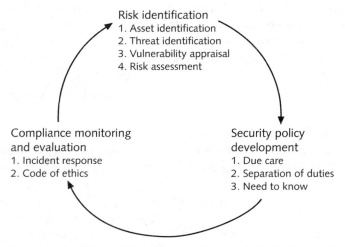

Figure 11-6   Compliance monitoring and evaluation

Incident Response

In spite of the best attempts to limit security attacks, an attacker will inevitably penetrate defenses to some degree. What steps should be taken to respond to the attack? An **incident response** outlines the actions to be performed when a security breach occurs. Most incident responses include the composition of an **incident response team (IRT)**. IRTs are composed of individuals from the following areas:

- *Senior management*—These decision makers need to be involved and must understand the actual function of the IRT. They are the ones to give valuable business decisions in times of crisis.

- *IT personnel*—The chief security information officer and other IT management personnel can provide detailed assessment of the damage caused by the attack.

- *Corporate counsel*—The corporate lawyer should always be aware of the activities of the IRT. From beginning to end, the counsel should be present to ensure that no applicable laws are violated concerning the company or an individual.

- *Human resources*—If the IRT comes across incidents that involve employees, then an immediate response from Human Resources is needed. This includes checking to see whether certain incidents actually violate existing policies, and in extreme cases whether employees should be terminated or merely counseled.

- *Public relations*—Public image is often a major priority of an organization. Public Relations personnel should know the nature of the security incident because they often advise or decide on what can and cannot be said to the general public.

NOTE There are several types of IRTs: public resource IRTs provide information to the general public in the aftermath of an attack; vendor IRTs provide information about restoring their own hardware or software; and commercial IRTs can be hired to come in after an attack to restore the IT functions of an organization.

After an incident is identified, the IRT must immediately convene and assess the situation. They quickly decide how to contain the incident. If the attack is coming electronically through the network, it may be necessary to take preventive measures to limit the spread of the attack, such as temporarily shutting off the wireless LAN. Other containment actions may include reconfiguring firewalls, updating antivirus software, or implementing an emergency patch management system. In extreme cases the connection to the Internet may even be terminated.

After the incident is contained, the next steps are to determine the cause of the attack, assess its damage, and implement recovery procedures to get the organization back to normal as quickly as possible. When the incident is over, a review of security is essential to ensure that a repeat attack is not successful.

Code of Ethics

Codes of ethics encourage members of professional groups to adhere to strict ethical behavior within their profession. For example, codes of ethics for IT professionals are available from the Institute of Electrical and Electronics Engineers (IEEE) and the Association for Computing Machinery (ACM), among others. Many businesses and other organizations are now also creating their own code of ethics.

The main purpose of an ethics code is to state the values, principles, and ideals that each member of an organization must agree to. In particular, the code is intended to uphold and advance the honor, dignity, and effectiveness of the organization. A code of ethics can also help to clarify some of the ethical obligations and responsibilities undertaken by users. This is important because no single set of rules could apply to the enormous variety of situations and responsibilities that exist. Although users must always be guided by their own professional judgment, a code of ethics will help when difficulties arise. A code of ethics also emphasizes to members of the public, employers, and clients that the members of an organization are professionals who are resolved to uphold their ethical ideals and obligations.

TYPES OF WIRELESS SECURITY POLICIES

Because a security policy is so comprehensive and detailed, most organizations choose to break it down into subpolicies that can be more easily referred to. The term *security policy* then becomes an umbrella term for all of the subpolicies included within it.

Table 11-7 describes examples of common types of security policies in an organization. Those policies that specifically relate to wireless networks include acceptable use policy, password management policy, public access network use policy, and virtual private network (VPN) policy.

Table 11-7   Examples of security policies

Name of security policy	Description
Acceptable encryption policy	Defines requirements for using cryptography in wireless transmissions
Analog line policy	Defines standards for use of analog dial-up lines for sending and receiving faxes and for connection to computers
Antivirus policy	Establishes guidelines for effectively reducing the threat of computer viruses on the organization's network and wired as well as wireless computers
Audit vulnerability scanning policy	Outlines the requirements and provides the authority for an information security team to conduct audits and risk assessments, investigate incidents, to ensure conformance to security policies, or to monitor user activity
Automatically forwarded e-mail policy	Prescribes that no e-mail will be automatically forwarded to an external destination without prior approval from the appropriate manager or director
Database credentials coding policy	Defines requirements for storing and retrieving database usernames and passwords
Dial-in access policy	Outlines appropriate dial-in access and its use by authorized personnel
Demilitarized zone security policy	Defines standards for all networks and equipment located in the DMZ
E-mail policy	Creates standards for using corporate e-mail
E-mail retention policy	Helps employees determine what information sent or received by e-mail should be retained and for how long
Extranet policy	Defines the requirements for third-party organizations to access the organization's networks
Information sensitivity policy	Establishes criteria for classifying and securing the organization's information in a manner appropriate to its level of security
Router security policy	Outlines standards for minimal security configuration for routers and switches
Server security policy	Creates standards for minimal security configuration for servers

Table 11-7   Examples of security policies (continued)

Name of security policy	Description
VPN security policy	Establishes requirements for Remote Access IPSec or L2TP Virtual Private Network (VPN) connections to the organization's network through a wireless connection
Wireless communication policy	Defines standards for wireless systems used to connect to the organization's networks

Acceptable Use Policy (AUP)

An **acceptable use policy (AUP)** defines what actions the users of a system may perform while using the wireless network. The users may be employees, vendors, contractors, or visitors, with different standards for each group. AUPs typically cover all computer use, including wireless, Internet, e-mail, Web, and password security.

An AUP should have an overview regarding what is covered by this policy, as in the following sample:

Wireless/Internet/intranet/extranet-related systems, including but not limited to computer equipment, software, operating systems, storage media, network accounts providing electronic mail, Web browsing, and FTP, are the property of Organization X. These systems are to be used for business purposes in serving the interests of the company, and of our clients and customers in the course of normal operations.

The AUP should also provide explicit prohibitions regarding security and proprietary information:

Keep passwords secure and do not share accounts. Authorized users are responsible for the security of their passwords and accounts. System level passwords should be changed every 30 days; user level passwords should be changed every 45 days.

All PCs, laptops, and wireless devices should be secured with a password-protected screensaver with the automatic activation feature set at 10 minutes or less, or by logging off when the host is unattended.

Postings by employees from an Organization X e-mail address to newsgroups should contain a disclaimer stating that the opinions expressed are strictly their own and not necessarily those of Organization X, unless posting is in the course of business duties.

Policy for unacceptable use (sometimes called an abuse policy) should also be outlined as in the following sample:

The following actions are not acceptable ways to use the system:

- *Introduction of malicious programs into the wireless network*

- *Revealing your account password to others or allowing use of your account by others. This includes family and other household members when work is being done at home.*

- *Using an Organization X computing asset to actively engage in procuring or transmitting material that is in violation of sexual harassment or hostile workplace laws in the user's local jurisdiction.*

11

- *Any form of harassment via e-mail, telephone, or paging, whether through language, frequency, or size of messages.*

- *Unauthorized use, or forging, of e-mail header information.*

Acceptable use policies are generally considered the most important information security policies that should be implemented. All organizations, particularly educational institutions and government agencies, should have an AUP in place.

See Appendix C for a complete sample acceptable use policy.

Password Management Policy

Although passwords often form the weakest link in information security, they are still the most widely used form of security. A **password management policy** should clearly address how passwords are managed. In addition to controls that can be implemented through technology (such as setting passwords to expire after 45 days and not allowing them to be recycled), users should be reminded of how to select and use passwords. For example, information regarding weak passwords can be included in the policy, as in the following sample.

Weak passwords have the following characteristics:

- *The password contains fewer than eight characters*

- *The password is a word found in a dictionary (English or foreign)*

- *The password is a common usage word such as:*
  - *Names of family, pets, friends, co-workers, fantasy characters, etc.*
  - *Computer terms and names, commands, sites, companies, hardware, or software*
  - *Birthdays and other personal information such as addresses and phone numbers*
  - *Word or number patterns like aaabbb, qwerty, zyxwvuts, 123321, etc.*
  - *Any of the above spelled backward or preceded or followed by a digit (e.g., secret1, 1secret)*

The policy should also specify what makes up a strong password, as in the following sample.

Strong passwords have the following characteristics:

- *Contain both upper and lowercase characters (e.g., a–z, A–Z)*

- *Have digits and punctuation characters as well as letters e.g., 0–9, !@#$%^&(_+|~-={}[]";'<>,)*

- *Are at least eight alphanumeric characters long*

- *Are not a word in any language, slang, dialect, jargon, etc.*

- *Are not based on personal information, names of family, etc.*

Public Access WLAN Use Policy

Because of the proliferation of public access wireless hotspots in coffee shops, restaurants, airports, hotels, and convention centers, business travelers frequently make use of these facilities to check e-mail or communicate with customers and vendors. However, these facilities rarely have any type of wireless security in place to minimize technical difficulties for users. Many organizations now enforce a **public access WLAN use policy** to address accessing public hotspots.

Some of the provisions of a public access network use policy may include:

- *Do not use a public access wireless network without first determining its level of security. A WLAN that does not use any security encryption or uses wired equivalent privacy (WEP) must not be used for the transmission of secure information and should only be used for general Web access. A WLAN that uses Wi-Fi protected access (WPA or WPA2) may be used for secure transmissions.*

- *All wireless devices must be configured for security. These configurations include:*
  - *Current antivirus software*
  - *Personal firewall*
  - *Current antispyware software*
  - *All operating system patches installed*
  - *Disable all file sharing*
  - *Password protect sensitive files*

- *All wireless network interface card adapters must be configured for security. These configurations include:*
  - *Do not allow the card to connect automatically to any available network*
  - *Do not use ad-hoc mode*
  - *Turn off the card unless the wireless device is connected to a WLAN*

- *Only access secure Web sites that are protected by Secure Sockets Layer (SSL).*

- *All documents transferred over a public access WLAN must be encrypted with PGP Desktop Professional version 9.0 or higher.*

NOTE

Almost all Web-based e-mail providers, such as Google Gmail, Hotmail, and Yahoo! Mail, contain a link such as "Sign In Using Enhanced Security" or "Submit Over SSL." If this link is not available, try entering the address using "https" instead of "http", such as *https://gmail.google.com*.

- *Do not use instant messaging unless it is properly encrypted.*

- *Do not connect to the organization's network without using the virtual private network (VPN).*

11

Virtual Private Network (VPN) Policy

Because VPNs are widely used to protect wireless transmissions, many organizations now implement VPN policies. The requirements contained in a VPN policy frequently include the following:

- *By using VPN technology with personal equipment, users understand that their devices become an extension of Organization X's network and as such are subject to all policies that apply to Organization X-owned equipment.*

- *Only approved employees and authorized third parties (customers, vendors, etc.) may utilize Organization X's VPN.*

- *The user is responsible for selecting an Internet Service Provider (ISP), coordinating installation, installing software, and paying any fees. Refer to Organization X's Remote Access Policy for additional information.*

- *Users will be automatically disconnected from the VPN after 10 minutes of inactivity. Pings or other artificial network processes may not to be used to keep the connection open.*

- *VPN use is to be controlled using either a one-time password authentication such as a token device or a public/private key system with a strong passphrase.*

- *When connecting to Organization X's corporate network all transmissions must use the organization's approved VPNs. No other transmissions will be allowed.*

NOTE End-user training is a key element in creating a secure wireless environment. Users must be aware of and fully understand these policies. Organizations often use annual "campaigns" to inform employees of new policies and heighten their awareness.

CHAPTER SUMMARY

- ❏ A security policy is a document that outlines the protections that should be enacted to ensure that the assets face minimal risks. The security policy cycle defines the overall process for developing a security policy. The first part of the cycle is risk identification, which seeks to determine the risks that an organization faces against its information assets. The next step is developing the security policy. Once the policy is completed, it must constantly be reviewed for compliance, known as monitoring and evaluation, the last step of the cycle.

- ❏ There are four steps in risk identification. The first step is to inventory the assets and their attributes. Then, it is necessary to determine what threats exist against the assets and by which threat agents. After the threats are identified, the next step is to determine whether vulnerabilities exist that can be exploited by surveying the current security infrastructure. The final step is to make decisions regarding what to do about the risks.

- ❏ A security policy development team should be formed to create the security policy. The team should be charged with developing the initial draft of the policy, determining which groups are required to review each policy, completing the required approval process, and determining how it will be implemented. Because security policies are formal documents that outline acceptable and unacceptable employee behavior, legal elements are often included in these documents. The three most commonly found elements are due care, separation of duties, and need to know.

- Compliance monitoring is the validation that the controls are in place and functioning properly. It is important that there are clear definitions of the controls and that the oversight is performed continually, usually by an external unit of the organization. Two elements of compliance monitoring are incident response (actions that are taken when a security breach occurs) and a code of ethics (which encourages strict ethical behavior).

- Because a security policy is comprehensive and detailed, most organizations choose to break it down into smaller subpolicies. The most common security policies for WLANs include acceptable use policy, password management policy, public access WLAN use policy, and virtual private network (VPN) policy.

KEY TERMS

acceptable use policy (AUP) — A policy that defines what actions the users of a system may perform while using computing and networking equipment.

Annualized Loss Expectancy (ALE) — The expected monetary loss for an asset because of a risk over a one-year period.

Annualized Rate of Occurrence (ARO) — The probability that a risk will occur in a particular year.

asset — An item that has a positive economic value.

asset management — The process of keeping records of assets.

attack tree — A visual image of the attacks that may occur against an asset.

change management — Managing the process of implementing changes in an organization.

due care — The obligations that are imposed on owners and operators of assets to exercise reasonable care of the asset and take necessary precautions to protect it.

Exposure Factor (EF) — The proportion of an asset's value that is likely to be destroyed by a particular risk, expressed as a percentage.

guideline — A collection of suggestions that should be implemented.

incident response — A security policy that outlines actions to be performed when a security breach occurs.

incident response team (IRT) — A group of employees who respond to security penetrations.

need to know — Restricting access to information by limiting it only to personnel who must have it to perform their assigned tasks.

password management policy — A security policy that outlines how passwords should be used and handled.

policy — A document that outlines specific requirements or rules that must be met.

public access WLAN use policy — A policy to address accessing public hotspots by organization employees.

risk assessment — An evaluation that determines the likelihood that a vulnerability is a risk to the organization.

risk identification — The process that seeks to determine the risks that an organization faces against its information assets.

security policy — A document or series of documents that clearly defines the defense mechanisms that an organization will employ to keep information secure.

security policy cycle — A process for developing security policies that involves risk identification, security policy design and development, and compliance monitoring and evaluation.

separation of duties — One person's work serves as a complementary check on another person's work.

Single Loss Expectancy (SLE) — The expected monetary loss every time a risk occurs.

standard — A collection of system-specific or procedural-specific requirements that must be met.

threat agent — Any threat that exists against an asset.

threat modeling — The process of constructing scenarios of the types of threats that assets can face.

vulnerability appraisal – An examination of the current security infrastructure to determine what risks exists against assets.

REVIEW QUESTIONS

1. A(n) _____ is a weakness that allows a threat agent to circumvent security.

   a. vulnerability

   b. exploit

   c. risk

   d. mitigation

2. The _____ defines the overall process involved with developing a security policy.

   a. security policy cycle

   b. risk identification cycle

   c. monitoring scope

   d. evaluation cycle

3. Each of the following is a step of risk identification except _____ .

   a. Inventory the assets

   b. Decide what to do about the risks

c. Determine what threats exist against the assets

d. Write the security policy

4. Each of the following is an asset except _____ .

a. data

b. wireless access point

c. antivirus software

d. loans

5. Each of the following is an attribute that should be compiled for a wireless access point when performing asset identification except _____ .

a. the name of the equipment

b. the manufacturer's serial number

c. the MAC and IP address

d. the number of wireless devices that associate with it

6. A tool that is used in threat modeling is a threat tree. True or False?

7. A vulnerability appraisal is the first step of compliance monitoring and evaluation. True or False?

8. It is possible to eliminate the risk for all assets. True or False?

9. A guideline is a document that outlines specific requirements or rules that must be met. True or False?

10. Two elements that must be balanced in an information security policy are trust and control. True or False?

11. _____ means that one person's work serves as a complementary check on another person's work.

12. A(n) _____ defines what actions the users of a system may perform while using the computing and networking equipment.

13. An information security policy should clearly outline that all information is provided on a strictly _____ basis.

14. A(n) _____ is policy that governs how an employee can use a hotspot.

15. _____ is defined as the obligations that are imposed on owners and operators of assets to exercise reasonable care of the asset and take necessary precautions to protect it.

16. Explain the difference between a policy, a standard, and a guideline.

17. What is a public access WLAN use policy and why is it important?

18. What are the actions that an incident response team should take when an attack occurs?

11

19. List and define the three actions an organization may take regarding risk.

20. What is threat modeling and how can attack trees be used?

HANDS-ON PROJECTS

Project 11-1: Online Security Policy Generator

One starting point for creating a security policy is to use one of the security policy generators available online. In this project, you will use the Cisco Security Policy Builder.

1. Use your Web browser to go to **www.cisco.com/en/US/netsol/ns339/networking_ solutions_small_medium_business_tools_index.html**.

Content on the Cisco Web site periodically changes. You might need to search the site for a link to the latest version of the Cisco Security Policy Builder.

NOTE

2. Click **Cisco Security Policy Builder**.

3. Click **Launch Security Policy Builder**.

4. Click **Security Policy Interview**.

5. Answer the questions to the best of your ability for your school or organization.

6. Read the policy and when prompted, enter your e-mail address and check **I accept the disclaimer above**. Click **Send Security Policy**.

7. Retrieve the policy and read it. Does it contain helpful information? Could you use this as a starting point for a security policy?

8. Close all windows when finished.

Project 11-2: Ethics Test

Online tools are available to gauge the effectiveness of ethics in an organization. These tools can help raise the level of awareness regarding ethics among employees. In this project, you will use an online test from the Ethics Resource Center.

1. Use your Web browser to go to **www.ethicsa.org/article.php?story=20030922090035509**.

2. Click **Download EEQT Short-form (203 kb) PDF file** and open the document.

3. Read through the instructions. Answer the questions to the best of your ability for your school or organization. Because many of the questions are detailed, it may be difficult to know the precise response, but use your best judgment. Be sure to compute your score at the end of each section.

4. At the end of the document a scoring profile will allow you to create your scoring profile, as seen in Figure 11-7.

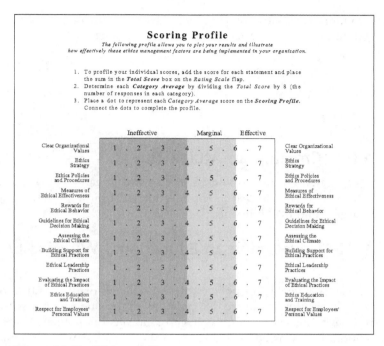

Figure 11-7 Ethics profile

5. Does this profile reflect the ethics at your school or organization? Do you feel that this tool would be helpful for employees and managers to take?

6. Close all windows when finished.

Project 11-3: Online Ethics Center

The Online Ethics Center for Engineering and Science contains specific ethical information and scenarios for engineers, scientists, and students in the fields of science and engineering. In this activity you read and make comments on computer ethical situations.

1. Use your Web browser to go to *www.onlineethics.org/*.

2. Click **Computers & Software**.

3. Click **Educational Resources**.

4. Click **Numerical and Design Problems with Ethical Content**.

5. Click **Computer Encryption Software**.

6. Read the introduction about the ethical situation.

7. Under **Questions on Ethics and Professionalism** record your answers to the questions.

8. Now compare your answers with other students. Discuss the reasons you made these choices. After listening to other students, would you now change how you answered the questions?

9. Close all windows.

CASE PROJECTS

Case Project 11-1: Creating an Attack Tree

Draw an attack tree for an attack against a wireless access point or gateway that you use. Try to think of the various types of attacks that might be launched against it. Limit your tree to four levels deep (vertically) and five different attacks (horizontally).

Case Project 11-2: Developing an Educational Wireless LAN Policy

Using the Internet, locate wireless LAN policies of four colleges or universities (these are almost always posted online). Now compare that policy with the one for your school (or if your school does not have one select a fifth college or university's policy). What are the strengths of your school's policy as compared to the other policies? What provisions is it lacking? Finally, draft a revised wireless LAN policy for your school.

Case Project 11-3: Evaluating Acceptable Use Policy Templates

Many acceptable use policy templates are available on the Internet. Locate three templates and carefully read them. Then, create your own acceptable use policy for your school or business. Share your policy with others for their feedback.

Case Project 11-4: Creating a Code of Ethics

Defining ethics and determining the ethical standards in an organization can be a challenging task. Using the Internet, research the definition of ethics and how it is used. Then, find two ethical policies of organizations. What are their good points? What are their bad points? Do they truly address ethics in the proper way? Finally, create your own technology ethics policy for your school.

Case Project 11-5: Security Policy Cycle

Create your own acceptable use policy for the computers and network access for your school or organization. Be sure to cover computer use, Internet surfing, e-mail, Web, and password security. Compare your policies with other students in the class. Finally, locate the acceptable use policy for your school or organization. How does it compare with the one you created? Which policy is more strict? Why? What changes would you recommend?

Fairvue Technology Consulting

G Charles Financial Services was recently the victim of a wireless attacker and it wants to revise its security procedures. Fairvue Technology Consulting has determined that the WLAN security policies that G Charles has on the books are incomplete and rarely enforced. Fairvue wants to hire you to work on this project.

1. Create a PowerPoint presentation that explains the security policy cycle and an explanation of the specific steps that are involved. Your presentation should be six to eight slides in length.

2. After seeing the presentation, G Charles has requested assistance in how to keep policies current so that this lapse does not re-occur. Write a one-page memo to G Charles regarding your recommendations for compliance monitoring and evaluation.

11

OPERATIONAL SUPPORT AND WIRELESS CONVERGENCE

After completing this chapter you should be able to do the following:

➤ List the features of a secure and scalable wireless local area network

➤ Describe the functions of wireless operational support

➤ Explain WLAN, WiMAX, and 3G convergence

The World of Wireless Security

The number of home wireless local area networks that are unprotected is staggering, according to most wireless industry analysts. By some estimates, 80 percent of home WLANs lack any protection at all, leaving them vulnerable to a wide range of attacks. The reason so many home users are not implementing wireless security, according to analysts, is the simple fact that most users cannot figure out how to set it up.

Wireless vendors are now trying to make it easier for home users to use wireless security. One of the first vendors to move in this direction is Linksys. Linksys's SecureEasySetup (SES) makes setting up a wireless network and installing wireless security as easy as pushing a button—because literally that's all it takes. First, the user presses the SES button on the Linksys wireless gateway. Then, she launches the SES software on the wireless device and clicks Start. SES initiates a "conversation" between the wireless device and wireless gateway that generates and installs a Wi-Fi Protected Access (WPA) key used by the devices for encryption. However, SES is only available on some Linksys wireless gateways or access points.

To overcome the limitation of only functioning on proprietary equipment, McAfee Wireless Home Network Security software automatically sets up encryption keys on a wide range of wireless gateways from different vendors. After loading McAfee's software on a wireless device like a laptop, the software detects an insecure wireless LAN nearby and asks if the user wants to protect the network. If the user answers "Yes" then the software puts a key on the laptop, sets up a secure connection to the wireless gateway, and then sets up the same key on that device. If another wireless device tries to enter the network, a message pops up on the first laptop indicating that a device is already on the protected LAN. That existing user can then either accept or reject the new participant.

Although the McAfee solution is attractive because it supports a variety of wireless hardware, it does have limitations. By default it uses wired equivalent privacy (WEP) encryption, which can be easily broken. If users opt for the stronger WPA or WPA2, they will have to manually change the setting. Also, the software costs $50 for 5 wireless devices with an annual $10 support fee for software updates.

The efforts to make home wireless security as easy as possible has attracted the attention of the Wi-Fi Alliance, the industry group that certifies Wi-Fi equipment. Wi-Fi has announced plans to create a standard for easy home security setup that vendors can build into their products. Devices that meet the standards can be certified by Wi-Fi as easy to use.

All networks require effective operational support to ensure that everything functions as intended. An organization that implements operational support will find that it is able to dramatically increase performance and security while decreasing network downtime and costs.

Because of the unique characteristics of a wireless local area network, operational support is even more important. Because of the nature of radio frequency (RF), certain events and conditions may unexpectedly impact wireless transmission that would have no effect on a wired network: interference from a newly installed access point in an office next door may cause the WLAN to become inoperable, the installation of a new wall can lower the wireless network's performance, a group of wireless users who take part in an online video teleconference can bring the wireless network to a crawl, and an employee who plugs in a rogue access point can instantly introduce security vulnerabilities into the WLAN. It is essential that operational support be in place to mitigate these issues.

Operational support is also important because of the new applications for WLANs that are being introduced. Applications that were almost unthinkable several years ago, such as mesh WLANs or voice-over WLANs, are rapidly becoming commonplace. One feature of these applications is that they are moving different types of wireless technology closer together. Instead of having one technology that supports a single application, multiple wireless technologies are becoming the foundation for different applications, resulting in a convergence of the technologies.

In this chapter you will examine operational support for WLANs and how convergence is changing the wireless landscape. Before looking into these topics, however, the foundation of what features a secure and stable WLAN should possess will be outlined.

FEATURES OF A SCALABLE AND SECURE WLAN

There is little value in attempting to implement operational support for a wireless LAN that is poorly designed. Such a network will continue to be the victim of attacks, while wireless network administrators "leap on fires" attempting to patch the latest vulnerability as other attacks are being launched. This approach results in administrator and user frustration, as well as an insecure WLAN.

On the other hand, a WLAN that has been designed from the outset to be secure and **scalable** (able to accommodate growth) will provide a solid foundation from which attacks can be thwarted and users can feel confident regarding the security of their work. What are the features of such a scalable and secure WLAN? Although there are several, some of the most important include continuous intrusion monitoring and containment, role-based access control, traffic filtering, strong encryption, scalable authentication, segmented network design, and fast handoff capabilities.

Continuous Intrusion Monitoring and Containment

One of the most important elements in a scalable and secure WLAN is continuous monitoring for intrusions (and then taking appropriate actions to contain any attacks). Monitoring a WLAN can be accomplished by using either a standard network management protocol or a system specifically designed for wireless networks. The Simple Network Management Protocol (SNMP) has been the standard network management protocol for both wired and wireless networks. SNMP allows computers and network equipment to gather data about network performance. However, SNMP also has several shortcomings, which include wasting bandwidth by sending needless information, complicated encoding rules, and the fact that SNMP may not be quick enough to provide satisfactory support in a WLAN because response time in a WLAN depends heavily upon the quality of the wireless connection.

Because of the weaknesses of using SNMP for wireless, alternative dedicated WLAN management systems are available. A WLAN management system, composed of a combination of hardware and software, provides a valuable function in managing the wireless network. Dedicated WLAN management systems use discovery tools to continuously monitor the RF for attacks. Monitoring the RF requires a special wireless probe sensor.

A more comprehensive solution to continuous monitoring for analyzing the overall activity of network traffic and detection of attacks is a wireless intrusion detection system (WIDS), which constantly monitors the radio frequency (using wireless probes) for attacks. If an attack is detected, the WIDS sends information about what happened but does not take any action. Containment of an attack can be achieved by using a wireless intrusion prevention system (WIPS). A WIPS is designed to stop an attack from occurring by uncovering and preventing an attack before it harms the WLAN. Wireless intrusion detection systems rely on probes to observe and then forward traffic summaries to a central analysis server.

 WIDS and WIPS are covered in more detail in Chapter 10.

NOTE

A characteristic of a secure and scalable WLAN is the installation and use of a WIPS, although a less-secure WIDS may be used in some environments where cost is a factor. Having the ability to identify an attack and mitigate its effects is critical.

Role-Based Access Control

Wireless authentication verifies that the person requesting access to the network is who they claim to be. Once users are approved and allowed to associate to the AP, they obviously cannot be given full privileges to all network resources. It is essential to restrict the user to accessing only the resources essential for the user to do his or her job. Known as access control, it is the mechanism for limiting access to resources based on the users' identity and their membership in various groups. Access control is typically used to control user access to network resources such as servers, directories, files, and printers through the operating system. In a wireless LAN access control is often performed by enterprise wireless gateways.

To determine what access privileges to assign, one model that should be used is role-based access control (RBAC). Instead of setting permissions for each user or group, permissions are assigned to a position ("role") and then users and other objects are assigned to that role. The users and objects inherit all of the permissions for the role. For example, instead of creating a user account *Jeff Butterfield* and assigning privileges to that account, the role *Comptroller* can be created based on the privileges that position should have. Then the user can be assigned to that role. Individuals can hold multiple roles in RBAC.

NOTE   RBAC is covered in more detail in Chapter 6.

The flexibility of RBAC makes it not only easier to establish permissions based on job classification but also facilitates enforcing those permissions. RBAC is considered a major step in keeping a WLAN secure.

Traffic Filtering

Traffic filtering restricts the traffic on a network based on specific criteria. There are a variety of different types of filters that can be applied. The three basic types of filtering include address filtering, which restricts access based on the media access control (MAC) address or IP address; data filtering, which limits a packet based on the contents of what that packet is carrying; and protocol filtering, which restricts specific protocols from being transmitted on the network.

Some access points can be configured to filter unwanted protocols from either entering or leaving the wireless network. An access point that receives an inbound or outbound packet that is using a specific protocol will drop the packet and not allow it to enter or leave the network.

Traffic filtering is difficult for an attacker to circumvent. It should be a key element in a scalable and secure WLAN.

Strong Encryption

At the heart of any secure WLAN is strong encryption. The original IEEE 802.11 encryption mechanism, wired equivalent privacy (WEP), provided a very weak degree of security. The stronger Wi-Fi Protected Access (WPA) is a subset of 802.11i and addresses both encryption and authentication. WPA replaces WEP with an encryption technology called Temporal Key Integrity Protocol (TKIP). WEP used a 40-bit encryption key that does not change. TKIP uses a longer 128-bit key and the keys are per-packet keys, meaning that TKIP dynamically generates a new key for each packet that is created. Per-packet keys prevent duplication of packets, which was one of the primary weaknesses of WEP.

NOTE

In mid-2006 the U.S. Department of Defense mandated that all its unclassified wireless networks must use IEEE 802.11i security.

A more secure version of encryption is Wi-Fi Protected Access 2 (WPA2), which is the second generation of WPA security. WPA2 is based on the final IEEE 802.11i standard ratified in June 2004. Encryption under the WPA2 personal security model is accomplished by using the block cipher Advanced Encryption Standard (AES). The AES algorithm processes blocks of 128 bits, yet the length of the cipher keys and number of rounds can vary, depending upon the level of security that is required. The available key lengths are 128, 192, and 256 bits, and the number of available rounds are 10, 12, and 14.

NOTE

Only the 128-bit key and 128-bit block are mandatory for WPA2.

A secure WLAN should use WPA2 for its encryption, although WPA may be required in older legacy equipment. WEP should not be used because of its weaknesses.

12

NOTE

WPA and WPA2 are covered in more detail in Chapter 5.

Scalable Authentication

Strong authentication that has the ability to grow as the needs of the organization change is another essential element in a secure and scalable WLAN. Based on the IEEE 802.11i security protocol, the WPA Enterprise and WPA2 Enterprise models utilize IEEE 802.1x port-based authentication. The port over which the device connects to the network is restricted until the device is approved. The credentials that are used for approval can be a username and password, a digital certificate signed by a certificate authority, biometric, or other credentials. The management protocol that controls port-based authentication is EAP. Because EAP messages are sent as cleartext by default, different protocols are used to encrypt and protect the transmissions, including EAP-TLS, PEAP, and others.

There are a variety of technologies that support IEEE 802.1x authentication. Although RADIUS (Remote Authentication Dial-In User Service) was developed in 1992, it has become the preferred scalable wireless authentication solution. A RADIUS client, typically a wireless access point, is responsible for sending user credentials and connection parameters in the form of a RADIUS message to a RADIUS server, which then authenticates and authorizes the RADIUS client request and sends back a RADIUS message response. The devices using RADIUS in a wireless network are illustrated in Figure 12-1. Because messages are never directly sent between the wireless device and the RADIUS server, attackers are unable to penetrate the RADIUS server and compromise security.

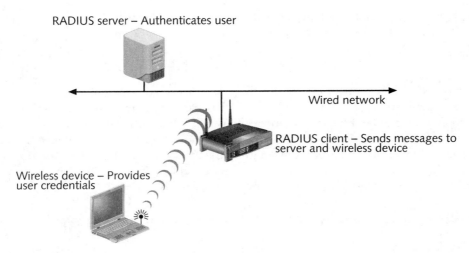

RADIUS server – Authenticates user

Wired network

RADIUS client – Sends messages to server and wireless device

Wireless device – Provides user credentials

Figure 12-1   Wireless devices using RADIUS

Scalable authentication for a secure WLAN should use RADIUS authentication. It provides the most robust and scalable solution.

RADIUS is covered in more detail in Chapter 8.

NOTE

Segmented Network Design

An important principle of good wireless network security design is dividing the network into smaller units, a practice known as segmentation. A network segment is a subset of a larger network. Segmentation was originally used to reduce the amount of traffic on a network, although for WLANs segmentation is primarily used to create smaller segments for security purposes. Network segments can help isolate computers that may not have the same level of security as other devices, can create more scalable networks, and may restrict the impact of an attack on a network. Wireless segmentation is illustrated in Figure 12-2.

Wireless segmentation can be accomplished through hardware devices. In addition to wireless gateways, wireless routers, and wireless switches, segmentation can be accomplished with firewalls, demilitarized zones, and devices with network address translation. Another way in which a wireless network can be segmented is through constructing a virtual local area network (VLAN), which is a logical grouping of network devices within a larger network. Because VLANs do not require that all of the devices be physically located together, they can be dispersed throughout the network. As with wired networks, wireless VLANs can be used to segment traffic. Although separating packets in a wireless VLAN can be done by the switch and each AP is connected to a separate port on the switch and represents a different VLAN, a preferred approach is for the access point to be responsible for separating the packets.

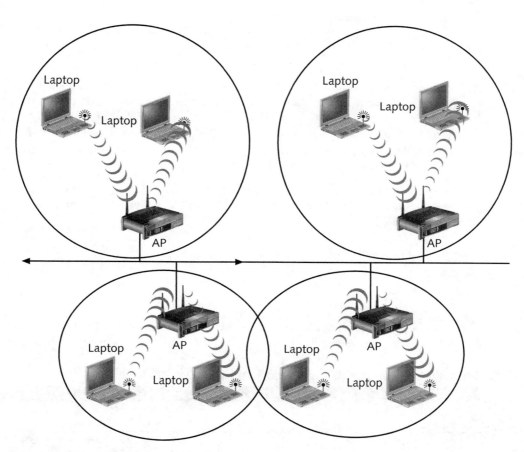

Figure 12-2   Wireless segmentation

Wireless segmentation and VLANs are covered in more detail in Chapter 7.

Segmenting a WLAN is important to wireless security. Dividing the network into smaller entities limits the effects of an attack.

Fast Handoff

The original 802.11 standard did not specify how communications were to take place between access points to support users roaming from one area of AP coverage to another. The result was that access points from different vendors did not always interoperate when a wireless user roamed from one vendor's AP to another vendor's. To solve this problem, the

IEEE 802.11F recommended practice was created. Using the Inter-Access Point Protocol (IAPP), 802.11F specified information that access points need to exchange to support WLAN roaming.

Although IAPP improved handoffs between access points, it did not address how quickly this handoff should occur, which can result in problems if voice-over WLAN (VoWLAN) is being used. A standard is being developed, known as fast handoff or IEEE 802.11r, that streamlines the transition process of a mobile client as it roams between APs. The protocol allows a wireless client to determine the quality of service (QoS) and security being used at a different AP before making the transition.

Because of its benefits, fast handoff is generally considered an important element in a secure and scalable WLAN. It allows users to implement a wider variety of applications with wireless technology.

Fast handoff is covered in more detail in Chapter 6.

NOTE

Table 12-1 lists the technologies and features of a secure and scalable WLAN. A network that has these characteristics provides a solid foundation for monitoring for attacks.

Table 12-1   Characteristics of a secure and stable WLAN

Technology	Benefit
Continuous intrusion monitoring and containment	Limits impact of attack
Role-based access control	Facilitates enforcing user permissions
Traffic filtering	Restricts attacks from entering network
Strong encryption	Prevents attacker from viewing transmissions
Scalable authentication	Provides strong authentication and easy to grow with organization
Segmented network design	Limits impact of attack
Fast handoff	Provides support for wider variety of applications

WLAN Operational Support

No network functions on its own. Instead, there must be operational support to ensure its continued functionality and reliability. Planning for sound operational support is considered a critical element for all organizations.

Some industry experts estimate that operational support consumes almost half of the total lifecycle costs of a WLAN.

NOTE

Operational support can be divided into three basic tasks: monitoring, configuration management, and user training.

Monitoring

Monitoring tools for wired networks do not provide the full array of features necessary for monitoring WLANs. Radio frequency interference, jamming, location of access points, and identification of unauthorized users—all of which are important in a WLAN—will be undetected by most wired monitoring tools. WLAN monitoring tools are also tuned to recognize uniquely wireless issues. For example, the increase of packet retries on an access point may indicate RF interference in that area of the facility or an increased number of collisions resulting from hidden nodes.

Network monitoring continuously measures attributes of the wireless LAN. Software and hardware tools for monitoring a WLAN will systematically examine each wireless user and AP and then provide a map of all network devices, including connectivity status, availability, performance, channel interference, and security settings.

12

Network monitoring tools are known for imposing a significant additional burden on WLAN traffic. The polling intervals for WLAN monitoring should be set to a rate that will accumulate the information but not impact WLAN throughput.

NOTE

WLAN monitoring tools can be used to identify the following elements:

- *AP settings*—WLAN monitoring tools can be used to provide documentation of the service set identifier (SSID), channel number, transmit power, and other settings of the AP. In addition, any changes to these settings may indicate that an attacker has compromised the AP.

If an AP has been tampered with, some WLAN monitoring tools can even reset the AP to its proper settings.

NOTE

- *Coverage*—The area in which the RF signal provides coverage for wireless users can also be monitored.

- *Network performance*—WLAN monitoring tools can continually measure the traffic utilization of APs as a means of determining when an AP is overloaded by users and more should be added to the area. These tools can also watch for RF interference.

- *Security audit*—The ability to audit the WLAN, such as the identification and approximate location of rogue access points, is one of the main features of a WLAN monitoring tool.

NOTE   Many of these tools have "triggers" that can be set so that the IT staff can be alerted through e-mail or a pop-up message that a specific problem has been identified.

Configuration Management

Configuration management, or controlling changes made to the WLAN after installation, is another key element of operational support. The types of changes made to an existing WLAN may include:

- *Applications*—Installing a new application that will be used on the wireless network, such as voice-over WLAN (VoWLAN), will require analysis to ensure that the network can support the application.

- *Coverage area*—When new walls are added to an office or other structural changes are made, it may be necessary to add more APs or move existing APs.

- *RF channel*—Because of interference from another AP, it may be necessary to change the channel number on which the AP is transmitting.

- *Security*—The installation or upgrade of WIPS or WIDS, updated security software, new firmware, and other security-based improvements are changes that should be properly managed.

- *Transmit power*—Increasing the power level of the AP in order to provide a wider area of coverage or decreasing the level to reduce interference may be required in order to "fine-tune" the WLAN.

Most organizations use a change request form process for configuration management. A **change request form** outlines the requested alteration in such a way that it can be determine what type of review is needed prior to accepting (or rejecting) the proposed changes. For example, adding a new application may require a review by security functions (to determine if the current level of security can protect the application), network functions (how it will impact performance), and management functions (whether this application is part of the business process).

In order for a change request form process to be able to thoroughly evaluate how a proposed change may impact the WLAN, it is first necessary to have established a **WLAN baseline**. This baseline provides the standard for the operation of network. Any proposed changes must be viewed from the perspective of how they will impact the baseline. A baseline will typically include a **configuration management database**, or a listing of all installed wireless components, configuration settings, and diagrams that document the current state of the wireless LAN. This database should include a listing of all hardware and software (including configurations) that are part of the wireless LAN. In addition, it can become a security checklist to ensure that all necessary security functions are implemented.

As configuration changes are approved, the WLAN baseline is, in effect, altered and must be changed. The configuration management database must be updated to reflect these changes.

Education and Training

A common misconception regarding security in an organization is that keeping wireless networks secure is the role of the technology staff and users have little to do with security. Nothing could be further from the truth. All computer users share responsibility for protecting the assets of an organization. Users need to receive training regarding the importance of securing information, the roles that they play in security, and the necessary steps they need to take to ward off attacks. Because new wireless attacks appear regularly and new security vulnerabilities are continuously being exposed, this training must be ongoing. User awareness is an essential element of security, demands that all users need continuous training in the new security defenses, and must be reminded of company security policies and procedures.

Education in an enterprise is not limited to the average employee. Human resource personnel also need to keep abreast of security issues because in many organizations it is their role to train new employees on all aspects of the organization, including security. Even upper management needs to be aware of the security attacks that the organization faces, if only to acknowledge the necessity of security in planning, staffing, and budgeting.

Organizations should provide education and training at set times and on an ad hoc basis. Opportunities for security education and training can be at any of the following events:

- A new employee is hired
- A computer attack has occurred
- An employee is promoted or given new responsibilities
- A department is conducting an annual retreat
- New user software is installed
- User hardware is upgraded

One of the challenges of security education and training is to understand how individuals learn. Users learn in different ways: for example, some individuals are visual learners, whereas others are auditory learners. Once it is understood how people learn, an organization can tailor training to meet those needs.

How Learners Learn

Learning involves communication: a person or material developed by a person is communicated to a recipient. However, learning is much more than telling someone what they need to know. Because different individuals learn differently, training should be varied to meet the learning styles of a variety of learners. Most people are taught using a *pedagogical* approach, which comes from a Greek word meaning *to lead a child*. However, for adult learners an *andragogical* approach (the art of helping an adult learn) is preferred. Some of the differences between the pedagogical and andragogical approaches to learning are summarized in Table 12-2.

Table 12-2   Pedagogical and andragogical traits

Subject	Pedagogical Approach	Andragogical Approach
Desire	Motivated by external pressures to get good grades or pass on to next grade	Motivated by higher self-esteem, more recognition, desire for better quality of life
Student	Dependent upon teacher for all learning	Student is self-directed and responsible for own learning
Subject matter	Defined by what the teacher wants to give	Learning is organized around situations in life or at work
Willingness to learn	Students are informed about what they must learn	A change triggers a readiness to learn or students perceive a gap between where they are and where they want to be

Adults learn in three ways, with most people using a combination of the styles and one being dominant. Visual learners learn through taking notes, being at the front of the class, and watching presentations. Auditory learners tend to sit in the middle of the class and learn best through lectures and discussions. The third style is kinesthetic, which many IT professionals tend to be. These students learned through a lab environment or other hands-on approaches.

NOTE

To truly aid in knowledge retention, trainers should incorporate all three learning styles into a course and present the same information using different techniques. For example, a course could include a lecture, PowerPoint slides, and an opportunity to work directly with software and replicate what is being taught.

Learning Resources

An organization can provide educational content in several ways. One way is seminars and workshops. These training sessions may be conducted by a variety of sources, such as by the organization itself on company security policies and practices. Most organizations have mandatory workshops for new employees and refresher sessions every three to six months. Other venues for workshops include those conducted by security vendors, trade shows, and local or regional user groups. Seminars and workshops are a good means of learning some of the latest technologies and networking with other security professionals in the area.

Although most seminars or workshops conducted by training vendors contain valuable information, remember that the vendor may present material from a slanted perspective. It is always good to compare information obtained from one vendor to that of other vendors as a counter-balance.

NOTE

Another resource for learning content is print media. Reputable publishers produce factual and unbiased material that contains solid information on security and defenses. Magazines and journals are also good sources for the most up-to-the-minute material.

The Internet contains a wealth of information that can be used on a daily basis to keep informed about new attacks and trends. Web sites can be classified as those maintained by vendors, trade associations, vendor-neutral organizations, and software tools. What may be more important than identifying a specific site is to become fluent with the use of search engines. Web sites come and go every day, and their addresses change frequently. Users who can use search engines to regularly locate solid sources of information can keep well informed of security procedures.

Appendix B lists a variety of Web resources pertaining to wireless security.

NOTE

12

THE CONVERGENCE OF WIRELESS TECHNOLOGIES

As new technologies appear, they initially are isolated and unrelated to other technologies. Often, however, as time goes on they become incorporated with other technologies. Consider the cellular telephone as an example. When it was first introduced, it was used exclusively for making mobile voice telephone calls. Today the cell phone is not only a telephone, but it is also a camera, watch, calculator, address book, text messaging device, and provides a host of other features.

The only constant regarding communication technologies is that of change. At its height in 1929, Western Union was transmitting over 220 million telegrams per year. In early 2006, it stopped this service after the number of telegrams sent annually fell below 20,000.

NOTE

The same is true with wireless networks. Initially WLANs were isolated entities providing local area network access. Today WLANs are converging with other wireless technologies to provide an impressive array of functions. This convergence of wireless technologies is poised to have a significant impact upon all types of communication in the very near future.

The convergence of wireless technology is most evident today in the blending of wireless LANs with wireless WANs. The two technologies that are supporting this unification in addition to WLAN are WiMAX and cellular 3G.

WiMAX

Of the basic wireless wide area network (WAN) technologies that are in use today, one technology holds the potential for dramatically changing the wireless landscape. Based on the IEEE 802.16 standard approved in June 2004, this technology is commonly called **WiMAX (Worldwide Interoperability for Microwave Access)**. Fixed WiMAX has been receiving a large amount of attention worldwide because of its potential for providing wireless access across large areas. Another variation of WiMax, known as Mobile WiMAX, has the potential for even greater impact.

Fixed WiMAX

The current 802.16 standard, known as **Fixed WiMAX**, is officially IEEE 802.16-2004. It renders the previous version of IEEE 802.16-2001 obsolete, along with its amendments 802.16a and 802.16c. Fixed WiMAX provides up to 50 kilometers (31 miles) of linear service range and is not line-of-sight dependent. WiMAX also provides shared data rates up to 70 Mbps.

NOTE   The shared data rate of 70 Mbps is sufficient bandwidth to simultaneously support more than 60 businesses with a T1 level of service and over 1000 homes at 1 Mbps.

The media access control (MAC) layer of WiMAX is different than that used in IEEE 802.11a/b/g (CSMA/CA) or IEEE 802.3 (Ethernet CSMA/CD). WiMAX uses a scheduling system and the device only has to compete once in its initial entry into the network. Once the device has been accepted, it is allocated a time slot. Although this time slot can enlarge and shrink, it remains assigned to that device and other devices must take their turn. This type of scheduling algorithm is more stable than CSMA/CA under heavy loads and is more efficient with bandwidth. The scheduling algorithm also allows the base station to control Quality of Service (QoS) by balancing the assignments among the needs of the subscriber stations

NOTE   Fixed WiMAX is making strides to become a worldwide standard. The WiMAX equivalent in Europe is called HIPERMAN. The WiMAX Forum consortium (like the Wi-Fi Alliance), is working to make 802.16-2004 and HIPERMAN interoperate seamlessly. Korea's standard, WiBro, has already agreed on interoperability with WiMAX.

The applications for Fixed WiMAX can be broken down into two major categories. The first is high-speed enterprise connectivity for businesses. Fixed WiMAX can be seen as an alternative to an organization's wired backhaul connection (the company's internal infrastructure connection between two or more remote locations).

In the past, companies may have used trunk-based leased lines or special high-speed circuits to connect remote sites, such as a T1 (1.5 Mbps over twisted pair copper wires), a T3 (44.7

Mbps), or a T4 (274.1 Mbps) fiber-optic connection. However, installing fiber-optic cables is both an expensive and lengthy process. Current costs to run fiber-optic cable can range as high as $200,000 to $3 million per mile (1.6 kilometer), with almost 85 percent of that amount spent on digging trenches and installation. Street trenching and digging are not only expensive but they also can cause major traffic inconvenience, displace trees, and sometimes even mar or destroy historical areas. Because of these disruptions, some cities are even considering a moratorium on street trenching. Also, laying fiber-optic cable can be a complex process, requiring the acquisition of right-of-ways, moving existing buried utilities, and burying fiber-optic cable. It is not uncommon for fiber-optic installations to take 6 to 8 months or more even between two buildings in close proximity. Because of the expense in installing these lines, Fixed WiMAX is considered a viable alternative.

The second application for Fixed WiMAX is as a competitor to cable and digital subscriber lines (DSL) as an alternative **last mile connection**. The last mile connection refers to the connection that begins at a fast ISP, goes through the local neighborhood, and ends at the home or office. Whereas the connections that make up the nation's data transmission infrastructure are very fast and well established, the last mile connection that links these high-speed transmission lines to the home or office are much slower and not universally available. These slow last mile connections are bottlenecks for users.

Fixed WiMAX could be used as an alternative to cable and DSL for the last mile connection. This competition could result in lower prices and higher speeds. Fixed WiMAX may also allow "upstart" companies to cheaply break into incumbents' markets, and even major ISPs could deliver content in each other's territories.

Mobile WiMAX

An amendment to Fixed WiMAX, known as **Mobile WiMAX**, is currently in development. As its name implies, Mobile WiMAX adds mobility components to the standard, allowing users to freely roam both indoors and outdoors for kilometers while remaining connected. There are two competing standards for Mobile WiMAX. The first is **IEEE 802.16e**. This technology is an extension of IEEE 802.16-2004 and is backward-compatible with it.

The second competing standard is also currently under development and is known as **IEEE 802.20**. It too sets standards for mobility over large areas. However, unlike WiMAX 802.16e that supports the WiMAX 802.16 standard, IEEE 802.20 is an entirely new specification. The IEEE 802.20 standard would permit users to roam up to 15 kilometers and to deliver those high-speed rates to mobile users even when they are traveling at speeds up to 250 kilometers per hour (155 miles per hour). This would make IEEE 802.20 an option for deployment in high-speed trains. The 802.16e standard will only support users traveling at "vehicular speeds" of 120 to 150 kilometers per hour (75 to 93 miles per hour).

Mobile WiMAX is both faster and has a longer range than IEEE 802.11 networks. A WiMAX base station installed by a wireless Internet service provider (Wireless ISP) can send high-speed Internet connections to homes and businesses in a radius of up to 50 km (31

12

miles). These base stations could easily cover an entire metropolitan area, making that area into a WMAN and allowing true wireless mobility within it instead of individual 802.11 networks.

3G

Cellular telephones have been available since the early 1980s in the United States. Since that time cell phone technology has changed dramatically. The first generation of wireless cellular technology is known appropriately enough as **First Generation (1G).** The first generation of wireless cellular telephony transmitted at 9.6 Kbps using analog **circuit-switch** technology. When a telephone call is made, a dedicated and direct physical connection is made between the caller and the recipient of the call through the switch. While the telephone conversation is taking place, the connection remains open between only these two users. No other calls can be made from that phone while the first conversation is in progress, and anyone who calls that phone will receive a busy signal. This direct connection lasts for the length of the call, at which time the switch drops the connection.

A 1G analog cellular telephone can only be used for voice communications. Although it was a pioneer in cellular telephony, it was soon replaced with improved digital technology.

The next generation of cellular telephony is known as **Second Generation (2G)**. The second generation of cellular telephony used circuit-switched digital networks and started in the early 1990s. The only major feature that 2G systems share with 1G is that they are circuit-switched networks. 2G systems use digital instead of analog transmissions. Digital transmissions provide several improvements over analog transmissions: digital transmission uses the frequency spectrum more efficiently, over long distances the quality of the voice transmission does not degrade as with analog, digital transmissions are difficult to decode and offer better security, digital transmissions use less transmitter power, and digital transmission enables smaller and less expensive individual receivers and transmitters.

The **2.5 Generation (2.5G)** is an interim step between 2G and 3G digital cellular networks. 2.5G networks operate at a maximum speed of 384 Kbps. The primary difference between 2G and 2.5G networks is that 2.5G networks are **packet-switched** instead of circuit-switched. Although circuit switching is ideal for voice communications, it is not efficient for transmitting data. This is because data transmissions occur in "bursts" with periods of delay in between. The delay results in time wasted when nothing is being transmitted. Instead of using circuit switching, 2.5G networks use packet switching. Packet switching requires that the data transmission be broken into smaller units of packets, and each packet is sent independently through the network to reach the destination.

Today the three leading wireless carriers in the United States are all in the process of rolling out **Third Generation (3G)** networks. With throughput rates for 3G averaging between 400 Kbps and 700 Kbps, this means for the first time the cellular telephone network can be used for wireless data communications. A laptop computer with a PC card and a VPN client will allow mobile workers to access remote networks wherever there is cellular coverage.

Where 3G is not yet available, the service is backward-compatible to 2.5G.

The characteristics of 3G technology for data communications are as follows:

- *Coverage areas*—3G wireless technology is not available on a widespread basis yet in the United States. It is estimated that by the middle of 2007 all major metropolitan areas in the United States will have 3G service available.

- *Throughput*—Speeds range on average from 400 to 700 Kbps for data coming into the device (downlink) up to a maximum of 2 Mbps. Data being sent out from the wireless device (uplink) is at a much slower speed of only 80 to 140 Kbps.

- *Devices*—A PC Card 3G wireless modem is required for laptop computers to access the 3G data network.

Mobile Wireless Data Convergence

IEEE 802.11 WLANs, WiMAX, and 3G are technologies that are converging to provide mobile wireless data connectivity to users almost anywhere. Users are no longer restricted to a specific distance from an access point or cellular tower; rather, almost unlimited freedom is potentially available for wireless data access.

12

 Dual-mode phone handsets based on Unlicensed Mobile Access (UMA) allow users to make VoWLAN calls when in the area of a WLAN or regular cell phone calls using 3G when there is no WLAN available.

In the near future, wireless WLANs, WiMAX, and 3G may all be used together to provide wireless data services. WLAN hotspots continue to spread, but this coverage can be spotty for business travelers who need more reliable access to data. Chipsets are available from Intel for laptop manufacturers that incorporate WiMAX connectivity. Many "road warriors" are installing combination 3G+WLAN PC Cards for full connectivity options. When they are in the vicinity of a WLAN, the card uses that technology and connects to the access point. However, when they are outside the reach of an AP, the slower 3G technology is used instead. And for those areas in which Mobile WiMAX is available, this is used instead. This approach provides the "best of all worlds" for users.

However, this triple option may not always be necessary. Some industry experts predict that Mobile WiMAX will eventually actually replace IEEE 802.11and 3G cellular data service for wireless area coverage in the wide area, because IEEE 802.20 supports fixed as well as mobile clients. The 802.11 and 3G technologies would then be found in more specialized applications. For example, IEEE 802.11 might be used indoors whereas 3G will only be used in rural areas where no other coverage exists.

How this convergence will ultimately play out is difficult to predict. Political, social, economic, and technological forces will all come into play. The only assurance is that in the future wireless data access will be more accessible than ever before. And according to several security experts, what is troubling regarding this convergence from a security standpoint is that adequate security mechanisms may not be in place to protect users. Security attacks on the emerging VoWLAN market have already resulted in several types of security attacks, including:

- Attackers listening to voice conversations without the participant's knowledge or approval
- User VoWLAN information, such as user account and password, captured and used to make free calls
- Conversations corrupted by attackers intercepting packets and modifying them to result in unintelligible noise or silent gaps in the transmissions
- Denial of service attacks against the VoWLAN device

Like the original IEEE 802.11 security standards that utilized WEP, these new wireless protocols may contain security vulnerabilities as well. Several security experts express concern that flawed security protocols among convergence technologies could result in widespread identify theft and injection of malware that would expose private information and open systems up to more attacks.

All this means that the wireless security professional, whether she is managing a WLAN or a converged network of new wireless technologies, can never truly rest. Constant vigil must be maintained to protect wireless systems against attacks. The wireless security professional must remain informed regarding the latest wireless vulnerabilities, attacks, and defenses by reading, attending workshops, enrolling in courses, and all other means available. Awareness and education are two key elements in stopping attackers. Although there is no end in sight for wireless attacks, a diligent and informed wireless security professional is the best defense available.

Chapter Summary

- Designing and building a secure and scalable wireless LAN is the essential foundation for the operational support of the network. Although a secure and scalable WLAN has several features, some of the most important include continuous intrusion monitoring and containment, role-based access control, traffic filtering, strong encryption, scalable authentication, segmented network design, and fast handoff capabilities.

- Operational support for a WLAN involves three key elements. Monitoring is essential to provide information regarding the status of the network and to build a baseline for auditing the network. Configuration management, which is controlling changes made to the WLAN after installation, is important to ensure that changes made do not negatively impact previous settings or configurations. A WLAN baseline is required in order to know the current configuration of the network.

❏ Education and training is also a key element in informing users regarding the need for wireless security and how they can implement it.

❏ Different wireless technologies are converging to create a seamless wireless mobility experience for mobile users. WiMAX is a wide area network technology of two "flavors": Fixed WiMAX and Mobile WiMAX. 3G is a digital cellular telephony technology that allows users to transmit over wide areas at relatively high speeds. Coupled with IEEE WLAN, these three technologies are poised to have a major impact on mobile communications.

KEY TERMS

2.5 Generation (2.5G) — An interim step between 2G and 3G digital cellular networks that operate at a maximum speed of 384 Kbps.

change request form — A form that outlines the requested alteration of the WLAN in such a way that it can be determine what type of review is needed prior to accepting or rejecting the proposal.

circuit-switch — A technology in which a dedicated and direct physical connection is made between the caller and the recipient of the call through the switch.

configuration management database — A listing of all installed wireless components, configuration settings, and diagrams that document the current state of the wireless LAN.

First Generation (1G) — The first generation of wireless cellular telephone technology.

Fixed WiMAX — A wireless wide area data transmission standard that supports up to 50 kilometers (31 miles) of linear service range and is not line-of-sight dependent, at shared data rates up to 70 Mbps.

IEEE 802.16e — A Mobile WiMAX standard that is an extension of IEEE 802.16-2004 and is backward-compatible with it.

IEEE 802.20 — A Mobile WiMAX standard that permits users to roam up to 15 kilometers and deliver high-speed data rates to mobile users.

last mile connection — The connection that begins at a fast Internet service provider, goes through the local neighborhood, and ends at the home or office.

Mobile WiMAX — A wireless wide area data transmission that adds mobility components to the WiMAX standard allowing users to freely roam both indoors and outdoors for kilometers while remaining connected.

packet-switched — A communications technology that requires that the data transmission be broken into smaller units of packets and each packet is sent independently through the network to reach the destination.

scalable — The ability to accommodate growth.

Second Generation (2G) — The second generation of cellular telephony that used circuit-switched digital networks and started in the early 1990s.

Third Generation (3G) — The third generation of cellular telephony with throughput rates for 3G averaging between 400 to 700 Kbps and allowing use for data communication.

12

WiMAX (Worldwide Interoperability for Microwave Access) — A technology for wireless data transmissions over a wide area.

WLAN baseline — A standard for the operation of a wireless network.

REVIEW QUESTIONS

1. The _____ has been the standard network management protocol for both wired as well as wireless networks.
   a. Simple Network Management Protocol (SNMP)
   b. 2.5G
   c. Single Line Internet Protocol (SLIPL)
   d. Wired Equivalent Management Standard (WEMS)

2. Each of the following can be used for wireless network management *except* _____.
   a. Simple Network Management Protocol (SNMP)
   b. WLAN management system
   c. Wireless intrusion detection system (WIDS)
   d. Wired management control system (WMCS)

3. _____ allows assigning permissions to a position instead of an individual.
   a. Role Based Access Control (RBAC)
   b. User Permission Settings (UPS)
   c. Channel Assignment Permission Control (CAPC)
   d. Management Assignment Protocol (MAP)

4. Each of the following is a type of traffic filtering *except* _____.
   a. data filtering
   b. address filtering
   c. device filtering
   d. protocol filtering

5. Each of the following is a standard for wireless data encryption *except* _____.
   a. WEP
   b. MAC
   c. WPA
   d. WPA2

6. Based on the IEEE 802.11i security protocol, WPA Enterprise and WPA2 Enterprise models utilize IEEE 802.1x port-based authentication. True or False?

7. A network segment is a superset of a larger network. True or False?

8. A virtual local area network (VLAN) is a physical grouping of network devices within a larger network. True or False?

9. The original 802.11 standard did not specify how communications were to take place between access points to support users roaming from one area of AP coverage to another. True or False?

10. Monitoring tools for wired networks do not provide the full array of features necessary for monitoring WLANs. True or False?

11. _____ is the controlling of changes made to the WLAN after installation.

12. A(n) _____ outlines the requested alteration in such a way that it can determine what type of review is needed prior to accepting or rejecting the proposed changes.

13. A(n) _____ provides the standard for the operation of network against which any changes must be compared.

14. A(n) _____ is a listing of all installed wireless components, configuration settings, and diagrams that document the current state of the wireless LAN.

15. The current 802.16 standard, known as _____ , provides up to 50 kilometers (31 miles) of linear service area range and is not line-of-sight dependent.

16. Explain how the media access control (MAC) layer of WiMax is different from wireless or wired networks.

17. What is the last mile connection?

18. How is Mobile WiMAX different from Fixed WiMAX?

19. What are the advantages of Third Generation (3G) cellular telephony networks?

20. Explain how WiMax could replace 3G and WLANs for wide area network data transmissions.

12

Hands-On Projects

Project 12-1: Monitoring the WLAN Using the Cisco Ping Test

Although specific tools are available for monitoring the WLAN in order to provide operational support, those tools may not always be available. In that case, other tools can be used that provide a limited set of information for the configuration management database. In this project you will use one of the tools on the Cisco Aironet access point to ping a wireless device while roaming to perform a survey of area of coverage. In order to perform this activity you will need a laptop computer that is associated with a Cisco Aironet access point.

1. Use your Web browser to open the Cisco Aironet access point interface.

2. Click **Association** to display the Association menu, as seen in Figure 12-3.

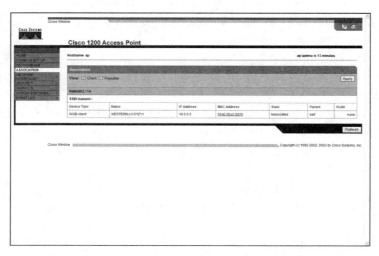

Figure 12-3   Aironet Association screen

3. Click the MAC address of the wireless device associated with this access point to display the association statistics, as seen in Figure 12-4.

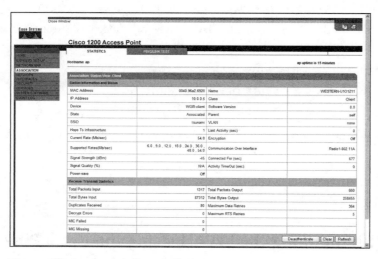

Figure 12-4   Association statistics screen

4. Click the **PING/LINK TEST** tab to display the PING/LINK TEST window, as seen in Figure 12-5.

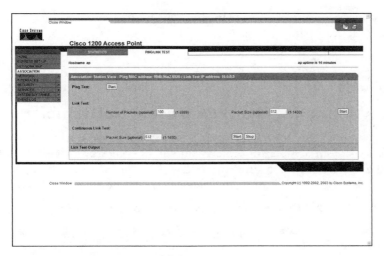

Figure 12-5   PING/LINK TEST screen

5. Under **Continuous Link Test** be sure the packet size is **512.** This is an average packet size for wireless packets and will provide good test results.

6. Click **Start.**

7. Roam through an area with the wireless notebook computer. The access point will continue to ping the notebook as you roam and display updated statistics, as seen in Figure 12-6.

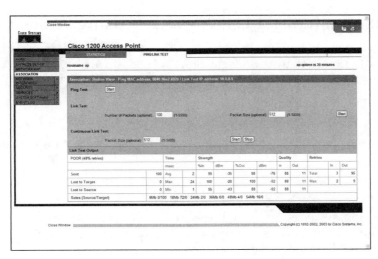

Figure 12-6   Ping results

12

8. Note areas as you roam under the **Strength** and **Quality** results from the table. What obstacles in your path may have caused these numbers to drop? Why?

9. Click **Stop** to complete the test.

10. Exit the Cisco Aironet access point interface.

Project 12-2: Monitoring the WLAN using NetStumbler

Although it is not considered a monitoring tool, NetStumbler can also be used for gathering information for basic site surveys. In this project you will use NetStumbler and will compare the results with the Cisco ping results in Project 12-1. In order to perform this activity you will need a laptop computer that is associated with a Cisco Aironet access point.

1. Click **Start**, point to **All Programs** and click **Network Stumbler**.

2. If your access point device does not appear click **Device** and select the AP. Expand the items in the left pane by clicking the **+** sign. Double click on the AP listed under **SSID**.

3. The column **SNR** gives the strength of the signal divided by the noise level and is measured in decibels. Roam with your laptop computer along the same areas you did in Project 12-1 when you used the Cisco ping test and observe the fluctuation of this value. Do the values change at the same locations where the Cisco ping test strength and quality levels changed?

4. Locate the access point that you are connected to in the right pane on Network Stumbler and double click on it to display a graphic of the SNR.

5. Close NetStumbler. Click **No** and do not save the settings.

Project 12-3: Monitoring a Linksys WLAN Using Windows

Consumer products such as Linksys do not include a site survey tool. However, the site survey process can be simulated by the information supplied by Microsoft Windows. In this activity you will perform a test on a Linksys wireless network.

1. Click **Start** and **Connect to** and the wireless connection for the wireless device. The Wireless Network Connection Status window will open, as seen in Figure 12-7.

2. Note that the signal strength is indicated in successive bars along with the connection speed.

3. Roam away from the Linksys access point and monitor signal strength and speed. What obstacles are affecting the signal strength? Why?

4. Return to the Linksys access point and reposition it in the same room to another location. Roam again with the notebook and observe the signal strength? Did moving the Linksys AP have any positive change?

5. Close the Windows Network Connection Status window.

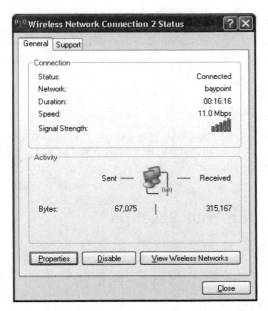

Figure 12-7   Windows Network Connection Status window

CASE PROJECTS

Case Project 12-1: Exploring Learning Styles

Interview four other students or friends about how they learn. Develop a set of questions that you ask each learner: how do you learn best, what do you not like about specific teaching styles, if you could learn something in any way what would be your choice, and so on. From that information, develop a training plan for each one of the learners as if they were new employees hired by your company and they were to be trained on the company's security. How could you teach them individually? How could you teach them if they all were together in the same room?

Case Project 12-2: Grade Your Network

Select an enterprise wireless LAN at school or your place of business for evaluation. On a scale of A through F, grade its scalability and security in terms of continuous intrusion monitoring and containment, Role Based Access Control, traffic filtering, strong encryption, scalable authentication, segmented network design, and fast roaming capabilities. For any items that received a score of C or less, include a recommendation regarding how you would improve it.

Case Project 12-3: WiMax Penetration

Where is WiMax currently available? Using the Internet search for areas in which WiMax is available. What is the cost for this service? What is the guaranteed bandwidth? Would you recommend purchasing it? Why or why not?

Case Project 12-4: 3G Service

One of the criticisms of 3G is its cost. Visit the Web sites of three of the major cellular providers and create a table that lists the costs, bandwidth, and availability of the service. Also, what cellular telephones or other products support 3G? How much more expensive are they than standard cell phones?

Case Project 12-5: Establishing Your Baseline

What is the baseline for your WLAN? Create a listing of all installed wireless components, configuration settings, and diagrams that document the current state of the wireless LAN to build a configuration management database. What changes are necessary to improve it? Why?

Fairvue Technology Consulting

Sunny Summer Vacations (SSV) wants to enhance the wireless support it provides in its offices to its employees. They have asked Fairvue Technology Consulting for help. Fairvue has examined their network and procedures and determined that SSV lacks a wireless operation support system. Fairvue has asked you for help in working with SSV.

1. Create a PowerPoint presentation that explains what an operational support system covers and why it is necessary. Your presentation should be six to eight slides in length.

2. After seeing the presentation, SSV sees the need for training its employees on wireless security. No formal training has ever been conducted. Create a one-page memo that outlines your recommendations for training SSV's employees. Be sure to include a variety of training to meet the needs of different employees.

CERTIFIED WIRELESS SECURITY PROFESSIONAL (CWSP) EXAM OBJECTIVES VERSION 2006

The Certified Wireless Security Professional (CWSP) certification is an advanced wireless LAN certification administered by Planet3 Wireless, Inc. This certification is designed to demonstrate that the user has mastered the necessary skills for securing a WLAN from attacks. The 2006 CWSP exam objectives, cross-referenced to chapters and headings within chapters of this book, are shown in Table A-1. Users must also complete the Certified Wireless Network Administrator (CWNA) exam in addition to the CWSP exam in order to receive the CWSP certification. The CWSP Web site is located at *www.cwnp.com/cwsp/index.html*.

Table A-1 CWSP exam objectives coverage

1.0. Wireless LAN Discovery		
Objective	**Chapter**	**Heading**
1.1. Describe and categorize the various methods of target locating and WLAN mapping: • Wardriving • Freeware discovery applications (Kismet, KisMac, Netstumbler) • Integrated Operating System Tools (Microsoft WZC Service) • PC card manufacturers' client utilities • Public online databases	3	Wardriving
1.2. Describe and apply the following methods of information gathering as they apply to the enterprise: • Social engineering • Search engines • Public records • Garbage collecting (dumpster diving)	3	General Information Gathering
1.3. Compare, contrast, and demonstrate hardware used to circumvent 802.11 Security: • Laptops & tablet PCs • Handheld PCs & PDAs • Wireless radio cards & antennas • Handheld Global Positioning Systems (GPS) devices	3	Wardriving
2.0. Network Attacks		
Objective	**Chapter**	**Heading**
2.1. Demonstrate how to recognize, perform, and prevent the following types of attacks: • Physical layer denial-of-service attacks • MAC layer denial of service • MAC layer protocol attacks • Rogue infrastructure hardware placement • MAC spoofing • Hijacking and peer-to-peer attacks • Eavesdropping	4 2	Wireless Infrastructure Attacks Vulnerabilities of IEEE 802.11 Security

Table A-1   CWSP exam objectives coverage (continued)

2.0. Network Attacks (continued)		
Objective	Chapter	Heading
2.2. Explain the commonality and demonstrate the simplicity of the following attacks against wireless infrastructure devices: • Weak/default passwords and SNMP community strings on wireless infrastructure equipment • Misconfiguration of wireless infrastructure devices by administrative staff • Describe and demonstrate preventative measures against attacks on wireless infrastructure devices	4	Basic Vulnerabilities
2.3 Explain and demonstrate the use of protocol analysis to capture the following sensitive information: • Usernames/Passwords/SNMP Community Strings • Encryption keys • MAC filter identification • Describe and demonstrate preventative measures against protocol analysis	2	Wireless Packet Sniffers
2.4. Explain and demonstrate security protocol circumvention against the following types of authentication and/or encryption: • WEP • PSK • LEAP • PPTP	2 8	Vulnerabilities of IEEE 802.11 Security Extended Authentication Protocols (EAP)
2.5. Explain and demonstrate the following security vulnerabilities associated with public access or other unsecured wireless networks: • Spamming through the WLAN • Viruses/spyware/adware • Direct Internet attacks through the WLAN • Placement of illegal content • Information theft	4 4	Vulnerabilities Associated With Using Public WLANs Vulnerabilities Associated With Implementing Unsecured WLANs

Table A-1   CWSP exam objectives coverage (continued)

3.0. Network Monitoring		
Objective	Chapter	Heading
3.1. Understand how to select and use an 802.11 protocol analyzer based on its security features.	3	Wireless packet Sniffers
3.2. Describe and demonstrate the different types of 802.11 Wireless Intrusion Prevention Systems (WIPS): • Integrated • Overlay • Integration-enabled	10	Wireless Intrusion Prevention Systems (WIPS)
3.3. Describe and demonstrate security features of 802.11 WIPS: • Device identification and categorization • Rogue triangulation vs. fingerprinting • Device tracking • Event alerting, notification, and categorization • Policy enforcement and violation reporting • Wired/wireless Intrusion mitigation and rogue containment • Protocol analysis with filtering	10 10	WLAN Management Systems Wireless Intrusion Prevention Systems (WIPS)
3.4. Explain 802.11 WIPS baselining and describe the following tasks: • Measuring performance parameters under normal network conditions • Understanding common false positives for a specific network configuration • Configuring the WIPS to recognize all APs in the area as authorized, monitored, or known so that rogues can be easily and quickly identified	10	Wireless Intrusion Prevention Systems (WIPS)
3.5. Describe and demonstrate the different types of WLAN management systems and their features: • Network discovery • Multi-vendor configuration and firmware management • Audit Management and policy enforcement • Network and user monitoring • Rogue detection • Event alarms and notification	10	WLAN Management Systems

Table A-1   CWSP exam objectives coverage (continued)

4.0. Security Solutions		
Objective	**Chapter**	**Heading**
4.1. Recognize and understand the following basic security concepts:	5	Personal Security Model
• Functionality and weaknesses of static and dynamic WEP	5	Enterprise Security Model
• Functional parts of TKIP and its differences from dynamic and static WEP		
• The role of TKIP in WPA		
• Appropriate use and configuration of WPA-Personal and WPA-Enterprise		
• Feasibility of WPA-Personal exploitation		
• The role of CCMP in WPA2		
• Appropriate use and configuration of WPA2-Personal and WPA2-Enterprise		
4.2. Identify the purpose and characteristics of 802.1X and EAP:	5	Enterprise Security Model
• Supplicant, authenticator, and authentication server roles	8	Extended Authentication Protocols (EAP)
• Functions of the authentication framework and controlled/uncontrolled ports		
• How EAP is used with 802.1X port-based access control for authentication		
• Strong EAP types used with 802.11 WLANs: PEAPv0, PEAPv1, EAP-TLS, EAP-TTLS, EAP-FAST		
• Explain the exploits of specific EAP types: LEAP, EAP-MD5		
4.3. Explain and describe legacy authentication protocols:	8	Extended Authentication Protocols (EAP)
• PAP		
• CHAP		
• MS-CHAP		
• MS-CHAPv2		

Table A-1 CWSP exam objectives coverage (continued)

4.0. Security Solutions (continued)		
Objective	**Chapter**	**Heading**
4.4. Recognize and understand the following concepts about VPNs: • Common VPN technologies, their appropriate use in wireless networks, and their strengths and weaknesses: PPTP, L2TP/IPSec, IPSec, SSH • Compare advantages and disadvantages of VPN technology and 802.1X/EAP types in 802.11 WLANs: protocol overhead, configuration complexity, scalability • Describe and demonstrate 802.11 WLAN hardware and software that use VPN technology: Access Points, Wireless Gateways, Client software, WLAN Switches/Controllers	9 9	Encryption for Virtual Private Networks (VPNs) VPN Advantages and Disadvantages
4.5. Describe client-side security software applications: • VPN policies • Personal firewall software • Antivirus/antispyware software	7 9 11	Wireless Device Security Encryption for Virtual Private Networks (VPNs) Types of Wireless Security Policies
4.6. Describe secure infrastructure management protocols: • HTTPS • SNMPv3 • SFTP (FTP/SSL or FTP/SSH) • SCP • SSH2	9	Encryption for Transmitting Documents
4.7. Explain the role and importance of VLANs in an 802.11 WLAN infrastructure	7	Network Segmentation
4.8. Describe and demonstrate configuration of 802.1Q VLANs on Ethernet switches and WLAN infrastructure devices	7	Network Segmentation
4.9. Explain the purpose of and features in role-based access control (RBAC), including the configuration of RBAC in WLAN Switches/Controllers.	6	Hardware Security Features

Table A-1   CWSP exam objectives coverage (continued)

4.0. Security Solutions (continued)		
Objective	Chapter	Heading
4.10. Describe and demonstrate the following types of authentication servers used with 802.11 WLANs: • RADIUS • Kerberos • LDAP	8	Authentication Servers
4.11. Explain what an AAA server is and explain the following concepts of AAA servers: • EAP standards support for 802.11 • Proxy services • LDAP integration • Explain AAA's role in RBAC (return list attributes) • Appling user and AAA server credential types (Username/Password, Certificate, PAC, Biometrics) • The role of AAA services in VLAN tagging • Benefits of mutual authentication between supplicant and authentication server	8 8	Defining Authentication Authentication Servers
4.12. Explain these authentication design models and their scalability aspects: • Single-site deployment • Distributed autonomous sites • Distributed sites, centralized authentication and security • Distributed sites and security, centralized authentication	8	Authentication Design Models
4.13. Explain 802.11i Authentication and Key Management, including: • AAA Key generation • PMK/GMK generation • PTK/GTK generation & distribution • 4-way handshake • Group handshake • STAKey handshake • Passphrase-to-PSK mapping	8	Extended Authentication Protocols (EAP)
4.14. Describe strengths, weaknesses, appropriate applications, and scalability issues of WLAN switches, access points, WLAN bridges, WLAN routers, and WLAN mesh Routers	6	WLAN Hardware

Table A-1   CWSP exam objectives coverage (continued)

4.0. Security Solutions (continued)		
Objective	Chapter	Heading
4.15. Describe and demonstrate configuration of major feature sets in WLAN Switches, access points, WLAN bridges, WLAN routers, and WLAN mesh routers:		
• 802.11e/WMM QoS support	6	Other Hardware Features
• Layer 2-7 Role-Based protocol filtering (per user or per group)	6	Hardware Security Features
• 802.11h dynamic frequency and power control	6	Other Hardware Features
• Automated site survey with automatic RF power and channel management	6	WLAN Hardware
• Fast Layer 2-3 handoff (roaming)	6	Other Hardware Features
• VLAN support with 802.1Q trunking	7	Network Segmentation
• Hot standby/failover support		
• 802.3af Power-over-Ethernet	6	Other Hardware Features
• WPA/WPA2 Personal and Enterprise security	5 / 5	Enterprise Security Model / Personal Security Model
• Secure management interfaces (HTTPS, SNMPv3, SSH2)	9	Encryption for Secure Management Interfaces
• Layer 3-7 VPN termination	9	Encryption for Virtual Private Networks (VPNs)
• Intrusion prevention	10	Wireless Intrusion Prevention Systems (WIPS)

Table A-1 CWSP exam objectives coverage (continued)

4.0. Security Solutions (continued)		
Objective	Chapter	Heading
4.16. Describe and demonstrate configuration of major feature sets in Enterprise Encryption Gateways (EEGs)	6	WLAN Hardware
4.17. Explain where infrastructure security devices fit into an enterprise wireless LAN topology	7	Network Segmentation
4.18. Explain the reason for network segmentation and its limiting factors on WLAN network design	7	Network Segmentation
4.19. Explain the functional differences and advantages of both directly connected and distributed APs in a WLAN Switch architecture	6	WLAN Hardware
4.20. Describe and demonstrate layered security solutions	7	Basic Principles of Security Design
4.21. Explain the impact of L2, L3, and L7 security protocols on client station reassociation	6	Other Hardware Features
5.0. Security Policy		
Objective	Chapter	Heading
5.1. Explain and apply the phases of security policy development: • Define and document • Management buy in • Communication • Monitoring and auditing • Response and enforcement • Revise and fine-tune	11	Designing the Security Policy

Table A-1 CWSP exam objectives coverage (continued)

5.0. Security Policy (continued)		
Objective	**Chapter**	**Heading**
5.2. Explain the purpose and goals of the following wireless LAN security policies: • Password policy • End-user and administrator training on security solution use and social engineering mitigation • Security marketing and propaganda campaigns to heighten awareness • Ongoing review (auditing) • Acceptable use & abuse policy • Traffic filtering • Obtaining the latest security feature sets through firmware and software upgrades • Consistent implementation procedure • Creation and maintenance of a WLAN security checklist • Centralized implementation and management guidelines and procedures • Inclusion in asset management program • Inclusion in change management program	11	Types of Wireless Security Policies
5.3. Perform a risk assessment for a wireless LAN, including asset analysis and legal implications	11	The Security Policy Cycle
5.4. Perform a baseline analysis of a series of WLAN attack scenarios and discuss their impact on the organization. Attacks include the following: • Information theft and placement • PHY and MAC Denial of Service • Client hijacking • Protocol analysis (eavesdropping) • Social engineering • Infrastructure hardware theft • Access to unsecured console interfaces	11	The Security Policy Cycle

Table A-1   CWSP exam objectives coverage (continued)

5.0. Security Policy (continued)		
Objective	**Chapter**	**Heading**
5.5. Describe appropriate installation locations for wireless LAN hardware in order to avoid physical theft and tampering, considering the following: • Security implications of remote placement of devices • Physical security for remote infrastructure devices	7	Hardware Placement
• Secure remote connections to wireless LAN infrastructure devices	9	Encryption for Secure Management Interfaces
5.6. Explain the importance and implementation of client-side security applications: • VPN policies • Personal firewall software • Antivirus/Antispyware software	7	Wireless Device Security
5.7. Explain the importance of layered security solutions	11	What is a Security Policy?
5.8. Explain the importance of ongoing WLAN monitoring and documentation: • Explain the necessary hardware and software for ongoing WLAN security monitoring • Explain the necessary criteria for ongoing WLAN security audits and reporting • Implement and conduct timely and consistent reporting procedures • Implement & maintain a wireless LAN security checklist	12	WLAN Operational Support
5.9. Summarize the security policy criteria related to wireless public-access network use	11	Types of Wireless Security Policies
5.10. Summarize the security implications of using non-standard security solution	12	Features of a Scalable and Secure WLAN

A

Table A-1   CWSP exam objectives coverage (continued)

5.0. Security Policy (continued)		
Objective	Chapter	Heading
5.11. Given a set of business requirements, design a scalable and secure wireless LAN solution considering the following security parameters: • Continuous intrusion monitoring and containment • Use of Role-Based Access Control and traffic filtering • Scalable, segmented network design • Use of strong encryption, scalable authentication, and fast roaming	12	Features of a Scalable and Secure WLAN

WIRELESS WEB SITES

This appendix provides a selection of Web sites that contain valuable information regarding wireless security and WLANs.

Wireless Standards Organizations and Regulatory Agencies

- *Institute of Electrical and Electronics Engineers (IEEE)*—The IEEE Web site contains a wealth of information about the current activities of working groups and task groups along with the technical IEEE 802 standards that can be freely downloaded. The Web address is *www.ieee.org*.

- *Wi-Fi Alliance*—The Wi-Fi Alliance organization has information on Wi-Fi standards, locating a hot spot, technical papers on wireless transmissions, and other material. The URL is *www.wi-fi.org*.

- *Federal Communications Commission*—Information regarding FCC proposed action, strategic goals, and consumer issues that relate to wireless transmissions can be found at *www.fcc.gov*.

- *WiMAX Forum* —The WiMAX Forum, located at *www.wimaxforum.org*, works to facilitate the deployment of broadband wireless networks based on the IEEE 802.16 standard.

Wireless Certifications

- *Certified Wireless Network Professional*—The CWNP Web site provides information regarding registering for a CWNP exam along with CWNP practice exams. It also has more than 1,000 free papers on wireless topics than can be freely accessed. The address of the site is *www.cwnp.com*.

- *Wireless Certification Program*—The WCP is designed for individuals who sell and market wireless products and is an overview of wireless that is not technically oriented. The URL is *members.ce.org/certifications/wireless_certifications/default.asp*.

- *Cisco Wireless LAN Certifications*—Cisco offers three levels of wireless LAN certifications for Cisco equipment: Cisco Wireless LAN Design Specialist, Cisco Wireless LAN Sales Specialist, and Cisco Wireless LAN Support Specialist. The Web address is *www.cisco.com/en/US/learning/le3/learning_career_certifications_and_learning_paths_home.html*.

Vendor Web Sites

- *Cisco Aironet*—Cisco offers detailed information about their Aironet product line. The main wireless page is *www.cisco.com/en/US/products/hw/wireless/index.html*.

- *Linksys*—The Linksys page, at *www.linksys.com/* provides product information and support for all Linksys products.

TECHNICAL SUPPORT

- *Cisco*—The Web address of the Cisco technical support site is *www.cisco.com/en/US/support/index.html*.

- *Linksys*—The Linksys support page is found by going to *www.linksys.com* and clicking on **SUPPORT**.

- *Microsoft*—The Microsoft TechNet site contains information about wireless at the address *technet.microsoft.com/default.aspx*.

- *Cisco Wireless LAN Software*—Cisco maintains a site that contains software and updates for its wireless hardware. The URL is *www.cisco.com/public/sw-center/sw-wireless2.shtml*.

WIRELESS INFORMATION

- *Palo Wireless Resource Center*—The Palo Wireless Resource Center contains technical articles on all aspects of wireless communication, including WLANs, WPANs, WMANs, and WWANs. The address is *www.palowireless.com*.

- *Microsoft*—Microsoft's "Cable Guy" Web site has monthly articles about networking and wireless technologies. The address is *www.microsoft.com/technet/community/columns/cableguy/default.mspx*.

- *Wireless Networking*—This site contains a broad wealth of information regarding wireless technologies. The address is *bengross.com/wireless.html*.

- *Wi-Fi Planet*—The Wi-Fi Planet Web site contains daily news, tutorials, and reviews of wireless hardware and software. It is located at *www.wi-fiplanet.com*.

- *Search Networking*—This Web site has detailed information on a variety of networking topics including wireless. The address is *searchnetworking.techtarget.com*.

SECURITY ORGANIZATIONS

- *Computer Emergency Response Team Coordination Center (CERT/CC)*—This organization was initially founded by the U.S. Department of Defense and is now part of the Software Engineering Institute at Carnegie Mellon University. CERT provides a wealth of information regarding computer and network attacks, ways to protect systems, and general information about attacks. Their Web site is *www.cert.org*.

- *Forum of Incident Response and Security Teams (FIRST)*—FIRST is an international security organization composed of over 170 incident response teams from educational institutions, governments, and business. FIRST's goal is to both prevent and quickly respond to local and international security incidents. Their Web site is *www.first.org*.

- *InfraGard*—The goal of InfraGard is to improve and extend information sharing between private industry and the government, particularly the FBI, when dealing with critical national infrastructures. Composed of a consortium of private industry and the U.S. federal government, and coordinated through the FBI, their URL is *www.infragard.net*.

- *Information Systems Security Association (ISSA)*—ISSA is an international organization that provides research and education regarding computer security. The ISSA also sponsors certification programs, including the Certified Information Systems Security Professional (CISSP), Systems Security Certified Practitioner (SSCP), and Certified Information Systems Auditor (CISA) programs. Their Web site is *www.issa.org*.

- *National Security Institute (NSI)*—The NSI provides information about a variety of security vulnerabilities and threats. Their Web site is *nsi.org*.

- *SysAdmin, Audit, Network, Security (SANS) Institute*—SANS provides information, training, research, and other resources for security professionals. The SANS Institute Web site is *www.sans.org*.

WIRELESS SECURITY INFORMATION

- *University of Maryland*—A very good starting point for learning about wireless security vulnerabilities is the University of Maryland's *www.cs.umd.edu/~waa/wireless.html*.

- *Wardrive*—The Wardrive Web site (*www.wardrive.net*) contains technical papers regarding wireless security threats.

- *The Unofficial 802.11 Security Web Page*—This site has numerous articles and links regarding wireless security. The URL is *www.drizzle.com/~aboba/IEEE*.

- *Wireless LAN Security FAQ*—The FAQ site contains questions and answers regarding wireless security (*www.iss.net/wireless/WLAN_FAQ.php*).

WIRELESS TOOLS

- *AiroPeek*—AiroPeek is a commercial packet analyzer for IEEE 802.11 wireless LANs to isolate security problems by fully decoding protocols and analyzing wireless network performance. AiroPeek can be found at *www.wildpackets.com/products/airopeek*.

- *Airsnort on Windows XP*—This Web site explains how to download and install the attack tool Airsnort on a Windows XP computer. The site is located at *airsnort.shmoo.com/win_setup.html*.

- *AP Vulnerabilities*—AP security default settings and their vulnerabilities are available at *www.remote-exploit.org/index.php/Wlan_defaults*.

- *Attack and Defense Tools*—Talisker Security maintains a Web site with links to numerous wireless attack and defense tools. The address is *www.networkintrusion.co.uk/wireless.htm*.

- *Default AP Passwords*—At the site *www.phenoelit.de/dpl/dpl.html* a list of default AP passwords can be found.

- *Default AP SSIDs*—A list of default SSIDs for access points can be found at *www.cirt.net/cgi-bin/ssids.pl*.

- *Kismet*—Kismet is an 802.11 layer2 wireless network detector, sniffer, and intrusion detection system. Kismet will work with many wireless cards and can detect 802.11b, 802.11a, and 802.11g traffic. The Web site is *www.kismetwireless.net*.

- *MAC Spoofing Utility*—A utility to spoof MAC addresses can be obtained at *www.klcconsulting.net/smac*.

- *Mirabilis*—Mirabilis supports online wireless modeling tools for exploring wireless throughput and interoperability with other protocols. The Web address is *www.mirabilisdesign.com/WebPages/mdi_demonstration/wireless/wireless802model/mdi_wireless_wlan.htm*.

- *Netstumbler*—Netstumbler software can locate wireless LANs and provide information about them. The URL is *www.netstumbler.com*.

- *Online Ethics Test*—An online ethics test can be found at *www.ethics.org/quicktest/index.cfm*.

- *Online Security Policy Generator*—A program that will produce a security policy is found at *www.cisco.com/en/US/netsol/ns339/networking_solutions_small_medium_business_tools_index.html*.

- *Password Generator*—A site that will create a unique password is *www.grc.com/pass*.

- *PrismStumbler*—PrismStumbler is a WLAN discovery tool that scans for beacon frames from access points by constantly switching channels. The Web address is *prismstumbler.sourceforge.net*.

- *Radio Theory and Link Planning for WLANs*—The Web site *www.swisswireless.org/wlan_calc_en.html* contains several calculators and explanations regarding RF frequencies and WLANs.

- *Security Tools*—A broad range of security tools are available for download at *www.sysinternals.com/Utilitie.htmls* and *www.foundstone.com*.

- *SSH Application*—A program that will enable secure transmissions is available at *www.chiark.greenend.org.uk/~sgtatham/putty/download.html*.

- *Test Antivirus Software*—The Web site *www.eicar.org/anti_virus_test_file.htm* contains tools that can be used to test antivirus software.

- *Wardriving Tools*—Descriptions and links to wardriving tools can be found at *www.wardrive.net/wardriving/tools*.

- *Wireless LAN Management Program*—An excellent WLAN management program is available at *manageengine.adventnet.com/products/wifi-manager/index.html*.

ONLINE NETWORKING MAGAZINES

- *Network Computing Wireless Channel*—This resource provides a wealth of up-to-date information and reviews of WLANs. The address is *www.networkcomputing.com/channels/wireless/*.

- *Network World Wireless in the Enterprise*—Located at *www.networkworld.com/newsletters/wireless/index.html* this site provides articles regarding WLANs and WiMAX technologies as they relate to organizations.

- *Wireless Week*—This site provides analysis of wireless technology as it relates to businesses. The address is *www.wirelessweek.com/*.

SEARCH ENGINES

- *Google—www.google.com*

- *Microsoft MSN—www.msn.com*

- *American OnLine—search.aol.com*

- *Yahoo—search.yahoo.com*

- *Ask—www.ask.com*

- *Dogpile—www.dogpile.com*

- *List of search engines*—A detailed list of different types of search engines can be found at *http://searchenginewatch.com/links/*.

SAMPLE ACCEPTABLE USE POLICY

ORGANIZATION X ACCEPTABLE USE POLICY

1.0 Overview

The intentions for publishing an Acceptable Use Policy (AUP) are not to impose limitations and restrictions that are contrary to Organization X's culture of trust and integrity. The purpose of this Acceptable Use Policy is to protect our employees, partners, and the company itself from illegal or damaging actions by individuals. It is the responsibility of every computer user to know these guidelines, and to conduct their activities accordingly.

All information-processing systems are the sole property of Organization X. These include but are not limited to local area network, wide area network, Internet, Intranet, and Extranet-related systems, computer equipment, software, operating systems, storage media, network accounts providing electronic mail, WWW browsing, and FTP. These systems are to be used for business purposes in serving the interests of the company, and of our clients and customers in the course of normal operations.

2.0 PURPOSE

The purpose of this policy is to outline the acceptable use of computer equipment at Organization X.

3.0 SCOPE

This AUP applies to all employees, contractors, consultants, temporary workers, and other workers at Organization X. This policy applies to all equipment that is owned or leased by Organization X.

4.0 POLICY

4.1 General Use and Ownership

1. Users should be aware that the data they create on the corporate systems remains the property of the organization. The management cannot guarantee the confidentiality of information stored on any network device belonging to it.

2. Employees are responsible for exercising due care regarding the use of Organization X's information resources. Guidelines concerning personal use of systems are clearly defined in the security policies. In the absence of any such policies, employees should be guided by departmental policies or should consult their supervisor or manager.

3. For security and network maintenance purposes, authorized individuals within Organization X may monitor equipment, systems, and network traffic at any time without the employee's consent.

4. Organization X reserves the right to audit networks and systems on a periodic basis to ensure compliance with this policy.

4.2 Security and Proprietary Information

1. Examples of confidential information include but are not limited to corporate strategies, competitor sensitive information, trade secrets, specifications, customer lists, and research data. Employees should take all necessary steps to prevent unauthorized access to this information.

2. Keep passwords secure and do not share accounts. Authorized users are responsible for the security of their passwords and accounts. User-level passwords should be changed every 45 days.

3. All computers and laptops should be secured with a password-protected screensaver with the automatic activation feature set at 10 minutes or less, or by logging off when the system will be left unattended.

4. Encrypt information when necessary.

5. Postings by employees from an Organization X e-mail address to newsgroups should contain a disclaimer stating that the opinions expressed are strictly their own and not necessarily those of the organization.

6. All computers used by the employee that are connected to the organization's network, whether owned by the employee or the organization, must be continually executing approved virus-scanning software with a current virus signature.

7. Employees should exercise caution when opening e-mail attachments received from unknown senders.

4.3. Unacceptable Use

The following activities are, in general, prohibited. Under no circumstances is an employee of Organization X authorized to engage in any activity that is illegal under local, state, federal, or international law while using company-owned resources.

The following lists are not exhaustive but attempt to provide a framework for activities that fall into the category of unacceptable use.

System and Network Activities

The following activities are strictly prohibited, with no exceptions:

1. Violations of the rights of any person or company protected by copyright, trade secret, patent or other intellectual property, or similar laws or regulations, including, but not limited to, the installation or distribution of software products that are not appropriately licensed for use by the organization.

2. Unauthorized copying of copyrighted material including, but not limited to, photographs, books, copyrighted music, and the installation of any copyrighted software for which the organization does not have an active license is strictly prohibited.

3. Using any hardware or software to scan the wireless radio frequency in order to intercept, examine, alter, or detect the presence of other wireless systems is prohibited.

4. Introduction of malicious programs into the network or server, such as viruses, worms, Trojan horses, etc.

5. Connecting an unauthorized wireless access point to Organization X's data network is prohibited.

6. Revealing your account password to others or allowing use of your account by others.

7. Using an organization computing resource to actively engage in transmitting material that is in violation of sexual harassment or hostile workplace laws in the user's local jurisdiction.

8. Making fraudulent offers of products, items, or services originating from any organization account.

9. Effecting security breaches of the organization's resources. Security breaches include, but are not limited to, accessing data of which the employee is not an intended recipient and accessing a server or account that the employee is not expressly authorized to access.

10. Effecting security breaches or disruptions of network communication. These include, but are not limited to, network sniffing, packet spoofing, denial of service, and forged routing information for malicious purposes.

11. Port scanning is expressly prohibited.

12. Circumventing user authentication or security of any host, network, or account.

13. Interfering with or denying service to any user other than the employee's computer.

14. Using a program or script with the intent to interfere with or disable another user's computer.

E-mail Activities

1. Sending unsolicited e-mail messages or other advertising material to individuals who did not specifically request such material is prohibited.

2. Employees must not engage in any form of harassment via electronic means, such as e-mail, telephone, or paging, whether through language, frequency, or size of messages.

3. The unauthorized use, or forging, of e-mail header information is forbidden.

4. Employees must not be involved in the solicitation of e-mail for any other e-mail address, other than that of the poster's account, with the intent to harass or to collect replies.

5. Creating or forwarding e-mail "chain letters" is prohibited.

6. The use of unsolicited e-mail originating from within the organization's networks is prohibited.

5.0 ENFORCEMENT

Any employee found to have violated this policy may be subject to disciplinary action, up to and including termination of employment.

6.0 DEFINITIONS

Term	Definition
Spam	Unauthorized and/or unsolicited electronic mass mailings.

7.0 REVISION HISTORY

Glossary

2.5 Generation (2.5G) — An interim step between 2G and 3G digital cellular networks that operate at a maximum speed of 384 Kbps.

AAA — The combination of authentication, authorization, and accounting.

AAA server — A network device that performs authentication, authorization, and accounting services.

acceptable use policy (AUP) — A policy that defines what actions the users of a system may perform while using computing and networking equipment.

access categories (AC) — Different streams of traffic under EDCA, prioritized for voice, video, best effort,

access control — The mechanisms for limiting access to resources based on the users' identity and their membership in various groups.

access point (AP) — A device that acts as a base station to receive signals from and transmit signals to wireless network devices, and to connect those devices to a wired network.

access point mode — A remote wireless bridge configuration in which the device functions as a standard access point only and does not communicate with other remote wireless bridges.

access restrictions — Restrictions placed on what a user can perform on a network after being accepted into the network.

accounting — The process of measuring the resources a user consumes during a network session.

ad hoc wireless mesh network — A wireless network that is designed so that wireless devices can be longer distances away from the access point.

Advanced Encryption Standard (AES) — A block cipher used in IEEE 802.11i.

adware — A software program that delivers advertising content in a manner or context that is unexpected and unwanted by the user.

AES-CCMP — The encryption protocol in the 802.11i standard.

algorithm — In cryptography, the underlying process or formula for encrypting and decrypting messages.

Annualized Loss Expectancy (ALE) — The expected monetary loss for an asset because of a risk over a one-year period.

Annualized Rate of Occurrence (ARO) — The probability that a risk will occur in a particular year.

anomaly detection — A type of wireless intrusion detection system (WIDS) that monitors the normal activity of the wireless LAN and "learns" its normal characteristics.

ANonce — A nonce sent from the authenticator to the supplicant.

antispyware — Software that helps prevent computers from becoming infected by spyware.

antivirus (AV) software — Software that can scan a computer for virus infections and isolate any file that contains a virus.

Arbitrary Inter-Frame Space Number (AIFSN) — Fixed slot times of the WMM standard.

asset — An item that has a positive economic value.

asset management — The process of keeping records of assets.

association — The process of being accepted into the wireless network.

association request frame — A frame sent from a device to an access point containing information about the device.

asymmetric encryption — Encryption in which two mathematically related keys are used instead of one; also known as public key cryptography.

attack tree — A visual image of the attacks that may occur against an asset.

authentication — The process of providing proof that a user is "genuine" or authentic.

Authentication Header (AH) — An IPsec protocol that authenticates that packets received were sent from the source identified in the header of the packet.

authentication server — A server on an IEEE 802.1x network that verifies the authentication of devices.

authenticator — A device that receives requests and forwards to an authentication server in an 802.1x network.

authorization — The process that determines whether the user has the authority to carry out such tasks.

backhaul — The wired connection from the access point to the wired Internet connection.

backhaul wireless mesh network — A wireless mesh network that connects wireless mesh routers together.

bands — Sections of the radio frequency spectrum.

baseline — The normal state of a network's traffic.

beacon frame — A frame from an access point that announces its presence and provides necessary information for other devices to join the network.

beaconing — The process in which an access point announces its presence and provides necessary information for other devices to join the network.

biometrics — Authentication based on the unique human characteristics of a person, such as a fingerprint.

block cipher — A cipher that manipulates an entire block of cleartext at one time.

bridge — Device used to connect two network segments, even if those segments use different types of physical media, such as wired and wireless connections.

broadcast — Sending a packet to all network devices.

broadcast domain — The area in which a broadcast occurs.

broadcast traffic — Traffic sent to all users on the network.

brute force attack — An attack in which an attacker attempts to create every possible key combination by systematically changing one character at a time.

built-in VPN — A type of VPN endpoint that handles all the VPN tunnel setup, encapsulation, and encryption so that wireless client devices are not required to run any special software.

Carrier Sense Multiple Access with Collision Avoidance (CSMA/CA) — A procedure used by IEEE WLANs to prevent multiple wireless devices from transmitting at the same time.

certification authority (CA) — A trusted third party that issues digital certificates.

challenge text — A block of text that must be encrypted by the wireless device in shared key authentication.

Challenge-Handshake Authentication Protocol (CHAP) — An older three-way authentication handshake that is accomplished during the initial authentication and may be repeated any time after the link has been established.

change management — Managing the process of implementing changes in an organization.

change request form — A form that outlines the requested alteration of the WLAN in such a way that it can be determine what type of review is needed prior to accepting or rejecting the proposal.

chipset — A group of integrated circuits that provides specific functionality.

cipher — An encryption algorithm.

ciphertext — An encrypted message.

circuit-switch — A technology in which a dedicated and direct physical connection is made between the caller and the recipient of the call through the switch.

cleartext — The original unencrypted text; also known as plaintext.

cold site — A disaster recovery option that consists of a remote site that provides office space in the event of a disaster, but the customer must provide and install all the equipment needed to continue operations.

collision — In wireless security, two packets that were created from the same initialization vector (IV).

collision domain — The area that encompasses all of the network devices that can cause collisions.

community string — An authentication string that functions like a password to allow or deny access to the information that was collected by SNMP (Simple Network Management Protocol).

configuration management database — A listing of all installed wireless components, configuration settings, and diagrams that document the current state of the wireless LAN.

contention window — Random slot times of the WMM standard.

Controlling the Assault of Non-Solicited Pornography and Marketing Act of 2003 (CAN-SPAM) — A U.S. law passed in 2003 to limit the effect of spam.

Cryptographic File System (CFS) — A Linux file encryption system.

cryptography — The science of transforming information so that it is secure while it is being transmitted or stored.

cyclic redundancy check (CRC) — A checksum value that is based on the contents of the text; used to verify that no bits have been changed or inserted in transmission.

decryption — The process of changing ciphertext into cleartext.

default key — A key value that is used to encrypt wireless data transmissions when they are sent.

default password — A standard password that is configured on all equipment.

definition files — Antivirus software updates; also called signature files.

delay spread — A technique that minimizes the spread of the signal so that it can reach farther distances.

demilitarized zone (DMZ) — A separate network that sits outside the secure network perimeter and is protected by a firewall.

denial of service (DoS) — An attack designed to prevent a device from performing its intended function.

deterministic techniques — Predictable techniques that are used by wireless intrusion detection systems to detect attacks.

dictionary attack — An attack that takes each word from a dictionary and encodes it in the same way a passphrase was encoded.

digital certificates — Electronic files that are used to uniquely identify users and resources over networks.

dipole antenna — An antenna that detects from all directions equally; also known as an omni-directional antenna.

Directory Access Protocol (DAP) — The X.500 standard that defines a protocol for a client application to access the X.500 directory.

directory information base (DIB) — The repository in which X.500 information is held.

directory information tree (DIT) — The tree structure of a directory information base.

directory service — A database stored on the network itself that contains information about users and network devices.

discretionary access control (DAC) — An access control model in which the user can adjust the permissions for other users over network devices.

distributed autonomous site deployment — An authentication model that uses local authentication with one or more RADIUS servers at each site, but the authentication database is replicated from one central site to each local site.

distributed sites with centralized authentication and security deployment — A deployment model in which the distributed sites with centralized authentication and security deployment rely on remote RADIUS servers to perform authentication.

due care — The obligations that are imposed on owners and operators of assets to exercise reasonable care of the asset and take necessary precautions to protect it.

dumpster diving — Looking through an outdoor trash receptacle as a source of secure information.

dynamic frequency selection (DFS) — A technology that detects other devices using the same radio channel and then switches the WLAN operation to another channel if necessary.

Dynamic Host Configuration Protocol (DHCP) — A part of the TCP/IP protocol suite that leases IP address to clients to use while they are connected to the network.

dynamic WEP — A proposed solution to solve the weak initialization vector problem by rotating keys frequently.

EAP with Transport Layer Security (EAP-TLS) — An authentication protocol that requires that the wireless device and RADIUS server both prove their identities to each other by using public key cryptography such as digital certificates.

EAP with Tunneled TLS (EAP-TTLS) — An authentication protocol that uses Windows logins and passwords instead of issuing digital certificates.

embedded probe — A probe integrated into an existing access point, used for monitoring the RF.

Encapsulating Security Payload (ESP) — An IPsec protocol through which confidentiality is achieved by encryption.

encryption — The process of encoding cleartext into ciphertext.

endpoint — The end of the tunnel between virtual private network (VPN) devices.

end-span — An Ethernet switch that has embedded Power over Ethernet (PoE) technology.

Enhanced Distributed Channel Access (EDCA) — A mode of IEEE 802.11e QoS that is contention-based yet supports different types of traffic.

enterprise security model — A wireless security model designed for medium to large-sized organizations such as businesses, government agencies, and universities in which an authentication server is available.

Exposure Factor (EF) — The proportion of an asset's value that is likely to be destroyed by a particular risk, expressed as a percentage.

Extended Authentication Protocol-MD 5 (EAP-MD5) — An authentication protocol that allows a RADIUS server to authenticate wireless devices by verifying a hash of each user's password.

Extensible Authentication Protocol (EAP) — An "envelope" that can carry many different kinds of exchange data used for authentication, such as a challenge/response, one-time passwords, and digital certificates.

failover support — The ability to absorb equipment failures by using redundant equipment.

false positive — Attack alert that turns out to be false.

fast handoff — A standard that streamlines the transition process of a mobile client as it roams between APs; also known as IEEE 802.11r.

Federal Communications Commission (FCC) — The primary regulatory agency for wireless communications in the United States and its territorial possessions.

File Transfer Protocol (FTP) — A protocol of the TCP/IP suite used to transfer files that is considered unsecure.

firewall — Hardware or software that prevents unauthorized access to a network.

First Generation (1G) — The first generation of wireless cellular telephone technology.

Fixed WiMAX — A wireless wide area data transmission standard that supports up to 50 kilometers (31 miles) of linear service range and is not line-of-sight dependent, at shared data rates up to 70 Mbps.

flash memory — A type of solid-state (microchip) technology in which there are no moving parts.

four-way handshake — An exchange of information for the master key that authenticates the security parameters that were negotiated, confirms the PNK, establishes temporal keys, performs the first group key handshake, and provides keying material to implement the group key handshake.

frame acknowledgment — A method in which CSMA/CA reduces collisions using explicit acknowledgment.

gateway — A network device that acts as an entrance to another network.

global positioning system (GPS) — A navigation system that allows a user to determine his precise location.

GNU Privacy Guard (GPG) — A free product for encrypting e-mail messages that runs on Windows, UNIX, and Linux operating systems.

Google phishing — A phishing technique in which attackers set up their own search engines to direct traffic to illegitimate sites.

Gramm–Leach–Bliley Act (GLBA) — A 1999 U.S. federal regulation that gives limited privacy protections against the sale of private financial information and obtaining personal information through false pretenses.

group keys (GK) — Keys that are used in the master key model when an AP sends the same packet to all wireless devices.

group master key (GMK) — A random number that becomes the starting point of the group key hierarchy in the master key model.

group temporal key (GTK) — A key created by a pseudorandom function that uses the GMK, the authenticator's MAC address and a nonce from the authenticator in the master key model.

guideline — A collection of suggestions that should be implemented.

handheld PC — A small computer that can be held in a single hand yet has many of the features of a notebook computer.

handoff — The process of switching associations from one access point to another.

handshake — An electronic exchange of information between two devices that typically contains acknowledgments of the receipt of the information.

hashing — A process of creating a ciphertext that is never intended to be decrypted but instead used in a comparison for identification purposes; the process of mathematically manipulating a value to disguise it.

Health Insurance Portability and Accountability Act (HIPAA) — A 1996 U.S. federal regulation that governs the privacy of personal health information.

highly directional antenna — An antenna that sends a narrowly focused signal beam.

hot site — A remote site that contains redundant equipment, supplies, and telecommunications infrastructure for a business in the event of a disaster, so that operations can continue nearly seamlessly.

hot standby — Equipment that is functioning alongside main equipment to provide failover support.

hub — A network device that joins multiple computers within one local area network (LAN) by sending packets to all attached devices.

Hybrid Coordination Function Controlled Channel Access (HCCA) — A mode of IEEE 802.11e QoS that is based upon polling.

identity theft — The theft of an individual's personal information to impersonate that individual with the intent to commit fraud or other crimes

IEEE 802.11 — A wireless local area network with a bandwidth (maximum throughput) of 2 Mbps.

IEEE 802.11a — A wireless local area network with a bandwidth (maximum throughput) of 54 Mbps and uses the UNII band.

IEEE 802.11b — A wireless local area network with a bandwidth (maximum throughput) of 11 Mbps and uses the ISM band.

IEEE 802.11e — The standard for wireless Quality of Service (QoS).

IEEE 802.11F — A recommended practice that specifies how roaming between access points should take place.

IEEE 802.11g — A wireless local area network with a bandwidth (maximum throughput) of 54 Mbps and uses the ISM band.

IEEE 802.11h — A standard that specifies how WLAN devices can share the 5 GHz spectrum with other devices.

IEEE 802.11i — A wireless security standard intended to replace the original WEP-based standard.

IEEE 802.11n — A proposed WLAN standard with a bandwidth (maximum throughput) between 300 600 Mbps.

IEEE 802.11r — A standard that streamlines the transition process of a mobile client as it roams between APs; also known as fast handoff.

IEEE 802.11s — A proposed standard for wireless mesh networks.

IEEE 802.11v — A protocol designed to assist with the management of WLAN devices.

IEEE 802.16e — A Mobile WiMAX standard that is an extension of IEEE 802.16-2004 and is backward compatible with it.

IEEE 802.1q — A standard for virtual local area networks (VLANs) that supports trunking.

IEEE 802.1x — A standard for authentication and key management that can be used for either wired or wireless networks.

IEEE 802.20 — A Mobile WiMAX standard that permits users to roam up to 15 kilometers and delivers high-speed data rates to mobile users.

IEEE 802.3af — A standard that defines the technology for sending power to devices through the unused wires of an Ethernet cable; also known as Power over Ethernet (PoE).

incident response — A security policy that outlines actions to be performed when a security breach occurs.

incident response team (IRT) — A group of employees who respond to security penetrations.

Industrial, Scientific and Medical (ISM) — An unregulated band used for WLAN transmissions.

inform request — A Simple Network Management Protocol (SNMP) feature that acknowledges the receipt of a message indicating an abnormal event with an SNMP response.

information security — The tasks of guarding information that is in a digital format, with the objective of protecting the integrity, confidentiality, and availability of that information.

initialization vector (IV) — A 24-bit value that changes each time a packet is transmitted.

Institute of Electrical and Electronics Engineers (IEEE) — An organization that establishes standards for networks.

integrated probe — A probe integrated into an existing access point, used for monitoring the RF.

integrity check value (ICV) — A checksum value that is based on the contents of the text; also known as cyclic redundancy check (CRC).

Inter-Access Point Protocol (IAPP) — A protocol used by IEEE 802.11F that specifies how roaming between access points should take place.

Internet Security Association and Key Management Protocol/Oakley (ISAKMP/Oakley) — An IPsec protocol that allows the receiver to obtain a key and authenticate the sender using digital certificates.

Inter-Switch Link (ISL) — A Cisco VLAN protocol that "wraps" the original Ethernet packet with 30 bytes of additional information. A proprietary alternative to IEEE 802.1q.

intrusion detection system (IDS) — A security management system that compiles information from a computer network or individual computer and then analyzes it to identify security vulnerabilities and attacks. The first generation of IDSs were for wired networks and focused on the detection of attacks.

intrusion prevention system (IPS) — A security system that is designed to stop an attack from occurring.

IP security (IPsec) — A set of protocols developed to support the secure exchange of packets.

Kerberos — An authentication system developed by the Massachusetts Institute of Technology (MIT) that is used to verify the identity of networked users.

key — The value that an algorithm uses to encrypt or decrypt a message.

key confirmation key (KCK) — A part of the pairwise transient key that is used by the EAP key exchanges to provide data origin authenticity.

key encryption key (KEK) — A part of the pairwise transient key that is used by the EAP key exchanges to provide confidentiality.

key-caching — A technology that stores information from a device on the network to improve roaming.

keystream — The output from a pseudo random number generator (PRNG).

keystream attack — An attack method to determine the keystream by analyzing two packets that were created from the same initialization vector.

KisMAC — A freeware discovery application for the Apple MacOS X operating systems.

Kismet — A freeware discovery application that runs under the Linux operating system.

last mile connection — The connection that begins at a fast Internet service provider, goes through the local neighborhood, and ends at the home or office.

Layer 2 Tunneling Protocol (L2TP) — A tunneling protocol that merges the features of the Point-to-Point Tunneling Protocol (PPTP) with Layer 2 Forwarding Protocol (L2F).

Layer 4-7 devices — Network devices that can provide intelligent traffic and bandwidth management based on the content of a session and not just on network connections.

license-exempt spectrum — Unregulated bands available nationwide to all users without requiring a license.

Lightweight Directory Access Protocol (LDAP) — A simpler subset of the Directory Access Protocol (DAP).

Lightweight EAP (LEAP) — An authentication protocol that requires mutual authentication and delivery of keys used for WLAN encryption.

Link Control Protocol (LCP) — An extension to the point-to-point tunneling protocol that establishes, configures, and automatically tests the connection.

logic bomb — A computer program that lies dormant until it is triggered by a specific logical event.

MAC address filter — A filtering mechanism on an access point that permits or prevents access based on the media access control number of a client device's wireless adapter.

malware — A general term used to describe worms, viruses, spyware, or other types of software with a malicious intent.

managed switch — A switch that provides all of the features of an unmanaged switch along with enhanced management features.

management information base (MIB) — The location where SNMP network traffic information is stored.

mandatory access control (MAC) — An access control model in which the user is not allowed to give access to another user to use or access anything on the network.

master key (MK) — A key from which all other keys are formed when using IEEE 802.1x authentication.

Media Access Control (MAC) address filtering — An access control method that restricts access based on the media access control address.

mesh network — A network that provides multiple data paths.

Message Integrity Check (MIC) — A technology that replaces the Cyclic Redundancy Check (CRC) that is designed to prevent an attacker from capturing, altering, and resending data packets.

Microsoft Challenge-Handshake Authentication Protocol (MS-CHAP) — The Microsoft implementation of CHAP as an Extensible Authentication Protocol (EAP).

mini PCI — A small card that is functionally equivalent to a standard PCI expansion card.

Mobile WiMAX — A wireless wide area data transmission that adds mobility components to the WiMAX standard, allowing users to freely roam both indoors and outdoors for kilometers while remaining connected.

Multiple-Input, Multiple-Output Enhanced WLAN (MEW) — A proposed WLAN standard with a bandwidth between 300 and 600 Mbps.

Multiple-Input, Multiple-Output (MIMO) — A proposed WLAN standard with a bandwidth between 300 and 600 Mbps.

nearest sensor — A method for determining the location of a wireless device that identifies the access point to which a wireless device is associated and computes how far the RF signal radiates from that access point.

need to know — Restricting access to information by limiting it only to personnel who must have it to perform their assigned tasks.

NetStumbler — The best-known freeware discovery application.

network access server (NAS) — A server in a point-to-point tunneling protocol configuration.

network address translation (NAT) — A technology that replaces the sender's actual IP address with another IP address.

nonce — A random value used in cryptography to prevent different types of attacks.

non-deterministic — Network traffic that is not created in a fixed or predictable fashion.

non-root mode — A remote wireless bridge configuration in which the device can only transmit to another bridge that is in root mode.

offline dictionary attack — An attack that hashes the encrypted PSK value and compares it with hashed values from a dictionary.

omni-directional antenna — An antenna that detects from all directions equally; also known as a dipole antenna.

one-way hash — A process of creating a ciphertext that is never intended to be decrypted but instead is used in a comparison for identification purposes.

open system authentication — An authentication method in which a wireless device sends a request to the access point.

overlay probe — A dedicated probe that monitors the RF and scans for attacks.

packet filter — Another name for a firewall that is designed to prevent malicious packets from entering the network or computers.

packet generator — A program that creates fake packets that flood the wireless network.

packet sniffer — A device or software that captures TCP/IP packets as they are being transmitted.

packet-switched — A communications technology that requires that the data transmission be broken into smaller units of packets and each packet is sent independently through the network to reach the destination.

pairwise master key (PMK) — A secondary key is derived from the master key.

pairwise transient key (PTK) — A key created by the wireless device and the access point after each device has its PMK.

passive scanning — The process of the wireless device listening for a beacon frame.

passthrough VPN — A type of VPN in which a separate VPN client application installed on the local device handles setting up the connection with the remote VPN server, and takes care of the special data handling required to send and receive data through the VPN tunnel.

password — A secret combination of letters and numbers that serves to validate or authenticate a user by what the user knows.

Password Authentication Protocol (PAP) — An older authentication protocol that was used to authenticate a user to a remote access server or to an ISP.

password guessing — A technique used by attackers to exploit weak passwords.

password management policy — A security policy that outlines how passwords should be used and handled.

password paradox — The paradox of needing lengthy and complex passwords, yet such passwords are difficult to memorize.

patch software — Software updates provided by vendors to improve operating system and application program security.

peer-to-peer attack — Attacks directed at other similar devices.

per-packet key — A technology that dynamically generates a new key for each packet and prevents collisions.

personal digital assistant (PDA) — A handheld device that was originally designed as a personal organizer.

personal firewall — A software-based firewall on a local device.

personal security model — A model for wireless security designed for single users or small office home office (SOHO) settings of 10 or fewer wireless devices.

pharming — A form of phishing that automatically redirects the user to a fake site.

phishing — Sending an e-mail or displaying a Web announcement that falsely claims to be from a legitimate enterprise in an attempt to trick the user into surrendering information.

PING (Packet Internet Groper) — A diagnostic program that sends a packet to a device and waits for a response to determine if it is properly functioning.

plenum — The air-handling space above drop ceilings (and sometimes even between the walls and under structural floors) in a building.

Plug and Play (PnP) — A service that allows the Windows operating system to automatically detect new hardware when it is installed on a computer.

point-to-multipoint — A remote wireless bridge configuration that is used to connect multiple LAN segments.

point-to-point — A remote wireless bridge configuration used to connect two LAN segments.

point-to-point protocol (PPP) — A widely used protocol for establishing connections over a serial line or dial-up connection between two points.

Point-to-Point Protocol over Ethernet (PPPoE) — A variation of PPP that is used by broadband Internet providers (with DSL or cable modem connections).

Point-to-Point Tunneling Protocol (PPTP) — The most widely deployed tunneling protocol.

policy — A document that outlines specific requirements or rules that must be met.

port address translation (PAT) — A technology similar to NAT, except it gives each packet the same IP address but a different port number.

port forwarding — An enhanced feature of SSH that can be used to provide secure access to other services that do not normally encrypt data during transmission; also known as tunneling.

port security — An authentication technique that blocks all traffic until the user is approved.

Power over Ethernet (PoE) — A technology that sends power to devices through the unused wires of an Ethernet cable.

pre-authentication — A technology that allows a device to become authenticated to an access point before moving into its range.

preshared key (PSK) — A technology that uses passphrases for generating encryption keys.

Pretty Good Privacy (PGP) — A program that encrypts e-mail messages using public and private keys.

private addresses — A series of IP addresses reserved for special use on an internal network.

private key — One key of asymmetric encryption that encrypts the message.

private key cryptography — Using the same secret key to encrypt and decrypt messages.

Project 802 — The original effort by the IEEE beginning in 1980 to establish network standards.

promiscuous mode — A mode that turns off the filtering mechanism and allows a wired NIC to capture all the packets it receives.

Protected EAP (PEAP) — An authentication protocol that uses Windows logins and passwords instead of issuing digital certificates.

pseudo-random number generator (PRNG) — A part of the process for encrypting packages using a shared secret key that generates a keystream.

public access WLAN use policy — A policy to address accessing public hotspots by organization employees.

public key — One key of asymmetric encryption that decrypts the message.

public key cryptography — Encryption in which two mathematically related keys are used instead of one.

public key infrastructure (PKI) — The use of digital certificates, CAs, and other registration authorities that validate each party of a transaction over a public network.

Quality of Service (QoS) — The capability to prioritize different types of frames.

radio frequency monitoring (RFMON) — A passive method of receiving WLAN signals.

radio frequency spectrum — The entire range of all radio frequencies.

RC4 — A cipher algorithm used in WEP.

Received Signal Strength Indication (RSSI) — A method for determining the location of a wireless device that measures the RF power loss between transmitter and receiver to calculate the distance to the device.

registration authority (RA) — A subordinate certification authority server.

rekey interval — The interval at which PSK keys are changed.

rekeying — The process of automatically changing PSK keys.

Remote Authentication Dial-In User Service (RADIUS) — An authentication server typically used on an IEEE 802.1x network.

remote wireless bridge — Wireless device designed to connect two or more wired or wireless networks together.

remote-access VPN — A virtual private network (VPN) from a single user to a LAN.

repeater mode — A remote wireless bridge configuration in which another remote wireless bridge may be positioned between two other bridges.

RF fingerprinting — A method for determining the location of a wireless device that creates an image of the wireless environment and then compares it to deviations in the real-time environment to locate the device.

risk assessment — An evaluation that determines the likelihood that a vulnerability is a risk to the organization.

risk identification — The process that seeks to determine the risks that an organization faces against its information assets.

roaming — Movement between WLAN cells.

Robust Secure Network (RSN) — A protocol that uses dynamic negotiation of authentication and encryption algorithms between access points and wireless devices.

rogue access point — A wireless device that is installed without permission.

role based access control (RBAC) — An access control model in which permissions are assigned to a position or role.

root bridge — A device that cannot communicate with another root bridge or any wireless clients.

root mode — A remote wireless bridge configuration in which the bridge can only communicate with other bridges that are not in root mode.

rootkit — A set of software tools used by an attacker to break into a computer and obtain special operating system privileges to both perform unauthorized functions and hide all traces of its existence.

round — An iteration in a block cipher.

router — A network device that transfers packets between networks.

rule base — A set of actions a firewall should take when it receives a packet.

Sarbanes-Oxley Act — A 2002 U.S. federal regulation that covers corporate governance, financial disclosure, and the practice of public accounting.

scalable — The ability to accommodate growth.

scanning — The process of a receiving wireless device looking for beacons.

script kiddies — Attackers that lack the technical skills of more advanced users and are sometimes considered more dangerous.

Second Generation (2G) — The second generation of cellular telephony that used circuit-switched digital networks and started in the early 1990s.

Secure Copy (SCP) — A protocol or client program based on the protocol that encrypts data by relying upon an underlying protocol such as SSH.

Secure FTP (SFTP) — An alternative to the unsecure File Transfer Protocol (FTP) for transmitting files.

Secure Hypertext Transport Protocol (HTTPS) — A version of HTTP that incorporates secure transmission standards between clients and servers.

Secure Shell (SSH) — A protocol originally based on a suite of UNIX commands for transmitting documents securely over the Internet but now replaced by a revised version known as SSH-2.

Secure Sockets Layer (SSL) — A protocol developed by Netscape for transmitting documents securely over the Internet.

security policy — A document or series of documents that clearly defines the defense mechanisms that an organization will employ to keep information secure.

security policy cycle — A process for developing security policies that involves risk identification, security policy design and development, and compliance monitoring and evaluation.

security vulnerability — A weakness or flaw in an information system that could be exploited to cause harm.

seed — The starting point for mathematically generating an encryption key.

segment — A subset of a larger network that is created by connecting equipment to a physical device.

segmentation — Dividing a network into smaller units.

semi-directional antenna — An antenna that focuses the energy in one direction.

separation of duties — One person's work serves as a complementary check on another person's work.

Service Set Identifier (SSID) — A unique number of up to 32 alphanumeric case-sensitive characters that serves as a WLAN network name.

shared key authentication — An authentication method in which a wireless device must encrypt challenge text before it can be authenticated.

shared secret — A passphrase in preshared key (PSK) authentication that must be entered in both the access point and wireless device.

signature detection — A type of wireless intrusion detection system that analyzes the information it gathers and compares it to large databases of attack signatures.

signature files — Antivirus software updates; also called definition files.

Simple Network Management Protocol (SNMP) — An industry-wide standard supported by most network equipment manufacturers.

Single Loss Expectancy (SLE) — The expected monetary loss every time a risk occurs.

single site deployment — The simplest type of authentication model that consists of one or more RADIUS servers accessing a centralized authentication database.

site-to-site VPN — A virtual private network (VPN) in which multiple sites can connect to other sites over the Internet.

sled — An external attachment for a PDA that can accommodate a wireless NIC or similar device.

slot time — The amount of time that a device must wait after the medium is clear.

smartphone — A cellular telephone that includes many of the functions of a PDA.

SNMP management station — An SNMP device that communicates with the software agents on each network device and collects the data stored in the MIBs.

SNMP trap — An abnormal event that is monitored on a network using the Simple Network Management Protocol (SNMP).

SNonce — A nonce sent from the supplicant to the authenticator.

social engineering — A technique that relies on tricking and deceiving someone to access a system.

software agent — SNMP software that is loaded onto each network device that will be managed.

spam — Unsolicited e-mail.

spear phishing — Phishing that targets specific users.

spyware — A general term used to describe software that violates a user's personal security.

standard — A collection of system-specific or procedural-specific requirements that must be met.

stateful packet filtering — A type of firewall that keeps a record of the state of a connection between an internal computer and an external server and then makes decisions based on the connection as well as the rule base.

stateless packet filtering — A type of firewall that looks at the incoming packet and permits or denies it based strictly on the rule base.

stream cipher — A cipher that takes one character and replaces it with another character.

subnet — Computers or other network devices grouped by Internet Protocol address; a "higher-level" software configuration compared to a segment, which is a physical network grouping.

supplicant — The wireless device that requires secure network access in an IEEE 802.1x network.

switch — A network device that joins multiple computers within one LAN by sending packets to only the intended recipient.

symmetric encryption — Using the same secret key to both encrypt and decrypt messages.

tablet computer — A small form-factor computer designed for truly mobile computing.

temporal key — A 128-bit encryption key used in TKIP; a part of the pairwise transient key that is used by the data-confidentiality protocols.

Temporal Key Integrity Protocol (TKIP) — A technology that replaces WEP encryption.

Terminal Access Control Access Control System (TACACS+) — An industry standard protocol specification that forwards username and password information to a centralized server.

thin access point — An access point with limited functions, used in conjunction with a wireless switch.

Third Generation (3G) — The third generation of cellular telephony with throughput rates for 3G averaging between 400 and 700 Kbps and allowing use for data communication.

threat agent — Any threat that exists against an asset.

threat modeling — The process of constructing scenarios of the types of threats that assets can face.

ticket — A token that is issued by a Kerberos authentication server.

TLS Handshake Protocol — A protocol that allows authentication between the server and the client and the negotiation of an encryption algorithm and cryptographic keys before any data is transmitted.

TLS Record Protocol — A protocol that is layered on top of a reliable transport protocol such as TCP, and ensures that a connection is private by using data encryption.

transitional security model — A model for wireless security that should only be implemented as a temporary solution before upgrading to a more secure model, either the personal security model or the enterprise security model.

transmit power control (TPC) — A technology designed to reduce interference from WLANs to other services by reducing the power level of the network.

Transport Layer Security (TLS) — A protocol that guarantees privacy and data integrity between applications communicating over the Internet.

transport mode — An IPsec mode that encrypts only the payload of each packet and leaves the header unencrypted.

triangulation — A method for determining the location of a wireless device that measures the angles between three or more nearby access points to determine the intersection.

trilateration — A method for determining the location of a wireless device that measures the distance between three or more access points; used by a GPS receiver to determine its location from satellite information.

trunking — Using a single cable for multiple virtual LANs.

tunnel mode — An IPsec mode that encrypts both the header and the data portion of the packet.

tunneling — An enhanced feature of SSH that can be used to provide secure access to other services that do not normally encrypt data during transmission; also known as port forwarding.

unicast — When a sending device on a LAN sends a packet that is intended for a single receiving device.

unicast traffic — Traffic destined for only one address.

Universal Plug and Play (UPnP) — A service that allows devices on a network to discover other devices and determine how to work with them.

Unlicensed National Information Infrastructure (UNII) — An unregulated band used for WLAN transmissions.

unmanaged switch — A switch that provides no management capabilities in the operation of the switch.

unregulated bands — Bands of the radio spectrum that are available to all users without requiring a license.

virtual local area network (VLAN) — A smaller logical grouping of network devices.

virtual private dial-up network (VPDN) — A user-to-LAN connection used by remote dial-up users.

virtual private network (VPN) — A technology that uses an unsecured network as if it were a private network.

virus — A program that secretly attaches itself to another document or program and executes when that document or program is opened.

voice over wireless LAN (VoWLAN) — A technology that uses an existing data WLAN for making and receiving telephone calls. Also called wireless voice over IP (wVoIP), voice over IP (VoIP), and VoWi-Fi.

VPN concentrator — A device that aggregates hundreds or thousands of virtual private network (VPN) connections.

vulnerability appraisal — An examination of the current security infrastructure to determine what risks exists against assets.

warchalking — The process of identifying wireless networks by drawing on sidewalks or walls around the area of the network.

wardriving — Driving through an area with a wireless device searching for an unprotected wireless signal.

warflying — Using an airplane to find a WLAN signal.

weak key — A cryptographic key that creates a repeating pattern.

weak passwords — Passwords that compromise security.

WEP2 (WEP Version 2) — An updated standard that addressed the limitations of WEP by adding two new security enhancements.

white-pages service — An X.500 service that provides the capability to look up information by name.

Wi-Fi Multimedia (WMM) — The Wi-Fi Alliance QoS specification, released in 2004.

Wi-Fi Protected Access (WPA) — A subset of 802.11i that addresses encryption and authentication.

Wi-Fi Protected Access 2 (WPA2) — The second generation of WPA security, based on the IEEE 802.11i standard.

Wi-Fi (Wireless Fidelity) Alliance — A consortium of wireless network equipment manufacturers and software providers.

WiMAX (Worldwide Interoperability for Microwave Access) — A technology for wireless data transmissions over a wide area.

wired equivalent privacy (WEP) — An IEEE 802.11 cryptography mechanism.

wireless authentication — The process of authenticating the wireless device prior to being connected to the network.

wireless client network adapter — The hardware that allows a mobile computing device to detect a wireless signal; also called wireless network interface card.

Wireless Ethernet Compatibility Alliance (WECA) — A consortium of wireless equipment manufacturers and software providers that has been superceded by the Wi-Fi Alliance.

wireless gateways — Devices that combine an access point, router, and network address translation features.

wireless intrusion detection system (WIDS) — The first generation of security management systems for wireless networks that focused on the detection of attacks by constantly monitoring the radio frequency.

wireless intrusion prevention system (WIPS) — A newer generation of security systems that attempts to uncover and prevent an attack before it harms the WLAN.

wireless location mapping — The formal expression used to refer to this passive wireless discovery or the process of finding a WLAN signal and recording information about it.

wireless mesh network — A wireless network that allows for multiple data paths for wireless transmissions.

wireless mesh router — A device that provides alternative data paths for the "backside" connection to the Internet.

wireless network interface card — The hardware that allows a mobile computing device to detect a wireless signal; also called wireless client network adapter.

wireless packet sniffer — Software or hardware that can be used to view the contents of wireless TCP/IP packets.

wireless probe — A special sensor that can monitor the airwaves for traffic.

wireless router — A network device that combines an access point with a router.

wireless switch — A network switch that contains authentication and encryption services for a WLAN.

Wireless Zero Configuration (WZC) — The integrated operating system tool connecting to and configuring wireless networks for Microsoft Windows XP and later Windows-based computers.

WLAN baseline — A standard for the operation of a wireless network.

worm — A malicious program that does not attach to a document to spread but can travel by itself.

X.500 — The International Standards Organization (ISO) standard for directory services.

yellow-pages service — An X.500 service that provides the capability to browse and search for information by category.

zero day attack — An attack based on a previously unknown flaw in software that provides no warning.

Index